Forgotten Heroes and Legends of Freedom Movement of India

N.C. Beohar

शहीदों की चिंताओं पर लगेंगे हर बरश मेले,

वतन पे मरने वालों का बाकी यही निशाँ होगा।

INDIA • SINGAPORE • MALAYSIA

Copyright © N.C. Beohar
All Rights Reserved.

This book has been published with all efforts taken to make the material error-free after the consent of the author. However, the author and the publisher do not assume and hereby disclaim any liability to any party for any loss, damage, or disruption caused by errors or omissions, whether such errors or omissions result from negligence, accident, or any other cause.

While every effort has been made to avoid any mistake or omission, this publication is being sold on the condition and understanding that neither the author nor the publishers or printers would be liable in any manner to any person by reason of any mistake or omission in this publication or for any action taken or omitted to be taken or advice rendered or accepted on the basis of this work. For any defect in printing or binding the publishers will be liable only to replace the defective copy by another copy of this work then available.

Dedication

I dedicate my book to those countless warrior- freedom fighters of our country who were either prominent front-line leaders or who were innumerable common-citizens who otherwise played a no- mean part under the banner of their selfless leaders, who laid down their lives, lost their personal liberty and convenience, who willingly lost their jobs and means of livelihood, who willingly abandoned their studies, who braved the lathis of the police force, who spent the best days of their lives in the deep-dungeons of the Black-Water jails or in jails abroad such as in Aden never to join their dear family members again, who otherwise spent their years in the local jails during the course of a struggle for resurgence spread over an indefinable period since the beginning of the eighteenth century ending up with the Tryst With Destiny or with the Freedom at Midnight on the 15th of August 1947 when an immortal Bharatvarsh or Aryavrata or Hindustan or India was freed from the shackles of political dominance or on the 14th of August 1947 when a new nation in the nomenclature of Pakistan was born. Salute of dedication to those thousands of brave soldiers of various armed forces who martyred themselves in the defense of democracy and for the restoration of humane values during the First World War and the Second World War and who thus laid the foundation of the freedom of their country. Dedication offered also to such of brave men and women who performed similar deeds of bravery, sacrifice and service in achieving emancipation from the foreign rulers and occupiers in other parts of the country.

Contents

Acknowledgments

The list of persons to whom I am indebted is very long andI want to thank them all. I have drawn and borrowed from the works of so many distinguished writers, authors, journalists and commentators. Google search and Wikipedia have also been a source of information to me. The books of these eminent writers have enabled me to form my views and to draw up my conclusions. I express my sincere thanks to all of them. I have drawn from the Collected Works of Mahatma Gandhi which have been published by the Publication Division of India. It has also to be said that many of these stories and pieces of history relating to these patriots are already in the treasury of memory of many of us although they are safely consigned in some remote corners of our memories. So I have drawn from my blurred memory also.

In the completion of a work of this nature, the encouragement from one's family members and colleagues is a condition precedent. My father late Shri Jiwanlal Beohar always encouraged me to write. My elder sister Smt. Dr. Shashi Srivastava has shaped my career considerably. My wife Rupali has been a source of strength to me in all my projects. I have received such encouragement and motivation in full measure from my all of my family members. I am very much thankful to them also.

My colleagues at the Bar have also been of considerable encouragement to me. I convey my thanks to them also.

My sincere thanks to the printer of my book who has done such a good job in bringing out an attractive book.

N. C. Beohar

Foreword

We normally remember only the most prominent and we are prone to forget those who are less prominent although their contribution towards the attainment of the goal so achieved is no less significant. In the history of the freedom movement of India, normally the names which come to our memory are Lokmanya Balgangadhar Tilak, Mahatma Gandhi, Mahamana Madan Mohan Malviya, Chakravarti Rajgopalacharya, Lala Lajpat Rai, Sir Feroze Shah Mehta, Justice Tyebji, Deshbandhu C. R. Das, Dr. M. A. Ansari, B. C. Pal, Hakim Ajmal Khan, Motilal Nehru, Sardar Vallabh Bhai Patel, Dr. Rajendra Prasad, Pt. Govind Vallabh Pant, Dr. B. R. Ambedkar, Netaji Subhash Chandra Bose, Maharshi Purushottamdas Tandon, Maulana Abul Kalam Azad, Jawaharlal Nehru, Rafi Ahmad Kidwai, Sir Tej Bahadur Sapru, Kailashnath Katju, some of the members of the Muslim League (till such times as they did not canvass the cause of Pakistan). The names of revolutionaries such as Sardar Bhagat Singh, Rajguru, Sukhdev, Chandra Shekhar Azad, Ramprasad Bismil, Sardar Udham Singh, Madanlal Dhingra and others immediately come to our mind. We also immediately remember the Last Mughal Bahadur Shah Jafar, खूब लड़ी मर्दानी वो तो झाँसी वाली रानी थी (khoob ladi mardani vo to Jhansi vali rani thi.) Maharani Laxmi Bai, Mangal Pandey, Tatya Tope, Thakur Kunwar Singh, Begum Hazrat Mahal, Haidar Ali and Tipu Sultan and others. The industrial sector also played a very significant part in the freedom struggle. We can name only a few here, for example Dada Bhai Naoroji,

Jamshedji Naoroji, the House of Modys, the House of Sarabhai, the House of Birlas, the House of Seth Jamnalal Bajaj, the Singhanias, the House of Godrej and others. But there are some other equally important industrialists who have to be remembered by us. Several doctors and physicians also contributed their respective shares in the patriotic cause. For example Dr. B. C. Roy whose birth day on July 1 is commemorated as the Doctor's Day, Dr. Keshav Baliram Hedgewar the founder of RSS, Dr. Bal Krishna Moonje, Dr. Satyapal, Dr. Patabhi Sitaramayyya, Dr. Lakshmi Sehgal Dr. Sushila Nayyar, Dr. Gopichand Bhargava, Dr. M. A. Ansari, Dr. Jivraj Mehta, Dr. H. L. Sharma and others. We have to remember other equally eminent contributors from amongst this sector of service. No less important was the role played by various writers, intellectuals and journalists who ignited the fire of patriotism in the hearts of their fellow country-men. In almost all the important revolutions all over the world, philosophers and thinkers have ignited the fire of change with their writings.

The significant contribution of the natives of India i.e. the aborigines, various tribes such as the Gonds, Bhils, Baigas, Santhals, Pradhan, Meenas, Kol, Mundas, Mizos, Khasis, Oraon and others in the freedom struggle of India has not been properly recognised. It is mostly believed that the independence of India has been won by the upper classes living in the bigger towns and metropolitans of India. But this is not a proper assessment of the history of the freedom struggle. Indeed it is the various tribes who raised the banner of revolt against the forces of the East India Company. It is true that their struggle was not purely political in nature simply because they were too simple to be politically volatile. But still then, they fought against the British policy of aggrandizement in their traditional homelands and also against the evangelical campaign of the foreign missionaries. But then not much could have been expected from the simpletons amongst the tribes who were armed with rudimentary weaponry as against the deadly fire power of the British. Salute to their bravery and sacrifice. It is welcome that the benefits of modern civilization, science and technology should be extended to all sections of society including those who are living in deep forests. It may also be arguable that with the expansion of urbanisaion from cities towards villages and then towards inaccessible forests may necessitate de-forestation. But then this contention may be applicable with more force in the prevailing imperatives of today when there is an equal awakening towards planting a greater number of saplings. Could this be the reason behind the forces of the East India Company in the early eighteenth century when they were launching their new forest rules and laws.

Besides these revolts, there were several other revolts also but mostly against the zamindars and money-lenders. If the British had not permitted exploitation at the hands of those agents, then the revolts might not have taken place at all. Some of these revolts are– Deccan riots of Poona now Pune and Ahmednagar of 1874, Peasants revolt in Punjab in 1901, Eka movement in Hardoi, Barabanki, Bahraich and Sitapur in Uttar Pradesh in 1921-22, Mappila Revolt in Malabar Kerala in 1922 against the zamindari system and against the complicity of the British which later turned out to be communal also, Bardoli satyagraha of 1927, All India Kisan Congress of Lucknow of 1936 against the exploitation of zamindars and money-lenders, Bakasht movement of Bengal of 1938 to 1947.

Mahatma Gandhi was undoubtedly the spear-head of the movement, but then he drew his strength from his colleagues and also from the countless number of his countrymen who gave up almost everything they had at his call to provide momentum to the several movements which he launched. It is difficult to research these silent workers because many of them kept a low profile in all the agitations. They also serve who wait and watch as they say.

Another important question arises- whether we have to remember only those persons who have led from the front and in doing so; they have suffered loss of their lives or have been badly injured or whether we should also pay tribute to those innocent persons who have lost their lives either while taking part in a procession of protest or have lost their lives in a police firing. The number of the second category is countless, but they are no less significant contributors and martyrs.

In a war or in a battle field, there are soldiers who have lost their lives but who cannot be traced out. For these unknown soldiers we have **the Tomb of an Unknown Soldier**. We have such a monument in New Delhi whereby we pay our homage to the acts of unknown supreme sacrifice. There are other similar monuments all over the country.

Similarly in the freedom struggle from the British rule for a period of about ninety years starting from 1857 to 1947, millions have lost their lives. Eminent author and Parliamentarian Shashi Tharoor has estimated that about thirty five million Indians and the British citizens included have lost their lives in these struggles between the same period. In Oudh alone where some of the fiercest battles were staged during the 1857 uprisings, about 150000 persons are reported to have lost their lives and the number of civilians was about 100000 out of the total number. There is no account of the rebels who were hanged or blown away by cannon fire after the 1857 uprisings. In the Bibighar massacre during the uprisings, about 206 women and children were put to death by engaging two butchers; the dead or the dying were thrown into a well or into the Ganges river. The family of the Last Mughal as described by eminent author William Dalrymple Bahadur Shah Zafar suffered the most, four of his sons including Mirza Mughal, Mirza Khazir Sultan and grand-son Mirza Abu Bakr were ordered by William Hodson to be shot dead near the Khooni Darwaza Delhi Gate. The family had to endure untold misery, torture and hardship. He was deported to Rangoon with some of his close family members never to return to his home-land.

During the 1857 up-risings, some of the Indian policemen and soldiers refused to fire upon the rebels. For example, Jamadar Ishwari Prasad the Indian commander of the Quarter Guard of the British Army refused to arrest Mangal Pandey. He was summarily quarter-martialled, sentenced and hanged.

Mufti Nizamuddin of Lahore issued a fatwa to rebel against British rule. His brother Mufti Yaqinuddin and brother-in-law Abdur Rahman Nabi Baksha rebelled against the Government. They were hanged in Delhi.

Very little is known about the Gurjar uprising of 1857 which was organized by their leader Chaudhari Kadam Singh. Similarly also little is known about the uprising in Bihar which took place alongside the 1857 up-rising. Thakur Kunwar Singh 80 years old Rajput Zameendar of Jagdishpur, Bihar organized a rebellion against the British. Some of the participant-rebels were his brother Babu Amar Singh, commander Kare Krishna Singh, Hussain Baksha Khan, Ghulam Ali Khan and Fateh Singh of Gaya. Thakur Vishwanath Shahdev organized a mukti bahinialong with zamindars Pandey Ganpat Rai and Nadir Ali Khan. So also it has to be remembered with respect that in September 1858, Rai Ahmad Nawaz Khan Khural, head of the Khural tribe, led a revolt against the British near Neeli Bar district near the fabled Sutlej, Ravi and Chenab rivers. Ahmad was killed in an encounter with the British forces

After a comparative lull after the take-over by the British Crown from the East India Company in 1858, and after the awakening launched by Lokmanya Bal Gangadhar Tilak in 1904, the fires of movement were re-ignited which were quelled only after the 15th of August 1947 and with the arrival of the last refugee both in India and in the newly created Pakistan in 1947. During this period, we have had several incidents of unnecessary mass-killings. In the Jallianwala Bagh killings, 379 persons lost their lives while attending a meeting. Their names are inscribed in the memorial in Amritsar. In the Chauri Chaura incident twenty two policemen were killed by an agitating mob which led the Mahatma to suspend the movement. In the 1942 Quit India Movement a large number of persons lost their lives in the different parts of the country.

It is remarkable that a large number of foreigners had sympahies with the Indian cause. They lent all possible support to the Indian leaders and to the public at large. Many of them arrived in India, took active part in the several movements, went to the jails, adopted India as their homeland and several of them engaged themselves in various projects of social service to the deprived sections of the Indian society. A separate chapter has been devoted in this book for them.

The Mahatma used to console that in the attainment of independence, the country had suffered a comparatively lesser figure of lives lost than in similar attainments in some other countries. There was a great amount of truth in this assertion, however, till such time as **the great-exodus** occurred following the independence of India and the birth of Pakistan. The exchange of population led to loss of life in an unprecedented number. Millions lost their lives, a larger number of them were injured mostly permanently. The great Calcutta killings and the subsequent reprisals of Bihar resulted in the loss of a countless number of innocent lives. The Direct Action launched by Mohammad Ali Jinnah in October 1946 earlier had brought about in its wake loss of lives in thousands. In the Calcutta great-killings of 1946, in the killings in Bihar and Punjab and in other places in the newly created Pakistan, lacs of persons were killed. A countless number of women and young girls had to suffer untold ignominy, Their estimate can only be approximate. Earlier, thousands had been killed in the Moplah disturbances.

The family members of mass-leaders suffered during the confinement of their bread-winners. They co-operated whole-heartedly. Their contribution is almost forgotten today. But they are no lesser heroes in their own rights entitled to full recognition. Kasturba Gandhi was a great source of inspiration to the Mahatma firstly in South Africa and then in India during the freedom movements. Let us remember her as a freedom fighter in her own right. Rajvanshi Devi the wife of Dr. Rajendra Prasad is an example worth note. Her husband was engaged in various movements all through out. He gave up his legal practice at the call of nation. Yet she endured valiantly. Janki Devi Bajaj burnt all her expensive clothes in 1921 and lived a life of simplicity. Kamla Nehru is yet another shining example of supreme self sacrifice. There are a very large number of such stout-hearted house-wives who allowed their illustrious husbands to sacrifice everything so that the nation might awaken. Let us remember these great ladies also.

In the First World War 1914-1919 and in the Second World War 1939-1945, thousands of Indian soldiers paid with ultimate sacrifice. Mahatma Gandhi had expected that the British would grant at least greater autonomy after the closure of the first war in return for the participation in the War. These brave soldiers were laying down their lives not only in the defence of democracy, but they also had a bright future ahead in their eyes their motherland would be liberated after the closure of the War. The Mahatma had worked hard for the enlistment of the Indian soldiers in the war effort. But his hopes were dashed afterwords. The British Government engaged the Indian soldiers in the second war despite the refusal of the Mahatma and the INC. In these two great wars, thousands of Indian soldiers lost their lives. They were engaged in them with a fervent hope that their country would become independent one day soon after the end of the war. Therefore, they were no less than martyrs in the cause of national duty. Their names are inscribed in the stone-pillars of the monuments in New Delhi.

Azad Hind Fauz of Netaji Subhash Chandra Bose is a shining chapter in the history of the freedom struggle. Brave soldiers of the Fauz martyred themselves in various battle-fields. Let us remember them also.

It has been my sincere effort to track down as many unsung heroes as possible. But then I suffer from a handicap that it is possible to miss out on many of them despite best efforts on my part. My sincere apologies for this inadvertent omission on my part. Even some facts may not be accurate.I may stand to correction there.

Secondly, it is difficult to say who are unsung heroes and who are still remembered today. There are several heroes who are commonly remembered today on their national days of remembrance. There are some others who are so prominent that their names are subject of common folk-lore. There are some other heroes who figure in the books of schools and colleges and they are remembered in this manner. Some other important heroes are remembered as subjects of academic research. Some others find remembrance in academic conferences and in similar group discussions and deliberations. Furthermore, it can also be a choice of personal assessment as to who is a forgotten hero. In other words, it is not easy to find all the unsung heroes. Perhaps it has also to be admitted that it is not possible to count and remember so many thousands of brave martyrs individually. Tributes are paid to them collectively on national festival days. I also believe that their names and their deeds should be compiled in a book shape as far as possible.

As said earlier, in almost all the countries the world over, there is a national monument erected and constructed in the memory of **the Unknown Soldier** who has laid down his life in the defence of his country. The grateful nation pays its homage by placing a wreath in this monument every year. My effort in writing this book is something akin to this expression of national gratefulness. There are monuments in the memory of the prominent leaders all over the country. If there are no such monuments in the memory of civilian lives lost, then it is recommended that such monuments can still be erected.

In the creation of this book, I have relied upon the secondary sources. I have tried my best to be reliable to the best of my ability. I have tried to place all the facts in an honest and truthful manner. Still then there is a possibility that some of the presented facts may be open to some correction. Some dates may not be accurate. Spellings of some names may not be correct. Even some names may not be correctly mentioned. However, if despite my best efforts and sincere desire, there are still some errors in the text of this book, then I will like to express my regrets apologies.

I have tried to cover as many freedom-fighters as it could be possible for me. Still then, some eminent freedom-fighters may have been left out inadvertently. I have also described some other freedom-fighters, eminent industrialists, journalists, intellectuals, writers and authors, doctors and spiritual leaders who are remembered today for their outstanding contributions. I have described them for the reason that I found that there are some remarkable stories about these great persons which have to be brought to the notice and knowledge of the readers. I have great respect for them. I would like to express my regrets if any errors or corrections are located.

Besides the British rule over India, there were other European powers also who made their presence felt here even though not as prominently as that of the British Raj. These powers are the Portuguese, the French, the Dutch and the Danes. No freedom struggles were staged against the Dutch, the French and the Danes. Such a struggle was waged only against the Portuguese occupiers in Goa and adjoining territories. A large number of freedom-fighters lost their lives in the Goanese territories. The native Goanese had to struggle for their liberation. I have made an attempt to deal with the encounters with these four other European powers also.

East India Company had entered into Subsidiary Treaties with a large number of Princely States in their drive of imperialism in a place which was susceptible to easy subjugation. Lord Wellsely had introduced this theory and practice. All of these treaties ceased to exist with the lapse of the paramountcy of the British Crown as a result of the independence of the sub-continent. Almost all of them chose to join either of the two unions. But Jammu & Kashmir, Hyderabad, Junagarh and Bhopal expressed their desire to remain independent except Junagarh who chose to join the Union of Pakistan. The dates of merger of these states with either of the two unions were much later than either the 14th of August or 15th of August which are the two respective dates for Pakistan and India respectively. There was substantial loss of life in these operations. In my book, I have dealt with these operations also.

In my book, I have added some allied subjects and topics also to be refreshed in our memory such as the National Flag, monuments and pensions for the heroes, jail literature etc. I believe stories regarding them need to be refreshed in our memory. There is a possibility of some errors with respect to some dates and facts. They are innadvertent and I sincerely stand to be corrected where needed.

It is heartening to learn that we have the good fortune of some freedom-fighters still amongst us. Only the other say, one of the leading dailies of the country has high-lighted the profile of Shri Datta Gandhi who has recently turned 100. His contact with Mahatma Gandhi once in Oundh Pune was one of the defining moments of his life. He left studies at the call of the Mahatma and took part in the Quit India Movement of 1942. He was confined to the Vispur jail for eighteen months. His brother Shankarbhai was also a noted freedom-fighter who spent six yeas in the British jail.

I do not know upto what extent I have succeeded in my humble effort. The nation is celebrating the 75th anniversary of independence. This is an auspicious occasion to pay my tributes to these valiant heroes in the shape of this book. I will also like to repeat that it is not easy to determine who is remembered and who is forgotten. Subjective discretion can differ. However, I have tried my best to be as investigative as possible. I shall be extremely happy if my esteemed readers are able to find some merit in my work. With these observations, may I place this book **Forgotten and Legends of the Freedom Movement of India** before my esteemed readers.

N. C. Beohar

Jabalpur

Chapter One

From the East India Company to the British Raj

It is difficult to find out who is the first indigenous force to rise in revolt against the foreign domination over the destiny of India. The East India Company arrived in India in 1600 during the rule of Jehangir to be followed by the French, the Danes and the Dutch. The Portuguese and the French were not able to establish themselves up to the extent the British were successful, although they had their pockets in different parts of India. The revolt against these European powers started almost the moment they entered into the Indian arena.

The three battles of Panipat have decided the destiny of India, the first between Babar and Ibrahim Lodhi of 1526 which helped in the establishment of the Mughal dynasty in India, the second battle of Panipat between the forces of Robert Clive for the East India Company and Nawab Sirajudowla of Bengal in 1556 in which the Nawab was defeated largely due to the treachery of Mir Jafar and Jagat Seth and the reigns of the Company were reinforced in India and the third battle of Panipat between Ahmad Shah Abdali and the Marathas on 14. 1. 1761. Earlier, the Peshwa and the Mughal Emperor of Delhi had entered into a bi-lateral treaty to help each other in times of need. But the Mughal nobility were divided into two camps, one camp sided with the local Muslims while the other faction sided with the foreign invaders. The ruler of Oudh sided with Abdali in the name of religion.

It was a fierce battle in which the Marathas were badly routed. Almost all of their generals were killed in the battle field. But we are here concerned more with the revolt against the East India Company or against the British establishment. The above facts, however, go to show why and how the foreign rule was established in India and also how by way of the Newtonian law of action is equal to rection and it is always in the opposite direction, the forces of opposition set in motion in Hindustan almost instantaneously. The locals were of different hues coloured by their personal vested interests. Some favored the foreign rulers, others decided to oppose them even at the cost of the supreme sacrifice. It is difficult if not impossible to determine who fired the first shot which ended up with the hoisting of the tri-colour from the ramparts of the Red Fort on the day of the Tryst with Destiny and also with the birth and creation of a new nation in the name of the Islamic Republic of of Pakistan.

Resentment against the East India Company started simultaneously with their ascension upon the rule over the country. So it is very difficult to determine who fired the first salvo against them. However, some approximate estimate and determination could be attempted. Reaction and resentment against the entrenchment of the East India Company started the very first day. Various rulers and kings all over the country offered their resistances. Since they were sporadic and not organized and united, they were unsuccessful in their efforts. But still then, a large number of Indians and rebel rulers lost their lives. Their accounts are not fully available. Resistance continued unabated. So it is not possible to assess the exact and accurate loss of life. They are also **the Forgotten Heroes.**

However, the British were not the only European power to enter into the Indian domain. Their presence here lasted from 1600 to August 1947 i.e. a total of 347 years although their rule over the entire country started from 1858 onwards when the British Crown assumed complete authority over Indian affairs from the East India Company. In 1600, Sir Thomas Roe arrived in India by anchoring in the Western coast. Emperor Jehangir patronized him with trading concessions little realizing that thereby he was facilitating the establishment of the mighty British Empire. Thereafter, the next 258 years the British East India Company spent in transforming itself from a mere trading assignment into the precursor of the occupier of the Brightest Jewel in the British Empire. In other words, from that day and date onwards, i.e. since 1858, they were here not for trade and commerce any more. But they were here progressively to transform themselves as masters to rule over their British Indian subjects. The East India Company of England was preceded by the Portuguese and they were followed by the Dutch, the French and the Danes. The British had out-shown other powers. This is the reason why more prominence is accorded to the domination of the British Raj and also to the freedom struggle of India against them.

Chapter Two

Some of the Early Warriors against the British East India Company

Maveeran Alagumuthu Kone (1728–1757) He fought the forces of the East India Company, but was defeated.

Puli Thevar (1715–1767)–He ruled astate in Tirunelveli and fought the forces of the East India Company. But then he ultimately lost and was executed in 1767.

Maruthu Pandiyar (1748–1801) He hailed from Madras, now Tamil Nadu.

Dheeran Chinnamalai (17. 4. 1756–31. 7. 1805)–He was a warrior from Tamil Nadu who fought against the British East India Company. In the battle of Coimbatore, he escaped and thereafter, he resorted to the guerilla warfare methods. He had a vast army which was trained by the French military who were the traditional rivals of the British. Dheeran helped Tupu Sultan in his crusades against the British. But then finally, he was caught by the British because of the treachery of one of his associates namely Nallappan. The Company forces hanged him along with his associates sometime in 1805.

Veerapandiya Kattabomman or Gettibommu (**3 January 1760 – 16 October 1799**)–He was a chieftain from Panchalankurichi in Tamil Nadu of the eighteenth century. He refused to pay taxes to the East India Company and also refused their domination. So he had to wage battles against the forces of the Company. In the battle of 1797-98, the Company forces were defeated. But then in the subsequent encounter, Kottabomman was defeated, captured and hanged on 16. 10. 1799. His capture was made easy by the traitorous help of another rival chieftain. However, Kottabommans brother Oomaidurai and his associate Duraisingam continued to defy the Company. They were also captured and hanged in 1801.

Veluyudhan Champakarman Thampi (1765- 1809) took part in the battle of Quilon against the British East India Company.

Ahmadullah Shah–1787-1858-He was a maulvi of Faizaabad who came to be known as the Lighthouse of the Revolution of 1857. He did not allow the British to enter Faizabad for nearly one year. He was ably supported by Subedar Ghamandi Siingh and Subedar Umrao Singh in the historic battle of Chinhat. He was betrayed by Raja Jagannath Rao which led to his capture and killing. The Company rewarded the Raja with Rs. 50000/ for his loyalty.

General Bakht Khan–1797–1859–He was the commander-in-chief of the rebel forces in the 1857 rebellion against the forces of the British East India Company. He was earlier a combatant in the Company forces and after the first Anglo- Afghan war, he rose to a higher rank in the Company forces as a subedar. But then he shifted his alliance with the rebels and he began to be called general by them for his several acts of valor. By July 1857, Bahadur Shah Zafar had been proclaimed the Emperor of India by the rebel forces. But then soon the revolt began to suffer and the Company forces achieved ascendancy. Bahadur Shah Zafar tried to take shelter in Humayun's tomb in the Nizamuddin area of Delhi. But then he was betrayed by one of his confidants which led to his capture, trial and final deportation to his resting place in Rangoon. Bakht Khan continued to fight until he was fatally wounded in a clash and died on 13. 5. 1859.

Sangolli Royanna (1798–1831)–He fought the forces of the East India Company. He was a military chief or shetsanadi in the kingdom of Rani Channamma of Kittur Karnataka. He wanted to install Shivligappa the adopted son of Rani Channappa and the King Mallasarju to the throne of Kittur. The East India Company opposed this move. They wanted to include Kittur in their expansion because the kingdom did not have a male claimant to the throne. But in the Hindu way of life an adopted son has the same value as a natural born son. Sangolli engaged the Company forces in a guerilla warfare knowing full well that he did not have much of a chance against the much larger force of the enemy face to face on the ground. But finally, he was caught due to an act of treachery and hanged in April 1830.

Uyalawada Narasimha Reddy–He led a revolt in Andhra Pradesh, but was defeated and martyred in 1847.

Maniram Dutt Barua (Dewan) 17. 4. 1806–26. 2. 1856–He was the pioneer in the field of establishment of the gardens and estates in Jorhat Assam in a truly commercial and organised basis. At that time, the Governor-General was Lord Wlliam Benthick. He encouraged the British entrepreneur to enter this lucrative field. This led to professional competition between them and consequently to hostility also. The British tried to wreck the monopoly of the Dewan. He had sympathy with the Nagas also and therefore, he canvassed the cause of them with the British. His ancestors had moved into Assam from Kannauj at the time of the rule of the Ahom kingdom. He wanted the restoration of the Ahoms. He decided to resort to revolutionary methods against the British in the company of Piyali Singh during the 1857 revolt. But he was soon caught by the British and hanged.

Chetram Jatav–He was one of the active participants of the 1857 revolt hailing from the Eta district of United Provinces. The Company forces captured him, hung him up from a tree and shot him into martyrdom.

Uyyalawada Narsimha Reddy (24. 11. 1806-22. 2. 1847)-He organised about 5000 peasants in the Coonoor district as a revolt against the new agrarian policy of the British East India Company of agrarian settlement. This policy was helpful to the Company and also to some of the bigger land-lords and various vested interests. But it was exploitry of the smaller tiller and cultivators. Narsimha Reddy engaged the Company forces in battle field. A large number of British soldiers and also perhaps a much larger number of freedom fighters were killed. Narsimha Reddy was captured and finally publicly hanged before a crowd of 2000 persons on 22. 2. 1847. Kurnool Airport commemorates his memory as it is named after him.

Jayee Rajguru–In 1804, there was a revolt against the British East India Company against the annexation of Odisha a year earlier by the Company. Jayee Rajguru was the foremost warrior of this revolt. He was captured and hanged and in this manner he became the first freedom fighter and martyr from Odisha.

Buxi Jagabandhu–In 1917, Buxi staged a revolt against the British East India Company with the help of an army of the Paikas.

Samantha Madhaba ChandraSamantaray–He led a revolt against the British in 1827.

Baji Rout– He refused to ferry the British troops across the Brahmani River. He was killed by them. He was hardly 12 years of age then.

Chaki Khuntia–He was one of the prominent freedom fighters of 1857 uprisings. He offered assistance to the legendary Rani Laxmi Bai in her crusadess against the British forces.

Surendra Sai–23. 1. 1806– He is at par with anyone of the more talked-about revolutionaries of the 1857 era or for that matter with anyone subsequently without trying to take anything away from these immortal martyrs. He hailed from the princely state of Sambalpur, Orissa now Odisha. After the demise of King Mahendra Sai in 1827, Surendra was entitled legitimately to accede to the throne. The British intervened to allow his widow Rani Mohan Kumari to succeed to the vacant throne. After some time, however, the British intervened again by deposing the Rani and replacing her with one Narayan Singh ignoring one more time the better claims of Surendra Sai. King Narayan Sai died in the year 1849 without a male heir-apparent to the throne. Governor-General Lord Dalhousie invoked the doctrine of lapse and annexed Sambalpur to the territories of the Company. Surendra Sai was a devoted tribal who wanted to safeguard the tribal traditions and culture from the onslaught of the missionaries. Surendra launched his campaign against the British when he was hardly 18 years of age and this confrontation ended with his passing away on 23. 5. 1884 in the remote confinement of the Asirgarh jail. He had earlier voluntarily surrendered in 1845 in the hope that some amicable rapprochement might be established with the British. But his hopes were dashed and he was again incarcerated for the next 17 years. After his release, he was again put behind the bars in 1865 and he spent the remaining part of his mortal existence of next 19 years in the Asirgarh confinement. In this manner, he spent about 36 years of his precious life in the British jails.

Surendra Sai was assisted by the following associates in his crusades— Madho Singh, Kunjal Singh, Airi Singh, , Bairi Singh, Uddat Sai, Ujjal Sai, Khangeshwar Deo, Saligram Bariha, Govind Singh, Pahar Singh, Rajee Ghasia, Kamal Singh, Hali Singh, Salik Ram Bariha, Loknath Panda, Mrityunjai Panigrahi, Sahabandu Hota, Padmanav Guru, Trilochan Panigrahi and many others.

Nawab Wajid Ali Shah–30. 7. 1822-1. 9. 1887–He ruled over Oudh for nearly nine years from 13. 2. 1847 to 11. 2. 1856 when he was deposed by the Company on the ground of mis-rule and he was exiled to an out-skirt of Calcutta on a pension. He was a great patron of arts, music. Dance and other fine arts. He was a great exponent of the kathak form of classical dance. He composed the popular song–बाबुल मोरा नैहर छूटो जाय (babul mora naihar chhooto jaye.)

Azimullah Shah–1830-1859 –He was one of the heroes of 1857. He was Prime Minister of Nana Saheb. He stood for Hindu-Muslim unity. He died of fever in 1859.

Qasim Nanautavi (1832–1880)-He founded the Darul Uloom Deoband and took part in the 1857 revolt. Mahmud Hasan Deobandi (1851–1920)was also a crusader against the British.

Syed Allauddin Hyder or Maulvi Alauddin —He was the Imam of Makkah Masjid Hyderabad, India and one of the Islamic divines of that period. But he was a great patriot also who wanted to rid his country of the British occupation. On 17. 7. 1857, he led an attack accompanied by 300 rebels upon the British Residency in Hyderabad. There were several casualties including some martyrs. Maulvi was captured, deported to the Cellular Jail where he died. He is credited to be the first rebel in the after-math of the revolt of 1857 to be deported to the Cellular Jail.

Bakhtawar Singh was hanged in February 1858 for his part in the up-rising. Diwan Gulab Rai, Chimalal and Bashir Ullah Khanwere also other heroes of 1857.

Peer Ali Khan 1812—1857–He used to pass on secret papers and information to the rebels of 1857. But then he was finally caught along with his associates on 4. 7. 1857. They were all publicly hanged by the Commissioner William Tayler along with 14 other rebels. They were Ghasita Khalifa, Ghulam Abbas, Nandu Lal alias Sipahi, Jumman, Maduwa, Kajil Khan, Ramzani, Peer Bakhsh, Wahid Ali, Ghulam Ali, Mahmood Akbar and Asrar Ali Khan.

Nana Saheb Dhondu Pant– Balaji Rao Bhatt commonly known as Nana Saneb was born in Bithoor Kanpur in 1824. After Shivaji's death in 1749, Nana Ji was hailed as the most powerful of the former Maratha Confederacy. Maharaja Shivaji did not leave behind any heirs. So he nominated the Peshwas of Poona now Pune as his heir. He organized Poona as a developed metropolis. In the 1857 revolt, he was one of the principal participants. He even defeated the British army in a battle in Kanpur.

Brijis Qadir–20. 8. 1843–14. 8. 1893–He was son of Nawab Wazid Ali Shah and Begum Hazrat Mahal. In 1856, Wazid Ali

Shah was deposed by the British on the charges of mis-rule and exiled to Calcutta. Begum Hazrat Mahal led the rebels in Oudh in 1857, they defeated the British forces in the battle of Chinhat and Qadir was installed as Nawab at age 11 by his mother. The rebels defended the city ably for a long time. But then they were finally routed. Begum and Qadir fled to Nepal. Later Qadir returned to Calcutta in 1893 and it is said that he was poisoned to death by his adversaries.

Maruthu Pandiyar ruler of Shivgangai state in TamilNadu resisted the imperialism of the British East India Company.

Dhan Singh Gurjar or Dhunna Singh was a kotwal of the city of Meerut when the war of 1857 broke out on 10. 5. 1857. He is one of the martyrs of 1857.

Shaheed Veer Narayan Singh took active part in the rebel activities in 1857 and worked in the 1856 famines. He fought the British forces in 1857, arrested and sentenced to death. He is the first martyr from Chhattisgarh. district.

Bheema Nayak—He was one of the heroes of the 1857 uprisings. He was captured by the British, confined to the Port Blair and Nicobar jails and finally hanged on 29. 12. 1876. The Government of Madhya Pradesh has launched a scheme known as Shaheed Bheema Nayak Pariyojna. There is a memorial Bheema Nayak Memorial in his village Dhaba Badwani

Ubaidullah Sindhi-(10. 3. 1872- 21. 8. 1944)—He was born in a Sikh Khatri family in the district of Sialkot now in Pakistan as Buta Singh Uppal. Some of his friends gave him a few books related to Islam. He was deeply impressed by the philosophy of Islam and he converted himself into this religion at age 16. He enrolled himself into the Darul ul Ullum Deoband where he came in contact with several Islamic scholars. He developed a theory of Pan-Islamic movement, but at the same time, he strove for Hindu-Muslim unity. He visited Afghanistan where he befriended the Afghan ruler Amir Habibullah Khan. He supported the plans of Raja Mahendra Pratap Singh for a Bolshevik revolution in India. He became Home Minister in the Provisional Govvernment of India in exile in Kabul with Raja Mahendra Pratap Singh as President and Maulana Barkatullah Bhopali as Prime Minister. He visited Russia in the midst of the First World War and spent six months there. He visited Turkey in 1923 and espoused the cause of freedom of India from that platform. Finally he returned to India. But owing to indifferent health, he passed away in Hyderabad in 1944. He is also known for the Reshmi Rumal Movement or Silk Letter Movement wherein he deals in details with the 1857 rebellion and the Faraizi Movement.

Seth Hirachandrai Vishnudas (1862-1928)–He hailed from Sindh Karachi now in Pakistan. He promoted Hindu Muslim unity. He was elected to the Karachi Municipality in 1888 and served till asMayor of Karachi from 1911 to 1921 and as President of the body for ten years. He beautified the city during his tenure as mayor. He was appointed to the Viceroy's Executive Council and he was an ex-officio member of the Privy Council till his death. He organised the annual session of the INC held in Karachi in 1913. He opposed the Simon Commission when it arrived in India in 1928. He was going towards the Assembly Hall to cast his vote against the Commission when all of a sudden he died on the way.

Chapter Three

Some of the other occupiers in India

1) Movement for the liberation of Goa

It is generally believed that the wars of independence were fought by the Indians exclusively against the British. This is the reason why nobody talks about almost anything about the earlier ambushes, troubles, sporadic encounters and bigger engagements between the local kings and queens on the one hand and the Portuguese or other foreign forces on the other hand. They have not been high-lighted in the pages of our history. The Portuguese arrived in India much earlier than the British, their colonies were established here much earlier. Vasco de Gama set sail east-word in a fleet of four ships on 8. 7. 1497 and arrived in India on 18. 5. 1498. The fleet anchored in the Malabar Coast. They were followed by the Dutch in 1595, by the British in 1600 by the French in 1602 and finally by the Danish.

It is rather surprising that the liberation of Goa has not received as much high-light in the history of freedom movements as has been accorded to the independence of India from the British rule. Goa was liberated on 19. 12. 1961. But this date has not received the same attention as 15. 8. 1947 when the British left the Indian shores. It is perhaps also surprising that the Indian leaders did not launch a concerted struggle for the liberation of Goa from the Portuguese and of other possessions which were under the control of the Dutch, the French and the Danes side by side along with the struggle for the emancipation of the mainland India from the British control. It is also possible that the leaders were expecting the Portuguese and other powers unilaterally to liberate their possessions in the wake of the independence of India. Portuguese remained adamant. However, the French withdrew pracefully after the Indian independence. The Indian independence day 15th August receives the same importance in Goa as anywhere in the entire country. But the liberation of Goa on 19. 12. 1961 does not receive the same highlight in any part of the country. It is perhaps due to the fact that even during the struggle for the independence of mainland India, hardly anybody paid the same quantity and quality of attention to the liberation of Goa. Of course, there were diplomatic efforts against the occupation of Goa by the Portuguese across thousands of nautical miles away in the UNO forum and elsewhere in various international meetings. But those efforts were a far cry from the various movements that were launched against the British Government.

The 17th century has been treated in the history books as the Age of Adventure and Discovery and Exploration, Renaissance, Scientific and Industrial Revolution. European powers registered great advancements. They felt the necessity to expand their horizons. Almost all the European powers of those days had developed strong naval fleets. So their monarchs issued charters and commands for the exploration of the East. They established their companies for trade and commerce with the Eastern world which could be thus discovered. India had already been trading upon the sea-waves much earlier. The Chola King Rajendra had been trading with Egypt and several other countries in the eleventh century. But after this dynasty, the naval power of the Indians did not develop because of the antipathy of the subsequent kings. So in a way this void was filled up by the influx of various Western powers in the Indian markets. There was almost no unity and cohesion between the kings and rulers of India of those times. These factors helped the new arrivals to diversify their initial interests from mere trade and commerce to territorial expansions and imperialistic ambitions. Four European powers were able to set themselves entrenched upon the Indian soil. They are the Dutch, Portuguese, the British, the French and the Danes. Spain was another European power to embark upon a similar expedition, but in a different sphere.

The Portuguese arrived in India much earlier than the British, their colonies were established here much earlier. Vasco de Gama set saileast-word in a fleet of four ships on 8. 7. 1497 and arrived in India on 18. 5. 1498. The fleet anchored in the Malabar Coast. Zamorin was the local ruler who immediately gave commercial and trading concessions to the Portuguese. By 1560, the Portuguese were able to establish their political control over Goa, Daman, Diu, Nagar and Haveli and the Anjediva Island thanks due to the efforts of their governor Francisco de Almeida. He constructed four forts in the region. Beginning with trade and commerce, the Portuguese developed territorial and expansionist designs. In 1511, they conquered the city of Malacca Islands and Hormuz. In 1526, they captured Mangalore. By 1559, they had consolidated their stronghold over these territories. They wanted to expand further East. But their designs were foiled by the Mughal Emperor who defeated them in an encounter in 1631 and they were deprived of their possessions in Hubli. By then, other European powers the British, the Dutch and the French had also arrived upon the

Indian theater. So the ambitions of Portuguese were stalled to mere the confines of Goa and the adjoining places.

Another factor which militates against the Portuguese was their evangelical ambition to convert the entire population to the Roman Catholic faith. They established Inquisition Board of 1561 to supervise the forcible the re-conversion of the locals who had earlier converted into Roman Catholic faith but who were suspected of secretly observing their previous religious practices. The Board acted ruthlessly. Thousands of the natives were summarily tried in the Portuguese courts, sentenced harshly and many of them were executed. The Portuguese Inquisition earned a bad reputation all over the world and it was given up in 1812. Rest of India was ruled over by the Mughal Empire. They also offered resistance and this is another reason why the Portuguese could not expand further. Those thousands who lost their lives in this manner are no less martyrs in their own rights and they have also to be remembered with reverence.

Probably the first attempt towards the liberation of Goa was in 1787 in the shape of the Conspiracy of the Pintos. There were several other unsuccessful attempts thereafter. Luis de Menzes Braganza founded his newspaper OHeraldo which served the purpose of igniting the spirit of freedom. The Portuguese retaliated by suppressing the freedom of speech and expression. Not much headway could be registered in the nineteenth century. But by the turn of the twentieth century, the movement for liberation gathered momentum along with the possibility of the freedom of India. Goanese leaders also gathered courage from the Indian leaders.

In 1928, Tristao de Braganca founded the Goa National Congress. The Portuguese Government passed the Acto Colonial((Colonial Act) which restricted political activities, movements and protests in 1930. A. G. Tendulkar became the President of the Goanese National Congress. Juliao Menzes is another prominent name in the Goanese struggle. From amongst the Indian leaders, Dr. Ram Manohar Lohia took active interest in the Goanese liberation. He visited Goa in 1946, stayed with Juliao Menzes and they began to organize public meetings. They were arrested but they were soon set free following popular uproar. By now, several other parties had been established with the common denominator of the liberation of Goa. Several revolutionary groups and revolutionaries merged upon the firmament such as the Azad Gomantak Dal which was founded by Vishwanth Lawande, Narayan Hari Naik, Dattatraya Deshpande, Prabhakar Sinai and others. They were arrested and rigorously sentenced. Many of them spent about 14 years in the Portuguese jails in Lisbon and Angola. The Azad Gomantak Dal succeeded in liberating some parts of Dadra and Haveli. The Portuguese governor responded by calling for more reinforcements to deal with the situation.

Several women also volunteered in the struggle. To name a few of them—Sudhakar Mahadev Joshi the wife of eminent Vedic scholar Pandit Mahadev Shastri Joshi, her sister Ashatai, Laxmi Pangukar, Mario Azaro, Prema Purav, Shalini Loyekarr, Shashikala Nodarkar, Sindhu Deshpande, Suryakanti Phaldesai and Vilasani Mahala.

In the meanwhile. India was freed in August 1947. But the Portuguese authorities refused to hand over their possessions to India. Dr. Ram Manohar Lohia, therefore, called upon the Goanese to carry out their struggle single handedly. He is one of the prominent leaders from the mainland to take part in the liberation of Goa.

In 1953, Tristao de Braganca founded the Goa Action Committee. Another prominent leader to be arrested was P. D. Gaitonde. Jan Sangh leader Jagannath Rao Joshi organized a mass protest. The authorities responded with police force and firing which resulted in the death of several volunteers. Praja Socialist Party was another party from the Indian side was the Praja Socialiist Party. Another prominent revolutionary was Shivaji Rao Desai who founded the Goa Liberation Army. They carried out several raids upon the Goanese establishments. The volunteers of the Rashtriya SwayamSevak Sangh began to take more active part in the struggle in the early fifties.

The Indian Prime Minister Pt. Jawaharlal Nehru appealed to the Portuguese Government to hand over their possessions willingly to India. But to no avail. On the contrary, their Prime Minister Antonio Salazar appealed to the NATO powers to exert pressure upon the Government of India from trying to liberate the Portuguese possessions in India. The Goanese freedom fighters had succeeded in liberating some portions of Dadra and Nagar Haveli. But the Government of India decided not to integrate them into the Union of IIndia. But by now, popular feeling in India was brewing up in favor of completing their independence by achieving departure of all the foreign powers from the Indian soil. The Indian Government could not keep themselves neutral any more. Accordingly in late 1961, the Indian Government sent military forces in the shape of the

Air Force and troops in the Goanese territory. They received almost no opposition. The Governor General of Portuguese Goa General Manuel António Vassalo de Silva signed an instrument of surrender. Major General Kunhiraman Palat Candeth was appointed Military Governor General of Goa. In 1963, the Government of India passed the 12th Amendment Act of 1963 formally integrating Goa in the Union of India. Goa, Daman, Diu, Nagar Haveli became Union Territories. In 1987, Goa was made a full fledged Union state.

So Goa stood liberated from 19. 12. 1962 from the Portuguese rule lasting 451 years.

2) The French Colonies in India–

The following are the French colonies in India—Pondicherry now Puducherry, Karaikal, Masulipatnam, Mahe on the Malabar Coast, Calicut, Chandernagar now Chandan-nagar in Bengal, Cossimbazar, Jugdia, Balam and Yanon (Andhra Pradesh on the Coromandel Coast.)

The French East India Company or La Compagnie française des Indes Orientales was formed under the rule of Cardinal Richelieu in 1642. The Company sent an expedition in 1667 under the command of Francois Canon accompanied by a Persian namely Marccara. They reached Surat in 1668. First French factory was set up inSurat in 1668, another such factory in Masulipatnam In 1669. Chandernagore now Chandan-nagar was established as a French colony in 1672 with the consent of the Nawab Shista Khan the Mughal chief of Bengal. In 1673, the French acquired Pondicherry. However, the British East India Company took over Surat, Masulipatnam and Balam from the

French East India Company. By now, there were three European powers namely the Portuguese, the Dutch and the British who had conflicting interests. There were constant conflicts between the French and the Dutch. The Durch were routed by the British and they had to leave the Indian scene.

Competent French Governors like Pierre Christophe Le Noir (1726-1735) and Pierre Benoit Dumas (1735–1741) consolidated their French stay in India. They tried to beautify the French colonies particularly Pondicherry. But with the advent of Joseph Franccois Dulex in 1741, their ambitions grew in the field of territorial expansion. Duplex was able to bring Hyderabad and Cape Comorin under their control.

Robert Clive arrived in India in 1744 and the fortunes of the East India Company took a turn for the better and conversely the fortunes of the French suffered a nose dive. The French sided with the Nawab of Bengal Sirajuddowla against the British forces under the command of Robert Clive. The Nawab and the French combine were defeated in the decisive battle of Plassey in 1757. The entire Bengal fell under the control of the British East India Company. The French Government recalled Duplex to Paris. They sent another competent governor, Lally Tollendal, to take revenge from the British. However, he was unsuccessful. The French lost Hyderabad in the battle of Wandiwash in 1760 and the same year they lost Pondicherry in the siege of Pondicherry 1760. The two powers were in constant wars in Europe whereby the British returned Pondicherry now Puducherry to the French in 1763. As a result of the Napoleonic War, the French recovered Chandernagore, Karaikal, Mahe, Yenon, parts of Masulipatnam, Kozhikode and Suural in addition to Pondicherry. In other words, they recovered almost the entire lost ground. Pondicherry changed hands between them a number of times until finally remaining with the French till 1954. Another aftermath of this war was that the British took control of several other territories of India such as Orissa also. This was their greatest expansionist achievement and this is how they began to scent to control the entire country gradually thereafter.

After the independence of India in August 1947 from British rule, France unilaterally and peacefully handed it over to India in October 1947 after some early hesitation. They declared Chandernagore as a free city in 1947. In June 1948, the French conducted a referendum in the French settlements and almost the entire population voted in favor of their merger with India. Chandernagore was made over to India on 2. 5. 1950 and the Government of India merged it with the province of Bengal. On 1. 11. 1954, France handed over Pondicherry, Yenon, Mahe and Karaikal to India and these territories came to be known as the Union Territory of Pondicherry or Puducherry.

This is how the French control over the Indian soil came to a peaceful end.

3) The Dutch in India–

In 1602, the United East India Company of the Netherlands was formed and was commissioned to trade in East India including India. They founded their first factory in Masulipatnam in Andhra Pradesh and then in Suratte and in the Dutch Bengal in 1616 and 1627 respectively. Portugal was already in control of Ceylon now Sri Lanka. But the Dutch took it over from them in 1656, Malabar Coast in 1671 and Nagapattinam near

Madras now Chennai. But then they were soon overpowered by the growing power of the expanding East India Company. Marthanda Varma the ruler of Travancore defeated the Dutch forces in the battle of Colachel in 1741. By virtue of the treaty of 1814 between the Dutch and the British in Europe, Dutch Coromandel and Dutch Bengal were returned to them by the East India Company. But then by another treaty of 1824 between them, all Dutch possessions were made over to the British East India Company. In this manner, the Dutch were devoid of all of their Indian possessions by 1825. There was another treaty between the two powers subsequently whereby the British left Indonesia in favor of the Dutch and the Dutch reciprocated by surrendering their interests in India in favor of the British East India Company. This is how they said an adieu to India.

4) Danish colonial possessions in India–

Denmark was another European power to have possessions in India. They are Thararangambadi or Tranquebar in Tamil Nadu, Serampore in West Bengal and the Nicobar Islands. The Danish ships arrived in Tharangambadi in 1620. Raghunath Nayak the ruler of the neighboring Thanjavur entered into a bilateral trade agreement with them giving them possession of this town as against an annual payment of rent worth Rs. 3111/. The Danes could trade mutual commodities in exchange.

The King of Denmark Christian IV issued a Charter in 1616 granting the Danish East India Company exclusive rights to trade with the Asian countries including India. First to arrive in India from Denmark was their explorer Marcelis de Boshouwer. The King issued Charter to two separate Companies. The first one was the Danish East India Company which functioned from 1616 to 1650 and the second one was the Asiatic Company which operated from 1670 to 1772.

In the Napoleonic War 1803 to 1818, the British Navy defeated the Danish naval force and as a result, the Danes lost their possessions in India to the British. They lost Serampore to the British in 1845. This is how the Danes were no more a political presence in India.

However, the Danes left behind some indelible impressions with their contributions. Some of them are as under–

- they developed Tranquebar as a beautiful seaside town,

- construction of the famous Dansborg Fort which is their second largest fort after the Kronborg fort which is in Denmark,

- they introduced Protestantism in India and they printed Bible in the Tamil language,

- they introduced an efficient educational system by establishing Catholic St. Theresa's Convent and the Tamil Evangelical Lutheran Church.

Chapter Four

Some of the Internal Dissensions

1) Operation Polo–Hyderabad—

British India consisted of 564 princely states and various provinces such as the United Provinces, Punjab, Bengal, Old CP & Berar, Maharashtra then Bombay, Madras and others As a result of the Indian Independence Act, 1947, announced by the Prime Minister of England Clement Atlee on June 3, 1946, the different Provinces automatically merged with the Union of India. Princely States had any one of the three options–

1. Accede to India

2. Accede to Pakistan and

3. Remain independent.

Out of 564 Princely States, many of them decided to merge with the Union of India while some others decided to merge with the newly created Islamic Republic of Pakistan. Three of the Princely States i. e Jammu & Kashmir, Hyderabad and Junagadh did not immediately express their desire to join the Union of India. The Nawab of Junagarh expressed his decision to join the Republic of Pakistan while the Nawab of Hyderabad began to play with the idea of remaining independent. First of all, he approached the Governor-General Lord Mountbatten to facilitate the independence of Hyderabad The later refused to oblige him by accepting Hyderabad as a constitutional monarchy within the British Commonwealth of Nations, the Nizam approached different nations of Europe and also of the British Commonwealth of Nations with his idea of independence. He received lukewarm response from them. He even approached the Security Council of the United Nations Organization by sending his emissary Moin Nawaz Jung on 10. 9. 1948. But later on, this approach was withdrawn on 22. 9. 1948 when Hyderabad had joined the Indian Union. Lord Mountbatten obviously had sympathies with the unity of India and he did not want any further balkanisation of India. The Nizam had even desired to purchase Goa from the Portuguese so that he could have an access to the sea route and so that Hyderabad could no longer remain a land-locked state to be permanently at the mercy of India. Hyderabad presented a complex situation, here the ruler was a Muslim while most of his subjects about 80% of them were Hindus. Nizam maintained an army consisting of razakars and many of the regular soldiers from his own community. He hoped to control the sentiments and even some possible revolt by the majority community with the help of his police and military strength. Just at that point of time, Nizam committed a grave mistake. He allowed his muscle power to unleash a reign of terror upon the majority community. Many of them fled to neighboring areas to save their lives and honor. This terrible situation compelled Prime Minister Pt. Jawaharlal Nehru and Home Minister Sardar Vallabh-bhai Patel to send their armed forces to quell the disturbances and to control the communal violence that was taking place in the state. It is also clear that they did not want Hyderabad to remain independent or to join Pakistan. Both the Prime Minister and the Home Minister tried their best to persuade the Nizam to continue to remain along with the Indian Union as it was since ages. But when all the efforts failed, the two leaders had to send their forces not only to restore law and order in the disturbed state but also to effect its merger with the Union of India.

At that point of time, Chakravarty Rajgopalachari was the Governor General and the Supreme Commander of India who sanctioned the military operation. The Indian forces landed into the territories of the reluctant state on September 13, 1948 ie. nearly thirteen months after the national independence of August 15, 1947. It was led by Major General JN Chaudhuri who later was promoted as the Commander-in Chief of the Indian Army. A fierce battle ensued between the Indian soldiers and the razakars at the Naldurg Fort on the Sholapur-Secunderabad Highway. The Govt of India deployed the might of the Air Force. This strategy proved to be decisive. Soon towns like Rajeshwar, Jaina, Mominabad, Bidar, Chitya and others fell like ninepins and by the end of the evening of 17. 9. 1948, entire Hyderabad had fallen under the sway of the Indian forces with the surrender of their Commander Major General Syed Ahmad El Edroos before Major General JN Chaudhary as he then was. The subsidiary treaty between the State of Hyderabad and the erstwhile British Government came to an end. The Nizam also accepted merger with the Indian Union by signing the Instrument of Accession

The operation was given the name Operation Polo because at that point of time, Hyderabad had the largest number of polo grounds in the world.

It is to be noted that a Stand-still Agreement was signed by the then Administration of Hyderabad and the Government of India on 29. 11. 1947 and, therefore, by logic, the Indian forces ought not to have entered into the Hyderabadi premises before that date. But then the Government of India could not have sat as silent spectator and let the ground realities deteriorate further almost beyond repair. The Standstill Agreement vested defense and foreign affairs of Hyderabad into the hands of the Government of India.

Hyderabad was the largest princely state in British India comprising such regions as Telugu speakingTelangana with the city of Hyderabad, Marathi speaking Marathwada and some areas of Karnataka and a small Kannada speaking area. A movement for separation of Telengana was already underway. Telangana went on to become a separate state much later.

Nizam-ul Malik, founder of the Asaf Jahi Dynasty ruled Hyderabad state independently from 1724. Second ruler of Hyderabad Nizam Ali concluded a Subsidiary Treaty with the British Governor General Lord Wellesely in 1798. He was the first Indian ruler to do so. His example was followed by the rest of the princely states so that finally this number swelled up to 564..

2) Junagarh

Muhammad Sher Khan Babai was the foundder of the Babi dynasty of Junagarh in1654. Following the disintegration of the Mughal Empire, the Babis became involved in fights against the Gaikwad dynasty of the Maratha Empire over the control of Gujrat during the reign of Muhammad Mahabat Khanji who declared independence from the Mughal governor of Gujrat and he founded the state of Junagarh in 1730. Junagarh came under the suzerainty of Company in 1807 and thus Junagarh became British protectorate When India became independent in

August 1947, Junagarh declared its resolve to accede to Pakistan. Nawab of Junagarh decided to accede to Pakistan although 80% of the population was Hindu who resented this declaration. At the same time, the adjoining principalities of Babariawad and Mongol declared their independence from Junagarh and they declared their intention to join India although the Sheikh of Mongol receded from his decision the very next day. Muhammad Ali Jinnah saw similarities in the cases of Jammu & Kashmir and Junagarh because Junagarh had a Muslim ruler and Hindu majority whereas J&K had a Hindu Maharaja and a vast Muslim majority, so that if the Indian Prime Minister hoped to hold a plebiscite in Junagarh; then by the same token of logic; another plebiscite should be held in J&K. Governor-General of Pakistan waited for one month to see the next step of the Prime Minister of India as a political manouvre. However, Pakistan did not comply with the resolutions of the Security Council to vacate their occupation from the POK and thus failed to pave the way for holding plebiscite in J&K.

Bhopal–

Bhopal today is the capital of Madhya Pradesh. It is believed that it was founded in the 11th century by the Parmar King namely Raja Bhoj who himself is a legendary name in Indian history. In the early 18th century, Bhopal was a small village in the Gond Kingdom. The modern city of Bhopal was established by Dost Mohammad Khan who was a soldier in the Mughal Army in the reign of Aurangzeb. He used to provide and arrange for mercenary forces to the needy rulers. He provided such services to Rani Kamlapati of Bhopal and in return, he received some territory of Bhopal and after her death, Khan usurped the entire kingdom of Rani Kamlapati. Thereafter, he began to develop Bhopal. State of Bhopal signed a subsidiary treaty with the East India Company in 1818 with the result that Bhopal became one of the 564 princely states under the protectorate system of the East India Company with residuary powers of local administration. Between 1819 to 1926, Bhopal was ruled over by four Begums. The last of them Kai Khusrau Jehan abdicated in favor of her son Hamidullah Khan who ruled from 1926 to 1947. Hamidullah expressed his desire to remain independent i.e. neither with India nor with Pakistan. Consequently, there were wide-spread agitations against him in December 1948. Shri Shanka Dayal Sharma who went on to become the President of India was one of the agitators who was arrested. Nawab had to give in. He signed the instrument of accession with the Union of India on 30. 4. 1949.

Chapter Five

The Revolt of the Tribals

Why Did the Tribals Revolt

The tribals or who are now called the Scheduled Tribes in the Indian Constitution have been the original residents of India since time immemorial. They have been living in deep forests surviving upon basic necessities of daily life on fruits and leaves and other natural resources of the forests. They were very simple people extremely susceptible to outside influence of modern civilisation. With the advent of the British East India Company as an imperialist force from merely a commercial adventure, the deep and serene jungles were penetrated by the agents of the Company. They thought that many of their commercial demands could be easily fulfilled by exploiting the abundance of the natural resources and timbers which were available in abundance in the forests. They entrusted the exploitation of the tribals to their agents such as zamindars, thekendras and money-lenders. This trend set in motion a chain of ruthless exploitation of the simple aboriginals and indiscriminate elimination of wildlife. It is also alleged that the missionaries set about evangelizing them into what they professed as a civilised way of life.

Many of these aboriginal tribes offered no resistance and accepted the so-called modern and more civilised way of life. But then there was another group amongst them who wanted to safeguard their primordial way of life.

The aborigines were the first to offer resistance to the forces of the East India Company. It could be debated whether their resistances were political in nature so that they wanted the British to leave their territories or whether they were primarily interested in the protection of their forests. It is certain that the officers of the East India Company were quick to realise that these vast forests of their newly acquired assets could easily meet their demands for natural resources which could help the smooth running of their mills and factories wayback in England. The aborigines were too simple to have systematic political awakening in the language of Hobbes, Locke, Rousseau, Montesquieu, Kant, Heigel, Machiavelli, the Mills and others. But it is certain that their revolts were contemporaneous with the more political revolts and rebellions of the rajaas, ranis, kings and other chieftains of those times such as Rani Abbakka of Chowta who fought out the rampaging Portuguese in 1556, Rani Velu Nachiar who fought out the British forces since 1772 till her death in 1796 and Rani Kittur Channamma who fought out the British in 1824 much before the more celebrated first revolt of 1857.

So it looks like that the credit of firing the first salvo against any foreign power nust go to Rani Abbakka Chowta of Ullal even though she took cudgels with the Portuguese adventurers.

But then the bravery of the aborigines is no less praise-worthy. They had traditional bows and arrows, ballam, axe and shields as weapons of offence and defence. Needless to say, these stone-age scruples could hold no front against the more sophisticated and modern weapons of the western powers. Moreover, insofar as they did not want any foreigner to intrude and encroach upon their lands and insofar as they wanted to expel them from their habitates, their struggles were motivated not only with the desire to protect and safe-guard their time-immemorial way of life and culture, but their struggles were indeed motivated by a political overtone howsoever embryonic in nature it might have been. It is, therefore, surprising that not much importance has been given in the Indian history records for the significant contribution of the tribals.

The aborigines were a separate group with a chieftain from amongst them who ruled over his subjects who willingly obeyed him. They lived an idyllic way of life far from the madding crowd almost in the original state of nature. They survived for centuries upon their jungles, woods and wildlife. They were separated from other non-tribes and other city-dwellers almost aloof from the external world. They did not brook any external interference in their ways of life. However, the administrators and right-thinking social reformers could not have felt comfortable with one group of population remaining bereft of the fruits of progress, prosperity and material advancement. They tried to extend their concept of civilisation into those dungeons. Frictions were natural to result. If the British and their agents had confined their efforts merely to bona fide intentions, then no reactions would have resulted. The propagators of civilisation instead resorted to economical exploitation and a completely new societal and cultural renovation by means of evangelisation and proselytisation. This resulted in several conflicts. Treated from this point of view, tribal confrontations were anti-colonial also.

Here are some of therevolts of the tribunals—

The Sanyasi Rebellion—

After the Plassey war of 1757 in which Nawab Siraj-ud-dowla was defeated and the battle of Buxar in which Mir Kasim was defeated by the forces of the East India Company, the Company was able to establish its sway over Bengal, Bihar and Orissa. They were awarded the exclusive rights of land-revenue collection from these large areas. The Company officers extracted land revenue in a very ruthless manner which spread resentment. Earlier a devastating famine had overtaken vast tracts of these areas with little or no aid from the ruling class. So poor peasants, farmers, wealthy landlords and even sanyasis rose up in a concerted revolt which came to be known as the Sanyasi revolt. The revolt was of course suppressed.

Tilka Manjhi Revolt–

He led the first organised revolt of the tribes against the might of the East India Company in 1772 against the policy of exploitation of the natural resources of the deep forests following the famine of 1770 when the British did hardly anything to ameliorate the sufferings of the drought-stricken. Tilkah fought the forces of the Company with his traditional weapons for 15 long years. But then he was finally caught, tied to four horses and dragged all the way to Bhagalpur. He hailed from the Chhota Nagpur hills of Bihar now part of Jharkhand. Robert Clive was perhaps one of the first exponents of the British policy of divide and rule by creating a division between the tribals of that area. He was successful in luring a few of them to his side. However, a large number of the tribes still decided to save their culture and habitates. So they came under the banner of Tilkah Manjhi. Governor General Lord Warren Hastings sent a large contingent of 800 soldiers to capture Tilkah Manjhi. After offering stiff resistance, he was finally caught and dragged all the way as described earlier in 1785. It is generally believed that 1857 is the first revolt against the might of the Company. There is significant truth behind this assertion and we do not want to take anything away from the sacrifices of the warriors of 1857. But history also tells us that there were numerous revolts big and small against the rampaging Company much earlier. Let us give full respect and recognition to the brave aborigines like Birsa Munda and Tilkah Manjhi and several others who had the valor to raise a David versus Goliath like confrontation with the mighty foreigners. The adivasis from across the entire country hailing from Bihar, Bengal, Orissa, Madhya Pradesh, Rajasthan, Madras, Maharashtra and other places revolted one after another. Jnanpith Award winner Mahashweta Devi has immortalized Tilka in one of her novels.

Birsa Munda (15. 11. 1875—9. 6. 1900) With the rise of industrialization in England in the nineteenth century, timber and woods were needed by them for their naval requirements. In India, these commodities were urgently needed to spread railway lines and tracks across the country. The British Raj thought that India with their vast forests could easily fulfill these demands. The British evolved a new forest policy called scientific forestry. They enacted new laws, rules and regulations. The Indian Forest Act, 1865 was enacted with this new perspective which was later amended in 1878 and finally in 1927. According to this new policy, the forests were divided into basically two groups, one as reserved forests or as the forest villages where other tribal villagers could not live as they were previously doing since ages and where only selected villagers could live and who would cut the jungle produce for the benefit of the Government. In the other set of forests, normal tribals could live. But the tribals in general were deprived of their regular means of livelihood as they could not cut the forests and they were not allowed to hunt the forest animals such as deers and other smaller animals for their diet. If any tribal killed any such wild-life, then he was treated as a poacher, if he cut any forest trees then he would be personally liable for criminal actions. The timber thus removed was sent to England for their commercial use.

The tribals have been inhabiting different parts of India since time immemorial. But they are primarily in Madhya Pradesh, Bihar, Orissa, Maharashtra and in the sister states of the East. Chhattisgarh has been carved out of the erstwhile Madhya Pradesh. Chhattisgarh now comprises Bastar, Jagdalpur and Sarguja districts where there are tribals in a large number. These tribals felt the heat of the new forest policy of the British the most in the early twentieth century and the late nineteenth century. The tribals of these areas gathered together to chalk out a common line of action. They wanted to drive the British out of their areas. They were not happy that they could not use their habitate for their personal needs and requirements as in the previous regular manner. They resented the ruthless deforestation of their time-immemorial habitates. They resented the killings of their wild-life. The needs of the British colonials were at odds with the needs of the millennial tribals. Wild-life had the utility confined to big-game and big-trophy to the British rulers while the wild-life meant everything to the tribals.

It is estimated that during the period between 1875 to 1925 i.e. about 50 years, over 80000 tigers, 150000 leopards and 200000 wolves were hunted out by the British and the local rulers and shikaries. The Maharaja of Sarguja alone killed about 1200 tigers and 2000 leopards till 1957. Sir George Yule ICS is reported to have killed 400 tigers. Lord Reading similarly is credited with a similar haul of big-trophies. Jim Corbett was another celebrated British shikari, but then he is associated with the preservation of wild life also.

The tribals of Bastar and Jagdalpur rose in an armed revolt against this exploitation in about 1910. The specific leader of the rebels is not clear. Yet it is believed that Gunda Dhur of village Nethanar in Bastar was their front line leader. The British with their better forces were able to suppress the up-rising. Yet the tribals put up a brave fight with their primitive arsenal of arrows and bows.

The aforesaid can also serve as a back-ground under which Birsa Munda waged his rebellion against the British. His revolt was two-fold, one to make his tribe free of the foreign rule and in this manner it was a struggle for political independence of the tribals of Chhota Nagpur Ranchi region of Bihar, and secondly it was a religious up-rising also led by Birsa Munda to save the time-immemorial old culture and heritage of the tribals against the drive of evangelization of their community. He had to convert into Christianity in order to seek admission into the German Missionary School of his area. But then he later returned to his old tribal culture and Hindu way of life. He began to preach these precepts to his tribal people. This is the reason why he is treated in the tribal areas of Chhattisgarh,

Jharkhand, Bihar, Orissa, Madhya Pradesh as a prophet. He is an icon to them. His photo hangs in the Indian Parliament. He used to give emotionally charged but powerful speeches before his Munda community. His method of war-fare was Maharaja Shivaji's exploits of guerilla-warfare which he raged between 1897 to 1900. But then, ultimately the superior arsenal of the British proved effective. Birsa was arrested by the British forces on 3. 3. 1900, tried and sentenced for two years. He died in jail custody on 9. 6. 1900. It is still argued that he was administered poison in jail confinement.

Sambalpur Revolt–

The British East India Company tried to exploit the simplicity of the tribals of Sambalpur Orissa, the area rich in natural resources. The tribes revolted under the leadership of Surendra Sai. They fought the British with their traditional bows and arrows. But finally they could stand nowhere against the latest weapons of the foreigners. The revolt was suppressed and the leaders were summarily hanged.

Kherwar Revolt–

This was a revolt against the exploiting zamindars and the Company who wanted to exploit the natural resources of several areas of Bihar. The four Murmu brothers namely Sidhu, Kanhu, Chand and Bhairow resorted to guerilla means of confrontation against the might of the Company. But they were no match. It is reported that about 15000 Santhals were killed with Sidhu and Kanhu amongst them.

Rampa Rebellion-

This revolt was staged by the Rampa tribes of Oraon Visakhapatnam Orissa in 1879 as a result of the exploitation unleashed by the Madras Forest Act of 1872. They were deprived of their traditional culture, way of life, their means of livelihood and their ancestral territories. Their leader was Alluri Sitaram Raju or Manyam Veerudu or the king of jungles. He was eventually caught and killed.

Peasants Uprising of Rangpur Bengal 1783

As said earlier, Bengal, Bihar and Orissa fell under the control of the East India Company in 1757 after their victories in the decisive battles of Plassey and Buxar against Nawab Siraj-ud-dowla and Mir Kasim respectively. Earlier than this event, the Company had to depend upon procuring resources from home. Now they had a novel idea of replenishing their demands from the lands of their new conquests. After some time, the tribals rose up in revolt under the leadership of Dirjinarayan. They looted the godowns of the Company. But this could not last long. They were caught and finally killed.

Uprising of the Bhils 1818

The Bhils of Khandesh rose up in revolt against the British in 1818.

Waghera uprisings

Waghera chiefs of Baroda state rose up against the Company because of their adverse policies. A peace treaty followed in November 1820.

Ahom revolt

This revolt in Assam took place following the First Burma War of 1824-26. The British tried to annex some territories of Assam, the Ahom area. Their leader was Gandhar Kanwar. The British had to relent. They returned the territories.

The Rebellion of Mysore 1830-1831

After the final defeat of Tipu Sultan in 1799, the British forced the subsequent rulers of Mysore to remit heavy land revenue. They engaged zamindars for this collection who resorted to ruthless methods. The peasants rose up in revolt under the leadership of Sunder Malle of Nagar area. The revolt was suppressed.

The Kol Uprising of 1831-32

The Kols of Singhbhoom rose up in revolt against the British who transferred large tracts of their lands to outsiders such as money-lenders and merchants The revolt spread over different areas of Bihar such as Ranchi, Hazaribagh, Palaman and Manbhum. The revolt was suppressed.

Kandh uprising

In this revolt, the areas covered were Ghumsar, China-ki-Medi, Kalahandi in Orissa and Patna in Bihar. These tribes were in the tradition of offering human sacrifices to propitiate their deities. The British tried to stop this practice. This resulted in revolt by the tribes concerned. The British used persuasion at first, but then they resorted to force. The British had tried to bring about some reforms in the Hindu community earlier with the help of Raja Ram Mohan Rai when they brought out an enactment to abolish the sati-pratha. Later they helped the Hindu community to enact the Sarda Act which laid down an age for the marriages of the Hindu girls. So it cannot be said that those attempts were not bona fide.

Revolts from the Eastren States–

Revolt by Tirut Singh–In 1829, the British tried to construct a road across the hilly areas of the north-west border of Assam. There were revolts by the Khasi tribe. Bar Manik the chief of the Mihim tribe led yet another rebellion and yet another revolt was generated by Tirut Singh the leader of the Nankhows tribe. The revolt started in 1829 and continued till 1833. The revolt was suppressed. Yet another revolt was started by the Singhows tribe in 1839 which again was suppressed. Another tribe Kapaschor revolted in 1935. It was also suppressed. Nagas revolted from 1849 to 1951.

The Kukis of Manipur and Tripura

Revolted against the Company forces in 1829, 1844 and 1849. The revolt was suppressed.

Tikendrajit Singh–29. 12. 1856–13. 8. 1891–Manipur was a British protectorate in the mid-19th century. After the death of Raja Chandrakriti in 1887, there was a tussle for accession to his throne. The British recognised Jugraj Kulachandra Singh as the King. But the decision raised a big controversy which resulted in the Anglo-Manipur War of 1891. Tikendra Singh fought the forces of the Company. But he was finally caught and put on trial along with two others namely Kulachandra and Thangal General. The three were sentenced to death. But then finally only two of them i.e. Tikendrajit Singh and Thangal were publicly hanged on 31. 8. 1891 in a polo ground in Imphal.

The Khonds tribe of Khondmals of Orissa

Offered resistance in 1846 to 1849, then again in 1855 and finally in 1914. All of them were unsuccessful. Kacha Nagas also revolted.

Some other tribes to revolt were the Poligars in North Arcot in 1801-1805, the Wagheras in Gujarat in 1818-1819, the Ramosis in the Western Ghats in 1822 and again in 1882. Bhils in Rajasthan offered resistance in 1913. Chuars in 1766-1768 in Manbhum and Barabham in Bengal defied the Company but were suppressed.

Kolis of Sahyadri Hills in Gujarat and Maharashtra

Revolted in 1824, 1828, 1839, 1844 to 1849, but were unsuccessful. **Koyas of Rampa** region of Andhra Pradesh rose up in revolt in 1840, 1845, 1858, 1861-62, 1879-80 and finally in 1922-24. But all these efforts were unsuccessful. Naikdas in PanchMahal in Gujarat revolted in 1858-59 and again in 1868. Their leaders were Rup Singh and Jora Bhagat. The revolts were foiled and both of them were executed. **Orams of Chhota Nagpur** revolted in 1914-15. It was a political revolt to drive the British away from these territories, although the revolt was crushed. **Thadou Kukis of Manipur** revolted in 1917-1919. Their leaders were legendary leaders Jadong and Rani Gaidinliu.

Po Togan defied the Company forces and their expansion in North-East after they had established their sway over the Khasi and Jaintia Hills. He was helped in the revolt by Po Gilsang Dalbot Sangma Kundapeshwar Singh and Po Goval Nangminja Sangma. They resisted the superior arms and ammunition of the British to the last moment with their traditional weapons. Pa Togan received a bullet injury on his chest and was martyred on the battlefield.

Chapter Six

Some Contemporary Revolts and Movements Against the British

Tipu Sultan Fateh Ali Saheb Tipu the Tiger of Mysore (1750- 1799)

Who fired the first significant shot of independence

The first significant revolt against the expansion of British rule can be credited to Tipu Sultan of Hyderabad who always fought against the might of the East India Company. His father Hyder Ali also fought the same opponents all his life. So the pride of place could go between the father and the son. But perhaps Tipu could breast the tape first in a photo-finish because his revolt was more organized. Tipu wanted to drive the British out of Madras. He defeated two British generals namely Col. Baillie and Col. Braithwaite seized Chittur from them in 1781. Marathas had defeated Hyder Ali in an earlier battle which resulted in a treaty between them whereby Hyder Ali had to pay a regular tribute to the Marathas. But Tipu stopped paying this tribute to them. In the decisive battle of Seringapatam, Tipu was defeated while defending the fort. He was killed in the engagement on May 4, 1799. He fought so valiantly that even the British praised him for his bravery and they called him a Tiger. This is how the Company was able to entrench themselves in the South. But they could not do so in the life-time of Hyder Ali and Tipu Sultan. Everybody remembers Tipu Sultan for his deeds of heroism. But hardly any-one recalls that he is perhaps the first ruler formally to rise in revolt against the Company. Similarly due recognition and appreciation should be given to Hyder Ali about whom there are several folk lores.

Freedom fighters from Hyderabad– Some historians believe that the first torch of revolt was ignited in Hyderabad in 1815 i.e. much earlier than 1857. It was taken up by prince Mubariz-ud-dowla son of Sikandar Jah Nizam III of Hyderabad. Noor-ul-Umara and Ram Rambha Nimbalkar also revolted in 1818. Although the revolt was soon suppressed by the Company forces with the help of better weaponry and also because of some help rendered to them by the adversaries of the Nizam.

Another chapter of the history of Hyderabad is its reluctance in 1946-47 to join the Indian Union. It is said that the Nizam wanted to join the newly created Islamic Republic of Pakistan. Shoebullah Khan, Makhdoom Mohiuddin, Ravi Narayan Reddy, Shaik Bandagi, Ramkrishna Rao, P. V. Narasimha Rao and others struggled for the assimilation of Hyderabad into the Indian Union. Swami Ramtirth also was an important participant in this struggle.

Jagannath Gajapatti Narayan Deo II of Paralakhemundi Odisah fought against the French powers from 1753 and thereafter, the British at Jelmur on 4. 4. 1768, he was defeated and he fled away. He continued to defy the British East India Company till his death in December 1771.

Kerala Verma Pazhassi Raja 1774, the Prince Regent of the Princely State of Kottiyoorin North Malabar fought a guerrilla war against the forces of the East India Company.

The Paik Revolt

Paika Bidorla 1804 the King of Khorda in Kalinga was deprived of his traditional rights of Jagannath Temple by the British, so he attacked the British forces in October 1804 at Pipli. Jayee Rajguru the chief of the Kalinga Army was killed on 6. 12. 1806. The reigns of revolt were taken over by Bakshi Jagabandhu. This is known as the Paik Rebellion and this may well be the first organized rebellion against the British advancement.

Revolt of Velu Thampi–He revolted in 1805 to 1809. He was Dewan of Travancore. The revolt was ignited by the reason of heavy financial burden imposed by the British upon the state by their subsidiary system. War broke out between the two sides. But the Dewan was defeated and Velu Thampi succumbed to the injuries.

The Vellore Revolt of 1806—This could very well be the first organized up-rising against the growing British rule in the shape of the East India Company. It took place on 10. 7. 1806 in Vellore which is now in Tamil Nadu. It lasted just one day. But it had far reaching consequences for the future. It could well be called the precursor of the much larger up-rising of 1857 because there are several notable similarities of the causes between the two epoch-making events in the history of India. The Vellore Revolt is, however, almost forgotten in the daily folk-lore.

Tipu Sultan the Tiger of Mysore had been defeated in the battle of Srirangapatna in 1799 and his family members had been kept in the Fort of Vellore by the East India Company as hostages by way of some safe-guard against future revolt. But then exactly the opposite took place. The rebel soldiers of the

British Indian Army of the Madras Army wanted to restore the Mysore Sultanate back upon its throne. There were some compelling religious reasons also behind the resentment of the soldiers from the Indian ranks. They apprehended that there was an attempt to spread Christianity amongst them in view of the fact that earlier many evangelist-priests had descended upon the arena fuelling the fears of their conversions. The susceptibilities of both the Hindu and Muslim soldiers were aroused. The commander of the British Army Sir Rollo Cradock tried to introduce certain reforms in the dress-code of the Indian soldiers which they resented.

On the fateful day, soldiers of Indian origin in the British Indian Army killed about 129 British officers and soldiers. Soon a reinforcement from Arcot arrived under the lead of Sir Rollo Gillespie. They barged into the Fort. The rebels were overpowered soon by the end of the same day, heavy reprisals followed soon with about 350 rebels killed and many more seriously injured. The family members of Tipu were later transported to Calcutta bringing the curtain down upon the incident which could claim to be the first serious resentment against the British aggrandizement.

The next up-rising was in 1857. There are striking similarities between the two major events. In 1806, the rebels tried to restore the son of Tipu Sultan namely Fateh Hyder to the Mysore throne, in 1857 the rebels tried to restore the glory of the Mughal empire under Bahadur Shah. Religious susceptibilities of both the Hindu and Muslim soldiers were hurt in 1806 and also later on in 1857. Religious conversion was apprehendd on both occasions.

Some other prominent rebels of 1857 are as under—Maulana Qaeim Nanautavi and Maulana Rashid Ahmad Gangohi who took up arms against the British, Brijish Qadir and Ahmad-ullah of Lucknow, Rao Saheb and Azimullah Khan of Kanpur, Jaidayal Singh and Hardyaal Singh of Rajasthan, Tufzal Hasan Khan of Farrukhabad Uttar Pradesh, Kundapareshwar and Maniram Dutta Barua of Assam and Surendra Shahi and Ujjawal Shahi from Orissa.

Wahabi Movement–This was primarily religious in nature but later it developed political shape also in1820. Later the Fairazi sect under the leadership of Shariat-ullah and Muslin or Dudhu also joined forces. Shariat-ullah died later while Dudhu Mian was arrested and confined in the Alipore jail..

Kittur uprising–Kittur is in Dharwad in Karnataka. Here in 1824-1829, Here the valiant Channamma and Royappa, Shivling Rudra Desai the chief of Kittur rose up in revolt in 1824. Here the policy of lapse was prectised by the British since the Rani did not have any male heir-apparent to the throne. Rani Channamma revolted. Desai Royappa declared unilateral declaration of independence with an adopted son as heir to the throne. But the revolt could not succeed. Royappa was captured and executed while the valiant Rani died in British custody

Movement of the Pagal Panthies–. It took place in Sherpur, East Bengal between 1925 to 1933. The leader was Karam Singh. It was both religious and political in nature. It was ultimately suppressed.

Parlakimidi revolt— This revolt took place from 1929 to 1935. The leader was Gayapati Narayan Rao Jagannath. His zamindari was attached by the British due to non-payment of high land-revenue. The revolt failed.

Satvadi Revolt– It took place in Maharashtra between 1839 to 1845. The Company deposed the existing ruler Khen Savant and appointed a British administrator in his place. This led to a mass uprising.

Gadkari revolt–It took place in Kolhapur Maharashtra between 1844 to 45 as a result of direct assumption of administration by the Company. The revolt by the Gadkaries was suppressed.

Raju rebellion– This took place in Visakhapatnam in Andhra Pradesh in1827 to 1833 led by Birbhadra Raju. The revolt failed.

Satara disturbances 1840-41–The people of Satara rose up in revolt under the leadership of Dhar Rao in 1840 and again under Narsingh in 1841 and seized Badami. Later Narsingh was defeated by the British and transported for life.

Revolt of Rao Bharmal- He raised the banner of revolt in Kutch and Kathiawar in Gujarat in 1861 against the expansionist policies of the Company. The revolt did not succeed. But a treaty of peace was entered into between the two parties.

Pabna Revolt– It took place in Bengal in1873 against the agrarian policy of the Company. It resulted in the enactment of the Bengal Tenancy Act of 1885.

Bundela Revolts of Saugar and Damoh– These are the areas of Bundelkhand. The Bundels revolted against the revenue policy of the Company. The leaders were Madhulkar Shah and Singh.

Contribution of Mahoba, Banda and Bundelkhand regions in the freedom struggle–

Even before the uprisings of 1857, there were earlier revolts against the British in many places starting with early nineteenth century. On such revolt took place in the Bundelkhand territory of India such as Sagor, Damoh, Narsinghpur and other places in 1842. After the Third Anglo Maratha War of 1818, the British annexed several territories of this area under their expansionist drive. Their methods of forcible and unjust revenue collection resulted in the creation of unrest in the minds of several malgujars, land-owners and local rajas and they rose in revolt. Some of the prominent rebels were Gaya Datta, Manik Chand Kochar, Chaudhary Shankar lal, Daryao Singh, Thakur Kundan Shah, Gond Rajas of Garha-Mandla, Bundelas, Thakurs and Lodhis of Sagar, Damoh and Narsinghpur, Ganeshju Bundela of Narhat, Jawahar Singh Bundela of Chandrapur, Madhukar Shah of Narhat, Gond king Dilhan Shah of Madanpur and Raja Hira Shah of Hirapur. The Company forces had to struggle for about one year before they could quell these revolts. However, they had a far reaching impact upon the coming history of India because the great uprising of 1857 soon followed in its wake 15 years thereafter.

In 1857, 16 freedom fighters were hanged from an imli or tamarind tree for their participation in the revolt.

Kalapahar in the Mahoba district of Uttar Pradesh has a special place in the history of the freedom struggle of India. Under the leadership of Bhagvan Das Balendu, foreign clothes were consigned to flames in 1921 at the calling ofMahatma Gandhi.

Others who took part were Balgovind Agrawal, Moolchand Tailor master, Abdul Razzaq and others. In 1929, Mahatma Gandhi visited Kalapahar and a public meeting was held Jantantra Inter College ground and the residents of this area collected a fund of Rs. 1500/ and they presented it to the Mahatma in the national cause. Yet another purse was presented to him by the missionary community of the area worth Rs. 150/.

Balendu participated in the historic Congress session of Lahore held in 1930 where a resolution for complete independence was passed on 31. 12. 1930. Balendus participation in the movements continued and he was arrested several more times along with Balgovind Agrawal, Ramdulare Dwivedi of Gourhari, Motilal of Jetpur, Vishweshwar Dayal Pateria, Raghuvir Dixit, Atte Dua and others. He was jailed for six years in 1942 for his participation in the Quit India Movement. Women of the area were also arrested in the national cause namely Kishori Devi Arjaria, Rani Devi Dwivedi, Saraswati Devi, Sarju Devi Pateria, Rani Rajendra Kumari and others.

Dr. Smt. Salma Jamal the well-known Hindi poetess has pointed out in her book relating to Mahoba that in the office of the Vikas Khand Mahoba- Hamirpur, there is a list of the following freedom fighters of the area–

1. Baijnath Tiwari

2. Vinnayya

3. Bilasi,

4. Vishveshvar Dayal,

5. Bodhilal,

6. Bhagwandas Balendu,
7. Munni alias Hiralal,
8. Mahadev Prasad Awasthi,
9. Mukund Lal,
10. Rajjab Ali Azad,
11. Raj Bahadur,
12. Rambharose,
13. Ramsevak Khare,
14. Ladle,
15. Lal Diwan,
16. Shankar Lal Jain,
17. Shri Ram Pachouri,
18. Sarju Rani Pateria,
19. Sukhaiya,
20. Hardayal Chourasia,
21. Hiralal Tiwari,
22. Smt. Yashoda Devi Tiwari,
23. Ram Asare,
24. Uma Dutt Shukla,
25. Kamta Prasad,
26. Kaluram,
27. Kashi Prasad,
28. Ganpat,
29. Chunnilal,

30. Jagannath Singh,
31. Jawaharlal,
32. Jujhar Singh,
33. Tijwa,
34. Deen Dayal Tiwari,
35. Devi Deen,
36. Devki Nandan Sullere,
37. Pt. Nathuram Tiwari,
38. Pyare,
39. Puranlal Vaishya,
40. Pancham Datt Choube
41. Brijlal Saxena,
42. Balram alias Balaiyan,
43. Baldev Prasad Gupt,
44. Baladeen.

Banda Bundelkhand has also a history of contribution to the freedom movement. Some of the freedom fighters of the area are –

1. Kaloo Ram Vaidhya,
2. Haji Gajju Khan,
3. Godeen Sharma,
4. Gopi Nath Dwivedi,
5. Chandrika Prasad Gupta,
6. Ganga Prasad Khare,
7. Chandra Bhushan Chaudhari,

8. Jumana Prasad Nigam,

9. Jugal Kishor Singh,

10. Deen Dayal Kanwariya,

11. Narain Das tailor master,

12. Badri Prasad,

13. Brij Mohanlal Gupta,

14. Man BodhanlalNigam,

15. Mahavirdas Baba,

16. Mithila Sharan Shivhare,

17. Ram Bhajan Nigam,

18. Smt. Raj Kumari Gupt,

19. Ramnath Gupt,

20. Ram Sanehi Bhartiya,

21. Vishvanath Vaishampayan,

22. Vishnu Karan Mehta,

23. Shiv Balak Ram Gupt,

24. Shiv Kumar Tripathi,

25. Har Prasad Singh and

26. Harun Rasheed

Various revolts in Bihar and in other places

Some where in the mid–eighteenth century, there were several uprisings organized by various zamindars and estate-holders against the progressive acquisition of control of the Indian territory by the East India Company. They could hear the dreading alarms. They refused to accept the authority of the Company. They refused to remit land-revenue into the coffers of the Company. One such revolt was organized by zamindar Chait Singh of Varanasi in 1781. This was promptly suppressed by the forces of the Company. But it was a precedent to other similarly situated zamindars. They also rose up one by one. Zamindar of Huseypur Fateh Bahadur Singh gathered an army, waged constant guerilla war against the forces of the Company, but he was defeated and killed in the battle-field. Zamindar of Kutumba in Aurangabad Raj Narain Singhrose up in revolt against the Company forces. But it was suppressed soon. Raja Akbar Ali of Gaya district also raised a banner of revolt against the Company forces, but in vain.

The Kuka Rebellion of 1886- This movement had its roots in the religious reforms and purification of the Sikh religion. It is the same as the Namdhari Movement. Some of the prominent members of this movement were Baba Balan Singh, Ram Singh and Jawahar Singh who founded this movement. They were against child-marriages, condemned the dowry system. They promoted simple marriages and inter-caste marriages between the upper castes and the untouchables. Indeed they performed one such marriage on 4. 1. 1863. Kukas killed some butchers who were suspected of kine slaughter. The British Government arrested some of the Kukas and they were hanged. It can be said that Kukas are the pioneers of the civil dis-obedience and non-co-operation philosophy which was later followed by Mahatma Gandhi because they had themselves adopted these means in their relations against the British Government of those days. The Kukas treated political activities as an indispensable part of one's religious beliefs. Mahatma Gandhi also similarly believed that political activities could not be alienated from one's religious beliefs although he extended this concept further by trying to spiritualise the political field and activities.

The Indigo revolt– It took place in 1917 in Champaran revenue circle of Bihar. This agitation brought Mahatma Gandhi, Babu Rajendra Prasad, Babu Brij Kishor, Dharnidhar and other leaders from Bihar into national prominence. It was against the exorbitant financial burden placed upon the local indigo planters by the British officials and also by the British land planters.

The Moplah Revolt of 1921

Malabar riot or Moplah genocide or Mapila Lahala 1921 was an armed uprising against the British in the Malabar region bythe agricultural tenants. These incidents were a culmination of a series of Mapilah agitations which were taking place in the region against the British administration throughout the 19th and the 20th centuries. The community of the area had resentments against the British against the way they had suppressed their Khilafat movement. The British Government suppressed again the agitation of the Moplahs. In the notorious Wagon tragedy, 67 out of 90 Mapillah prisoners were suffocated to death in a closed wagon in which they were being transported to the Central Prison in Podanur. It is also said that the agitation took a communal angle also in which a large number of lives were lost. It is said that about ten thousand persons lost their lives although according to the official figures 2337 persons had lost their lives and about 1652 were injuredand many more were imprisoned.

There is a difference of opinion about the nature of the Moplah agitation between communal nature and national nature. However, the contemporary opinion is that it was political in nature as against the British Government and there were communal troubles also. Mahatma Gandhi condemned those atrocities while Jinnah defended them as an act of reprisal.

Important leaders who were participants in the agitation, who were prosecuted and sentenced to death were–Ail Musaliyar, Kunhi Kadir, Varian Kunt Kunjahammad Haji, Kunhi Koya Thangal, Koya Thangal, Chembrasseri Imbici Koya Thangal, Palakam Thodi Avocker Musaliyar and Konnar Mohammad Koya Thangal.

The Dandi March of 1930

Mahatma Gandhi organized this historic march to protest against the monopolistic policy of the British Government to manufacture salt all alone. It started from the Sabarmati Ashram of almost constant walk from Ahmedabad on 12. 3. 1930 and ended at the Dandi Navsari sea beach on 6. 4. 1930. In other words, the pedestrians took 240 days on almost constant foot to cover up 240 miles. The Mahatma was accompanied by 79 other followers which comprised mostly 39 marchers from Gujarat, 14 from Uttar Pradesh, 5 from Punjab, and others from Kerala, two from Sindh now in Pakistan, Odisha or Orissa, Karnataka, Maharashtra, Andhra Pradesh, Rajasthan and from Bihar. The Mahatma picked up a pint of sea water from the sea thereby signaling an epoch-making event. Others in the group followed suit.

The Marchers were–This event is one of the celebrated events of Indian history of this period. But the marchers are not that well known. They are– Pyarelal Nayyar, Chhaganlal Joshi, Pandit Narayan Moreshwar Khare, Ganpat Rao Godse, Prithviraj Asar, Mahavir Giri, Bal Dattatraya Kelkar, Jayanti Nathubhai Parekh, Rasik Desai, Vitthal Liladhar Thakkar, Harakhji Ramjibhai, Tansukh Pranshankar Bhatt, Kantilal Hiralal Gandhi, Chhotubhai Khushalbhai Patel, Valjibhai Govind Desai, Pannalal Balabhai Jhaveri, Abbas Varteji, Punjabhai Shah, Madhavjibhai Thakkar, Nanjibhai, Maganbhai Vora, Dungarsibhai, Somanlal Pragjibhai Patel, Hoshmukhram Jakbar, Daudbhai, Ramjibhai Vankar, Dinkarrai Pandya, Dwarkanath, Gajanan Khare, Jethalal Raparel, Govind Harkare, Pandurang, Vinayakrao Apte, Ramdhirai, Bhanushankar Dave, Munshilal, Raghvan, Ravji Nathalal Patel, Shankarbhai Bhikabhai Patel, Jeshbhai Ishwarbhai Patel, Sumangal Prasad, Thevarthundi Titus, Krishna Nair, Tapan Nair, Haridas Varjandas Gandhi, Chimanlal Shah, Shankaran, Subramaniam, Ramniklal Maganlal Modi, Madan Mohan Chaturvedi, Harilal Mahimutre, Matibas Das, Harridas Majumdar, Anand Hingorani, Mahadev Martand, Jayanti Prasad, Hari Prasad, Anugrah Narain Sinha, Keshav Chitre, Ambalal Shankarbhai Patel, Vishnu Pant, Premraj, Durgesh Chandra Das, Madhavlal Shah, Jyotiram, Surajbhan, Bhairav Dutt, Lalji Parmar, Ratanji Boria, Vishnu Sharma, Chintamani Shastri, Narayan Dutt, Manilal Mohandas Gandhi, Surendra Krishna Mohoni, Puratan Buch, Kharag Bahadur Singh Giri and Jagat Narayan besides the Mahatma himself.

This is to highlight these marchers who are not talked of today even though the Dandi March of 1930 is one of the most important events of the entire freedom movement. The Dandi March has been compared to the earlier **Long March of March 1893** which started from Newcastle Natal towards Volkrust into

Transvaal, South Africa. The party consisted of 127 women, 57 children and 2037 men. An route, Mohandas was arrested, released on bail, moved on and again arrested. On one such occasion, he was taken from the gaol to the court of law in the routine uniform of an undertrial but without any protest from him. These two marches inspired the famous **Washington March of 1960** organized by Dr. Martin Luther King and James Bavel and other civil right-agitators.

But it has to be noted that much earlier than the Dandi March of 1930, salt agitations had taken place in Surat in 1844 and 1850 against high salt duty. The heavy duty was reduced substantilly.

Vedaranyam Salt March–Several similar marches were organized by other leaders such as the one led by Chakravarti Rajgopalchari from Tiruchirapalli Madras to coastal village Vedaranyam. The party consisted of 150 marchers. It started on 13. 4. 1930 and it ended on 28. 4. 1930 covering a distance of about 150 miles or 240 kilo-meters. Prominent members of the party were Rukmani Lakshmipathi, K. Kamaraj, Aranthangi C. Krishnaswami, M. Bhaktavatsalam, CR Narsimhan, A. Vaidyanath Iyer, G. Ramachandran and Panthule Iyer.

Qissa Khwani Bazaar, Peshawar movement–

Khan Abdul Gaffar Khan the Frontier Gandhi organized Salt Satyagraha in Peshawar in the Frontier region. He was arrested on 30. 4. 1930. Earlier he led the satyagraha of Khudai Khidmatgar volunteers. The police opened fire in the Qissa Khwani Bazaar area of Peshawar killing about 250 satyagrahis. Charan Singh Garhawali and other soldiers refused to open fire. They were tried and sentenced to life imprisonment.

The Chimur incident:

This incident took place after the culmination of the Quit India Movement of 1942. The British Government suppressed the Movement with all the strength in their command. There were agitations and protests all over the country. One such incident took place in Chimur, a part of Chanda district which is in old C. P. and Berar now Maharashtra. Sant Tukdoji set the ball rolling by singing a bhajan upon his khajari, a musical instrument. He exhorted the people to protest against British rule. The police responded with force and opened fire resulting in several deaths. About four hundred suspects were tried for various offenses, 29 were sentenced to death and 43 to life imprisonment. All the national parties such as the Indian National Congress, the Muslim League and the CPI appealed for mercy to the condemned persons which resulted in commutation for life to 14 of them.

This incident is notable for the long fast of Professor J. P. Bhansali to protest against the police excesses. The fast started on November 12, 1942 and ended on 12. 1. 1943 i.e. a duration of 61 days.

A committee known as the Capital Punishment Relief Society CPRS was set up to provide relief to the families of the convicted to death on 7. 2. 1943 in Nagpur. Dr. N. B. Khare the first Premier of the state was its Chairman with G. T. Mudholkar, Veer Harakare, advocate Rambhau Manohar and advocate P. K. Tare, E. S. Patwardhan and A. N. Udhoji as members.

Some of the prominent women activists in these protests were Vimlabai Deshpande, Dwarkabai Deoskar, Vimala Abhyankar, Ramabai Tambe and Durgabai Wazalkar.

Chapter Seven

Forgotten Women Heroes

In the history of the freedom movement of India and particularly in the saga of 1857, there are some brave queens and Ranis who took the British by their horns in the various battlefields and fought them like their male counter-parts. Their acts of bravery and sacrifice are in no manner less chivalrous than those of the legendary Maharani Laxmi Bai of Jhansi. Still then, these brave women patriots are either completely forgotten or they have not been accorded the lime-light and high-light which is certainly due to them. This is not to take away anything from the credit which is given to the heroic Maharani of Jhansi who is reckoned in world history along with such braves as Joan of Arc of France. But still then, it has to be said that due coverage and lime-light have to be given to other equally significant contributors like a few which are being mentioned below.

Rani Abbakka Chowta of Ullal—After the arrival of Vasco da Gama in the eastern coast of India in 1498, several parts of India fell under the control of the Portuguese. They might have remained unchallenged throughout the 16th century. After capturing Mangalore, they tried to bring Ullal under their control. Rani Ullal refused to come under their control. So a battle ensued between the two forces in 1556. The Portuguese were unable to subdue the Rani in this battle. However, they regrouped themselves with a larger force. Even this time, they were pushed back by the Rani. However, the third time in 1581 they were able to defeat the Rani with the help of the treachery of some of the earlier associates of Rani. She was caught unprepared and the Portuguese engaged her in a decisive battle. She lost the battle and was killed in the battle field. In 2003, the Government of India issued a special stamp in her honor and the Indian Navy named one of its vassals in her honor as Rani Abakka of Chowta.

Rani Velu Nachiyar (1730-1796)–Rani Velu Nachiyar the queen of the Sivaganga state in South India is widely regarded as the first queen who fought against the British colonial power in India.

Born as princess of Ramanathapuram she took training in handling different weapons, in martial arts, horse riding and archery, and was also proficient in languages like English, French and Urdu. She was married to the King of Sivagangai, Muthuvaduganathaperiya Udaya Thevar. After the British soldiers and son of Nawab of Arcot conquered Sivaganga and killed her husband, she fled with her daughter and lived at Virupachi under the protection of Palayakarar Kopala Nayakkar, build her army and joined hands with Gopala Nayaker and Sultan Hyder Ali to wage war against the British and regained her kingdom. She is also credited as the first person to apply human bomb technique.

Velu Nachiyar was born on January 3, 1730, in Ramanathapuram, Tamil Nadu, India, to Raja Chellamuthu Vijayaragunatha Sethupathy of the Ramnad kingdom and to Rani Sakandhimuthal. Since they had no male child, Velu was reared up by them just like a boy. She was trained like any other male warrior and she acquired proficiency in archery, horse-riding and in almost all the methods of warfare. She also achieved proficiency in several languages such as English, French and Urdu.

From 1730, Muthuvaduganananthur Udaya Thevar was in charge of the administration of Sivagangai, the first independent state from Ramnad, while his father ruled as the King. Muthuvaduganananthur Udaya Thevar became the King of Sivagangai in 1750 and he ruled the state for more than two decades till his death in 1772. Nachiyar and Muthuvaduganananthur Udaiyathevar had a daughter named Vellachi.

In 1772, Sivagangai was invaded by the forces of the East India Company helped by the Nawab of Arcot. Her husband was killed while fighting the forces led by Col. Smith in the Kalaiyar Koli battle field. Velu tactically fled with her daughter Vellachi and she took shelter in Virapachi near Didigul. Here she associated herself with Hyder Ali. She conversed with Hyder in Urdu language. She immediately impressed him with her intelligence, resolution and her qualities as a warrior. Hyder could easily appreciate that Velu wanted to take on the Company forces again in the battle field to regain her estate. By this time, she had collected her forces also. Hyder also provided her with man-power and weapons to fight the Company.

Velu confronted the Company forces in 1780. First of all, she blew up the arms garrison of the Company by employing the tactic of a human-bomb. One of her soldiers, namely Kuyilli, came forward to become a human bomb. She doused herself with ghee, set herself afire and then jumped into the Company arsenal with the result that it was blown up. She thus went into records as the first human bomb. (Incidentally this tactic is being followed so often today). She regained her estate Sivagangai and she ruled over it till her death in 1796 at age 66. In Tamil culture, she was called as Veeramangai or the brave queen.

Kittur Rani Chennamma (23 October 1778–)–She was the queen of the princely state of Kittur which is now in Karnataka. The state did not have a male member to ascend the throne of this princely state. So they intended to take it over by the doctrine of lapse. Rani Kittur resisted the forces of the East India Company in a battle in 1824, i.e. much earlier before the uprising of 1857. She died while fighting out the Company forces.

She is venerated in Karnataka folklore along with other brave queens such as Abbakka Rani, Keladi Chennamma and Onake Obavva.

Bhima Bai Holkar defeated Col. Malkam of the East India Company in a guerilla war in 1817. Some of the earlier women warriors are Rani Tace Bai, Rani Jindon, Baiza Bai, Chouhan Rani, Devi Chandramani, Pandey Queen. Rani of Tulsipur and Tapaswini Maharani. They fought the battles just like their counter –parts, suffered imprisonment or death.

Rani Avanti Bai Lodhi (1831-1858)——Rani Avanti Bai was the wife of King Vikramaditya of Ramgarha which is today's Mandla of Madhya Pradesh. When Vikramaditya fell ill, she took over the reins of her kingdom and sometimes later on, he died. She continued to rule over her subjects in a proper manner. The British adopted the policy of lapse earlier promulgated by Lord Dalhousie. They refused to recognise Avanti Bai as the legitimate ruler of Ramgarh and in 1851, they annexed Ramgarh to the British Empire declaring Ramgarh as a Court of Wards and appointed their own administrator for Ramgarh.

Avanti Bai accepted the challenge of the British, raised an army with the help of the neighboring kingdoms and embattled them in the fields of Kheri. However, her forces were no match to the superior strength of the Company. Rani was defeated, her capture seemed inevitable and imminent. Therefore, she killed herself rather than face an ignominy in the British captivity.

Uda Devi (—1858) Uda Devi belonged to the dalit community of Pasis. She was married to Makka Pasi who was a soldier in the army of the Nawab of Oudh. She also enlisted herself in the women's wing of the Oudh army. The British attacked Oudh on 10 June 1857. Uda Devi decided to take the British bravely in the battle-field. She disguised herself as a man, climbed atop a peepal tree and from that perched position, she shot dead 30 British soldiers before she herself was shot dead by the British forces. This battle took place in the Sikandar Bagh of Lucknow. About two thousand brave patriots were martyred in this battle.

Begum Hazrat Mahal of Lucknow (— 1879) The British wanted to annex Oudh to their Empire and, therefore, they deposed the Nawab Wajid Ali Shah from the throne. Begum refused to surrender her Oudh. She regrouped her forces with the help of her followers Sarafand-ud-daula, Maharaj Bal Krishna, Raja Jailal, Mammu Khan, Rana Beni Madho Baksha of Baiswara, Maulvi Ahmad Ullal Shah of Faizabad and Raja Man Singh. She crowned her eleven year old son Briji Qadir as the Nawab of Oudh. She fought the might of the Company as long as she could, but finally, she was no match to the might of her opponents. She took shelter in Nepal and she died there in 1879. Some of the fiercest battles of 1857 were fought in Oudh. It is estimated that about 150000 people lost their lives in Oudh alone during these up-risings, about 100000 being civilians.

Some other women soldiers in the army of Rani Laxmi Bai who deserve remembrance are Jhalkari Bai, Durga Bai, Mander, Sundari Bai, Mundari Bai and Moti Bai. Jhalkari Bai was a look-alike of Rani Laxmi. One of the close confidants of the Rani namely Dulha Ju played a traitor and opened one of the doors of the fort to allow the British forces entry into it. When the Company forces were near the fortress of Jhansi, she disguised herself as the Rani and took up the challenge of the Company by herself. The Company forces were under a mistaken belief for quite some time. Though Jhalkari Bai was ultimately martyred, yet the Rani was able to make her escape even though for a brief period before she herself could be martyred into immortality. Some of the close confidants of the Rani of Jhansi are the two valiant gunners Ghulam Gaus Khan and Khuda Baksha, Lala Bhau Bakshi, Diwan Raghunath Singh, Diwan Jawahar Singh, Dost Khan Brijish Qadr and Bakht Khan.

Similarly, some of the brave women of Muzaffarnagar took up the challenge during this interlude. They fought out the British bravely until such time as they were either killed or were hanged on capture. Some of them are Asha Devi, Bakhtavari, Habiba, Jamila Khan, Bhagvati Devi Tyagi, Indra Kaur, Man Kaur, Raj Kaur, Shobha Devi and Umda.

Matangini Hazra (17 November 1869 – 29 September 1942)–Matangini Hazra was born in a village by the name Hogla near Tamluk in 1869. She was married early, but she was widowed at age eighteen. She joined the national movement in 1905. She began to take part in national duties regularly since then. She was arrested twice in 1930 for taking part in the Salt Satyagraha. Once she was injured by a police baton while taking part in a procession.

In 1942 during the Quit India Movement, she was leading a procession of mainly women volunteers despite prohibitory orders issued under Section 144 of the Criminal Procedure Code near Tamluk. She was critically injured and died as a result at age 72 with the tricolor in one hand and singing Bande Mataram. Her memory has been perpetuated by erecting a statue in Kolkata at the spot where she was shot and died. A postal stamp has been issued by the Postal Department of the Government of India in her memory.

Women heroes-(of the freedom movement period)

The Nehru women

Swarup Rani Nehru 1868 – 1938

She was the wife of the leading lawyer Motilal Nehru and mother of the first Prime Minister of India Pt. Jawaharlal Nehru. She took active part in several freedom movements such as the Civil Disobedience Movement, Salt Movement and Swadeshi Movement. She called upon the women to give up foreign clothes for the national cause.

Kamla Nehru (1 August 1899 – 28 February 1936)

She was the wife of Pt. Jawaharlal Nehru and the mother of Smt. Indira Gandhi. She took active part in various freedom movements such as the movement of 1920-1921. She suffered incarceration along with her mother-in-law, Smt. Sarojini Naidu and other ladies twice. She took active part in the swadeshi movement by calling upon the women to give up foreign clothes. She opened a dispensary in the Swaraj Bhavan to help the needy persons. After her death, the dispensary was named as the Kamla Nehru Memorial Hospital, Allahabad.

Kamla did not keep good health as she was suffering from T. B. which was almost incurable at that point of time. She was rushed to sanatoria in Germany and Switzerland and back to India for treatment. In 1935, Netaji Subhash Chandra Bose took her to Badenweiler Germany for her admission there in a sanatorium. But she could not recover and she died on 28. 2. 1936 at age 37.

Jawaharlal Nehru has referred to her illness, her treatments and her contribution towards her father-in-law and her husband so that they could devote greater times for the national duty in his Auto-biography. It is a no mean achievement on her part that her husband could give up perhaps the most lucrative of the legal practices of that time and that he could go to jail no less than nine times during the struggle for independence. He has referred to the contribution of his entire family in general and to Kamla in particular in the following words–

" From 1923 onwards I found a great deal of solace and happiness in my family life, though I gave little time to it. I have been fortunate enough in my family relationships, in times of strain and difficulty they have soothed me and sheltered me. I realized, with some shame of my own unworthiness in this respect, how much I owed to my wife for her splendid behavior since 1920. Proud and sensitive as she was, she had not only put up with my vagaries but brought me comfort and solace when I needed them most. " 1 An Autobiography, Jawaharlal Nehru pages 105 and 106

Jawaharlal has referred to her arrest also in his autobiography which took place in 1931. "...I was pleased, for she had so longed to follow many of her comrades to prison. Ordinarily if they had been men, both she and my sister and many other women arrested long ago. But at that time the Government avoided as far as possible, arresting women, and so they escaped for so long. And now she had her heart's desire! How glad she must be, I thought. But I was apprehensive, for she was always in weak health, and I feared that prison conditions might cause her much suffering. "2 An Autobiography Jawaharlal Nehru page 240

Rameshwari Nehru (1886-1966)–She was born into the family of Raja Narendra Nath Raina and Rooprani of Lahore. She hailed from an aristocratic family with relationship to the family of Motilal Nehru. She married Brijlal Nehru in 1902 who was the youngest son of Nandlal Nehru the brother of Motilal Nehru and thus Brijlal and Jawaharlal were cousins. Despite such sophisticated back-ground, Rameshwari was endowed with liberal views. Although Rameshwari was essentially a social worker with special orientation towards the welfare of the women of India, yet she was a participant in the freedom movement of her country with equal distinction. She came in close contact with Mahatma Gandhi and almost all the front-line leaders of that era. She took part in the freedom movements organized by the Indian National Congress under Mahatma Gandhi.

Rameshwari started her public career by bringing out a journal for the women, namely Stree Darpan in 1909 from Allahabad. Through this vehicle, she ventilated the cause of the women in such diverse fields as eradication of the system of child-marriages, rehabilitation of the prostitutes and eradication of the devadasi system, spread of education amongst the women and all other causes. When the British Government appointed the Age of Consent Committee in 1928 to recommend the age of girls for their marriages, Rameshwari was invited by them to take part in these deliberations. Like Mahatma Gandhi, she also believed that if a minor girl loses her equally minor husband at an early age, then that girl could not be called a widow. Accordingly, she presented her paper before the Committee. The final report of the Committee paved the way for the legislation of the Child Marriage Restraint Act, 1929 more famously known as the Sarda Act after the presenter of this Bill in the Central Legislation.

She was one of the founders of the All India Women's Conference and she presided over the Conference in 1942.

Following the partition of India in 1947, Rameshwari worked tirelessly for the rehabilitation of the refugees coming from different parts of Pakistan either West or East. She will be more particularly recalled for her work in the Purana Qila locality of New Delhi where a large number of refugees were sheltering. She worked in the rehabilitation and acceptance of the women who were abducted in thousands during the great exodus of 1946-1947 along with Lady Mountbatten, Dr. Sushila Nayyar, the Sarabhai ladies, Smt. Indira Gandhi, Smt. Kamla Chattopadhyaya, Smt. Rajkumari Amrit Kaur and others. She was appointed Honorary Advisor to the Ministry of Rehabilitation simply because she refused a salary for this humanitarian work. She was awarded Padma Bhushan in 1955 and the Lenin Peace Prize in 1961.

Uma Nehru (8 March 1884 – 28 August 1963)–Uma Nehru is yet another member of the Nehru family of India who played important roles in the struggle for independence. She was imprisoned for her part in the Salt Satyagraha of 1930and in the Quit India Movement of 1942. She was elected to the Lok Sabha twice after independence and she was a member of Rajya Sabha from 1962 until her death in 1963.

Vijaya Lakshmi Pandit (18 August 1900 – 1 December 1990)–She is the daughter of Motilal and Swarupa Nehru. She married Ranjit Sitaram Pandit in 1921. He was a successful barrister of Bombay and a scholar of great caliber and a leading freedom fighter in his own personality.

She followed her family tradition by taking active part in the freedom struggle of India. She started her public career by entering Municipal Corporation of Allahabad. Then she became a legislator of the United Provinces in 1937 and she was made the minister of Local Self Government and Public Health in the Pt. Govind Vallabh Pant ministry. But then the entire Government resigned in 1939 following a protest against the unilateral decision of the British Government to involve India in the World War II. She thus became the first woman to hold the post of a minister. She was imprisoned for her participation in the Quit India Movement of 1942. In 1945 general elections, she was elected to the Constituent Assembly of India.

Smt. Pandit entered into a very distinguished diplomatic career after independence. She was a part of the Indian delegation to the United Nations Organization between the periods 1946-1948 and 1952-1953. She was India's Ambassador to the Soviet Union from 1947 to 1949 and to America and Mexico from 1949 to 1951. She was elected as the President of the General Assembly of the United Nations in 1953 and in this manner, she became the first woman to achieve this honour. She was made the Indian High Commissioner to Great Britain from 1954 to 1961. She was made the Governor of Maharashtra in 1962 and served as such till 1964. She successfully contested the Lok Sabha elections in 1964 for a term ending in 1968.

Other women warriors

Bhikaiji Rustom Cama or Madam Cama (24 September 1861 – 13 August 1936)–She was one of the leading Parsi women of prominence in the freedom struggle of India. She hailed from the reputed Parsi family of Sorabji Framji Patel and Jaijibai Sorabji Patel. Her father Sorabji was a well known merchant and lawyer at the same time. She received her education in the prestigious Alexandra Native Girls English Institution. In August 1885, she married Rustom Cama who was a pro establishment lawyer. The marriage did not prove to be successful and, therefore, Bhikaji devoted herself to the social service and national causes.

In 1896, the Bombay Presidency was hit by famine and then by the bubonic plague. She engaged herself in the relief work. As a result, she herself caught the disease. She went to England for treatment. There she came in contact with Shyamji Krishna Varma and Dada Bhai Naoroji. She helped Shyamji in founding the Indian Home Rule Society in London in February 1905. The British Government took note of these activities of Bhikaji. They did not allow her to return to India unless she gave a written undertaking that in return, she would not take part in anti- British movements. She refused to do so. Instead, she went to Paris to carry out her work for Indian independence. She founded the Paris Indian Society along with S. R. Rana and Munchershah Burjorji Godrej. She published revolutionary literature in weeklies *Vande Mataram* and *Talwar* in Netherland and Switzerland.

She attended the Second Socialist Congress held in Stuttgart Germany on 22. 8. 1907. It is here that she hoisted the flag of Indian independence. The flag signified the aspirations of the entire India. The green and the crescent moon stood for Islam, orange for Buddhism and Hinduism was signified by the red and the sun in the flag. The word vande-mataram was inscribed in the devanagari script of Hindi. The eight lotuses signified the eight provinces of the British India. This design was duly adopted in the Berlin Committee in 1914 which was later known as the Indian Independence Committee. The original design is now available for public display in the Maratha and Kesari Library in Pune.

Impressed by the activism of suffragette Christabel Pankhurst and Margaret Cousins, she advocated the cause of voting rights to the Indian women also and also for all other legal and civic rights for them.

Bhikaji remained in exile till 1935 when the British Government allowed her to return to India in view of her age and failing health. So she returned to India in November 1935 after a self-imposed exile of about thirty years. However, she died nine months into her return. But she donated most of her personal assets to the Avabai Petit Orphanage for Girls and Rs 54000/ to the family fire temple in South Bombay.

Basanti Devi (23. 3. 1880–7. 5. 1974)–She was the wife of Deshbandhu C. R. Das. She participated in the freedom movements in her own individual personality. After the arrest of her husband in 1921, she came forward, took the lead and her personal example was followed by a large number of women. She was the first Indian woman activist to be imprisoned by the

British Government. She was decorated as Padma Vibhushan by the Government of India in 1973. Basanti Devi College, Kolkata is named after her.

Begam Shareefa Hamid Ali (1883-1971)–She was the daughter of Ameena Tyebji and Abbas Tyebji who was a cousin of Badruddin Tyabji Chief Justice of Baroda High Court and a close associate of Mahatma Gandhi. The Tyebji family was of nationalist outlook and progressive in thinking. Begam was similarly of a broad mind. She advocated social reforms in her community. She was opposed to the purdah system. She attended the Congress session of 1907. She supported the swadeshi movement. She was one of the keen supporters of the Child Marriage Restraint Act 1929 popularly known as the Sarda Act of 1929. She was one of the prominent activists in the All India Womens Conference which looked after the issues related to the womens cause. She represented India in several international conferences.

The Parsi ladies in the front

The Parsi community of India has played a very important role in the freedom movement of India. They are comparatively a small community in terms of number. But their deeds of social service, philanthropy and charity are at par with any other community any where. They are primarily a business community specializing in such sectors as textiles, pharmaceuticals, drugs and medicines, liqueurs and other commodities. They have donated generously both at the time of the freedom movements and also thereafter. During the movements, they were one of the leading contributors to the Congress funds despite the fact that Mahatma Gandhi had launched a picketing campaign against the sale of liquor. This is the best evidence of their patriotism and benevolence. Dada Bhai Naoroji has been recognized as the Grand Old Man of India. He was the first Indian to be elected to the British Parliament. From that platform, he introduced the aspirations of his countrymen to the British public at large and also to the British establishment. It will be no exaggeration to assert that after the 1857 up-risings, it is to the credit of Dada Bhai that he gave the clarion call of Indian nationalism and patriotism. He is also the pioneer of the renaissance of Indian industry, business and entrepreneurship, trade and commerce. Jamshedji Naoroji Tata is one of the makers of modern industrial India followed by the house of Godrej, Wadia, Petit and others.

It is remarkable that the Parsi ladies have also contributed significantly to the nationalistic cause particularly during that period in the Indian history when women in general were supposed to remain within the confines of their domestic responsibilities. Many of the Parsi ladies came out in open to provide an incentive and lead to the other women all over the country. Let us here recall the various sacrifices and contributions of some of these out-standing Parsi ladies.

Perin Ben Captain –Her parents were Ardeshir the eldest son of Dada Bhai Naoroji Tata and Virbai Dadina. After her initial education in Bombay, she moved on to Paris for her further studies in the Sorbonne Nouvelle University at Paris. During her stay in Paris, she came in contact with Bhikaji Cama and Vinayak Damodar Savarkar. Along with them, she attended several conferences and meetings such as the Egyptian National Congress. She returned to India in 1911. She came in personal contact with Mahatma Gandhi in 1919 and she immediately began to take part in national agitations such as in the Civil Disobedience Movement of 1920 and the Swadeshi Movement of 1930. She herself presented an example by putting on the khadi clothes. She was jailed for her involvement in the national movements. She was elected as the first woman President of the Bombay Provincial Congress Committee in 1930. Similarly in 1930, she was made the General Secretary of the Gandhi Seva Dal.

When the Padma awards were initiated by the Government of India in 1954, she was awarded the Padma Shri.

Gosiben Captain-

She was a follower of the Gandhian ideals. She took part in his movements. She was one of the trustees of the All India Village Industries Association.

Mithuben Hormusji Petit (11 April 1892 – 16 July 1973)—Mithuben came from the well-known family of her industrialist father Sir Dinshaw Maneckji Petit.

She was one of the marchers in the Dandi Satyagraha. She lifted a pinch of salt from the sea along with Mahatma Gandhi on 6. 4. 1930 in Dandi and on 9. 4. 1930 in Bhimrad. In the photo of that occasion, she is seen standing just behind him. She was also active in the Bardoli movement of 1928. She picketed the liquor shops during these drives. She was imprisoned for her role in the movements.

She set up an ashram in Maroli called Kasturba Vanat Sabha for the benefit of the harijans and the Scheduled Tribes.

She died on 16. 7. 1973. She was awarded the citation Padma Shri in 1961.

Nargis Captain was yet another of the prominent Parsi ladies who took part in the national and social mainstream of India.

Umabai Kundapur —She was born in Mangalore. She founded the Bhagini Mandal and she was a member of the women's wing of the Hindustan Seva Dal which was founded by Dr. Hardikar. They organized the All India Congress session of 1932 which was held in Belgaum. For her role in the freedom struggle, she wasarrested and kept in Yerwada Jail for four months.

Ansuiya Bai Kale (1896-1958)–Her father Sadashiv Rao Bhate was one of the leading lawyers of his place Satara. He was a widower and he married the second time to the mother of Anasuya. She married in 1916 to a widower. It is clear from this back-ground that Anasuya hailed from a family with broad-mind and large thinking.

Anasuya began to take part in the social service sector very early. She was appointed a member of the Central Provinces Legislative Council in 1928, an Inspector of Women's Prison, in 1929 a member of the International Labor Commission Nagpur unit and as such she took the ILO representatives to different areas of the Central Provinces and Berar to study labor problems and needs. In 1930, she resigned her membership of the Central Legislative Council and accompanied Mahatma Gandhi on an extensive tour of the Old C. P. and Berar to campaign against untouchability. She became the President of the Nagpur Congress Committee in 1935. In 1935, she was elected to the C. P. & Berar Legislative Council and was made its

Deputy Speaker in the ministry headed by Pt. Govind Vallabh Pant. The British Government involved the British Indian forces in the W. W. II unilaterally much against the wishes of the National Congress. The ministry resigned much to the delight of the Muslim League. She took part in the deliberations of the All India Womens Association in 1937 and onwards and she canvassed the causes relating to the needs of the women.

She was imprisoned for her participation in the Civil Disobedience Movement. In 1942, a number of Scheduled Tribes were convicted and sentenced to death. Anasuya took up their cause, fought a legal and social battle and ultimately saved them from the inevitable and imminent galows. Anasuya was returned to the Lok Sabha in 1952 and 1957.

Rani Gaidinliu (26 January 1915 – 17 February 1993)–She belonged to the Heraka religious movement which was started by her cousin Haipou Jadonang. This sect opposed the conversion of the Nagas to Christianity because they wanted to save their ancient culture and heritage. Conversion was fast spreading among the Nagas. Her cousin was also in the fore-front of these oppositions. So he was arrested and killed summarily. Thereafter, Gaidinliu took over the leadership. She called upon her people not to obey the unjust laws of the British Government. She asked them not to pay taxes. In this manner, she opened up a front against the Government. She went into exile. The police launched an extensive search for her. An inducement of tax-waiver for ten years to anyone helping the police upto her arrest was announced by the Government. Finally, she was arrested along with many of her associates on 17. 10. 1932. She was tried for the offences of murder while many of her associates were summarily eliminated by the police. She was jailed for a sentence of life imprisonment in 1932 and she remained in imprisonment right upto the dawn of the independence when she was released from captivity in 1947 on an order of the first Prime Ministe r of India Jawaharlal Nehru after spending nearly 15 years in different itinerary jails from one jail to another.

The Rani was awarded Tamrapatra Freedom Fighter Award 1972, Padma Bhushan in 1982 and the Vivekanand Seva Mandal in 1983.

The Rani had to fight on two fronts, one against the British and the other against the local Nagas most of whom were converted into Christianity. Rani was anxious to protect the ancient culture and heritage of the Nagas. Therefore, she found herself in the opposite camp of the Naga National Council who demanded secession from the Indian Union and who were carrying out insurgent activities in the Naga areas. She found herself opposed to the Naga leader Phizo also simply because she demanded more autonomy for her people but within the Indian union. Gaidinliu was called Rani by the Prime Minister Nehru who personally met her after independence. She died in February 1993.

Other lady patriots

Moolmati

She was the mother of the immortal martyr Ram Prasad Bismil. Ram Prasad inherited the qualities of valour and independent line of thinking from his mother. He has written in his auto –biography which he had written in the Gorakhpur Jail that if it had not been for his mother, then he would have lived his life like any other ordinary human being. Ram Prasad was hanged after his conviction and sentence to death on 19. 12. 1927 for his involvement in the Kakori Rail Robbery case. When his mother came to meet him for the last time with hand-made food, he was in tears but not the mother. She gave him courage and fortitude even at that crucial time. This is the contribution of Moolmati, the mother in the independence movement of India.

Raj Kumari Gupta——She was born in Banda Kanpur in the year 1920. She was married to Madan Mohan Gupta at age thirteen. Madan Mohan was himself a Congress worker. But then Raj Kumari differed from her husband in the sense that she began to subscribe to the revolutionary ideals of Ram Prasad Bismil, Chandra Shekhar Azad and other members of the Hindustan Socialist Republican Association HSRA. They planned to rob a train which was bound to Lucknow from Kakori railway station to raise funds for the Association. She was entrusted with the responsibility of supplying arms and other materials to the revolutionaries clandestinely. But she was caught, tried along with other revolutionaries, convicted to jail terms while Ram Prasad Bismil was sentenced to death. She was later disowned by her husband and his family. Raj Kumari served jail terms in 1930, 1932 and 1942.

Abadi Banu Begum or Bi Amman of Lucknow——She was the mother of Maulana Mohammad Ali and Maulana Shaukat Ali the legendary Ali Brothers who were very close associates of Mahatma Gandhi since the Khilafat days until the dawn of the Pakistan movement. When one of her sons was arrested in 1917, she came out in open in burqa and addressed a public meeting calling upon the people to continue the struggle. She was of the opinion that the Indians had helped the British against their own kings and it is the reason why they were now under their domination and secondly, the Indians were not united within themselves and it is the reason why they were defeated in 1857.

Lado Rani Zutshi of Lahore- She was one of the fore-most women leaders of Punjab. She was the wife of Pandit Ladi Prasad Zutshi, a leading lawyer of Lahore. She came out in open in freedom movement in 1919 during the Rowlatt Act, martial law and Jallianwala Bagh days by being very much vocal in her protests. She was in the fore-front of the picketing of the foreign clothes and liquor shops, in support of the swadeshi demands, the Civil Disobedience Movements of 1921 and the Non-Co-operation Movement of 1931. In 1931, she was sentenced for one year only to be released early under the Gandhi-Irwin general amnesty. She was again arrested in 1932 and this time also she was released early on medical grounds.

Parvati Bai—She was arrested in Meerut while she was taking part in a procession. She was arrested, convicted and sentenced to two years in 1922.

Sarla Devi Chaudhurani or Sarla Ghosal (9 September 1872 – 18 August 1945)–Sarla hailed from a well-known family of Bengal. Her father Jankinath Ghoshal was a secretary to the Indian National Congress while her mother Swarn Kumari Devi was the daughter of Debendra Nath Tagore and she was the elder sister of the Poet Rabindra Nath Tagore. In this manner, she inherited nationalistc and literary fervor from her parents' sides. She also inherited spiritual bent from her father's side since they were followers of the Brahmo sect of Raja Ram Mohan Roy.

Sarla Devi knew French, Persian and Sanskrit languages. She could sing very well also. She rendered the national song in the Congress session held at Benaras. She is also credited with composing the music for the national song *Vande Mataram*In 1905, she married Rambhuj Chaudhari of Lahore who was a lawyer by profession, but he was also a staunch nationalist, follower of the Bramho Samaj of Maharshi Dayanand Saraswati. He was himself jailed for participation in the freedom struggle. In 1910, she established the Bharat Stree Mahamandal, a social welfare organization for women, which has been regarded by many observers to be the first such organization for the women of India. Rambhuj was arrested in 1919 in connection with his activities relating to the Rowlatt Act. Although she was equally vociferous in her protests against this draconian law, yet the British chose not to arrest her in their wisdom. She was an ardent follower of the Mahatma. He used to stay in her house in Lahore during his visits to Lahore. Her son Dipak later married Radha, one of the grand-daughters of the Mahatma. She died on 18 August 1945 in Kolkata.

Sarojini Naidu or Sarojini Chattopadhyaya 13 February 1879 – 2 March 1949)—-Sarojini Naidu was born in Hyderabad in the family of Aghorenath Chattopadhyay a Bengali Brahmin who was the principal of the Nizam›s College in Hyderabad and her mother Barada Sundari Devi. She hailed from a cultured family. One of her brothers Virendranath had radical views while her another brother Harindra Nath was a talented artist. After doing her matriculation from Madras now Chennai, she went for higher studies to England after a break of about four years after her matriculation. A scholarship provided by the Nizam Charitable Trust enabled her to proceed to England where she studied in the King's College London and then at the Girton College Cambridge. At age nineteen, Sarojini came in contact with Govindarajulu Naidu who was a doctor hailing from Andhra Pradesh. Sarojini was a Brahmin while Paidipati was a Telugu. But the two families did not object to such an inter-caste marriage. So they were married. Smt. Padmaja Naidu was one of their children who was herself a freedom fighter and who went on to become the Governor of Uttar Pradesh.

The partition of Bengal in 1905 disturbed her a great deal. Some time thereafter, she came in contact with such great figures of Indian polity as Gopal Krishna Gokhale, Poet Rabindra Nath Tagore and Mahatma Gandhi. She emulated Mahatma Gandhi by extensively touring length and breath of the country for three years 1915 to 1918 delivering several speeches and at the same time she accumulated invaluable first hand knowledge of her people. The movement for the enfranchisement of the women launched by the suffragette in England attracted her also. So she accompanied Smt. Annee Besant to London in regard to this movement. She also helped in the establishment of the Women's India Association in 1917. By that time, Smt. Annee Besant had already pioneered the Home Rule Movement. Therefore, she again went to England along with Smt. Annie Besant to take part in the meeting of the All India Home Rule League.

Upon return, she found that the country was embroiled in such events as the Jallianwala Bagh, the Khilafat and the Civil Disobedience Movement of 1920. She joined the nationalist fervor of these movements. She was one of the active participants in all the movements initiated by the Mahatma such as the Salt

Satyagraha of 1930 and the Quit India Movement of 1942. She was arrested and jailed. She suffered them number of times totalling nearly two years. In the meanwhile, she had presided over the annual session of the Indian National Congress which was held in Cawnpore now Kanpur in 1929. She accompanied Mahatma Gandhi and other Congress leaders in the Second Round Table Conference held in 1932 in London.

After independence, she was appointed as the Governor of the United Provinces now Uttar Pradesh. She remained in office till her death in 1949. She is the first woman governor of any province. She was an eloquent speaker. She could leave her audience spell-bound.

She worked tirelessly for Hindu-Muslim unity firstly along with Mohammad Ali Jinnah and after Jinnah moved into the Muslim League folder, along with Mahatma Gandhi.

Sarojini was an eminent poet of English literature. Her poetry has been admired by almost all the critics of eminence like Aldoux Huxley. She has been called the Nightingale of India.

Nanibala Devi (1888-1967)—She was married at age eleven but widowed at age sixteen, she joined the Jaguantar Party which was founded by Amarendranath Chattopadhyaya. She used to give shelter to the revolutionaries. The police were on her look-out and therefore, she went under-ground. She fled to Peshawar where she was finally caught. She was badly tortured. She was released on a general amnesty in 1919. She spent two years in imprisonment. Afterwards, even her family refused to join her in their relationship. She died in 1967 almost unknown despite a Government pension which was sanctioned to her.

Rajkumari Amrit Kaur —Rajkumari belonged to the princely state of Kapurthala of Raja Sir Harnam Singh Ahluwalia and her mother was Lady Pricilla Golaknath. She was brought up in Anglican Christian way of life. But her parents saw to it that she was fully conversant with the traditional Hindu and Indian way of life and also in the Sikh traditions.

After completing her education in England, she returned to India. She was thus both rooted In the Indian ethos and in the Western thought-process. But she had such a family back-ground that she was soon drawn into the national mainstream. Her father used to be a host to national and Congress leaders of those times.

She was drawn into the freedom movement by the happenings in Jallianwala Bagh in 1919. She was one of the co-founders of the All India Women's Conference in 1927 and she served as its Secretary in 1930. She took part in almost all the movements initiated by Mahatma Gandhi such as the Civil Disobedience and Non-Co-operation, the Salt Satyagraha of 1930 and the Quit India Movement of 1942. She was she was imprisoned. She spent some time in the Sabarmati Ashram in 1934 with the result that she could assimilate herself all the more with the systems of austerity and simple living in spite of her princely back-ground. A delegation of the Indian National Congress visited Bannu area which is a part of Khyber-Pashtunistan now in Pakistan. The British did not approve of this act of the INC. She was arrested along with other leaders and imprisoned. She was again arrested and imprisoned in 1942 because of her participation in the Quit India Movement of 1942.

Rajkumari was the Chair-person of the All India Women's Education Fund Association. She was an executive member of the Lady Irwin College Delhi. Because of her contribution in the field of education and literacy of women, she was sent as a representative of the Indian delegation to the UNESCO conferences which were held in London 1945 and Paris 1946. Mahatma Gandhi appointed her as a member of the All India Spinners Association.

In 1946, Rajkumari was elected to the Constituent Assembly of India. She was a member of the Sub-Committee on Fundamental Rights and also of another Sub-Committee for Minorities.

Following India's independence, she was made the Minister for Health in the first cabinet of Jawaharlal Nehru. She thus became the first woman to hold the rank of a cabinet minister. She is instrumental in the establishment of the All India Institute of Medical Sciences, New Delhi. She was closely associated with the Red Cross Movement in India being its Chair-person for 14 years. She did pioneering work in the field of eradication of tuber –closis and leprosy. She also helped in the founding of the National Sports Club of India.

In 1957, she was elected as member of Rajya Sabha which honor she held until her death in February 1964.

Smt. Lilavati Munshi (11. 5. 1899—20. 2. 1978)–She was the wife of eminent lawyer, scholar and freedom-fighter K. M. Munshi. She took part in several movements of freedom struggle such as the Civil Disobedience Movement of 1922. Salt Satyagraha of 1930 and the Quit India Movement of 1942. She was jailed also. She was elected an M. L. A. in the Bombay

Legislative Assembly from 1937 to 1946 intermittently. She was member Rajya Sabha from 1952 to 1958. She was instrumental in the establishment of the Institute of Hotel Management, Catering and Applied Nutrition, Mumbai in 1954.

Kamaladevi Chattopadhyaya (3 April 1903 – 29 October 1988)–Born in Bangalore now in Bengaluru in the family of Ananthaiah Dhareshwar and Girijabai, Kamla was married at the age of fourteen. But then the equally child-like husband died just two years into their marriage leaving her as a so-called child –widow. A few years later, she entered into another wed-lock. This time to Harendra Chattopadhyay who was a very talented person. But then incompatibility intervened which compelled them to decide that it was better to separate mutually. So Kamla found herself to fend for herself. How well did she do thereafter, that is a remarkable story.

She was in England when she decided to join the nationalism of the Indian National Congress under the leadership of Mahatma Gandhi. On return, she joined the Seva Dal. She had also met Margaret Cousins, the leader of the suffragette movement which was agitating for the voting rights of women. She was definitely impressed by such revolutionary philosophy. Therefore, she chalked out a future plan for herself. She founded the All India Women's Conference and she took upon herself the responsibility of its secretaryship. She set up several social and community service programmes for women. In 1930, she was a part of the agitators in the Salt Satyagraha along with another woman walker Avanti Bai Gokhale. She also helped in the establishment of the Lady Irwin College for Women. In 1940, she toured several parts of the world espousing the cause of the freedom of India.

But her most remarkable contribution was to come in the field of the rehabilitation of the refugees who flooded in different parts of India from what are now Pakistan and Bangladesh during the partition days. Along with other equally devoted women like Rameshwari Devi, Dr. Sushila Nayyar, Lady Mountbatten and others, she worked tirelessly for the welfare and acceptance of the recovered women. She established the Indian Cooperation For Rehabilitation of the Displaced Persons Union. She set up colonies for the residential requirements of the displaced persons such as in places like Faridabad and outer Delhi. In one such colony, about 50000 refugees were rehabilitated.

After independence, she devoted herself to the promotion of fine arts, music, culture, theater drama and indigenous crafts. In Delhi, she set up Theater Crafts Museum and National School of Drama. In 1964 she set up Natya Institute of Kathak and Choreography in Bangalore now Bengaluru.

She was decorated with Padma Bhushan in 1955, Padma Vibhushan in 1987. Earlier in 1966, she was awarded the Ramsay Magsaysay citation by the Philippine Government in recognition of her contribution in the field of social and community services. She authored eighteen books also. Kamladevi passed away on 29. 10. 1988.

Begam Safia Abdul Wajid——She was born in Etah Uttar Pradesh in 1905. She took part in the Quit India Movement of 1942.

Begum Qudsia Aizaz Rasul (4 April 1908 – 1 August 2001)—She was born as Qudsia Begum into the family of Sir Zulfiqar Ali Khan and Begam Mahmuda Sultana. In 1929, she was married to Nawab Aizaz Rasul. In 1935, both of them joined the Indian

Muslim League. In the elections of 1937, she was elected to the Central Provinces Assembly on a Muslim League ticket and she remained a member till 1952. She was in the opposite camp in the Assembly from the Muslim League while the Congress Government was headed by Pt. Govind Vallabh Pant. The Government had to resign prematurely. She was elected to the Constituent Assembly of India in 1946. Begam was opposed to the demand for separate electorates for the Muslim community and also to the system of zamindari. The Indian Muslim League was dissolved after the partition of India. So she joined the Indian National Congress. She was elected to the Rajya Sabha in 1952 and to the Uttar Pradesh Legislative Council in 1969 upto 1989. In2000, she was conferred the Padma Bhushan.

Premaben Kantak (1906-1985)– She was one of the close associates of Mahatma Gandhi in her ashrams at Sabarmati and then at Sevagram. She looked after the management of the Ashram.

After obtaining a degree from the Bombay University, she joined the national main-stream guided by Mahatma Gandhi. After the Sabarmati Ashram was disbanded by the Mahatma in the year 1933, he established another one namely the Saswad Ashram in 1934. Later the Mahatma established his final ashram at Sevagram. She looked after this establishment also. Premaben hailed from Maharashtra and therefore, she was made a representative to the Kasturba Gandhi Trust as their representative.

Prema Ben was very active in almost all the movements which were launched by the Saint under the Congress banner. In 1940, she was jailed four times for her participation in the freedom movements. She was again imprisoned in 1942 for her role in the Quit India Movement of 1942 for 18 months. She was released in January 1944. She did not accept higher posts and offices in the Congress hierarchy and was content to keep her activity to the management of the idyllic ashrams of the Saint.

Bibi Amtus Salam—She was born in a zamindar Pathan family of Abdul Majid Khan. Her father was an aristocrat yet conservative in nature. Amtus was not allowed schooling by her orthodox parents. Still then, she was of progressive and nationalistic views. She joined Mahatma Gandhi in the Sabarmati Ashram and stayed with him till the days of partition of India. She was one of the close confidants of the Mahatma. She associated herself with all the movements for independence. But she will always be remembered for her association with the Mahatma in the extensive tours of Bengal and particularly in Noakhali during the 1946 communal disturbances. She even took a fast of 21 days in Noakhali for the restoration of communal harmony. It is to be noted that Mahatma did not allow many persons to undertake such fasts simply because he thought that not everyone was fully qualified to do so. She also joined other ladies such as Dr. Sushila Nayyar, Rameshwari Nehru and others in bringing relief to the women who were abducted to and from India and Pakistan in the midst of this frenzy. She was deeply disturbed when her family members decided to migrate to Pakistan. She established several institutions such as the Kasturba Seva Mandir in Rajpura.

Abha Gandhi—She was one of the 'walking-sticks 'of Mahatma Gandhi, the other being Manu Gandhi. Mahatma was in the habit of placing both of his hands upon the shoulders of these two young girls for support during some of his last days. It was an entirely innocuous act on the part of the Mahatma who perhaps derived some comfort while walking along with them with his head looking down in deep thought-process. However, there were some orthodox protestations from some quarters and he left the practice thereafter. Abha was with the Mahatma literally upto the last moment of his mortal existence with his head in her lap after being shot point blank by the assassin in the Birla Bhavan now the Smriti Bhavan, New Delhi.

Before her marriage to Kanu Gandhi, one of the grand-sons of the Mahatma, she was Abha Chatterji. She was with the Mahatma ever since she was 13 years of age and served him till the last moments of the fateful 30th of January 1948.

Her husband, Kanu Gandhi was a photo-grapher who shot some of the iconic pictures of his grandfather. They moved on to Rajkpt after January 1948 where they established some institutes to perpetuate the memory of Kasturba Gandhi, for example, Kasturbadham the place where Kasturba had been arrested during her agitation in the Rajkot movement of 1928 and the Rshtriyashala Institute, Rajkot.

Manu Gandhi or Mridula Gandhi was the daughter of Jaisuhkhlal Gandhi. After the death of her mother in 1942, Jaishukhlal entrusted her into the care of the ashram to learn English and other subjects. But then she was drawn into the movements once she was an inmate in the Ashram. She looked after the management of the Ashram and also the comforts of the Mahatma. In the 1942 participation, she was arrested and jailed in the Aga Khan Palace confinement in Poona now Pune.

She witnessed the passing away of Mahadev Desai and then Kasturba in the Palace. She was by the side of Mahatma when he was fatally shot in the Birla Bhavan or Smriti Bhavan New Delhi on the fateful evening of January 30, 1948.

Prabhavati Devi 1906 – 15 April 1973—-She was the daughter of Babu Brijkishore who was a leading lawyer of Champaran and also one of the active participants in the freedom struggle of India. She was married to Jai Prakash Narayan. Shortly after their marriage, Jai Prakash had to go to America for higher studies. He studied Marxism in the University of Wisconsin. During his stay abroad, she was entrusted into the company of Mahatma Gandhi by their father. This is how her initiation into the mainstream of Indian nationalism started. She began to subscribe to the ideals of the Ashram one of which was to take a a vow of celibacy compulsorily. Prabhavati herself had no difficulty in doing so. But when Jai Prakash returned from America in 1929, he felt a little bit embarrassed. By that time, he had developed radical views though not exactly on the extreme left.

Indumati Chimanlal Sheth —-She was born in Ahmedabad in 1906 to Manekba and Chimanlal Nagindas Sheth. She had her studies in Govt School Ahmedabad Girls School, Ahmedabad and then in the Gujarat VidyaPith in 1926. She took up a teaching job in the Vidyapith. And thereafter, she came under the spell of Mahatma Gandhi. She took part in the 1920 movement i.e. Civil Disobedience. She took active part in 1942 Quit India Movement for which she was imprisoned by the British.

She took part in the swadeshi movement and promoted khadi. She had by now become an active member of the INC.

In 1937, he was elected to the Ahmedabad Municipal School Board. In 1946, she was elected as an M. L. A. of the Bombay Assembly. She was also a member of the University Grant Commission. In 1970, she was decorated as Padma Shri by the Government of India.

Durgābāi Deshmukh or Lady Deshmukh (15 July 1909 – 9 May 1981)–Durgabai was married at age 8 to Subbarao. Durgabai Deshmukh had to discontinue her studies it seems because she attended the Congress conference in 1923 when it was held in her district Kakinada. She was hardly 14 years of age at that time. It is said that she did not allow Pt. Jawaharlal Nehru to enter into the conference premises because he could not show his ticket for entry. He was permitted to enter by her only when he was able to show his ticket. Nehru praised her for her sense of duty. It is further remarkable that late in 1953 when she married Chintaman Rao Deshmukh who was a member in the Nehru cabinet, Jawaharlal was one of the witnesses to the marriage between them. Deshmukh was an equally broad minded person.

She took part in the Salt Satyagraha in 1930 and she was arrested three times between 1930 and 1933. But after her release, she continued her studies. She obtained an M. A. in Political Science and then LL. B. She started her practice as late as in 1942. She was able to establish a good practice at the Bar soon in the High Court in Madras.

She was elected to the Constituent Assembly of India in 1946. She was a Member of the Planning Commission of India. She canvassed the cause of the setting up of family courts for expeditious relief to the needy women. The effort bore fruit in 1984 when the Family Courts Act 1984 was legislated. During the Constituent Assembly debates, she advocated the cause of Hindustani as the national language which was an ad-mixture of Hindi and Urdu. But otherwise she was not in favor of imposition of Hindi upon any one.

She was the first chairperson of the National Council on Women's Education, established by the Government of India in 1958. Under her leadership, the Committee made several recommendations for introducing better facilities for spreading education amongst girls all over the country. Here are some of her awards–Paul G Hoffman Award, Nehru Literacy Award, UNESCO Award (for outstanding work in the field of literacy) and the Padma Vibhushan.

Bellary Siddamma —She was born in 1903. She is one of the front-line nationalists of Karnataka. She took active part in the freedom struggle. In 1938, she was arrested while trying to hoist the national flag in a place where public meeting was prohibited by the administration. She was imprisoned for one month. She took part in the Aranya Satyagraha of Chitradurga in the year 1939. She also took part in the Quit India Movement of 1942

Hansa Jivraj Mehta (3 July 1897 – 4 April 1995) —Hansa was the daughter of Manubhai Mehta who was the dewan of the Barode State. After graduating in Philosophy in 1918, she studied in England. She married Dr. Jivraj Mehta who was an eminent physician and a prominent freedom fighter.

In England, she came in contact with Smt. Sarojini Naidu and this meeting must have helped inmolding her future line of action. On return to India, she came in contact with Mahatma Gandhi. She immediately joined various movements under his leadership. She took part in the picketing of the shops selling foreign clothes and liquor. In 1931, she was arrested and imprisoned. She was elected to the Legislative Council of Bombay and in 1945-46 for the Constituent Assembly of India. Here she was a member of the Advisory Committee and Sub-committee on Fundamental Rights. She was the President of the All India Women's Conference in 1945-46, Vice Chancellor of the Maharaja Sayajirao University of Baroda. She was a member of the UN Human Rights Commission in 1947 and its Vice Chair-person in 1950 and Executive Member of the UNESCO. She supported Dr. Bhimrao Ambedkar in his effort to legislate the Hindu Code Bill and the Uniform Civil Code in the Union Parliament.

Hansa was an eminent writer and translator also with several books to her credit. She was awarded the Padma Bhushan by the Government of India in recognition for her services in 1959.

Padmaja Naidu (1900 – 2 May 1975)–Padmaja was the daughter of the Nightingale of India Smt. Sarojini Naidu and Govindrajulu Naidu of Andhra Pradesh. So she inherited patriotism and social service from her eminent mother.

At age 21, she was instrumental in the establishment of the Indian National Congress branch in the Nizam ruled state of Hyderabad. She was imprisoned for her participation in the Quit India Movement of 1942. She was friendly with Ruttie Petit, the wife of Mohammad Ali Jinnah. She was also very close to the Nehru family. She was the Governor of West Bengal for a period of ten years. But before she took over this responsibility, she was elected to the Lok Sabha, although due to ill health, she could not complete her term. She was also associated with

Indian Society of Red Cross, Bharat Sevak Samaj, All India Handi-crafts Board and the Nehru Memorial Board.

She died in May 1975.

Maniben Patel (1903 – 1990)

Maniben Patel was the daughter of the Iron Man of India Sardar Vallabh Bhai Patel. She was born in Karamsad, Bombay in April 1903. She lost her mother at age six. So she was looked after by her uncle Vitthal Bhai Patel who was also one of the front-line Congress leaders and freedom fighters. Therefore, she inherited patriotism from her father and uncle in equal measure.

She was educated in the Queens Mary High School Bombay and immediately thereafter, she joined the movements of Mahatma Gandhi.

She actively participated in the Bardoli Satyagraha 1928 against high taxation of the poor peasants along with Mithuben Petit. This agitation is well known for the adroit leadership of Vallabh Bhai Patel and after this movement, he began to be called Sardar. She next participated in the Rajkot Satyagraha of 1938 which was directed against the mis-rule of the Diwan of that princely state. Kasturba Gandhi also participated in this movement because she hailed from Rajkot and, therefore, she could not tolerate atrocities upon her people. Maniben also fasted in this movement. The Diwan had to relent and reforms were soon announced by him. She took active part in the Non Cooperation Movement of 1921, Salt Satyagraha of 1930 and the Quit India Movement of 1942. She suffered incarcerations several times and in her involvement in the 1942 movement, she was put in the Yerwada Central Jail.

After independence, she was elected to the Lok Sabha on four occasions i.e. in 1952, 1957, 1973 and in 1977 this time on a Janta Party ticket. Between 1964 to 1970 she was a member of the Rajya Sabha.

She held several important assignments such as Vice President Gujarat Provincial Congress Committee besides being related to Gujrat Vidyapeeth, Vallabh Vijayanagar, Bardoli Swaraj Ashram and the Navjeevan Trust. She died in 1990. It is said that she did not get due recognition for her services to the nation after independence to which she was so rightly entitled.

Rehana Tyebji (1901-1975)

Rehana Tyebji was born in the family of Badruddin Tyebji and Amina Tyebji in Vadodara in Gujarat. Badruddin was an eminent judge, a close associate of Mahatma Gandhi and an active freedom fighter. Rehana inherited all these qualities from her father. It goes to the credit of the Tyebjees that they allowed Rehana to lead an independent life of almost an ascetic and an admxture of the best in the two religious orders. She was an ardent follower of her religion and at the same time, she was a devotee of Lord Krishna. She used to recite bhajans and devotional songs from her religion in the daily prayer meetings of the Mahatma. In the meetings of the Indian National Congress, she used to render Vande Mataram. She also helped him learn Urdu. Although Mahatma had himself read the Holy Book, Rehana used to explain to him the all the points of her religion. She was one of the close inmates of the Sabarmati Ashram and also of the Sevagram later. In this manner, Rehana had an idyllic and utopian way of life after her mentor the Mahatma. She herself was no less than a Saint in her own individual personality.

Rehana took part in almost all the freedom movements such as the Non Cooperation Movement of 1921 and 1931, the Swadeshi Movement of 1931, the Salt Satyagraha of 1930 and the Quit India Movement of 1942. She was arrested and imprisoned in the 1942 Movement. Rehana passed away in 1975.

Begum Anis Kidwai (1906- 1982)

She was born in 1906 in Barabanki Uttar Pradeshin the family of Shaikh Wilayat Khan. She was married to Shafi Ahmad Kidwai. Both her father and husband were nationalist Muslims and freedom fighters in their own individual personalities. Her brother-in-law Rafi Ahmad Kidwai was also a freedom fighter of note. The entire family took part in the Khilafat Movement and in the movements for independence.

Begam Anis will be remembered for her role in the restoration of communal harmony following the exodus of populations from across the borders, for rehabilitations of the abducted women along with such workers as Rameshwari Nehru, Dr. Sushila Nayyar, Mridula Sarabhai, Subhadra Joshi and others. Her husband was killed in the communal frenzy of 1946. However, she continued her work undaunted. She was called Anis Aapa or Sister Anis by the women.

She wrote books reminiscing her experiences of the events of the partition. She was honored by the Sahitya Kala Parishad. She died on 16. 7. 1982.

Violet Alva (24 April 1908 – 20 November 1969) *and*

Joachim Ignatius Sebastian Alva or Joachim Piedade Alva (21 January 1907 – 28 June 1979)

It is difficult to include the Alvas in this list. They appear so new and fresh to our memory as if it was only yesterday that they were referred to. Yet it is equally true that not many talk of them these days. But they are certainly a remarkable husband-and-wife combine in every sphere of their lives, they were the first and perhaps the only such a couple to be Members of Parliament at the same period of time. Acharya J. B. Kripalani and Smt. Sucheta Kriplani were also Parliamentarians, but they were not together as such.

Perhaps the greatest contribution of the Alvas lay in their effort to encourage Indian Christians to take part in the freedom movements of India. They were certainly very broad-minded, large-hearted and dynamic Christians. Violet hailed from a Protestant Christian family back-ground while Jochim, born a year earlier than her, was a Catholic Christian from Belle near Udupi Mangalore.

Both of them were educated in Bombay, both of them were law students in the same law college, i.e. Government Law College Bombay now Mumbai. Both of them practised law. Violet addressed a Full Bench of High Court and thus she became the first such lady lawyer to get this distinction. They combined together in the fields of journalism, social service and nationalism. Both of them joined the national mainstream by actively taking part in various movements such as in the Quit India Movement of 1942 for which cause Violet was imprisoned while carrying her second son Niranjan in her pregnancy. Jochim was incarcerated twice for taking part in the Salt Satyagraha and the Bardoli Satyagraha. In the jail premises, he had the felicity of the company of such stalwarts as Sardar Vallabh Bhai Patel,

Jai Prakash Narayan, Morarji Bhai Desai, J. C. Kumarappa and others. He did not let his time in jail go for no avail. He wrote two books while in jail confinement—namely Men and Supermen of Hindustan and Christians and Nationalism which were published later.

The Alvas collaborated in the field of journalism also. While Violet started The Begam later renamed as the Indian Women in 1944, the two started together the FORUM a news weekly on 9. 8. 1943 which was the first anniversary of the Quit India Movement of 1942.

Violet had her stint as a parliamentarian in the Rajya Sabha. She was elected to the Upper House in 1952. She was Deputy Minister for Home Affairs from 1957 to 1962, Deputy Chair-person of Rajya Sabha from 1962 to 1969. Jochim was elected to the Lok Sabha in 1952 and 1957. Thus they were Parliamentarians on two occasions at the same time.

Her daughter-in-law Margaret Alva is another distinguished person in public life.

Violet died on 20. 11. 1969 while Jochim died in 1979.

Aruna Asaf Ali (Aruna Ganguly) (16 July 1909 – 29 July 1996)

Aruna Ganguly was born into the family of Upendranath Ganguly and Ambalika Devi in Kalka Punjab. She had early education in the Sacred Heart Convent, Lahore and then in the All Saints College, Nainital. She married one of the leading barristers of that time Asaf Ali in September 1928 when she was 19 years of age and Asaf was 20 years her senior in terms of age. She defied the family opposition to do so. Asaf was equally involved in the freedom struggle perhaps before their marriage. Therefore, Aruna also joined the Indian National Congress immediately after her marriage. Aruna was one of the fore-front leaders of the socialist movement of India being a sympathizer with the progress of the proletariat movement of the Soviet Union. This is the reason why she did not fully subscribe to the traditional means and methods of agitations. On the other hand, even if she was not a fully radical practitioner of anarchical violence, she chose to carry out many of her activities while imposing a self-created exile as an under-ground activist. The British Government were always wary of her hide-outs, always in look-out for her, announcing once an award of Rs. 5000/ to any one leading up to her arrest during the Quit India Movement days of 1942. She surfaced herself out from her Karol Bagh hide-out on an appeal and assurance from Mahatma Gandhi to carry out her patriotism in open and visible. Her activities were similar to those of Jai Prakash Narayan, Dr. Ram Manohar Lohia, Maniram Bagri and others.

She participated in freedom movements initiated by the Indian National Congress such as the Salt Satyagraha of 1930. She was arrested, but then she was not released on a general amnesty of 1931 as a consequence of the Gandhi-Irwin Agreement of 1930 on the allegation that she was not a political prisoner. But then the British had to relent under public furore by releasing her from confinement. In 1942 she was one of the principal participants in the Movement. While most of the Congress leaders and field-workers were detained and arrested with almost no main leader available for leading from the front. Aruna stepped in by hoisting the national flag in a public meeting in the Gowalia Tank Maidan, Bombay now Mumbai.

Thereafter, she again went under-ground, her property was seized and auctioned-sold by the Government. She supported the Royal Navy Mutiny of 1946 and in this manner she earned the dis-approval of Mahatma Gandhi.

She was a member of the Congress Socialist Party of Acharya Narendra Dev, Ashok Mehta and other leading lights of the socialist movement in India. She edited some of the left-leaning journals such as the Inquilab, Patriot and after independence the Link. She joined the CPI in 1951. She was elected Mayor of Delhi in 1958. She passed away in July 1996 aged 87.

Hardly any-one has been decorated like Smt. Aruna Asaf Ali. International Lenin Peace Prize 1964, Jawaharlal Nehru Award for International Understanding in 1991, Padma Vibhushan in 1992 and finally the Bharat Ratna posthumously in 1997 are some of the national and international recognitions which have been given to her.

Accamma Cherian 14. 2. 1909– 5. 5. 1982)

She is one of the front-line freedom fighters from Travancore Cochin. She started her career as a school teacher in St. Marys English Medium School in Edakkara in Travancore. But then she left this job to join the national cause. She took part in almost all the movements such as the Civil Disobedience and Quit India Movements of 1942. She was jailed a number of times for her participation in them. The Diwan of Travancore Cochin Sir C. P. Ramaswami Ayyar had banned the State Congress Party. Accamma was leading a protest march of about twenty thousand volunteers when the police chief decided to open fire upon them. Accamma openly challenged them to fire first at her because she was their leader. For this act of bravery, Mahatma

Gandhi called her as the Rani Jhansi of Travancore. She was active even after independence. She was elected as a member of the State Legislature in 1947 and she also served as a member of the Freedom Fighters Pension Advisory Board.

Rosamma Punnoose (12. 5. 1913–28. 12. 2013)

She was the younger sister of Accamma Cherian, another leading freedom fighter of the area. She started her career with the State Congress Party in 1938 and took part in several movements. She was sent to jail along with her elder sister for three years. She joined the Communist Party of India in 1948. Her husband P. T. Punnoose was a CPI member. Rosamma was elected to the State Assembly in 1952 and she retained the seat in the 1957 elections. However, she was ousted as such by an adverse court order. She regained the seat again in the 1957 general elections. In the meanwhile, her husband had been elected to the Lok Sabha in 1952 and he retained this seat in the 1957 Parliamentary elections. Thus they became the first husband and wife duo of legislators.

Anna Mascerene-(6. 6. 1902-19. 7. 1963)–

She was a contemporary of such prominent figures as Accamma Cherian, Rosamma Punnoose, Pattom Thanu Pillai and others. She took part in several freedom struggle movements and also in the Quit India Movement of 1942. She joined the Travancore State Congress Party in 1938 when it was started there. She was elected to the State Legislative Assembly and in 1946, she was elected to the Constituent Assembly of India which became the Provisional Parliament of India after India became free on 15. 8. 1947. She was elected to the first Parliament of free India in the 1951 general elections. A bronze statue of her installed in Vazhuthacaud Thiruvananthapuram commemorates her achievements.

Mridula Sarabhai (6 May 1911- 26 October 1974) Mridula Sarabhai was drawn into the national mainstream very early in her early teens. She joined the Vanar Sena of Indira Priyadarshani as she then was and Smt. Indira Gandhi later on and then she worked for the organization of the Youth Conference 1927 held in Rajkot. In 1930, she joined the Congress Seva Dal, she took part in the Salt Satyagraha and the Swadeshi Andolan of the early thirties. As a result, she was imprisoned.

Mridula worked for the organization of the Congress Party from within, particularly the involvement of the women in the Party. In 1934, she was elected to the All India Congress Committee as a delegate from Gujarat. In 1946, she was elected as a member of the All Congress Working Committee. In the wake of the exodus of the populations in 1946 and 1947, she was one of the active workers in bringing relief to the displaced persons from across the border. In the subsequent years, she developed some differences with the Party.

Dakshyani Velayudhan (4. 7. 1912–20. 8. 1978)

She belonged to the Pulaya community of Kerala which is a depressed class. Despite such handicaps, she had several firsts to her credit. She was the first under-graduate from her community having received a B. A. in 1935. Thereafter, she took up a teaching assignment in two Government schools one in Trichur and another in Tripunithura till 1945. She was nominated as a Member of the Legislative Council of Cochin. She was married to R. Velayudhan in Sevagram Ashram by Mahatma Gandhi and Kasturba in a simple ceremony. Her husband was also a

Scheduled Caste and also a Member of Parliament. She was elected to the Constituent Assembly of India in 1946. She was one of the eight female Members of the Constituent Assembly of India and also the only one belonging to the depressed class.

In the Constituent Assembly debates, she was always vociferous with respect to the issues relating to the women and the interests of the depressed classes. She was an ardent follower of both Mahatma Gandhi and Dr. B. R. Ambedkar.

Captain Lakshmi Sehgal (1914—2012)

She was a brave soldier of the army of Netaji Subhash Chandra Bose of the Indian National Army (INA) or the Azad Hind Fouz. She was Lakshmi Swaminathan in her maiden name. Her father was S. Swaminathan an eminent lawyer of the Madras High Court and her mother was A. V. Ammukutty or in short Ammu Swaminathan. She obtained her degree of M. B. B. S. in 1938 from the Madras Medical College and then she completed a diploma in Gynecology and Obstratrics. She served for some time in the Government Kasturba Gandhi Hospital Chennai for some time. She married Prem Kumar Sehgal and therefore, she was called Lakshmi Sehgal.

She left for Singapore in 1940 where she came in contact with the Indian National Army or the Azad Hind Fouz of Netaji Subhash Chandra Bose. Netaji wanted to develop a regiment of the women forces. Lakshmi responded to the exhortation of Netaji and she stepped forward to organize this women force where she herself was in the rank of a Captain. This is the Rani Lakshmi Bai Regiment of the INA.

In 1942, the British Indian soldiers surrendered in thousands in Singapore before the Japanese forces and they constituted the bulk of the Indian National Army or the Azad Hind Fouz. The Japanese marched ahead at a fast speed into the Burma border in March 1942. This created a panic in British India. But then the events turned the other way. The Allied forces defeated the Axis forces in all parts of the arena of war as also in the Burmese border. Captain Sehgal was also taken prisoner along with other POWs.

After independence of the country, Lakshmi continued to take active part in the Indian polity. She joined the ranks of the Communist Party of India and she was elected as a member of the Rajya Sabha. Later she contested the Presidential election against the ultimate winner President A. P. J. Kalam. The Government of India decorated her as Padma Vibhushan in 1998.

Saraswati Rajmani —She was a member of the Azad Hind Fouz of Netaji Subhash Chandra Bose and she worked as an intelligence officer. She donated her entire jewelry to the Fouz.

Dr. Sushila Nayyar or Sushila Nayar (1914 – 2001)

She was born in Kunh Gujrat now in Pakistan. She obtained her degree in medicine from the Lady Hardinge Medical College, New Delhi. Thereafter, she joined the national mainstream under the leadership of Mahatma Gandhi in 1939. She combined her passion for medical care with her cause for the independence of the country. She was the younger sister of Pyarelal Nayyar who was one of the secretaries of Mahatma Gandhi, the other being Mahadev Desai.

She was primarily motivated by her ambition to provide affordable and essential medical care and facilities to the un-privileged and needy persons. Therefore, she opened a small clinic in the Sevagram Ashram in 1944. After some time, the leading industrialist Ghanshyam Das Birla donated a small but handy clinic in Wardha at her disposal which was called the Kasturba Gandhi Hospital and which finally blossomed into the Mahatma Gandhi Institute of Medical Sciences, Wardha. Leprosy was widely prevalent in Wardha at that point of time. Dr. Nayyar did a remarkable service in the control of this disease in Wardha.

She was very active in the Quit India Movement of 1942. She was imprisoned for her role in this historic moment along with other leaders and workers. She was kept along with them in the Aga Khan Palace cum-confinement. She was very close to Kasturba. She looked after the medical requirements of the Mahatma in the Ashram.

Some attempts were made upon the life of the Mahatma, one of them being in 1944. She testified before the Kapur Commission in this regard in the year 1948 following his assassination in January 1948.

In 1948, Dr Sushil Nayyar went to the United States of America for further studies in medicine. She obtained two degrees from the John Hopkins School of Public Health.

After independence, she was elected to the Legislative Assembly of Delhi in 1952. She was made the Union Minister for Health in the Nehru cabinet and she served as such between 1952 to 1955. Thereafter she was the speaker of the Delhi Vidhan Sabha from 1955 to 1956. In 1957, she was elected to the Lok Sabha from the Jhansi constituency till 1971. She was made the Union Minister for Health again in 1962 to 1967. She developed differences with Smt. Indira Gandhi joined the

Janata Party. Thereafter, she retired from active politics. Dr. Sushila Nayyar passed away on January 3, 2001.

Pritilata Waddedar (5 May 1911 – 23 September 1932)-- She was born in the family of Jagabandhu and mother Pratibha Mayi. She had her education in Chittagong and Calcutta, now Kolkata.

Immediately after her education, she was attracted to revolutionary philosophy. She joined the group of Surya Sen. Initially, there was a feeling that women should not be permitted in these acts. But the group allowed Pritilata in the rebel work. The group decided to attack the European Club namely Pahartali European Club at Chittagong. Some of the other members of the proposed raid were Kalishankar Dey, Bireshwar Roy, Prafulla Das, Shanti Chakravarti, Mahendra Chowdhry, Sushil Dey and Panna Sen. Since Kalpana Datta was already apprehended earlier, the leadership was entrusted to Pritilata. However, the raid was foiled by the intelligence and repulsive action of the police. Pritilata was injured. But to evade arrest, she consumed potassium cyanide. Her dead body was recovered a few days later.

Pritilata is today venerated both in Bangladesh as well as in India. There are many monuments erected in both of these countries in her memory.

Pushpalata Das (1915-2003)– She hailed from Lakhimpur in North Assam. She took part in several Civil Disobedience Movements and she was incarcerated. After independence, she was nominated to the Rajya Sabha in 1951 and 1961. She was a member of the Congress Working Committee in 1958. She was returned to the Lok Sabha in 1967 and 1971from the Dhekiajuli constituency. She was an active khadi promoter also. She was decorated with the Padma Bhushan in 1999.

Sucheta Kripalani or Sucheta Mazumdar

Sucheta Mazumdar as she was before her marriage, had her education in several institutions such as an M. A. in History from the St. Stephens College New Delhi, Kinnaird College Lahore, Indraprastha College New Delhi and the Punjab University. Thereafter, she took up the job as an Assistant Professor in the Banaras Hindu University. She joined the independence movement under the banner of the Indian National Congress. In the later part of her career, she successfully contested for the Lok Sabha on a ticket of the party raised by her husband Acharya J. B. Kripalani whom she married in 1936 braving opposition from her family members. She was returned to the Lok Sabha on three occasions in all, i.e. in 1952, 1957 and finally in 1967. She also has the distinction of being elected as the first woman chief minister of a state i.e. of Uttar Pradesh. Her term as the chief minister is noted for her adroit handling of a long-drawn strike which terminated to her credit.

She took part in almost all movements initiated by the Congress Party and she suffered incarceration also. She was very active during the Quit India Movement of 1942.

During the communal frenzy of 1946-47, she was very active in restoring peace and harmony. She accompanied the Mahatma during his Noakhali tours to quell communal disturbances. She rendered the Vande Mataram in the Parliament House shortly before the Tryst With Destiny speech of Jawaharlal Nehru in the midnight of 14 and 15 August 1947.

Shortly before her death in 1974, she donated all her personal belongings to a public welfare committee in charity.

Smt. Subhadra Joshi (2. 03. 1919–30. 10. 2003)–She hailed from Sialkot now in Pakistan. She had her education in Lahore and Jalandhar. She was attracted to the national cause while she was in college. During this period, she visited the Sevagram Ashram at Wardha. She participated in the Quit India Movement of 1942 as a student leader. After independence, she worked for the rehabilitation of the refugees after the communal frenzy of 1947 along with other eminent workers. She worked for the restoration of communal harmony in the country between the various communities. She set up Sampradayikta Virodhi Samiti in 1968 and the Qaumi Ekta Trust in 1971. She was a member of Lok Sabha in 1952, 1957, 1962 and 1971. She was instrumental in the enactment of such as the Bank Nationalization Act of 1970, Abolition of Privy Purses Act, 1971, the Special Marriage Act and the Code of Criminal Procedure (Amendment) Act 1960 which made it criminal any speech or act which led to communal disturbance.

Usha Mehta (25 March 1920 – 11 August 2000)–Usha had the distinction of taking part in patriotic activities even when she was hardly eight years old. Children of that age used to shout small protests against the British Raj and Usha was one of them. When the Simon Commission visited India in 1927, these children shouted slogans 'Simon Go Back' perhaps with little realization of what they were shouting for and why. But these experiences were sufficient in them to instill the favor of patriotism. But from amongst them, it is only Usha who carried the torch ahead to great heights.

When the Mahatma gave the call of Quit India on August 8, 1942 from the historic Gowalia Tank Maidan now the August Kranti Maidan, Mumbai, the British arrested almost all the leading Congress leaders. So it was left to the younger brigade of the Party to step in. Usha came forward immediately. She hoisted the national flag on 9. 8. 1942 in the same ground. Thereafter, she started a secret radio to broad-cast pro-independence news and appeals. This radio functioned for four months only. But still then by that time, it had fulfilled its purpose. After being caught and arrested, she was tried, convicted and sentenced to four years in the Yerwada Jail. She was released in March 1942.

After the attainment of independence, she continued her studies. She obtained a Ph. D. in Political Science and began to teach the subject in the Bombay University. She was elected as the President of the Gandhi Smarak Nidhi and also of the Gandhi Peace Foundation New Delhi. She was also associated with the Bhartiya Vidya Bhavan of K. M. Munshi. The govt. conferred upon her Padma Vibhushan in 1998. She passed away in August 2000 aged 80 years.

Kanaklata Barua (22 December 1924 – 20 September 1942)– She was born in Darrang district of Assam to Krishna Kant and Karneshwari Barua. She lost her parents early. Therefore, she could not get a proper and full education. She had to look after her brothers and sisters in the family.

She joined a revolutionary group namely Mrityu Bahini in 1942. On September 20, 1942 the Bahini decided to hoist the national flag at the local police station. She was shot with the national flag in her hand. She died shortly afterwards. Another revolutionary Mukunda Kakoti was also shot and he also achieved martyrdom. Kanaklata was 17 years of age at that time.

Tara Rani Shrivastava

She hailed from the Saran district of Bihar. She was married to Phulendu Babu of Saran Bihar. Both of them joined the freedom movement. They were a part of the procession on 12. 8. 1942 during the Quit India Movement of 1942 in pursuance to the call of the Mahatma dated 6. 8. 1942 issued from the Gowalia Tank Maidan Bombay now Mumbai. The police opened fire upon the procession. Her husband sustained injuries as a result of which he died. But still then, Tara Rani continued her march. Tara Rani continued to take part in the freedom movements till the country achieved independence.

Parbati Devi–(19-1-1926–17. 8. 1995)–She was born in the Sambalpur district of Odisha. She joined the freedom movements while still in her early teens. She traveled across Odisha teaching the values and importance of khadi, spinning and simple living. She took part in the 1942 Movement and was jailed for two years.

After independence, she started an orphanage for women and orphans in Matru Niketan at Nasinghati and another for destitutes called Dr. Santra Bai Niketan at Birasinghi Ghar at Sambalpur. For her record of social services, she was called Mother Teresa of Odisha.

Tarkeshwari Sinha (26 December 1926–14 August 2007)–- She was born in Tulsigarh, Nalanda Bihar. She had her early education in Patna. She was active in students' politics in her college days. She joined the struggle when she was hardly sixteen years old. She was the President of the Bihar Students Congress.

She was an M. Sc. in Economics from the London School of Economics.

She took active part in the Quit India Movement of 1942 and was imprisoned.

After independence, she was elected to the Lok Sabha in 1952 at age 26. In the Nehru Cabinet, she became a Deputy Finance Minister, thus she became the first woman to hold this honour. She was returned to the Lok Sabha in the elections of 1957, 1962 and 1967. But thereafter, her electoral fortunes took a turn for a series of continuous struggles. She fell out with Smt. Indira Gandhi, joined the rival group and lost four elections thereafter.

She set up a hospital in the memory of her brother Captain Girish Nandan Singh, a pilot with Air India who had lost his life in an air crash.

Hausabai Patil of Satara:–She was hardly seventeen years of age when she had joined the Toofan Sena, a revolutionary party of that area who used to attack Government property such as buses and trains to reign terror in the mind of them in the wake of the Quit India Movement of 1942. She was badly treated by the police. Later in 1944, she also took part in the movement to liberate Goa.

Some of the women freedom-fighters of Madras and Karnataka

Rukmini Lakshmipathi, Kamla Devi Arya, Kuttiammal, Chalaiammal, Meera Krishna Swami from Madurai, Narayan Ammal from Ramnad and Anchal Ammal from South Arcot, Subbarayulu Naidu, Salem Angachi Ammal, Thirumalacharia,

Padmashini Ammal, Krishnabai Panagikar, Umadevi Kundapur of Karnataka, Lakshmibai Dhashwatara, Shantibai Koppala, Lakshmibai Suhani, participants of the Forest Satyagraha of 1931, 1932, Mukambi, Nagaratnamma Hiremath, Bellary Siddamma, Muradhalli Thimmakka, Turuvannur Bhimakka, Babytanda Mudamma andothers.

Some of the women from Kerala who broke the Salt Law in 1930

A. V. Kuttimalu, Kamla Prabhu, C. Kunnakkavu Amma, Kunhi Lakshim Amma, Margarate Pavamani, M. R. Janaki Amma and Ishwarri Amma.

Some of the women workers from Madras Tamil Nadu

Rukmani Laxmipathi, Dhamayanthi, Ignatius Ammal, Janaki Ammal, Kahalaxmi, Padma Singh, Saraswati Ammal, Solai Begiya Laxmi Ammal, Mrs. Kamladevi Arya, Maya Joseph, Manjubhashini, G. Janaki, P. Susheela, Thangamma, Thirupura Sundari, Vasugi Ammal, Parvathi Kumarmangalam and others.

Some of the women freedom fighters from Odisha–

Laxmi Panda–She was a member and soldier in the Indian National Army of Netaji Subhash Chandra Bose.

Ramadevi Choudhari–She took part in several Civil Disobedience and Non-Co-operation Movements and she was jailed a number of times.

Malti Choudhari–She took part in several movements for freedom after 1934. She accompanied Mahatma Gandhi in his padyatra of Odisha when he toured Odisha and similarly, she accompanied Sant Vinoba Bhave when he toured Odisha in his Bhoodan Andolan movement. She was elected to the Constituent Assembly of India in 1946.

Chapter Eight

Revolutionary Movements in India

It is not easy to pinpoint who should be credited with the start of the revolutionary thought and revolutionary movements in India. The revolution of 1857 is generally said to be the first genuine war of independence although even before 1857, there were revolutionary activities in different parts of India. In 1806 and in 1816, there were revolts against the forces of the East India Company. The revolt of 1857 was almost spontaneous. There was no concerted planning. The entire country was far too wide and there were no easy and fast means of communications. Furthermore, all the princesses, rulers and principalities had their irreconcilable differences which could not be solved all that soon. Some rulers had their individual vested interests and they had been won over by British diplomacy. Many rulers announced their neutrality and non-alignment in the revolt. Some others declared their support to the Company. The immediate causes of the revolt were easy to understand. The army of the Company consisted of Hindu and Muslim soldiers. The problem arose when the Company tried to induct Enfield rifles in their arsenal. The cartridges contained animal fat which covered them and before use, the fat had to be removed by teeth. The fat was of pig and cow and both of them are forbidden in their respective religions. The soldiers of both communities suspected that the Company was trying to destroy their religious beliefs. Another cause of grievance was the drive of evangelisation and proselytisation by the Christian missionaries. Both the communities again suspected that the Company wanted to convert them into their religion. All these events were far too intolerable for the revolutionary blood like that of Mangal Pandey, Tatya Tope, Thakur Kunwar Singh and several others. The first fire was ignited on 10th of May 1857 in the Meerut Cantonment. It spread like wildfire in the affected areas. As we will see shortly, revolutions have taken place successfully in England in 1648 i. e the Glorious Revolution of 1648. In France in 1789, in Russia in 1917 and more recently in Algeria and Vietnam. What were the conditions in India which were different from their counterparts in these countries, we will shortly look into them.

India did not have political philosophers who could ignite political fire in every nook and corner of the country. India did definitely have philosophers in the field of spirituality, ethics and morality from ages. If the West had political thinkers like Socrates, Plato and Aristotle, the Epicureans, the Stoics, Cicero and others who are supposed to be the harbingers of Western political edifice and system, India had to offer the wisdom of spirituality, ethics and morality in the shape of the four Vedas, Upnishads, Maha Bharat, Shrimad Bhagwat Gita, Ramcharit Manas and other epics. Rishis and munis and other spiritual teachers of the ancient past have transmitted light to the entire world. These epics are acknowledged even by the Western scholars and philosophers to be the beacon of wisdom. But these epics did not provide political or revolutionary wisdom. Saint Kabir preached communal amity and exposed the dangers of superstitions. In the Vedic times, of course, we had Chanakya or Kautilya who preached saam, daam, dand and bhed. It is certainly apt to suggest that it is from his philosophy that the 16th century Italian thinker Nicole Machiavelli drafted his state

-craft which preached that the end justifies the means; i.e. the king may resort to any means, fair or foul, to achieve his stately objectives. This may also mean that while the West was engrossed in their political stabilization and consolidation, East was during the same period of time developing an edifice of a stronger and more stable personal and family way of life. So, therefore, this spiritual historicity was not conducive to the implementation of the wisdom of Chanakya nor did the history of ages produce an atmosphere here of political revolutions with the help of shedding of blood. It is true that several revolutionary activities have taken place in India during the struggle for independence. Several brave martyrs willingly laid down their lives at the altar of their motherland. But they were not full-fledged revolutions in the Western sense.

Sri Aurobindo and his brother Barin Ghosh and Bhupendranath Dutta can be said to be the initiators of revolutionary thought and activities in India by the beginning of the twentieth century. Sri Aurobindo was involved in the Alipore conspiracy case. He was acquitted in that case while some others were sentenced to different terms. He thereafter went on to become a mystic at Pondicherry now Puducherry. Jugantar Party and Anushilan Samiti can be said to be their products. However, some historians regard Bipin Chandra Pal to be the Father of Revolutionary Thought. Earlier, Bankim Chandra Chattopadhyaya had written and published Anand Math a novel with revolutionary ideas.. The novel also contained Vande Mataram वंदे मातरम, (In English Vande Mataram)– a patriotic song which infused the masses with patriotic and nationalist fervor. At the same time, the national song critically divided the Indian society into two irreconcilable groups on communal lines.

Hindustan Republican Association- (HRA)–

This revolutionary organisation was founded in Bhulachang now in Bangladesh

In 1924 by Sachindranath Sanyal, Narendra Mohan Sen and Pratul Ganguly. They wanted to establish an Indian republic free of British control by means of an armed revolution. Earlier Mahatma Gandhi had withdrawn the movement of 1921-22 following the Chauri Chaura incident of 1922. Many Indians had begun to feel that the country was on the verge of attaining independence and that the movement ought not to have been withdrawn. They began to feel that the Gandhian methods of non-violence were not adequate and proper to deliver the goods. Hence they chose the method of revolution. Revolutionary fire was ignited in many parts of the country, but particularly in Bengal, Punjab, Bombay now Maharashtra, Bihar and other places.

However, it has to be added that even those revolutionary activities did not succeed in bringing independence to the country immediately even though they succeeded in their mission of striking a reign of terror in the thought-process of the British Government that it was no longer safer for them to remain pernmanently in India as a minority of foreigners who could no longer contain the simmering discontent of the local freedom fighters.

Several conspiracies and raids were conducted by these valiant martyrs in different parts of the country such as the Alipore bomb case, the Chittagong conspiracy case, the Kakori train robbery case, the Benares conspiracy case and others. A large number of brave young men were martyred and a larger number of participants had to face long jail terms and inhuman torture in the British jails. The foregn domination continued for a few decades more. Why. The reason could perhaps be that there was no cohesion between these dare-devils throughout the affected areas. The periods of the events were also far distant such as 1906, 1926, 1931 and so on. They were great acts of sporadic attempts somewhat similar to the first revolution of 1857 which did not succeed due to almost the same situations and circumstances.

HRA attracted Chandra Shekhar Azzad, Sardar Bhagat Singh, Rajguru, Sukhdev, Ram Prasad Bismil, Roshan Singh, Ashafaqullah Khan, Rajendra Lahiri and other martyrs.

Hindustan Socialist Republican Association (HSRA)–

Ram Prasad Bismil and his colleagues opposed the motion to withdraw the C. D. Movement 1921-22 in the annual session of the Indian National Congress in Gaya in 1922. Mahatma Gandhi refused to rescind his decision. This led to a division in the INC into two groups of liberals and rebels. This was the second such division in the INC after the rift of the Surat session of 1907. In Gaya the liberals were Motilal Nehru and CR Das while the rebels were the revolutionaries Ram Prasad Bismil and others. In this manner, HSRA was instituted from HRA. Ram Prasad Bismil, Sachindra Nath Sanyal and Dr. Jadugopal Mukherji drafted the constitution of HSRA in 1923 with working branches in Agra, Allahabad, Benares, Kanpur, Lucknow, Saharanpur and Shahjahanpur. They soon began to implement their plans. On 9. 8. 1925, they raided a train bound towards Kakori which resulted in the Kakoritrain robbery case. The participants Ram Prasad Bismil, Ashafaqullah Khan,

Roshan Singh and Rajendra Lahiri were sentenced to death and hanged subsequently.

Lala Lajpat Rai was lathi-charged in a protest rally against the Simon Commission in Kanpur. As a result of those injuries, he died on 17. 11. 1928. Collector J. A. Scott had ordered the lathi-charge. HSRA decided to take revenge. Sardar Bhagat Singh, Rajguru, Chandra Shekhar Azad and Jai Gopal were called upon to execute the plan. Another British officer Saunders was shot dead by Sardar Bhagat Singh, Rajguru and Sukhdev. They were later hanged into martyrdom in the Lahore Jail. Chandra Shekhar Azad was involved in a fierce battle with the British police in the Albert Park Allahabad. The martyr shot himself to avoid being caught by the police.

Chapter Nine

Indian Revolutionaries Who Worked from outside but Are Almost Forgotten Today

There are many freedom fighters who operated from outside the Indian shores. They stationed themselves in several countries outside of India and brought the cause of Indian freedom in the focus of the world community. This is a great service they did to the cause. The Ghadar Party is one such organization of revolutionaries who played a very prominent role in bringing to the attention of the world community. Some of the pioneers of the Ghadar Party are as follows.

Abdul Hafiz Mahomed Barkat-ullah, Maulana Barkat-ullah (1854-1927)

Barkat-ullah was an Indian revolutionary with sympathies for the Pan- Islamic movement. He was a strong proponent of Hindu-Muslim unity. He fought for the independence of India from such places as England, Egypt, Afghanistan, Japan, Philippines and Germany. He wrote in several news-papers there and made fiery speeches to promote the cause of Indias freedom. While in England, he came in contact with other revolutionaries such as Lala Hardayal and Raja Mahendra Pratap. Along with them and some others, he was one of the founders and active workers of the Ghadar Party. He met such world leaders of that time as Kaiser Wilhelm II, Amir Habibullah Khan of Afghanistan, Ghazi Pasha, Vladimir Lenin, Adolf Hitler, Shyamji Krishna Verma and others. In December 1915, he established the Provisional Government of India in exile in Kabul during the First World War. The Bhopal University is named after him.

Bhai Parmanand (1876-1947)

Bhai Parmanad was an active and a prominent worker of the Hindu Mahasabha. But at the same time, he developed leaning towards the philosophy of the Arya Samaj because his father Tara Chand Mohyal was an active member and propagator of Arya Samaj.

In 1905, he visited South Africa where he stayed with Mahatma Gandhi. There he associated himself with the cause of the British Indians. He was one of the founders of the Ghadar Party along with other revolutionaries. Back in India, he engaged in radical activities for which he was arrested in 1915 with regard to the First Lahore Conspiracy case, found guilty and sentenced. He was consigned to the dreaded Andaman and Nicobar prisons. He entered in a hunger strike against inhuman treatment which was meted out to the inmates in jail. His protest lasted about two months. In 1920, he was released on a general amnesty.

Taraknath Das (1884-1958)

He spent most of his time in America from where he espoused the cause of the freedom of India. He took up some minimal jobs there to keep both the ends meet and then he got himself educated. Climbing the ladder, he was appointed as the Professor of Political Science in the California University Berkeley. He founded the Indian Independence League there. He moved on to Canada from America where he started the *Free Hindustan* to espouse the cause of the freedom of India and in 1907, he founded the Hindustani Association. He also promoted the cause of the Indian immigrants abroad. He was one of the founders of the Ghadar Party along with such revolutionaries as Lala Hardayal. Raja Mahendra Pratap Singh, Barkat-ullah and others. After a self-imposed exile of about 46 years, Das finally returned to India in 1952 for a while. He returned to America where he died in 1958.

Lala Hardayal (14. 10. 1884-4. 3. 1939)

He turned down a prospective career in the ICS for the cause of the freedom of India abroad. He was of the left inclination and he was influenced by the writings of Shyamji Krishna Verma, Vinayak Damodar Savarkar, Guisseppe Mazini, Karl Marx and Mikhail Bakuin and others. He wrote radical pieces in several periodicals such as *Indian Sociologist* in England. From there, he moved on to France where he edited the *Vande Mataram* from 1909 onwards. From there, he moved on to America where he espoused the cause of the Arya Samaj and the Vedic philosophy. There he involved himself in semi-anarchist activities. He also helped in the comforts of the Indians abroad particularly in America and Canada. He established Guru Gobind Singh Scholarships for the Indian students abroad. He was one of the founders of the Ghadar Party.

In 1914, he was arrested by the American Government for spreading anarchist propaganda there. He escaped and fled to Germany. After working for the cause of Indian freedom there for some time, he moved on to Sweden. Even though he was engaged in the spread of revolutionary thought and action, he found time outto continue his studies and obtained the degree of Ph. D in 1930 from the University of London. He was a prolific writer with about ten books to his credit.

The founder-members of the Ghadar Party—

1. Sohan Singh Bhakna President
2. Kesar Singh Vice President
3. Kartar Sngh Sarabha Editor
4. Baba Jwala Singh Vice President
5. Sant Baba Wasakha Singh Dadehar
6. Bhagwan Singh Gyanee
7. Balwant Sngh
8. Kashi Ram Treasurer
9. Harnam Singh Tandilat
10. G. D. Verma
11. Lala Thakur Das Dhuri Vice President
12. Munshi Ram
13. Bhai Parmanand
14. Nidhan Singh Chugha
15. Santokh Singh
16. Master Udham Singh
17. Baba Chhattar Singh Ahluwalia
18. Baba Harnam Singh
19. Mangu Ram Mugowalia
20. Karim Baksha

21. Amar Chan

22. Rahmat Ali

23. V. G. Pingle

24. Maulvi Barkatullah

25. Harnam Singh Saini

26. Tarak Nath Das

27. Pandurang Sadashiv Khankhoje

28. Ganda Singh Phanguresh

29. Bhai Randhir Singh

30. Baba Prithi Singh Azad

31. Wadhwa Singh Warwal

32. Rana Singh

33. Bana Singh

Raja Mahendra Pratap Singh (1886-1979)–He was educated in the Aligarrh Muslim University. He espoused the cause of the freedom of India abroad in such countries as Afghanistan, Germany, Turkey, Russia, Hungary, Switzerland, China, Tibet, Siam and America. He met several world leaders of that time. He was one of the founders of the Ghadar Party along with such revolutionaries as Lala Hardayal, Maulana Barkat-ullah and others. He established the Provisional Government of India in exile in Afghanistan in 1915 along with other radicals and was its President. During the second World War, he was in Japan to espouse the same cause. Back in India after a self-imposed exile of about 32 years, Raja canvassed the cause of grass-root democracy. He was elected as the President of the Freedom

Fighters Association after independence. In 1957, he was elected to the Lok Sabha as an independent candidate beating Atal Bihari Vajpayee who was contesting on the Jan Sangh ticket.

M. N. Roy (1887-1954)–Manabendra Nath Roy or Narendra Nath Bhattacharya was an Indian revolutionary, anarchist activist, a leading Marxist philosopher of his era and an ardent patriot of India's freedom movement. He was one of the leading lights of the Communist movement of India and was one of the founders of the Communist Party of India.

Like many of the young men of Bengal of that period, M. N. was influenced by the writings of Bankim Chandra Chattopadhyaya and particularly his Anandmath which preached bravery and action. Anandmath contained one of the national songs of India Vande Matram i.e. I salute my mother land. Of course, earlier Raja Ram Mohan Roy and Keshab Chandra Sen had heralded the gospel of social re-thinking in Bengal which was further propelled by Sir Ishwar Chandra Vidyasagar with his broad-minded renaissance, yet the fire of nationalism was ignited by the message of Vande Matram. Swami Vivekanand was the next great source of inspiration to the Bengal youth, but then from the Swami they picked up Vedantic spirituality. So in fine, this is the ideological back-ground of the Bengal youth of the late nineteenth century and early part of the next century.

The radical thinking of M. N. Roy started in the company of such dynamic thinkers as Hari Kumar Chakravarti, Satcowri Bannerji, Sailes Kumar Bose, Shyamsundar Bose, Phani Chakravarti, Narendra Chakravarti, Barin Ghosh, Moksha Charan Samadhi Yoga, Prafulla Chaki and others.

Like other radicals, M. N. Roy was convinced that the freedom of India could not be achieved by peaceful and constitutional means, but that blood had to be shed in order to become free of British domination.

He tried to procure arms and ammunition from Germany in the belief that Germany was at logger-heads with Britain. But he could not succeed in doing so. Therefore, he moved on to America where soon he reinforced his radical thinking and tilt towards Bolshevism. He began to contribute to radical periodicals such as El Pueblo. These writings impressed the Commintorn International and, therefore, he was invited to attend the Second Congress of the Communist Party of Russia which was held in Moscow in 1920. M. N. Roy duly attended. He was welcomed by no less a leading personality than Vladimir Lenin himself and also by Joseph Stalin.

After a long exile, M. N. returned to India in 1930. He was immediately arrested by the British police. He was tried for allegedly committing an offense of waging a war against the duly constituted Government of His Majesty and trying to overthrow the same by means of force. In a fiasco of trial, he was found guilty and sentenced to twelve years in jail. In an appeal, the sentence was later reduced to six years. His health deteriorated while in jail custody. But this could not dim his radical thinking.

But after release and towards the later part of his life, he lost some of his sheen towards radical-anarchism primarily because of the rise of totalitarianism in countries like Germany and Italy. He now began to preach radical-democratism i.e. rapid social changes by democratic means. In other words, he was now preaching democratic humanism.

Baba Gurdit Singh- (25. 8. 1860-28. 7. 1954) He canvassed the cause of the freedom of India from Canada.

Kartar Singh Sarabha (24. 5. 1896-16. 11. 1915)–But finishing his early education in his village Sarabha, he was sent to the United States for higher studies. But then his mind was not set on the course of education. He joined the movement for the independence of his country by becoming a member of the Nalanda Club of Indian Students who were espousing the same cause from there. When the Ghadar Party was formed in America and in Canada, he was influenced by its philosophy and, therefore, he became a member of the Party. Some of the members of the Party conspired to raise revolts in some places like Mia Mir, Ferozepur, Ambala and Delhi. But then one Kripal Singh turned a betrayer and he helped the British in the arrest of several rebels such as Harnam Singh Tundilat and Jagat Singh in addition to Kartar Singh himself. After a brief trial on the charges of sedition, they were gicen capital punishment and were executed in the Central Jail, Lahore on 17. 11. 1915. Kartar Singh faced the gallows valiantly. He refused to file an appeal. Sardar Bhagat Singh drew inspiration from him.

Chapter Ten

Some of the Dare-Devil Conspiracies Which Rocked the British Government but Which Are Almost Forgotten Today

1. Muzaffarpur Conspiracy case 1908

This conspiracy was hatched and executed by two young revolutionaries namely Khudiram Bose and Praful Chaki to kill the cruel Chief Presidency Magistrate D. H. Kingsford of Muzaffarpur. They threw the bombs targeting the vehicle carrying him. But he could not be hit. Instead two English women, the daughters of barrister Kennedy were killed. Praful Chaki committed suicide apprehending his arrest, but Khudiram was arrested, tried, sentenced to death and finally hanged. He is the youngest patriot to be hanged at age 18 while Chaki was 19 years at that time. Police officer Nandlal Banerjee who arrested Khidiram Bose was shot dead by Narendra Nath Banerjee

2. Delhi Conspiracy case 1912

This conspiracy was master-minded by some of the revolutionaries of Punjab and Bengal such as Rash Behari Bose, Basant Kumar Biswas, Amir Chand and Awadh Bihari to assassinate the Viceroy of India Lord Hardinge. The attempt was unsuccessful. They were arrested, tried, sentenced to death and finally hanged.

3. Kanpur Bolshevik Conspiracy case 1924

Some of the Communist leaders tried to throw out the British regime by Bolshevik methods. They were M. N. Roy, Muzaffar Ahmad, S. A. Dange, Shaukat Usmani, Nalini Gupta, Singaravelu Chettiar, Ghulam Hussain and some others. Their attempt was not successful. They were arrested and charged with the offence of attempting to overthrow the regime of His Majesty by unlawful and violent means. They were tried and convicted to life imprisonment and to other terms.

4. Kakori Conspiracy case 1925

In order to terrorise the Britishi into submission and to leave the country, a revolutionary organisation namely Hindustan Socialist Republican Association (HSRA) organised a plan to rob a train which was carrying valuable currency to the extent of Rs 8000/ which could be of use to them in their future activities. This is known in Indian history as the Kakori Train Robbery case. The master-mind was Ram Prasad Bismill and his associates were Ashfaqullah Khan, Rajendra Lahiri, Chandra Shekhar Azad, Sachindra Bakshi, Keshab Chakravarti, Manmathnath Gupta, Murarilal Gupta (Khanna), Mukundi Lal, Thakur Roshan Singh and Banwarilal. The incident took place in a small and remote place namely Kakori which is about 16 k. m. away from Lucknow on 9. 8. 1925. They wanted to target the British citizens, but by accident a non–British was killed. They used German mauser pistols in their operation. After a deep search, 40 suspects were arrested, tired of various offences and finally Ramprasad Bismil, Thakur Roshan Singh and Ashfaqullah Khan were convicted and sentenced to death. Rest of them were given transportation for life. They were consigned to the dreaded Cellular Jail in Port Blair.

5. Alipore Bomb Case or Muraripukur Conspiracy Case or the Maniktala Bomb Conspiracy Case or the King Emperor vs Aurbindo Ghosh and others 1908

Revolutionary political and nationalistic consciousness was brewing in Bengal since the early 19th century. Social consciousnesss had already been aroused by such reformers as Raja Ram Mohan Roy, Keshab Deb Sen, Sir Ishwar Chand Vidyasagar and others. Literary consciousness had already been aroused by such stalwarts as Bankim Chandra Chattopadhyaya, Rabindra Nath Tagore, Nazarul Islam, Nandlal Bose, Sarat Chandra Chatterji and others.

Another epoch-making event took place in Bengal in 1905 with the partition of Bengal by Lord Curzon. The peace-loving and devotees of fine arts, music and culture, the Bengali gentry and the commons did not approve of the physical bi-section of their *Sonar Bangla.* They revolted and as a result, the partition was revoked in 1911. Sri Aurobindo and Bipin Chandra Pal wrote revolutionary dissents in the local newspapers such as Jugantar and Sandhya. Bramhabhan Dev Upadhyaya, an editor who helped the Poet Tagore establish the Shantiniketan was imprisoned for his work as an editor and ventilator of revolutionary views. He died in police custody and thus he became the first freedom fighter to achieve martyrdom in this manner.

The partition of Bengal was followed by yet another significant event i.e. the founding of the Indian Muslim League in 1906 in Dacca. This was just like adding salt to the wound in the psyche of the Bengali consciousness.

Anushilan Samiti

These events gave rise to the establishment of several revolutionary societies all over Bengal with the avowed purpose of throwing out the British Government by violent means. One of them was the Anushilan Samiti founded by Satish Chnadra Basu with the support of the well-known Barrister Pramatha Mitra, the other by Sarla Devi and the third one by Aurobindo Ghosh.

Here it is pertinent to point out that Sri Aurobindo cannot be included in this list of the forgotten heroes of the struggle. However, it is necessary to recollect to the readers the history behind the Alipore Conspiracy which is related to the celebrated mystic. Aurobindo Ghosh would otherwise have become an ICS officer because he was successful in his competitive attempt. But patriotic sentiments impelled him to return to India. He took up an academic job in Baroda. It is here that he came under the spell of Lokmanya Bal GangaDhar Tilak. The partition of Bengal in 1905 inspired Aurobindo and also the entire b*hadralo*k of Bengal. Aurobindo decided that the British would not leave India by peaceful persuasion and that only the revolutionary means and methods would be successful against them. He embarked upon the path of revolution. He enlisted the support of his younger brother Barindra Nath Ghosh.

In 1906, Aurobindo, Subodh Malik and Bipin Chandra Pal started the Bengali language newspaper **Jugantor** and its English translation *Vande Mataram*. At the same time, the Dhaka branch of Anshuman Samiti under Pulin Das also became active. They enlisted the co-operation of yet another radical namely Ullaskar

Datt. The group made two attempts. In the first one, they tried to attack the train which was transporting the Governor of Bengal Andrew Fraser but unsuccessfully. Thereafter, Bibhuti Bhushan Sarkar and Prafulla Chaki detonated a bomb carrying the Governor near Midnapore. The Governor again escaped.

Some of the other revolutionaries in these activities were Hem Chand Kanungo, Bhupendra Nath Dutta, Sushil Sen, Prafulla Kumar Chakrovorti and Avinash Bhattacharya. In the meantime, an earlier attempt to kill the British magistrate by Prafulla Chaki and Khudiram Bose had already failed in which two daughters of barrister Pringle Kennedy were killed accidentally. By this time, however, the police were on full alert and all the participants of the Anshuman Samiti such as Aurobindo, Barindra Nath Ghosh and others were apprehended, arrested put on trial for various offences amongst others of attempting to overthrow by violent means the legally constituted regime of the King Emperor. They were arrested from different places but primarily from their main hide-out in 36 Muraripukur Lane in the Maniktala suburb of Calcutta now Kolkata. However, even before the trial could proceed a distance, Barin Ghosh, Ullaskar Dutta, Indubhushan Roy and Bibhuti Bhushan Sarkar confessed to their involvement even though they knew that such an admission would result in bringing to them the capital punishment. The trial started on 5 May 1908 in the Alipore Sessions Court Calcutta. One of the accused persons, Narain Goswami turned hostile and he became an approver in return for a pardon and reprieve. He was, however, killed in the jail custody by two other under-trials Kanailal Dutta and Satyen Basu. The trial commenced in the court of Additional Sessions Judge Charles Poten Beachcroft who had appeared in the ICS examination along with Aurobindo and it is note-worthy that the future mystic was successful ahead of his future prosecutor. Finally, Barin Ghosh and Ullaskar Dutt were found guilty and sentenced to death. The ultimate punishment was later on commuted into life imprisonment. They were consigned to the dreaded Cellular Jail. But they were released in 1920 in a general amnesty.

Thirteen other accused persons namely Upendra Nath Bannerjee, Bibhuti Bhushan Sarkar, Hrishikesh Kanjilal, Birendra Sen, Indra Nandi, Abhinash Bhattacharya, Soilendra Bose, Hem Chandra Das, Indu Bhushan Roy, Poresh Mullick, Sishir Ghosh and Nirapado Roy were sentenced to ten years rigorous imprisonment while Ashok Nandy, Balkrishna Kane and Sushil Sen were awarded seven years jail life. Aurobindo Ghosh and sixteen others were acquitted. The Alipore trial turned out to be a turning point in the career of Aurobindo Ghosh. He disengaged himself from such political activities, set up a spiritual ashram in Pondicherry now Puducherry and preached spirituality. The Ashram gained international name and fame and Aurobindo has been recognized as one of the great mystics India has ever produced.

However, the Bengal revolutionaries did not rest with this result. New leaders emerged such as Bagha Jatin, Amerendra Chatterjee and Naren Bhattacharya who carried the torch of radicalism ahead in Bengal.

6. Howrah-Shibpur Conspiracy Case 1910

In trial, 47 Bengal revolutionaties were put on trial for various offences including murder under section 302 IPC. The three persons killed were inspector Samshul Islam who was inspecting the murder of the crown witness Narain Goswami, Ashutosh Biswas a lawyer who was in charge of this trial and of the police officer Narain Bannerjee who had arrested Khudiram Bose. Thirty three of the accused persons were acquitted and the remaining were sentenced to different terms.

7. The Peshawar Communist Party Conspiracy Cases 1922-1927

This is a set of five cases against the cadres of the nascent Communist Party of India which came into existence in Tashkent on 17. 10. 1920 following the establishment of the dictatorship of the proletariat in the erstwhile Soviet Union under the leadership of Vladimir Ilyevich Lenin on 7. 11. 1917 or in other words of the establishment of the rule of a class-less workers and labors Government in that country. Lenin had succeeded in over throwing the Czarist rule which stood for the monopoly of the capitalist, imperialist and feudal values of rich land-lords and property owners to the exploitation of the working and productive classes. Lenin had adopted Bolshevik or violent means and methods to uproot the regime of the Czar monarchy. Thereafter, the philosophy and ideology of Communism spread like wildfire across several countries of Asia and Europe who were already facing similar exploitation at the hands of the foreign imperialistic empires. India was one such country with a similar problem and history.

The newly founded members of the Communist Party of India thought out a plan to liberate their countrymen by adopting the Bolshevik methods of proletariat violence to overthrow the foreign dominance. Many of them received indoctrination and training in the Soviet Union and thereafter, they attempted to sneak into India with the avowed purpose of Bolshevik revolution. The British Government set about to foil their attempts. They were arrested and tried for various penal offences directed towards an attempt to overthrow the duly constituted regime of the King Emperor of the British India by violent means. These are the details of the five such cases—

The first case was Crown Vs Muhammad Akbar Qureshi in which Hafizullah Khan and his associates were tried and sentenced in May 1922. The second case was launched against Mohammad Akbar Qureshi on breach of jail discipline. In the third Peshawar Conspiracy case, the accused persons were Akbar Shah and seven others who were tried by the Magistrate of Peshawar on 7 March 1923. Two years rigorous imprisonment was awarded to each of Muhammad Akbar Shah and Gawhar Rehman Khan, while one year rigorous imprisonment was awarded to each of Mir Abdul Majid, Ferozuddin Mansur, Habib Ahmad, Rafiq Ahmad and Sultan Mahmud as passed on 19 May 1923. Crown vs. Mohammad Shafiq was the fourth case. He was sentenced to three years rigorous imprisonment. The fifth and final Peshawar Conspiracy case was instituted against Fazal Elahi Qurban in 1927. He was given five years rigorous imprisonment. The accused filed an appeal against the conviction. The additional judicial commissioner maintained the conviction but reduced the sentence to three years of rigorous imprisonment

It was not the only case which became popular and galvanized the imagination of the young population of the Indian Subcontinent, there were similar such cases. Among them, the Kanpur Bolshevik Case of May 1924 can be quoted as a substantiating case.

8. Kanpur Bolshevik Conspiracy Case (1924 AD)

This is a case which was conducted by the British Government against the members of the newly constituted Communist Party of India such as M N Roy, Muzaffar Ahamed, S A Dange, Shaukat Usmani, Nalini Gupta, Singaravelu Chettiar, Ghulam Hussain. They were charged with an attempt to deprive the King Emperor of his sovereignty of British India, by complete separation of India from imperialistic Britain by a violent revolution. They were found guilty and sentenced to various jail terms.

9. Meerut Conspiracy case 1929

This case was initiated against thirty two members of the Communist Party of India in March 1929 and it was concluded in 1933. The British Government foisted criminal charges against thirty-two members of the Party for offences under section 121 A of the Indian Penal Code 1860. They were charged to have conspired to overthrow the duly constituted regime of the King Emperor of British India by violent means. Twenty seven out of thirty two accused persons were awarded various terms of convictions. It was clear to almost every right thinking person either in India or even in England that it was a case created by the British Government with the purpose of containing the influence of the communist influence in the British India and to nip in the bud the nascent stage of the trade unionism in India. The trial was noticed in England where a satirical play Meerut was staged by the theater group Red Megaphones which highlighted the evils of the colonization and industrialization.

The case soon became *a cause celebre*. The accused persons were defended by Jawaharlal Nehru and M. C. Chagla. Out of the thirty two accused persons, there were three Englishmen also in the dock who sympathized with the Indian cause. They were Philip Spratt, Benjamin Francis Bradley and H. L. Hutchinson. Some of the other accused persons were—K. N. Sehgal, S. S. Joshi, Shaukat Usmani, A. Prasad, G. Adhikari, R. P. Mitra, Gopen Chakravarti, Kishorilal Ghosh, L. R. Kadam. D. R. Thengdi, Goura Shankar, S. Banerjee, K. N. Joglekar, P. C. Joshi, Muzaffar Ahmad, M. G. Desai, D. Goswami, R. S. Naimbkar, S. S. Mirajkar, S. A. Dange, S. V. Ghate and Gopal Basak.

The Sessions Court of Meerut passed stringent sentences upon the accused in January 1933. Out of thirty two accused persons, 27 persons were convicted with various terms of jail sentences. Muzaffar Ahmed was transported for life. S. A. Dange, Philip Spratt, Ghate, Joglekar and Nimbkar were each awarded 12 years rigorous imprisonment. On appeal, in August 1933, the sentences of Ahmed, Dange and Usmani were reduced to three years by Sir Shah Sulaiman Chief Justice of the Allahabad High Court, on the grounds that the accused had already undergone a sufficient period in the jail confinement awaiting their trial and also because the nature of the alleged offences was primarily political. The convictions of other accused persons such as Desai, Hutchinson, Mitra, Jhabvala, Sehgal, Kasle, Gauri Shankar, Kadara and Alve were also set aside in this appeal.

10. Nasik Conspiracy Case

In this case, Arthur Mason Tippetts Jackson was an ICS officer. He was killed by a young man aged about seventeen or eighteen years of age on the suspicion that he had information about the Abhinav Bharat Society of Poona which was alleged to be a radical organization and that he was responsible for the arrest of Vinayak Damodar Savarkar which led to his arrest and subsequent deportation to the Cellular Jail. Jackson was an Indologist who contributed several learned research papers on Indology and History. He was well versed in Sanskrit also, He was even called Pandit Jackson. He was officiating as a magistrate of Nasik and he was transferred to some other place. He was attending a function in his honor and a drama by name Sharda was about to be staged when Anant Kanhere jumped before him and shot him four times. Jackson died on the spot. There was wide-spread consternation for this act because Jackson was sympathetic to the cause of Indian aspirations. The arrest of Babarao Savarkar for printing a 16-page book of songs of Kavi Govind and his prosecution was the last straw. Jackson was instrumental in getting Babarao arrested and prosecuted.

There were three alleged conspirators namely Krishnaji Karve, Vinayak Deshpande and Anant Kanhere. It was decided between them Anant would first try to shoot Jackson and in case he failed in his attempt, then Vinayak Deshpande would step into shoot. On 21 December 1909, while the play could start, Anant carried out his plan. He was arrested before he could commit suicide as planned by him earlier. The three were put on trial, sentenced to death and finally hanged within four months of the incident.

11. Benaras Conspiracy Case

The period immediately following the First World War witnessed a surge in revolutionary philosophy across the country especially West Bengal, Punjab, Bihar, Maharashtra and United Provinces. The Bolshevik revolution and the installation of the dictatorship of the proletariat in Lenin's Soviet Union was also a catalyst for radicalism both in precept and practice in several parts of the world particularly those of them which were struggling under imperialism. Several revolutionary committees developed such as the Anushilan Samiti of Dacca and its Benaras branch, the Jugantar Party, the Vijaya Sangh and the Ghadar Party of Punjab.

Sachindra Nath Sanyal and Ras Behari Bose tried to raise a rising in the proportion of the up-rising of 1857. However, the mission could not succeed because of lack of coordination and because of so many internal differences due to several reasons. Perhaps the plan was also too ambitious for easy implementation. Most of the accused hailed from Benaras. They were arrested, tried and sentenced.

12. The Ghadar Mutiny of 1915

During the midst of the First World War, Indian revolutionaries planned many attempts to overthrow the British Raj by force. One such effort was what is now known as the Ghadar Party Mutiny or the Hindu-German Mutiny. It was planned by a concerted effort of the Ghadar Party of US and Canada whose members were mostly drawn from Punjab, by its local branches in Punjab, the Berlin Committee of Germany, The German Foreign Office stationed at San Francisco, by the Singapore unit and others. It is also known as the Hindu-German Mutiny. However, the British intelligence thwarted the attempt and the proposed plan could not materialize. The British Government was alarmed and alerted. Lest there be a repeat of such events, the Government came out with such draconian laws as the Ingress Into India Ordinance 1914, the Foreigners Act 1914, the Defence of India Act 1915 and the Rowlatt Act. The Raj came out heavily upon the insurgents. The Jallianwala Bagh massacre was one of the after-math of these developments.

13. Royal Indian Navy's Revolt of 1946

It began on 18. 2. 1946 shortly before independence. Although the Navy men were demanding better working conditions, better accommodation, treatment at par with the British officers and work-force, the real cause of action was their sense of protest and indignation towards the trial of the soldiers of the Azad Hind Fauz in the Red Fort premises. The soldiers were defended by Pt. Jawaharlal Nehru, Dr. Kailash Nath Katju, Barrister Asaf Ali and others. Sailors from different harbors such as Karachi, Jamnagar, Cochin, Calcutta, Poona, Madras, Mandapam and Andman and Nicobar Islands also joined in the strike. 66 men of war also joined in the revolt. The strike ended on 23. 1. 1946 as a result of mediation by several leading leaders. Perhaps the British Government had by then realised that they could no longer afford to deal with another similar incident on the lines of 1857. So they decided to call it a day.

14. The Jabalpur Rebellion of 1946

It took place on 14. 02. 1946 in the STC premises of Jabalpur. They were protesting against some of their British officers who abused some of them and they were also protesting against the trial of some of the warriors of the Azad Hind Fouz which was taking place in the Red Fort, New Delhi. These rebels were about 1700 in number comprising of almost all political parties such as the National Congress and the Indian Muslim League. When the revolt seemed to be going out of control for the British, then the Commander-in -Chief of the British Indian Army General

Sir ClaudeAuchinteck sent an urgent cable to London about the ominous signs of this revolt. The British Government hastened their decision to depart from India. This historic rebellion deserves to be better remembered in the history of the freedom movement of India.

Chapter Eleven

Some of the Prominent Revolutionaries Almost Forgotten Today

Jatindra Nath Mukherjee-Bagha Jatin (1879-1915)–In his early days, Jatin was influenced by the teachings of Swami Vivekanand and Sister Nivedita which helped in the development of his spiritual views. He had great strength of physic and mental character. Once he was confronted with a Royal Bengal tiger in a forest. He fought out the mighty beast even though he was badly mauled by the beast. But then finally he succeeded in killing it with a khukuri.

Jatin was instrumental in the founding of the Anushilan Samiti in 1900 with the object of terrorizing the British Government in leaving India. Just about this time, Jatin came in contact with Aurobindo Ghosh, Barindra Ghosh and other radical thinkers.

Jatin was instrumental in the founding of yet another revolutionary party namely Jugantar Party. Just about this time, the Alipore Bomb case was being prosecuted and it had an impact upon the psyche of Jatin. In 1910, Jatin was suspected to be involved in a number of anarchist activities, but there was no clear evidence yet against him. But then finally, he was arrested along with 46 other suspects in the Howrah-Shibpur Conspiracy case. They were charged with the offence of waging a war against the British Government and also inciting the soldiers against the Government. The trial failed with regard to Jatin.

Jatin was in contact with revolutionaries outside India such as Taraknath Das, Lala Hardayal, Guran Dutt Kumar, Surendra Mohan Dutt and others. The Jugantar Party tried to procure arms and ammunitions from Germany in a bid to oust the British Government by armed force. The British intelligence, however, unearthed this conspiracy. Jatin was under a threat of arrest. So his friends advised him to move into some other safer place. Accordingly, he moved his home into Balasore in Orissa. Jatin and others were chased there and traced out. A fierce battle ensued between them and the British police. There were several casualties on both sides. Jatin himself was mortally wounded and he succumbed to his injuries on 10. 9. 1915.

Amarendranath Chatterjee-(1. 7. 1880-4. 9. 1957)-He was one of the close associates of Raja Priyamohan and his son Rajendranath Mukherjee, Jatin Mukherjee or Bagha Mukherjee, Premnath Karer or Sri Yukteshwar Giri, Hrishikesh Kanjilal, Pandit Samadhiyari and several others. He was a leading figure in the Indo-German conspiracy. He was imprisoned for sometime in the year 1923. He was elected as an MLA in 1929. He took part in the 1930 Dandi March and he was imprisoned for one year.

Bhupendranath Dutta-(4.. 9. 1980-25. 12. 1961)-He was a younger brother of Narendranath Datta later to be known as Swami Vivekananda. Another brother Vishwanath Datta was an attorney in the Calcutta High Court. He started his career by joining the Bengal Revolutionary Society formed by Premanath Mittra in 1902. But then he joined the Jugantar Party and became the editor of its journal. He was also a close associate of Sri Aurobindo and Barindranath Ghosh. In 1907. He was charged with the offence of sedition and sentenced to one years imprisonment. After his release, he went to the United States and he obtained a degree in M. A. from Brown University. In the USA, he became a member of the Ghadar Party. During the First World War, he went to Germany and there he became a member of the Indian Independence Committee. In 1921, he visited Moscow to attend the Comintern where Manabendra Nath Roy and Barindranath Dasgupta also participated. He continued his studies and obtained a Ph. D in Anthropology from the University of Hamburg in 1923.

After returning to India, he became a pacifist. He joined the Indian National Congress and became a member of the All India Congress Committee in 1929. He was a polyglot who was conversant with Bengali, Hindi, German, English and Bengali languages. He wrote the following books—

1. Baishnab Sahitya Samaj Tattva (in Bengali 1946)

2. Bhratri Dwitiya Swadhinta in Bengali 1983

3. Bhartiya Samaj Paddhati in Bengali 1983

4. Dialectics of Hindu Rituals 1950

5. Studies in Indian Social Polity 1983

6. Swami Vivekanand Patriot Prophet: A Study 1954

Bhavbhushan Mitra—(1881-1970)—Also known as Bhaba Bhushan Mitra or Swami Satyanand Puri, he was closely associated with such activists of those days as Bagha Jatin, Baldev Roy, Phani Roy Kushtia, Shiv Kumar Ghosh, Jyotish Majumdar Chandi, Amaresh Kanjilal, Suresh Majumdar Paran, Atul Krishna Ghosh, Nalinikanth Kar, Kshitish Sanyal, Satish Sarkar, Jnan Mitra, Charu Ghosh, Nani Gopal Sengupta, Surendranath Tagore, Sarla Devi Chaudhrani, Sister Nivedita and others. He was convicted in a conspiracy case and jailed between 1910 to December 1914. He also took part in the various Civil Disobedience Movements from 1921 to 1942.

Madan Lal Dhingra (18 September 1883 – 17 August 1909)– Madanlal Dhingra:was one of the many revolutionaries of that era who laid down their lives most willingly, who commanded their last journeys to the gallows with a patriotic cheer upon their lips, who simply wanted to avenge the wrongs their countrymen had to face for so long at the hands of the foreign occupation of their motherland. The struggle was waged not only by peaceful active resistors, not only by constitutional petition-writers, but also by such martyrs who gave up their physical mortal existence so that their country-men could live under peaceful environments of liberty and opportunities.

Madanlal hailed from a distinguished family of Amritsar. His father was an ophthalmologist and Civil Surgeon of Amritsar. Two of the brothers of Madan Lal were doctors, one of them being MRCP and two others of them were barristers. But only Madanlal chose the path of national patriotic duty. He achieved a Diploma in Civil Engineering from University College, London 1906-1909.

While in London, he met Shyamji Krishna Varma, Veer Savarkar and other revolutionaries. The meeting place was the India House which belonged to Shyamji Krishna Varma. This was a hostel to lodge Indian students who were studying in England. The seeds of revolution developed there. Dhingra planned to avenge by killing a few of the British officialdom, such as Lord Curzon the Viceroy, ex-Governor of Bengal Bramfield Fuller, but they escaped some-how or other. Then finally the plan centered down upon Curzon Wyllie who was an army officer of high rank and who was collecting secret intelligence about Veer Savarkar. Dhingra got his chance on 1. 7. 1909 when Curzon Wyllie was leaving the Indian National Association in the Imperial Institute building after a function. Dhingra pounced upon him and pumped five bullets point blank into his physique. He died instantaneously. Madanlal was over-powered. The subsequent trial ended in his conviction and the inevitable sentence of capital punishment.

The trial evoked mixed reactions even in England, There was a section of the British who pleaded for the lesser sentence of transportation for life. Even in the British Cabinet, there were some sympathizers with the Indian cause. But the sentence was carried out on 19. 8. 1909.

These are last words of Madanlal Dhingra before he was hanged–

"I believe that a nation held down by foreign bayonets is in a perpetual state of war. Since open battle is rendered impossible to a disarmed race, I attacked by surprise. Since guns were denied to me I drew forth my pistol and fired. Poor in wealth and intellect, a son like myself has nothing else to offer to the mother but his own blood. And so I have sacrificed the same on her altar. The only lesson required in India at present is to learn how to die, and the only way to teach it is by dying ourselves. My only prayer to God is that I may be re-born of the same mother and I may re-die in the same sacred cause till the cause is successful. Vande Matram. "

Vanchinathan Iyer–1886-1911–The plot to kill Robert Ashe the Collector of Tirunevelli was master-minded by Nilkantha Brahmchari who recruited Vanchinathan Iyer and Shankar

Krishna Iyer in the plot. On 17. 6. 1911, Ashe boarded the Minuchin Mail bound towards Kodaikanal along with his wife. Vanchi jumped into the first class compartment and shot him dead point blank with a Belgian made Browning pistol. In order to avoid arrest, Vanchi committed suicide.

Krishnaji Gopal Karve–1887-1910–He was a member of the Abhinav Bharat Society of Nasik. On 21. 12. 1909, he along with Anant Laxman Kanhere and Vinayak Narayan Deshpande, killed Collector Jackson of Nasik. He was hanged in Thane.

Anant Laxman Kanhere–He shot dead Collector Jackson of Nasik along with Krishnaji Gopal Karve and Vinayak Narayan Deshpande on 21. 12. 1909. They suspected that Jackson was responsible for the arrest of Ganesh Savarkar elder brother of Vinayak Damodar Savarkar. He was hardly 17 years at that time. He was hanged on 19. 4. 1910.

Vinayak Narayan Deshpande– He was associated with Krishnaji Gopal Karve and Vinayak Narayan Deshpande in the murder of Collector Jackson of Nasik on 21. 12. 1909. He was tried, found guilty and hanged.

Thakur Roshan Singh (22 January 1892 - 19 December 1927)–Thakur Roshan Singh was yet another revolutionary of the Kakori Train Robbery case along with Ram Prasad Bismil, Ashfaq Ullah Khan and Rajendra Nath Lahiri. Like his other immortal revolutionaries, he was also involved with the Hindustan Socialist Republican Association HSRA. He was tried along with the aforesaid immortals in the aforesaid case, found guilty and hanged on 19. 12. 1927.

Ambika Chakrabarty (1892-1962)- In 1930, he took part in the Chittagong armory case along with Surya Sen and other revolutionaries. They succeeded in destroying the entire communication system with the result that the city was totally cut off from the rest of the country for a few days. This raid is ranked as one of the most daring acts of revolutionary activities anywhere. Besides Surya Sen and Ambika Chakrabarty, the other participants were Anand Gupta, Ardhendu Dastdar, Sasanka Datta, Kalpana Datta, Pritilata Wadedar, Naresh Roy, Nirmal Sen, Jiban Ghoshal, Anant Singh, Lokenath Bal, Ganesh Ghosh, Subodh Roy, Harigopal Bal Bagra and others. He was caught in his hideout, sentenced to death, lodged in the Cellular Cell. But his sentence was later reduced to life imprisonment. He was released in 1946. After independence, he joined the CPI and was elected as an MLA in 1952. Unfortunately, he died soon thereafter

Surya Sen (1893-1934)–Surya Sen was a member of an organization which believed that the British could be ousted from India only by forceful means. This organization comprised of such revolutionaries as Ganesh Ghosh, Lokenath Bal, Ambika Chakrovarti, Harigopal Bal Tegri, Ananta Singh, Anand Prasad Gupta, Tripura Sen, Bidhubhushan Bhattacharya, Pritilata Waddedar, Kalpana Datta, Himanshu Sen, Binod Bihar Chowdhry, Subodh Roy, Manoranjan Bhattacharya, Debi Prasad Gupta and others. These dare-devils created a plot to raid the Chittagong armory of the British arsenal and to take the British as hostages, to loot some banks and to sever rail-way connectivity between Chittaggong and Calcutta. On 18 April 1930, some 65 of these radicals took part in a raid. But the British intelligence had got the scent of this conspiracy much earlier and this raid was rendered unsuccessful by arresting many of them before they could embark upon their plan. They were operating under the banner of the Republican Party of Chittagong Branch. Other operatives of these radical party were Manoranjan Sen, Rajat Sen, Swadesh Roy, Phanindra Nandi, Subodh Chowdhry, Deba Gupta, Jiban Ghoshal and Tarkeshwar Dastidar. But soon, an armed conflict took place between them and the British police in which 80 troops of the British force and 12 revolutionaries were killed. Pritilata Waddedar was injured. Among those killed in the encounter were Deba Gupta, Manoranjan Sen, Rajat Sen and Swadesh Ranjan Roy. In the subsequent trial during the period 1931 to 1932, 12 of them were sentenced to life imprisonment, two of them were given three years imprisonment and 32 of them were acquitted. Surya Sen and Tarkeshwar Dastidar were later arrested because of a traitor's role played by Netra Sen. They were later hanged by the British Government.

Bhai Bal Mukund (1889-1915) He tried to kill Lord Hardinge the British Governor by hurling a bomb upon him. He escaped. Balmukund was arrested and sentenced to death.

Sohan Singh Josh (12. 11. 1898-29. 7. 1982) He was a writer and he published a revolutionary daily namely Kirti and edited Jang-e-Azadi. He was a close associate of Sardar Bhagat Singh.

Sardar Udham Singh (26. 12. 1899—31. 7. 1944)– Shaheed-e-Azam Sardar Udham Singh was born as Sher Singh in Sangrur Punjab. He lost both of his parents very early, first his mother then his father by the time he turned seven years in his childhood. He was looked after in the Central Khalsa Anathalaya Amritsar.

The Jallianwala Bagh incident took place when Udham Singh was an impressionable 14 years old teen-ager. The atrocity definitely left an indelible impression upon his psyche. Thereafter, he came in contact with yet another immortal revolutionary i.e. Sardar Bhagat Singh while they were lodged in a jail in Lahore. Revolutionary Ram Prasad Bismil was yet another source of inspiration to him. He secretly planned to avenge the Jallianwala Bagh atrocity. He traveled to England on a passport under a different name, lived there incognito for several years and then finally he got the chance for which he was there. The Governor of Punjab of 1919 General Michael O'Dwyer was attending a function or meeting of the Royal Central Asian Society in the Caxton Hall on 13. 3. 1940. Udham Singh had kept his weapon secretly in a box which was carved out of two books. He shot the General dead. He made no efforts to escape. He was apprehended, tried almost summarily in a trial which was over in about two months and finally hanged on 31. 7. 1940 i.e. after about 21 years of a wait since after the actual incident dated 13. 4. 1919 the Baisakhi Day.

Atul Krishna Ghosh–1890–1966–He was a close friend of Jatindranath Mukherjee or Bagha Jatin, a follower of the Jugantar Movement and a member of the Anushilan Samiti. He was involved in the Indo-German conspiracy of the First World War period.

Ganesh Ghosh (22. 6. 1900–16. 10. 1994)–He was a member of the Jugantar Party and he took part in the Chittagong armory case on 18. 4. 1930. He was arrested, tried and found guilty. He was lodged in the Cellular Jail Port Blair for 14 years in 1932 to be released in 1946. After independence, he joined the

Communist Party of India and after the split in this party in 1964, he joined the CPI Marxist. He was elected to the Bengal Legislative Assembly in 1952, 1957 and 1962 and to the fourth Lok Sabha in 1967.

Ashfaqulla Khan (22 October 1900 – 19 December 1927)– His parents were Shafiqur Rahman and Mazharunnisa. He was born in Shahjahanpur in the North Western Provinces. He was by temperament and talent of poetic disposition. He used to compose Urdu poetry and he wanted to popularize Urdu. At the same time, he was a fierce nationalist who had come in contact with such revolutionaries as Chandra Shekhar Azad and Ram Prasad Bismil. They founded the Hindustan Socialist Republican Association HSRA. When Mahatma Gandhi with-drew the Civil Disobedience Movement following the Chauri Chaura incident of 1922, a large number of youth across the country were disappointed because they felt that independence was round the corner. They engaged themselves in revolutionary activities. Ashfaq was one of them.

Ashfaq was one of the accused persons in the Kakori Train Robbery case along with Ram Prasad Bismil, Thakur Roshan Singh, Rajendra Nath Lahiri and others. Their plan was to collect funds for the purpose of independence-related activities. They were caught subsequently, tried and sentenced. Ram Prasad Bismil, Thakur Roshan Singh, Rajendra Nath, Lahiri and Ashfaqullah Khan were sentenced to death and their sentences were executed. Ashafaq was hanged on 19. 12. 1927.

Sagarmal Gopa (3. 11. 1900-4. 44. 1946)- He wrote revolutionary books such as Azadi Ke Diwane, took part in several movement, he was imprisoned where he was tortured to death in jail custody.

Rajendra Nath Lahiri (1901–1927)—Rajendra Nath was an associate of such revolutionaries as Ram Prasad Bismil, Ashfaq Ullah Khan and Thakur Roshan Singh in the Kakori Train Robbery case. Earlier, he was implicated in the Dakshineshwar bomb case also. He absconded from there and escaped into Benaras where he began to study. But then he was caught while the proceedings for the Kakori case were under-way. For the earlier charge, he was sentenced to ten years rigorous imprisonment. But then, he was sentenced to death along with the three other revolutionaries. He was finally hanged on 17. 12. 1927.

Ullaskar Dutta –He was born in Brahmanbaria now in Bangladesh. After passing the entrance examination in 1903, he entered the Presidency College of Calcutta. Thereafter he moved on to London for higher studies and he obtained a degree from the University of London. He was of a fiery nature. Once Professor Russell did not speak kindly about the Bengali community. Ullaskar attacked him. He was suspended from the College. On 30. 44. 1908, Ullaskar Dutta Khudiram Bose and Prafulla Chaki tried to kill judge Kingsford by hurling a bomb. But instead two daughters of Barrister Kennedy were killed. They were tried and sentenced. They were lodged in the Cellular Jail where Ullaskar was given extreme torture. He was released in 1920. He continued with the same activities. As a result, he was again arrested in 1931 This time for 18 months. He died on May 17, 1965. Two streets are named after him in Kolkata and Silchar. He wrote the following two books–Amar Karajiban (My Life in Prison and Dwipantarer Katha or Tale of Deportation).

Gaya Prasad

Gaya Prasd was a member of Hindustan Socialist Republican Association. The members were engaged in the manufacture of bombs under the camouflage of the dispensary of Dr Gaya Prasad. All the other revolutionaries were to hide their identities by posing as compounders, house-keepers and other works. They put on such hidden names as—

Shiv Verma: Ram Narayan Kapoor

Vijay Kumar Sinha: Bacchu

Mahavir Singh: Pratap Singh

Chandrashekhar Azad: Pandit ji

Sukhdev: Balejar

Jaigopal: Gopal

Bomb factories were started in Ferozepur, Saharanpur. They had to be moved to different places to defy their arrest. However, Gaya Prasad could not avoid his arrest for all time to come. One day he was caught unawares. As he opened the door of his factory, he was confronted by a policeman with the help of a desertor namely Kalu Ram. Shiv Verma and Jaidev were also arrested. Gaya Prasad was taken to Lahore where he was tried in the Lahore Conspiracy case along with other co-workers. He was given life imprisonment, transported to the Cellular Jail. Here he went on a hunger strike of 46 days duration to protest against the bad treatment to him. In 1937, he was removed from the Cellular Jail. But then he was brought here again. He was finally released in 1946. He died on 10. 2. 1993.

Rajkumar Gupta was yet another prominent participant in the Kakori raid case.

Ananta Lal Singh–(1. 12. 1903- 25. 1. 1979) In the beginning of his career, he joined the Non Cooperation Movement in 1921. But then he soon joined hands with radicals like Surya Sen, Ganesh Ghosh, Jiban Ghoshal, Nirmal Sen and others. He was involved in a robbery case at the treasury office of Assam Bengal Railway. He was arrested in Calcutta, but he was let go probably for lack of evidence. He was again arrested in 1924 in another case and this time he was jailed for four years. In April 1930, he was involved in the Chittagong armory case. He again fled along with Ganesh Ghoshal and Jiban Ghoshal. He took shelter in the French Embassy in Chandernagore. But then he surrendered after some time and in the subsequent trial, he was sentenced to life imprisonment and lodged in the Cellular Jail in Port Blair. After some time, he was removed from Port Blair and brought back to mainland India. He was finally released in 1946. After independence, he joined the CPI. But after some time, he founded a more radical party namely Revolutionary Council of India. He was again arrested in 1969 this time by the Government of India and released in 1977. He developed cardiac problems by now and he died soon thereafter.

Sachindra Bakshi-(25. 12. 1904–23. 11. 1984)-He was one of the founding members of the Hindustan Republican Association HRA later to be known as the Hindustan Republican Socialist Association. He took part in the Kakori train robbery, was convicted and sentenced to life imprisonment.

Baikunthnath Shukla-1907-1934- He belonged to a family of great patriots. His nephew Yogendra Shukla was one of the founders of the Hindustan Republican Socialist Association

HSRA. His early acquaintance was Kishori Prasanna Singh and this friendship turned him into this line of thinking. HSRA was Bolshevik in philosophy. One Phanindra Nath Ghosh betrayed them, police caught him and subjected him to great torture. So he revealed the names of other revolutionaries. Some of the revolutionaries tried to take revenge by trying to kill him. However, Baikunth Shukla and Chandrama Ghosh succeeded in killing him on 9. 10. 1932 in his shop. Baikunthnath was arrested on 6. 7. 1933, tried, found guilty and hanged on 14. 4. 1934 in the Gaya Central prison.

Durgavati Devi-(7. 10. 1907-15. 10. 1997)–She was a member of the Hindustan Republican Socialist Association HSRA and wife of another revolutionary Bhagwati Charan Vohra. Therefore, other members of the party used to call her as Durga Bhabhi. She was also an active member of the **Naujawan Bharat Sabha**. She helped Sardar Bhagat Singh and Rajguru manage an escape from prison after killing J. P. Saunders. She later attempted to kill Lord Haily who, however, escaped. She was caught, sentenced to three years rigorous imprisonment. She sold her ornaments and thus raised an amount of Rs3000/ to help Sardar Bhagat Singh and others in their trials. She died at age 90.

Manmath Nath Gupta- (7. 2. 1908–26. 11. 2000) He was an eminent writer, member of the HRSA and he was involved in the Kakori train robbery case and jailed for 14 years. He was jailed again in 1939.

Loknath Bal (5. 8. 1908-4. 9. 1964)- He was an associate of Surya Sen and he was involved with others in the Chittagong armory raid in 1930. On 22. 4. 1930, he was involved in a gun fight with British forces In the fight, he lost such associates as his brother Hargopal Tagra, Jiban Ghosh and others. He was able to escape to Chandernagore, a French colony. But he was caught later on, sentenced to life imprisonment and sent to Cellular Jail Port Blair. He was released in 1946 and after independence, he joined the Indian National Congress. He was appointed as Deputy Commissioner of Calcutta Corporation.

Jogesh Chandra Chatterji- 1895-1969-He was one of the co-founders of the HSRA and he was also a member of the Anushilan Samiti. He was involved in the Kakori robbery case of 1926 and was transported for life. Earlier than that, he was arrested several times for different acts of revolutionary activities. After independence, he joined the Congress Party and was a Rajya Sabha member from 1956 till his death.

Barindra Kumar Ghosh–(5. 1. 1880-18. 4. 1959) He was involved in the Alipore bombing case.

Hemchandra Kanungo -1871-1950- He was one of the associates of Aurobindo Ghosh and he was involved in the manufacture of bombs.

Bhavbhushan Mitra-1881-1970- He took part in several Civil Disobedience Movements and the Quit India Movement of 1942. He was arrested several times.

Bhagvati Charan Vohra– He was an ideologue amongst the revolutionaries. He wrote manifestos of Naujawan Bharat Sabha and Republican Socialist Association of Hindustan and the notable ' Philosophy of the Bomb'. He joined the revolutionary movement after the withdrawal of the Civil Disobedience Movement as a consequence of the Chauri Chaura incident. He was impressed by the philosophy of the proletariat and of M. N. Roy. He associated himself with Jaichand Vidyalankar, Sardar Bhagat Singh and Sukhdev who had formed the Naujawan Bharat Sabha in1926. Yashpal co-authored ' The Philosophy of the Bomb'. The motto of the Sabha was ''Service, Suffering, Service ''. He died on 28. 5. 1930 by the banks of river Ravi while testing a bomb.

Pramod Ranjan Bannerji–He was a follower of Netaji Subhash Chandra Bose. He was involved in the Chittagong case and was kept in the Dhaka and Dum Dum jails and also in the Cellular Jail in Andaman Nicobar. He also took part in the Quit India Movement of 1942. His wife Manorama was also a freedom fighter who took part in the 1942 Movement.

Baswon Singh Sinha (23. 3. 1909)–As a school student, he came in contact with revolutionaries like Yogendra Shukla and in 1925, he joined the HSRA. For his radical views, he was rusticated from the school. Later he joined the Sadaqat Ashram in Patna. He was involved in several conspiracy cases such as Lahore Conspiracy case, Bhusawal, Kakori, Tirhut and Deluaha conspiracy cases. He was also associated with Chandra Shekhar Azzad and Keshav Chandra Chakravarty. He spent nearly 19 years in the British jails. He was lodged in different jails from time to time such as Bankipore Central Jail, Bhagalpur Central Jail and Gaya Central Jail. In the Gaya Central Jail, he undertook a fast unto death as a protest against ill-treatment of political prisoners. He was on fast for 58 days and finally, he terminated his fast only when he was assured by Mahatma Gandhi that all of his demands had been met. In 1936, he was released but with restrictions on his moments. He was an active trade union leader since 1936. He was arrested along with J. P, Narayan and Rambriksh Benipuri and spent six months in jail. During the Second World War, he was arrested under the Defence of India Ordinance for 18 months. In 1941, he went to Afghanistan to collect arms and ammunition. On return, he was arrested on 8. 1. 1943, spent more than three years there and was released in 1946. Earlier in 1938, he was arrested in Dalmianagar for organising a trade union strike. During the Second World War, he was arrested for delivering an anti war speech. He was convicted and jailed for 18 months. He was kept in the Hazaribagh Jail and he was released in 1941. He took active part in the 1942 Movement and he was black-listed in Group A along with such prominent leaders as Deep Narayan Singh, Rambriksh Benipuri, Narayan Prasad Verma and Bir Chand Patel. He facilitated the escape from prison of several leaders as Pandit Ramnanda Mishra, Suraj Narayan Singh and Gulab Sonar. During imprisonment sometimes, he was kept under fetters in addition to handcuffs. After independence, he was actively involved in socialist activities. In was elected to Parliament in 1952 from Dehri-on-Sone and again in 1957. He was a member of the Legislative Council from 1962 to 1968. During the days of emergency, he remained under-ground for nearly 20 months. After the emergency was lifted, he was again elected to the Parliament from Dehri-on-Sone and he served as Union Minister for Labour, Planning and Industry under the Janata Government. He was married to Kamla Singh, a grand-niece of Shyama Charan Mukherjee founder of Jan Sangh. She was twice elected to the Rajya Sabha from 1990 to 2000. She also served as ambassador to Suriname and Barbados. She also worked as Union Minister for State for external affairs under Shri I. K. Gujral. She was a MISA detenu during the emergency days. Basawon Singh was a widely traveled man who had visited Rangoon, China, Japan, Soviet Union and America. He died on 7. 4. 1989. A commemorative stamp was issued by the Postal Department on 32. 3. 2000 in his honor. An indoor stadium is named after him in Hajipur, Bihar.

Batukeshwar Dutt (1910–1965) ——It is strange to include Batukeshwar Dutt in this list of forgotten heroes although he is in the class of Sardar Bhagat Singh, Rajguru, Sukhdev, Chandra Shekhar Azad, Ram Prasad Bismil Sardar Udham Singh and similar other legendary revolutionaries. But then Batukeshwar Dutt is not only forgotten today, but he also faced neglect rest of his life. He was released from the dreaded Cellular Jail which is commonly called as the kala-pani saza. The waters of the Indian Ocean are so deep and fathomless that they appear to the common eyes like black-waters. Hence the dubious nomenclature. Moreover, many of the unknown freedom fighters went there never to come back to the main-land of their home-land

After his release, Batukeshwar raised a family, married Anjali at age 37 in 1947. But then he was recipient of no state pensions or any type of pecuniary assistance. He took up petty jobs such as an agent in a cigarette company. He raised a biscuit factory which had to be soon closed because it was bringing loss instead of some profit to the owner. There was some recompense in late 1964 when he was nominated to the State Vidhan Sabha, Bihar. But then he soon fell ill and was hospitalized in a Government hospital in Patna. From here he was removed to the Safdarjung Hospital, New Delhi, finally to the All India Institute of Medical Sciences AIMS, New Delhi where he breathed his last on 20. 7. 1965.

Batukeshwar was born in Oari village in West Bengal. He graduated from Kanpur. He was a member of the Hindustan Socialist Republican Association, HSRA in short. The dreaded Defense of India Act 1915 was in force at that time with the help of which the British could detain or arrest any one without charges and trial. The Central Legislative Assembly was deliberating upon yet another legislation namely the Trade Disputes and the Public Safety Bill 1929. The Government would have been saddled with more authoritarian powers. These were in short the reasons why there was resentment against these oppressive measures.

Sardar Bhagat Singh and Batukeshwar Dutt decided to make their protesting voices heard. So they threw a series of bombs in the empty seats of the Central Legislative Assembly, New Delhi on 8. 4. 1929. No one was injured, nor was it their intention to hurt anyone. They just wanted to make a statement. The two did not make any effort to escape. They were easily apprehended, put on trial before the Sessions Judge, New Delhi, found guilty and awarded life imprisonment, both of them were consigned to the Mianwali Jail from where Dutt was transported to the Cellular Jail. Later, Sardar Bhagat Singh was awarded death sentence along with Rajguru and Sukhdev, tried, sentenced to death and finally hanged on 23. 3. 1939 in a Lahore Jail.

In the Cellular Jail confinement, Dutt went on strike twice once in 1933 and then again in1937 against bad treatment to them and also to other inmates. He was brought to the Bankipur

Central Jail, Patna and he was finally released in 1945 in the eve of independence. In this manner, he was incarcerated for nearly sixteen years.

Binod Bihari Chowdhry (10. 1. 1911-10. 4. 2013)–In 1927, Binod joined the Jugantar Party in the company of Surya Sen and others in the Chittagong armory case. They wanted to raid and loot the armed depots in Chittagong, they succeeded in disrupting all the means of communication in such a manner as transport and telegraphic communication with the result that Chittagong was cut off with the rest of the country for a few days. But soon the British forces ambushed them with the result that 12 revolutionaries were killed and 80 British troops were also killed in the fierce battle. Binod Bihari was wounded and captured along with other revolutionaries. They were tried and different sentences were awarded to them. After independence, Chittagong fell under East Pakistan which is now Bangladesh. He died in Fortis Hospital undergoing treatment. He was awarded with the Independence Award which is the highest civilian award of Bangladesh.

Bina Das (24. 8. 1911–26. 12. 1986) She attempted to murder Stanley Jackson the tyrant British Governor by firing five rounds on him. He, however, escaped. She was caught and sentenced to 9 years. Thereafter, she took part in the Quit India Movement of 1942 and was again arrested.

Kishorilal (1912—1990)–He was one of the fiery revolutionaries of Punjaba long with the legendary Sardar Bhagat Singh. In 1928, he joined the Naujawan Bharat Sabha which was founded by Sardar Bhagat Singh. He was involved with the Hindustan Socialist Republican Association. In 1929, he was arrested along with Sardar Bhagat Singh, Rajguru and Sukhdev for their involvement in the manufacture of bombs in a factory in Lahore. In the ensuing trial, Sardar Bhagat Singh, Rajguru and Sukhdev were given capital punishment while Kishorilal was given life imprisonment which he served out till his release in 1946.

While still in jail, he joined the Communist Party. He took part in the agitation to liberate Goa in 1962.

Kalpana Datta (1913-1995)

Kalpana was born in Chittagong which is now in Bangladesh. She was a part of the Republican Party Chittagong Branch which wanted to raid the British armory on 18. 4. 1930. However, the British intelligence foiled their attempt, several of the revolutionaries were arrested Kalpana being one of them, she was released on bail, she jumped bail but was again re-arrested on 19. 04. 1933. In the trial thereafter, she was sentenced to life imprisonment. But she was released in 1939 after serving out six years in jail. After independence, she joined the CPI and married another notable CPI member P. C. Joshi. She was an active relief worker in the Bengal famine of 1943 and during the blood-bath generated by the partition of Bengal in 1947.

Benoy Krishna Basu, Badal Gupta and Dinesh Gupta– Dressed as Europens, they walked into the Writers Building in Calcutta now Kolkata on 8. 12. 1930 and shot dead the oppressive British officer Col. N. S. Simpson who treated freedom fighters very badly in the jails. Later soon after they committed suiccide to escape from being caught and tortured.

Subodh Roy (1915-2006)–He was born in Chittagong now in Bangladesh. He was the youngest participant at age 14 in the Chittagong armory case. In the year 1930-31. He was lodged in the Port Blair Jail in 1934 after conviction and was released from there in 1940. After independence, he joined the CPI, but after split in the Party in 1964, he joined the Marxist group.

Hemu Kalani (23.. 3. 1923 –21. 1. 1943)–Hemu is one of the youngest of the revolutionaries to be hanged by British rule, He was at that time two months shy of his 20th birthday when he was hanged in a Sindh jail.

He was a very talented young man, good at studies and in swimming where he was awarded for his skill asa swimmer. But then, he was soon attracted by the national duties. He took part in the boycott of the foreign goods and clothes during the Swadeshi Andolan of the early thirties. He raised slogans during the Quit India Movement of 1942. He was involved in an attempt to remove fish-plates from a goods train running between his home town Sukkur and passing by another station by name Rohadi. He was there doing this rebel work along with some of his companions. The train was carrying a large consignment of arms and ammunition which were meant to be used by the British police to suppress the patriotic rebels. Hemu was caught before he could carry out his plan. He was badly tortured in a Sindh jail. But he did not divulge the names of other conspirators. He was given death sentence. The citizens of Sindh petitioned with the British Government for commutation of the sentence into an imprisonment. He would have been thus let off leniently. But Hemu did not comply with the condition. Finally, he was hanged on 21. 1.

1943. On his way to the gallows, Hemu was still cheerful and he had a copy of Shrimad Bhagwat Gita with him. There are about 30 monuments all over the country to commemorate his martyrdom.

Chapter Twelve

Great Patriots and Freedom-Fighters

Ganesh Vasudeo Joshi (9 April 1828 – 25 July 1880)

He was a great social reformer, a lawyer by profession and precursor of the renaissance of modern political awakening of India. Along with Justice Ranade, he started the movement for the manufacture of daily-need consumer goods such as candles, soap, ink, umbrellas and other items. He promoted khadi also. This is how he believed that the Indians could free themselves from the expensive British goods. In this manner, it can be said that he is the pioneer of the spirit of local and indigenous manufacture of the goods of daily needs. Later on, Mahatma Gandhi developed this theory on a larger scale in the name of his Swadeshi Andolan which he launched in 1930 onwards. He was affectionately called as Sarwajanik Kaka.

Womesh Chunder Bonnerjee or Umesh Chandra Banerjee (29 December 1844 – 21 July 1906)

He was one of the founders of the Indian National Congress which held its first session under his Presidentship in Bombay now Mumbai from 28, 12, 1885 to 31. 12. 1885. He was again President of the Allahabad session of 1892. He was one of the leading barristers of his time.

Sir Dinshaw Edulji Wacha (1844–1936)–He was one of the leading names in the Parsi community in Bombay and one of the pioneers in the cotton industry. He was one of the founding fathers of the Indian National Congress. He presided over its annual session of 1901. He was a member of the Bombay Legislative Assembly, the Imperial Council and the Viceroy's Council.

Badruddin Tyabji (10 October 1844 – 19 August 1906)

He was one of the leading lawyers of Bombay and the first Indian to argue a case before the Bombay High Court. He was one of the founding fathers of the Indian National Congress and he presided over the third session of the INC. He promoted Hindu-Muslim harmony. He was opposed to the argument of Sir Syed Ahmad Khan that his community should not take part in national movements. He called upon his community members to become part of the national mainstream. He was elevated as a judge of the Bombay High Court and then he became the Chief Justice of the same court also.

Vasudev Balwant Phadke–(4. 11. 1845–17. 2. 1883)

He was one of the first revolutionaries who hailed from Shridhan Panvel, Maharashtra. He founded Poona Native Institutions, PNA later to be known as Maharashtra Education Society which today administers about 77 institutions all over Maharashtra. He collected a revolutionary group from amongst the tribes of the area such Kolis, Bhils and Dhangars of about 300 insurgents who raided British institutions and gathered money to be spent amongst the famine stuck areas. He hid himself in Hyderabad and collected more revolutionaries in that area. But then some traitor betrayed him which led to his arrest after a fierce fight on 20. 8. 1877. He was brought back to Pune where he was defended by the well-known lawyer Ganesh Vasudev Joshi popularly called Sarvajanik Kaka. He was given life-imprisonment and he was confined to the Aden jail. He escaped from the confinement only to be re-arrested again. Finally he died on 17. 2. 1883. Bankim Chandra Chattopadhyay's novel Anandmath has been inspired by the life and heroics of Vasudev. In 1984, the Indian Postal Department issued a stamp in his honour. A chowk in South Mumbai near the Metro Theater is named after him.

Sir Surendranath Banerjee (10 November 1848 – 6 August 1925)–The founding of the Indian National Congress in December 1885 was preceded by the establishment of another body of like-minded Indians when Sir Surendra Nath founded an earlier association called the Indian Association which was founded in July 1876. Even before the INC came into being, it was widely realized by many Indians that there ought to be a body of like-minded Indians who could deliberate upon the problems which they were facing. Hence this Association founded by Sir Surendra Nath.

Kashinath Trimbak Telang (20 August 1850 – 1 September 1893)–Kashinath Trimbak Telang was a member of the famous triumvirate, the other two members were Sir Phirozeshah Mehta and Badruddin Tyebji. He was one of the leading lawyers of Bombay who was later elevated as a Judge of the same High Court. He had the distinction of being allowed by the Bombay High Court to practise on the original side of the High court of Bombay and in this manner, he became the first Indian to hold this honour.

He was proficient in the English language and in Sanskrit. He was an indologist of great distinction. He translated Shrimad Bhagwat Gita in English. He was also a writer of eminence in his mother tongue Marathi.

He has the distinction of being the first Secretary of the Indian National Congress when it was started in 1885.

Swami Shraddhanand (22. 02. 1856–25. 12. 1926)–He was born in Talwan village of district Jalandhar. His first name was Brihaspati Vij and he was also known as Mahatma Munshi Ram. A few disturbing events early in his life had a profound effect upon his psyche and he became an atheist. He was a lawyer for sometime. He came under the influence of Maharshi Dayanand Saraswati. Therefore, he was drawn towards the Arya Samaj movement. He started his political career with the Indian National Congress under the influence of Mahatma Gandhi. He attended the Congress session of 1920 following the Jallianwala Baag incident. But by this time, he drifted away not only from the policies of the INC, but he also began to concentrate more in the field of reforms in the Hindu society and community. By 1923, he launched the Shuddhi-karan movement and in this manner, he courted controversy which finally resulted in his assassination on 25. 12. 1926.

Mathuradas Trikumji —He was grand-son of sister of Mahatma Gandhi namely Muliben and son of Mulibens daughter Anandiben. He was already impressed by the work of Mahatma Gandhi in South Africa, He met him in 1915 and thereafter, he associated himself in almost all the activities of the Mahatma during the struggle for independence. He compiled and collected the philosophy of the Mahatma and also translated some of his works from English and Marathi. He was elected to the Bombay Municipality. He was so close to him that he could advise him on at least two occasions once in 1924 and then again in 1934 to leave the Congress in view of the fact that there were so many differences of opinion by other leaders with the Mahatma and it appeared to him that not many of them were listening to him, It is to be noted that the Mahatma himself took a break from active politics some times during the mid-thirties and devoted his time for social service projects such as removal of untouchability and the opening of the temples to them through-out the country.

Ganesh Agarkar (14 July 1856 – 17 June 1895)–He was one of the prominent social reformers of Maharashtra. He was a companion of Bal Gangadhar Tilak since their college days. They edited two periodicals namely Maratha and Kesari which are responsible for the resurgence of nationalism in India by the end of the nineteenth century. Agarkar edited the Marathi language Kesari while Tilak edited the English language Maratha. But after some time, they fell out and Agarkar started his own Sudharak. While Agarkar emphasized the social aspect before the political aspect, Tilak laid stress upon the political aspect before the social aspect. Agarkar opposed the caste system, untouchability and other social evils, He promoted widow-remarriages.

Gooty Kesava Pillai Diwan Bahadur Pattu Kesava Pillai (1860 – 1933)–Gooty Kesahv Pillai started his career as a journalist with the Hindu as a correspondent of Gooty and therefore, he was called Gooty. He was the representative from this place in the first session of the Indian National Congress which was held in Bombay in 1885 December. He was one of the leading legislators of the Madras Legislative Council. He was elected to this body for a period of 22 years consecutively after winning eight electrons in a row. He fought for better treatment to the freedom fighters in the British jails. He also promoted jail reforms. He was also a member of the Madras Forest Commission.

Sushil Kumar Rudra (7. 1. 1861—29. 6. 1925)–Sushil Kumar Rudra was the first Indian principal of the prestigious St. Stephens College of New Delhi. The School prospered under his leadership. He was also one of the founding members of the equally prestigious Modern School of New Delhi.

He was very sympathetic with the national cause for freedom. Mahatma Gandhi stayed in his residence immediately after his return from South Africa. Deshbandhu C. F.. Andrews was friendly with him. He was close to almost all the leading lights of the freedom movements.

Sir Prabhashankar Pattani (15. 4. 1862 -16. 2. 1938)–-He was the Prime Minister of Bhavnagar State of Gujarat. He was one of the close associates of Mohandas since his school days in Rajkot. While Mohandas was in South Africa, he remained in close touch with him and he took keen interest in the welfare of the British Indians there. When Mohandas returned to India in 1915, Pattani associated himself with him in the affairs of India. But he differed with Mohandas with respect to his methods of non violence, its interpretation and the results. When the movement of 1922 resulted in violence in some parts of the country, Pattani advised Mohandas that such violence was bringing adverse publicity to the doctrine. So Mohandas withdrew the movement. He advised him to attend the second RTC in London. He was a philanthropist and he donated freely to the needy persons. He was knighted by the British Government for his services.

Hakim Ajmal Khan (1868-1927)–He was one of the founders of the Jamia Millia Islamia University, New Delhi and also of the Unani Tibbia College, Karol Bagh New Delhi. He used to contribute to the Urdu paper *Akmal-ul-Akbar* which was launched by his family.

He was one of the members of the delegations of the Muslim leaders under the Aga Khan who waited upon the Viceroy in Simla in 1906 with a charter of their demands wherein they demanded rights and interests for their community. He is one of the founders of the Muslim League in India in Dacca in December 1906. He also founded the Unani Dawakhana in Delhi. He is one of the pioneers of the Unani system of medicine in India. He was a nationalist crusader who had the distinction of presiding over the sessions of both the Indian National Congress and the Indian Muslim League. He was friendly with Mahatma Gandhi, Maulana Abul Kalam Azad, the Ali Brothers and almost all the leaders of those times. He participated in the Khilafat Movement and was a member of the Khilafat Committee.

Amritlal Vithaldas Thakkar–Thakkar Bapa (29 November 1869 – 20 January 1951)–Thakkar Bapa is an example of a civil engineer turned social worker-social-reformer whom Mahatma Gandhi popularized as Thakkar Bapa.

He obtained his degree in Civil engineering from Poona University in 1890. Thereafter, he went to East Africa on an assignment where he helped Uganda in the construction of their first railway line. He was a civil engineer with the Bombay Municipality and he was the Chief Engineer in Sangli. Just then he had an opportunity to come in contact with the poor colonies of Bombay which totally changed his perception towards life.

He resigned from the service as an engineer in 1914 and he decided to devote his entire life for the up-liftment of the poor sections of the Indian society in general but the members of the Scheduled Castes and Scheduled Tribes like the Bhils of Orissa, Madhya Pradesh and Bihar. He had already joined the Servants of India Society in 1917 and he aligned his social-services through the channel of the Society. He established the Bhil Seva Mandal in Dahod Gujarat in 1922. In 1939, he set up an Ashram in Rayagada for the benefit of the SC and ST boys and girls and an association with the Servants of India Society.

Thakkar Bapa was very close to Mahatma Gandhi in all of his movements. He accompanied him in Noakhali in 1946-47 during the carnage following the partition of the country. He was a member of several of the Gandhian associations.

Dr. Balkrishna Sivram Moonje (12. 12. 1872–3. 3. 1948)– Born in Bilaspur in old C. P. and Berar which is now in Chhattisgarh, he obtained his M. B. B. S. from Grant Medical College Bombay now Mumbai in 1898. He was appointed as Medical Officer Bombay Municipal Corporation. He served in the Boers War of 1901 in South Africa as a Kings Commissioned Officer. On return to India, he joined the freedom struggle by firstly participating in the Surat Session of the Indian National Congress of 1907. He joined the extremists wing of the Party by siding with Bal Gangadhar Tilak. He launched the Marathi news-paper Daily Maharashtra from Nagpur. He left the INC in 1920 arising out of his differences with Gandhiji on the policy of total non-violence. He joined the Hindutva philosophy of Hindu Mahasabha. He was the President of the Hindu Mahasabha from 1927 to 1937. He helped Dr. Hedgewar in founding the Rashtriya Swayamsevak Sangh in 1925.

Maulana Shaukat Ali (10. 3. 1873–26. 11. 1938)–Maulana Shaukat Ali and his brother Maulana Mohammad Ali Jauhar are known in the history of the freedom movement as the Ali Brothers. For his role in the agitation against the Rowlatt Act and the Jallianwala incident, he was jailed in 1919. He was one of the leading lights in the Khilafat Movement. He presided over the Khilafat Conference. He was very friendly with Mahatma Gandhi and he toured the entire country extensively along with him. But later he moved away from him and also from the Congress Party under the influence of the Pakistan Movement. Until that point of time, he was actively associated with various civil and non –cooperation movements and he was jailed in 1921 to 1923. He opposed the Nehru Report of 1928 on the issue of separate electorates for Muslims and then he joined the Indian Muslim League in 1936. He now began to support the policies of Mohammad Ali Jinnah for a separate state for his community. In the company of his younger brother Mohammad Ali, he founded a Urdu weekly Hamdard and an English weekly Comrade

Mangalamma Ganapathi Agraharam Annadhurai Ayyar Natesan (25 August 1873–29 April 1948) He was born in Thanjavur district of Madras, now Tamil Nadu. After graduating in Arts from the Presidency College Madras, he started his career as a publisher by starting his own publishing company styled as G. A. Natesan & Co. - in 1987. In 1900, he started the Indian Review, a monthly publication in English. When Mohandas visited Madras in 1915 from South Africa during his tour of the country for one year in 1915 or so, he stayed in the house of Natesan at Thambu Chetty Street George Town from 17. 4. 1915 to 8. 5. 1915.

In politics, he was a liberal and he believed in constitutional methods rather than the agitational means. He published a biographical book written on Mahatma Gandhi by H. S. L Pollock in 1909. In 1911, he published another book on the same subject written by one of his closest friends Dr. Pranlal Ji Mehta. He left the Indian National Congress in 1918 and joined the National Liberal Federation of India.

Some of the subjects of his publications were Sir William Wadderburn, Sir Dinshaw Eduljee Wacha, John Morley, P. C. Ray, Mahatma Gandhi and others.

Syed Fazl-ul-Hasan or Maulana Hasrat Mohani (14. 10. 1875–13. 5. 1951)–Maulana Hasrat Mohani was one of the truest and genuine champions of communal harmony. He decided to remain in India after partition. He was a noted Urdu poet, a practising Muslim and yet a lover of Krishna consciousness who composed lyrics in praise of Lord Krishna. He was such an unique blend of secular and cosmopolitan philosophy. Functions are held both in India and Pakistan to pay tributes to him each year on his death anniversary. Despite this record, this great patriot has not received the same highlight which he deserves.

He was associated both with the Indian National Congress and the Indian Muslim League since its inception in 1906. He was a product of the Muhammadan Anglo Oriental College, Aligarh which later came to be known as the Aligarh Muslim University. He demanded complete independence for India as early as in 1921, the same year when he coined the legendary slogan " Inqilab Zindabad ' which became the clarion call of all the great revolutionaries such as Sardar Bhagat Singh and Ram Prasad Bismil.

Maulana was a true champion of the interests of his community. But still then, he did not support the partition of India and the Pakistan Movement. He did not stand for the Two-Nation theory of Mohammad Ali Jinnah. He was elected to the Constituent Assembly of India and was associated with Dr. B. R. Ambedkar in the framing of the Constitution of India. After partition and birth of Pakistan, he opted to stay on in India. In one of the debates in the Constituent Assembly, he famously said that he was here to safeguard the interests of his community. Maulana was a no mean journalist also. He started Urdu-i-Mualla in Urdu from Lucknow and Mustaqil from Kanpur. Many of his ghazals are still popular even today both in India and Pakistan.

Inayat-ullah Khan Mashriqi–He founded the Khaksar movement of 1930 and he opposed the partition of India. He preached the university of all religions. He stayed back in Pakistan and he died in Lahore on 27. 8. 1963.

Abdul Qayum Ansari–He was the President of the All India Momin Conference. He opposed the two-nation theory of Mohammad Ali Jinnah and he also, therefore, opposed the partition of India

Babu Brij Kishor Prasad (1877- 1946)–He was one of the leading lawyers of Champaran, Patna and Bihar. He took a very active part in the Champaran Movement of 1917 along with Mahatma Gandhi, Dr. Rajendra Prasad and others. His daughter Prabhavati was married to Babu Jaiprakash Narayan. He associated himself with all the activities of the Mahatma when-ever he visited Bihar.

Maulana Mohammad Ali Jauhar (10. 12. 1878–4. 1. 1931)– The younger of the celebrated Ali- Brothers, Mohammad was a product of the Aligarh Muslim University. He was educated in London College, Oxford. Hismother Abadi Begum known as Bi Amma was of nationalist thinking and later his wife Amajadi Bano Begum also took part in the freedom movements. He was a member in the Dacca Conference of 1906 which led to the founding of the Indian Muslim League. He presided over the conference of the IML in 1918. He was one of the founders of Jamia Millia Islamia. He was a member of the Indian National Congress also. But then he distanced himself away from INC because of his opposition to the Nehru Report of 1928. Like his brother Shaukat, he was also one of the leading figures in the Khilafat Movement. He was also opposed to the suspension of the Civil Disobedience Movement of 1921 following the Chauri Chaura incident. He then moved towards the policies of Mohammad Ali Jinnah and of the Muslim League for a separate state. He was jailed a number of times. He attended the First Round Table Conference in London in 1931. He died in London shortly there-after. He was laid to rest in Jerusalem as per the wishes of his well-wishers.

About twenty three monuments, roads and institutions have been named after him in India, Pakistan, Bangladesh and Singapore.

Mohanlal Pandya—He was one of the first associates of Mahatma Gandhi in all of his movements for freedom along with Narhari Parikh and Ravi Shankar Vyas.. He was also a social reformer in the fields of prohibition, illiteracy and removal of untouchability. Mahatma used to call him as dungi-chor or thief of onions because he had removed them from a field which had been attached by the British Government. Mahatma thought that although it was legally wrong to do so, yet it was morally correct to do so because it was not wrong to disobey an order which was wrong and harmful.

Professor J. P. Bhansali: ——He was a true Gandhian philosopher. He stayed in the Sevagram Ashram and looked after its management. He took part in freedom movements and was jailed a number of times. He fasted twice while in the Ratnagiri jail in 1931 and 1932. First time, he was not allowed by the jail authorities to do the bhangi work and the other time he was not permitted by them to do the spinning work. He went on fast on both of these two occasions. Mahatma Gandhi also wrote letters of protest to Major E. E. Doyle the jail Superintendent. He had to relax and Bhansali was permitted to do his choice.

He entered into a 61 days fast in 1942 immediately after the Quit India Movement was over which resulted in police atrocities and violence all over the country. One such large incident took place in Chimur and Asthi in the Chanda district of old C. P. and Berar. The epic fast started in November 1942 and ended on 12. 1. 1943. Even Mahatma Gandhi used to envy the ability of Bhansali to embark upon such arduous fasts.

Pt. Ravishankar Shukla (02. 08. 1877–3. 12. 1956)–Pt. Ravishankar Shukla is one of the leading freedom fighters from this part of the country. He was attracted towards the national cause even from his early days of college education. He hailed from an illustrious family of national fervor. Despite the family wealth and plenty, Pt ji chose to lead a life of simplicity devoted mainly to the national cause. He was educated in Rajnandgaon now in Chhattisgarh, Jabalpur and finally in Hislop College Nagpur. He was initiated to the national cause in 1898 when the 13th session of the Indian National Congress took place in Amravati. His teacher Bhagirati Prasad took him there to attend this session. The local administration did not take this lightly. The teacher was suspended from the school.

Pt Shukla took a very active part in the relief work during the 1900 famines which swept that part of the country. By this time, he came in contact with some prominent patriotic workers such as Bhagvati Charan Dubey, Moolchandra Tiwari, Pyare Lal Mishra, Madhav Rao Sapre, Biharilal Khajanchi, Devi Prasad Choudhari, Seth Govind Das, Dwarka Prasad Mishra, Prof. M. D. Mishra and others who were prominent workers in their own rights. In 1903, he joined the Theosophical Society of India and in this manner, he became known to Smt Annee Besant. By this time, he also developed a successful practice in the Raipur bar and he became known in all the nooks and corners of that part. His areas of activities were part of the area which is today called Chhattisgarh, several parts of old C. P. & Berar including Nagpur, Amravati and Yavatmal and that part which is today known as Mahakoshal.

He attended the 1915 annual session of the INC held in Benaras. Here he came in contact with Pt Madan Mohan Malviya. He began to take active part along with Seth Givind Das in the propagation of Hindi as the Rashtra Bhasha. He became active in the activities of the Hindi Sahitya Sammelan and in the 1922 session of the Sammelan held in Nagpur, he moved a resolution to the effect that Hindi should be established to the throne of Rashtra Bhasha of India.

He took part in almost all the Civil Disobedience and Non-co-operation Movements launched by Mahatma Gandhi including the Quit India Movement of 1942 and he suffered imprisonment in the British jails. For example, in 1930, he was arrested and jailed for a period of two years. But following the Gandhi-Irwin Pact, he was released early as a political prisoner. In 1935, he founded a newspaper namely Mahakoshal from Nagpur to arouse national feelings. Subsequently in 1938, he started another journal namely Nagpur Times with the same view in mind. In 1931, the British Prime Minister announced the Communal Award. Mahatma Gandhi opposed this Award with a fast. Thereafter, he toured almost the entire country espousing the cause of the down-trodden for about one year. Pt Shukla arranged his tour in this part of the country. He walked and traveled about 600 miles along with the Mahatma.

At the local level, he was the President of the Raipur District Council from 1927 to 1937. He was elected to the C. P. & Berar Legislative Council in 1937 and he was given the portfolio of Education. However, the Ministry of Dr. N. B. Khare had to resign along with all other INC ministries all over the country in protest of the unilateral decision of the British Government to involve India in the Second World War.

Pt. Ravishankar Shukla had the distinction of being the Premier of the old C. P. & Berar and of being the Chief Minister of the newly formed Madhya Pradesh. He died in office on 3. 12. 1956. Two of his sons were very prominent public figures. Pt. Shyama Charan Shukla was Chief Minister of Madhya Pradesh while Vidya Charan Shukla was a Union Minister. Pt. Ravi Shankar Shukla is reckoned as the maker of modern Madhya Pradesh.

Satish Chandra Dasgupta (14. 6. 1880–24. 12. 1979)–After achieving an M. Sc. in Chemistry from the Calcutta University, Satish Chandra associated himself with Acharya P. C. Roy in his laboratory in an important research project in his Bengal Chemicals and Pharmaceuticals. In the Cocinada INC session held in 1921, he came in contact with Mahatma Gandhi and this meeting changed his entire life. While he continued with his scientific works, such as he invented a fire extinguisher namely Fire King and the popular brand of Sulekha Ink, he devoted thereafter more to the cause of the freedom of his country. He realized that independence could be achieved by resorting to the swadeshi methods such as weaving and carting, spinning and charkha and common looms. To meet these indigenous needs, he established an ashram of his own design but something like the two ashrams of Mahatma Gandhi, one in Sabarmati and the next one in Sevagram if we could not for the time being consider the two ashramas of South Africa namely the Tolstoy Farm and the Phoenix Settlement. This is his dream project live even today in the outskirts of Calcutta known as the Gandhi Pratishthan, Sodepur or better still as Sodepur Ashram. This Ashram produced and manufactured almost all the commodities relating to khadi. It also taught the art of spinning and weaving, operating charkha and takli. Khadi and khadi products were manufactured here for common consumption. His wife Hemprabha Dasgupta joined him in this work of national importance.

Mahatma Gandhi used to stay in this Ashram during his visits to Calcutta. He spent a week here from 9. 8. 1947 to 13. 8. 1947 while the entire country and millions of the countrymen were readying themselves up to usher in a new dawn of independence. He used to call this place as his second home. Today this Ashram has been recognised by UNESCO as one of the World Heritage Ashrams of India where Satyagraha was undertaken.

Satish Chandra was a successful writer/author also with such books as The Cow in India, Home and Village Doctor and Fountain Pen and Ink to his credit. He also translated My Experiments With Truth, an Autobiography by Mahatma Gandhi into Bangla language.

After independence, Satish Chandra refused to accept a pension and a Tamra Patra from the Government of India stating that he suffered for the welfare of his country and that he had learnt a great deal from his service to his country.

Dr. Mukhtar Ahmed Ansari (25 December 1880 – 10 May 1936)—-Dr Ansari obtained his first degree in medicine from the Medical College, Madras. He then moved on to England where he obtained several degrees in medicine and surgery, such as an M. D. and an M. S. in 1905. In 1910 he obtained yet another degree in Master of Surgery from the University of Edinburgh. He thereafter worked for sometime in the Lock Hospital London. Thereafter, he went to Vienna Austria, Paris, Lucerne and some other places in Europe where he met a number of world-authorities in the field of medicine and surgery. He specialized in the field of organ-transplantation and grafting.

In return, he set up a leading practice in Daryaganj, New Delhi. In the early stages of his political career, he took part in the meetings of both the Indian National Congress and the Indian Muslim League. In the Lucknow session of the Party, he was one of the participants instrumental in the drafting of the Lucknow Pact. He was an active participant in the Khilafat Movement of 1917. In 1918 and 1920, he presided over the sessions of the Muslim League. But then since the ascendancy of Mohammad Ali Jinnah as a communal leader, he almost parted company with him and also with the Muslim League and moved closer to Mahatma Gandhi. He became a personal physician of Mahatma Gandhi. He treated some members of the Gandhi family very carefully. He was one of the members of the Indian medical team which provided service in and during the Balkan Wars.

He was the General Secretary of the Congress for a number of years and its President in 1927. He was one of the founders of the Jamia Milia Islamia College New Delhi and also its Vice Chancellor in the year 1927.

Madhav Shrihari Ane (1880- 1968)–He was one of the disciples of Lokmanya Bal Gangadhar Tilak along with N. C. Kelkar, Kaka Saheb Khadilkar, Gangadhar Deshpande, Dr. B. S. Moonje, Moreshwar Abhyankar, T. B. Paranjape and Vaman Malhar Joshi. Soon after the death of the Lokmanya, Ane joined the leadership of Mahatma Gandhi and involved himself in freedom movements. He started his career by joining the Home Rule in 1918. He founded the Lokmat paper from Yeotmal to spread nationalistic messsages. In 1921, he was elected as the President of the Vidarbha Pradesh Congress Committee. He was pracitising as a lawyer at that same time. But the British Government suspended his sanad as a lawyer for his participation in various movements. He was imprisoned a number of times by the British. He was very popular amongst his fellow lawyers and they came to his help financially. The house in which he lived was converted into Lokmanya Aney Mahila Mahavidyalaya largely due to the financial help of his colleagues in Yeotmal.

He was a member of the Swatantra Party of Pt. Motilal Nehru and C. R. Das. In 1923, he was elected to the Central Provinces Legislative Assembly. In 1928, he founded the New English High School Yeotmal known as the Lokmanya Bapuji Aney Vidyalaya, Yeotmal.

The Motilal Nehru Report recommended dominion status for India vide its Report dated 10. 8. 1928 for free India. Aney was its secretary of the Committee and other members were Sir T. B. Sapru, Mangal Singh, Shuaib Quraishi, Netaji Bose, G. R. Pradhan, Imam Ali besides Pt. Motilal Nehru and C. R. Das themselves.

In 1930, he participated in the Forest Satyagraha of Pusad and for his qualities as a leader, he was called Lokmanya. In 1933 he was the President of the Indian National Congress and earlier he was a member of the Congress Working Committee. In 1941, he was appointed to the Viceroy's Council under Lord Linlithgow. He represented the Princely states of India as a member in the Constituent Assembly of India. He was Governor of Bihar from 12. 1. 1948 to 14. 6. 1962. He became bed-ridden due to several physical problems, but still then he was active in his duties to the national cause. He was twice elected to the Lok Sabha in 1959 and again in 1962. But he lost in the 1967 elections to the Lower House. He was awarded the Padma Vibhushan on 26. 1. 1968, the day when he passed away.

Pandurang Mahadev Bapat (12 November 1880 – 28 November 1967)–Pandurang Mahadev Bapat was born in Ahmednagar, Maharashtra. After his early schooling, he went to Scotland where he studied Mechanical Engineering in the Heriot Watt College, Edinburgh. While in Europe, he came in contact withsuch radicals as Damodar Balwant Bhide, Professor Franxis William Bain, a British who had sympathy with the India cause. In the India House in London, he met Veer Savarkar, Krishna Shyamji and others. He also read through **The Poverty In India** written by Dada Bhai Naoroji. This book had a profound impression on the psyche of Pandurand. He must have leaned towards radical thinking just at that point of time. He began to learn the science of the manufacture of explosives.

Back in India, he wanted that there should have been a concerted armed revolt all over the country to throw the British away from the shores. But way back in India, there could not be such a revolt simultaneously all over the country. Instead there were sporadic incidents of armed revolts here and there. As a result, the entire scheme failed and it was foiled by the intelligence of the British govt. There were revolts and revolutionary activities such as the Alipore Conspiracy Case, the Maniktala Conspiracy and others. Pandurang was wanted in the Maniktala case. But when he went underground, he remained like this for a period of about six years putting on different physical features to hide his identity. The principal approver was incidentally killed while in jail custody.

In the early twenties, the Tata and Company were constructing a dam near Mulla and Neli rivers in Poona, now Pune. The project required compulsory acquisition of lands of peasants and cultivators of 54 villages. Many of them were satisfied with the compensation that was to be awarded to them. But many of them were not willing to give their lands away. A satyagraha was already underway conducted by Vinayak Rao Bhuskute. Pandurang joined this agitation. It is after his successful handling of this agitation that he began to be called as Senapati by his admirers and supporters. The proposed name of the dam was Musli dam. Therefore, the agitation is known in Indian history as the Musli agitation. He was imprisoned for six years as a result of his part in the Musli agitation.

But then, he had to undergo imprisonment again when he met Netaji Subhash Chandra Bose in a Mumbai public meeting, he was again to be imprisoned after his part in the Hyderabad agitation. It seems there was no end to his imprisonments. He spent nearly twenty years under imprisonments. While in jail, he lost his parents and his daughter.

Senapati Bapat was an admirer of Mahatma Gandhi. But then he differed with him on the issue of the means and methods. He believed that force and violence could be resorted to when the non- violent means were not bringing the desired results.

Kopalle Hanumantha Rao (1880–1927)–He founded his institutions in Machilipatnam Andhra Pradesh to train young men and women as to how to implement the Constructive Programme of Mahatma Gandhi. He believed that this was the way to win independence for the country.

Bhogaraju Pattabhi Sitaramayya (24 November 1880 – 17 December 1959)—Bhogaraju Pattabhi Sitaramayya obtained his degree of medicine MBBS from the Madras Medical College, started his medical practice and soon set up his mark in this field. But then the national cause attracted him towards itself. He was now in the freedom main-stream.

He attended the Lucknow session of the Congress held in 1916. It is because of his initiative that a separate chapter of Congress was established in Andhra Pradesh in 1918. He went on to become its President in 1937 to 1940. In the 1939 session of the Indian National Congress held in Tripuri, Sitaramayya was the official candidate sponsored by Mahatma Gandhi. The old brigade was of the opinion that the election to this post should be unopposed according to the old tradition. The young Turks in the Party fielded Netaji Subhash Chandra Bose as their candidate. In the division that followed, Netaji was the winner by a wide margin. Mahatma Gandhi took it as a personal defeat, there could be no rapprochement, Netaji resigned his membership of the Party, went on to form the Forward Block and then the Indian National Army or the INA or the Azad Hind Fauz and the rest is Indian history. But later on in 1948, Sitaramayyay was elected Congress president.

In 1923, he founded the Andhra Bank which today is one of the leading corporate banks of India.

Sitaramayyaa was an active participant in the Quit India Movement of 1942. He was imprisoned for his role and sentenced to three years. In the year 1946, he was elected to the Constituent Assembly of India. After independence, he was made a member of the Rajya Sabha. He was Governor of Madhya Pradesh from 1952 to 1959.

Dr. Sitaramayya has authored the comprehensive history of the Indian National Congress which till today is supposed to be the authoritative interpretation of the history of this national Party.

Bhavbhushan Mitra (1881-1970)-He was born in Berhampur now in Bangladesh. He came in early contact with Bagha Jatin. He was one of the founders of the Anushilan Samiti in 1902. He was closely associated with the Tagore family and with almost all the leading lights of Bengal of that time. For his revolutionary activities, he was interned in 1916 under the Defance of India Act and was released in 1920.

Jairam Daulatram (1881-1979)–He was one of the leading lawyers of Karachi. Under the influence of Mahatma Gandhi, he left his practice to take part in almost all the freedom movements starting from the Civil Disobedience Movement of 1920 to the Quit India Movement of 1942. In 1930, he was seriously injured while taking part in the Salt Satyagraha in Karachi. He had to suffer incarceration on a number of occasions for his participation. He was elected to the Bombay Legislative Council in 1926. In 1933, he had the distinction of being the President of the Indian National Congress.

He had a career as a journalist also. He edited the Hindu, the Hindustan Times and *the Harijan*. He was a member of the Congress Working Committee from 1928 to 1940 and he a was also General Secretary of the Party twice in 1929 and 1939. He was also the General Secretary of the All India Hindu Muslim Conference. He was a member of the Central Board of the Village Industries Association. He was elected to the Constituent Assembly of India in 1946. He was instrumental in the incorporation of Sindhi as a national language in the Constitution of India. In the Nehru Cabinet, he was made the Union Minister for Food and Agriculture. He was also the Governor of Assam from 1952 to 1957.

Bidhan Chandra Roy (1 July 1882 – 1 July 1962) ——Born to Prakash Chandra Roy and Smt. Aghore Kamini Devi in Bankipore Bihar and into the princely descendants of the King of Jessore Maharaja Pratapaditya, Bidhan inherited the qualities of service before self. He had his early education in Patna and Calcutta with his medical degree from the Medical College Calcutta. Thereafter, he moved on to England for further studies in medicine. He had to make several attempts to get admitted to England. But finally, he was admitted into the St. Bartholomew Hospital and College. Within a short period of about two years, Bidhan Chandra accomplished the rare feat of becomingF. R. C. S and M. R. C. P. On return to India in 1911, he started teaching medicine and surgery in Calcutta besides establishing a successful career as a physician and surgeon in Calcutta. He had the distinction of being a treating physician to Mahatma Gandhi in 1933 in the Parna Kuti in Poona now Pune when and where he was convalescing after his fast.

He was a pioneer in the field of establishing medical health and treatment in West Bengal. He was instrumental in establishing a chain of medical facilities in West Bengal such as Jadavpur T. B. Hospital, Chittaranjan Seva Sadan Calcutta, Kamla Nehru Memorial Hospital, Victoria Institution and Chittaranjan Cancer Hospital Calcutta. In 1942, he was the Vice Chancellor of the Calcutta University when Burma was invaded by the Japanese forces. There was an apprehension of their advancement into West Bengal. This resulted in a large-scale migration of the population from Calcutta and other places. Dr. Roy provided shelter and other medical facilities to the fleeing and needy persons.

Dr. Roy had already joined mainstream India by becoming a member of the West Bengal Legislative Assembly by beating the stalwart Sir Surendra Nath Banerjee. He was elected to the All India Congress Committee in 1928 and he was made a member of the Congress Working Committee in 1930. But before that, he had taken part in the 1930 Salt Satyagraha. He was arrested in 1930 on the allegation of being a member of an unlawful assembly.

Dr. Roy was mayor of Calcutta from 1931 to 1933. He became the Chief Minister of West Bengal on 32. 1. 1948 and he had a long and a very successful term as the Chief Minister of that state.

He was honored with the Bharat Ratna on 4. 2. 1961. First of July is celebrated each year as Doctors Day.

Shri Krishnadas Jaju (1882-1955)–He was one of the followers of the Mahatma in his movements for independence and also in the implementation of the Constructive Programme of the Indian National Congress. He was one of the members of the Working Committee and also Secretary of the All India Spinners Association and also one of the trustees in the Board of Management of the All India Village Industries Association.

Maganlal Gandhi (1883-1928)–Maganlal was the son of Khushal Chand Gandhi, one of the nephews of the Mahatma. He went to South Africa with the intention of building up his future there. But then he soon aligned himself entirely with his uncle when he realized that he was completely devoted to the services of the British Indians there. He worked in the Ashramas of the Mahatma, he looked after the publication and management of the Indian Opinion there. When Mohandas returned to India in January 1915, it was his responsibility to arrange the journey back of the party along with the Mahatma on the way back.

Back in India, he started from where he had left in Johannesburg. He joined the Sabarmati Ashram and he was soon almost the sole manager of the Ashram. He was opposed to the entry of the dhed family of the dalit Dudha and Lakshmi in the Ashram and so also was Kasturba of the same view. But later Maganlal realized that it was better to adjust with the views of the Mahatma. He was a very strict disciplinarian in the Ashram. He helped the Mahatma with sufficient time away from the Ashram responsibilities to be able to devote more time to national cause. So much so that when Maganlal passed away early in his age, the Mahatma was completely broken and he paid very rich tributes to the promising career of the early departee.

Shiv Prasad Gupta (28 June 1883 – 24 April 1944) ——Shiv Prasad Gupta of Benaras or Varanasi was a rich land-lord and zamindar but with a difference. He devoted himself entirely to the national cause of independence of the country and to several philanthropic projects of the Indian National Congress. Mahatma Gandhi bestowed upon him the decoration of Rashtra-Ratna in recognition of his selfless services to the nation.

He was one of the principal donors to the funds of the Indian National Congress. When the Congress held its first annual session in Varanasi in the year 1928, the venue was his residence Seva Upwan and he bore the entire finances of the session. He had purchased the building which was designed by the well known British architect Sir Edwin Lutyen in the year 1916 and Mahatma Gandhi renamed it as Seva Upwan. All the national leaders such as Mahatma Gandhi, Pandit Madan Mohan Malviya, Jawaharlal Nehru and others used to stay in his residence during their visit to Varanasi.

He helped in the establishment of the Bharat Mata Mandir which is a national heritage monument. He was also instrumental in the establishment of the Mahatma Gandhi Vidyapeeth in Varanasi. He also established a city hospital which today is known as Shiv Prasad Gupta Hospital in Varanasi. In 1920, he founded the daily Aaj news-paper as a product of the Jnana Mandal Limited to espouse national views. This paper soon became one of the leading national dailies of the country. When Mahamana was planning to found the Banaras Hindu University, Shiv Prasad was amongst the first to offer financial help to him by donating an amount of Rs. 101000/. He also donated 100 acres of land in mouza Akbarpur to the Indian National Congress to set up the first Gandhi Ashram in the country for the purpose of the manufacture of the khadi clothes.

Shiv Prasad was a close associate of Lala Lajpat Rai also. He visited several countries along with him such as America and Japan and spent a lot of time there to introduce the world to the aspirationsof his countrymen.

Shiv Prasad was the treasurer of the Indian National Congress for several years. In the national cause, he was imprisoned several times.

Khursheed Framji Noriman (1883—1948)After taking a degree in law, Khurshed practised law for some time. But then he soon entered the national politics of the freedom movement. He was President of the Bombay Provincial Congress Committee and Mayor of Bombay from 1935 to 1936. He was elected as a member of the Bombay Legislative Assembly in 1937.

Earlier he had come in prominence for exposing the scandal involving the British engineer George Buchanan for his involvement in the Bombay Backbay Reclamation scandal.

The prestigious Nariman Point in Mumbai is named after him and also a road is in his name as the Veer Nariman Road.

Ravi Shankar Vyas (25. 2. 1884—1. 7. 1984) He was one of the closest associates of Mahatma Gandhi along with Mohanlal Pandya, Ravishankar Vyas and Darbar Gopaldas Desai. Like them also, his arena was largely Gujarat.

He came in contact with the Mahatma in 1915 and began to take part in various movements from 1920 onwards. He participated in movements such as the Borsad movement of 1923, The Bardoli movement of 1928 when he was imprisoned for six months, the Dandi March of 1930 for which he was jailed for two years. He was active in the relief work of 1927. He took part in the Quit India Movement of 1942.

After independence, he joined the Bhoodan Aandolan of Sant Vinoba Bhave. He traveled along with him six thousand kilo-meters between 1955 to 1958.

Master Tara Singh (24. 6. 1885–22. 11. 1967)–Born on the aforesaid date in Rawalpindi now in Pakistan in a Hindu family of Gopichand, he accepted Sikhism as his religious creed. He started his career as a teacher and this is the reason why he was called Master. He gave up this job in 1921 and took up journalism. This work brought him in close contact with the people from all walks of life.

He is one ofthe pioneer-builders of modern Punjab. He was one of the founders of Shiromani Gurdwara Parbandhak Committee which controls the management of the gurudwaras across the country. He was also instrumental in the foundation of the Akali Dal which continues to be the most representative political party in Punjab.

He was opposed to the partition of Punjab in the wake of the partition of India. He did not accept the assurances of Mohammad Ali Jinnah that the Sikhs would be safe in Pakistan. He agitated for an Azad Punjab since 1942 along with other prominent Sikh leaders such as Sardar Joginder Singh, Giani Kartar Singh, Sardar Mohan Singh and Sardar Ujjal Singh. But then once the partition was done, he continued his agitation for a separate Punjab on linguistic basis. He was arrested by the Indian Government in 1949, 1953, 1955 and 1960 for his agitations. As a result however, a separate Punjab was created with effect from 1. 11. 1966.

Master was a noted freedom fighter also. He took part in the 1930 movement and was arrested. He was released following the Gandhi-Irwin Pact of 1931. He passed away on 22. 11. 1967.

Abdul Majid Khwaja (1885-1962) He was a prominent lawyer of Aligarh. He was attracted to the philosophy of non-violence and ahimsa of Mahatma Gandhi. He supported the Aligarh Movement which saw the establishment of the Aligarh Muslim University. But then he did not support the two-nation theory of Sir Syed Ahmad Khan, nor did he support the partition of India on the lines of religion as propounded by Mohammad Ali Jinnah. He worked along with Mahatma Gandhi for the promotion of the Hindu Muslim unity. He had the reputation of being a liberal and a nationalist Muslim.

He gave up his lucrative practice to devote towards the nationalist cause. He took part in the Khilafat Movement of 1917 and the Civil Disobedience Movement of 1920. He suffered imprisonment for six months. He had to return to his legal practice again due to family reasons and needs. Poor health kept him away from active politics thereafter although he continued his affiliation with the Jamia Millia Islamia and the Indian National Congress.

Dr. Satyapal —Dr Satyapal obtained his degree in medicine from Peterhouse Cambridge. On return, he soon set up a good practice in Amritsar. But he was soon engaged in national duties.

After the closure of the First World War, the economy of British India had suffered a down-ward slide, so also has England suffered irreparably. There was discontentment in India on account of high prices in all the basic commodities. The discontment gave rise to revolutionary fervor which was already at boiling point in Punjab. Just then the Hindu festival of Ram Navmi fell on 9. 4. 1919. The festival presented unprecedented communal harmony between the two communities. They decided to celebrate Ram Navmi as Rashtriya Ekta Diwas or the National Unity Day. Preparations were underway since about two months preceding the Ram Navmi day. Two general strikes had already been staged in Amritsar once in March 1919 and the other in April 1919. The British were terrified. They even apprehended the repeat of 1857 history. So they legislated the controversial Anarchical and Revolutionary Crimes Act, 1919 or in short the Rowlatt Act, 1919.

Dr. Satyapal and Dr Kitchlu were the two most prominent and popular leaders of Punjab. Lt Governor Michael O'Dwyer and Sir Miles Irwin ICS the Deputy Commissioner of Amritsar decided to whisk the two leaders away from Amritsar acting under the provisions of the Defence of India Orders and this is exactly what happened when the two were removed by a police escort to Dharamshala which is today in Himachal Pradesh. The news of their detention spread like wildfire. People gathered near the residence of the Dy. Commissioner. They decided to hold a peaceful protest meeting on the day of Vaisakhi i.e. on 13. 4. 1919 in the Jallianwala Bagh premises. What happened on that fateful day is now a record of history which needs hardly to be repeated.

Dr Satyapal joined the Indian National Congress and soon progressed in ranks in the Party such as President Congress Committee and General Secretary AICC in 1924.

Earlier in June 1919, Dr. Satyapal and Dr Saifuddin Kitchlu were tried along with other co-accused in the Amritsar Conspiracy Case for the charges of trying to over-throw the duly constituted Government of the King Emperor by unlawful means and methods. The other co-accused persons are—Badr-ul-Islam Ali Khan, Mohammad Bashir, Pandit Kotu Mal, Narain Das Khanna, Gurdial Singh, Bhawan Nand, Dina Nath, Gurbaksh Rai, Ghulam Nabi, Ghulam Mohammad, Abdul Aziz, Mohammad Ismail and Motiram Mehra.

Dr. Satyapal and Dr. Kitchlu were given life imprisonment. Mohammad Bashir was sentenced to death.

Dattatreya Balkrishna Kalelkar or Kaka Kalelkar (1885-1981) He hailed from the village Kalechi in Maharashtra and hence the name Kalelkar. He did his B. A. with Philosophy as his subject in the year 1907 from Pune and then he started his career as a correspondent with a Marathi daily namely Rashtramat and then he became a teacher in a school in Baroda in the year 1910. On the return of Mohandas from South Africa in 1915, he joined his Ashram at Sabarmati and began to teach in the Rashtriya Shala of the Ashram. For sometime, he edited the periodical Sarvodaya which was issued from the Ashram. He took part in almost all the movements started by the Mahatma and he was imprisoned several times. He was instrumental in the establishment of the Gujrat Vidyapeeth in Ahmedabad and he was its Vice Chancellor from 1928 to 1935. He was a member of the Rashtra Bhasha Samiti which was meant to popularize Hindi as the national language of the country. He was also associated with the Gandhi Smarak Nidhi from 1948 till his death. He was a member of the Rajya Sabha from 1952 to 1964. He was also the Chairman of the first Backward Classes Commission which was set up in the year 1953. The Commission placed its recommendations before the Govt identifying the backwards classes and the necessary remedies for their welfare. In 1959, he presided over the Gujarati Sahitya Parishad. He was part of the establishment of the Gandhi Vidyapeeth in the year 1967 in Velchhi and he was also its Vice Chancellor. He authored a number of books also. Mahatma Gandhi used to call him Sawai Gujrati i.e. someone more than a Gujrati.

The Sahitya Akademi Award was conferred upon him in the year 1971 and the Padma Vibhushan in 1964.

Moraeshwar Vasudev Abhyankar (16. 8. 1886–2. 1. 1935) He was one of the leading barristers of Nagpur. He was a member of the Indian National Congress but on the side of Lokmanya Tilak and with equal respect for Mahatma Gandhi. He participated in the Home Rule Movement and also in the various Civil Disobedience and Non Cooperation Movements. He was known for his generous charities and donations for the national cause. In 1933 when Mahatma Gandhi visited Nagpur propagating the cause of the harijans and soliciting funds for the national cause, Moreshwar donated gold ornaments of his wife for this purpose. The Moreshwar Public School, Indore perpetuates the memory of this outstanding patriot.

Anugrah Narayan Sinha- (18. 6. 1887–5. 7. 1957)–He was always a brilliant student starting from his elementary education upto his finals where he always topped the lists. He obtained an M. A. in History and, therefore, he was appointed as a Professor of History in the Bhagalpur University. He rose to national prominence in 1917 when he actively participated in the Champaran movement along with other leaders. He organised the annual session of the Indian National Congress in 1922 held in Gaya. In 1923, he was appointed as one of the General Secretaries of the All India Congress Committee AICC. He took active part in all the movements such as those of 1921. 1930 and 1942 and he was jailed accordingly. He worked hard during the Nepal-Bihar earthquake of 1934 to provide relief to the victIms. He was elected to the Central Council in 1935 and to the Bihar Legislative Assembly in 1936. In 1937, he was made Deputy Prime Minister cum Finance Minister in the Bihar ministry which had to resign in 1939 in the wake of the Second World War. In 1942, he was arrested and released in 1944. He led a delegation of Food and Agriculture to Nepal and was a member of the delegation to the International Labor Organization to Canada and Switzerland. He is considered to be one of the architects of modern Bihar along with another stalwart Dr. Sri Krishna Sinha. His son Satyendra Narayan Sinha was a freedom fighter in his own right and he later became Chief Minister of Bihar. He was called Bihar Vibhuti.

Dr. Sri Krishna Sinha (21. 10. 1887–31. 1. 1961)–He was a product of the Patna University. He worked as a lawyer in

1915. He soon gave this work to join the national movements for freedom. He rose to national prominence along with other leaders for his participation in the Champaran movement of 1917. Thereafter, he took part in almost all the movements and he had to suffer imprisonment for a total period of nearly eight years.. He became the Prime Minister of the Bihar Ministry in 1937. But the Ministry had to resign in 1939 in the wake of the Second World War. He facilitated the entry of the down-trodden to the Vaidyanath Temple, Deoghar Bihar at the call of Mahatma Gandhi. He abolished the zamindari system in his state and in this manner he became the first Chief Minister in the country to do so. He took very active part in providing relief to the victims of the Nepal-Bihar earthquake of 1934. He was a member of the Constituent Assembly of India in 1946. He is considered to be one of the architects of modern Bihar. In 2016, the Postal Department of India issued a stamp in his honor.

Hridaya Nath Kunzru (1 October 1887 – 3 April 1978) Hridayanath was a Kashmiri pandit. After his B. A. from the Allahabad University, he moved on to England from where he did his B. Sc. in Political Science. He started his career in the public domain by joining the Indian National Congress. But then he left the Congress and formed a new party namely National Liberation Front along with Mahamana Madan Mohan Malviya and Sir Tej Bahadur Sapru. He did not believe in the agitational methods of mass protests, instead he stood for the constitutional methods to achieve all the political demands. This was the point of his difference with the Indian National Congress and also with Mahatma Gandhi for whom he continued to reserve highest regards.

He joined the Servants of India Society under the influence of Smt. Annee Besant and Gopal Krishna Gokhale. He crusaded against such social evils as untouchability, caste system, he advocated divorce and property rights to women. He was a member of the C. P. Legislative Council during 1921-1926, of the Central Legislative Assembly during 1926-1930, Council of States 1936, the Provincial Parliament 1950 and member Rajya Sabha 1952-1964. He was the Chairman of that committee in 1944 which recommended that all the existing railway companies should be consolidated into one combined Indian Railways. He was also the chairman of the committee in 1948 which recommended the formation of the National Cadet Corps NCC. He was a member of the States Reorganization Committee 1953-1956. He was instrumental in the formation of the Indian Council of World Affairs and the Indian School of World Affairs. He was also the chairman of the committee which recommended the formation of the National Defence Academy NDA which is in Khadakwasla. He was a member of the University Grants Commission UGC from 1953-1966. He was also one of the founders of the Indian Scouts and also the first commissioner of the Bharat Scouts and Guides. In 1968, the Government of India decided to confer Bharat Ratna upon him. But he refused the honor.

Gopaldas Ambaidas Desai (1887—1951) He hailed from the princely family of Gujrat. But then he gave up his stately glamor to jump into the national movements. He took part in almost all such movements as the Civil Disobedience Movement and the Quit India Movement of 1942. He was jailed also. He was thus the first prince to sacrifice for the freedom of the country.

George Joseph (1887-1938) After his studies at the Madras Christian College, he went to England from where he did his M. A. in Philosophy from the University of Edinburgh. He studied for law there and he was called to the Middle Temple, London in 1908. During his stay in London, he came in contact with several patriots of the freedom struggle. On return, he started his legal practice in Madras and soon he shifted to Madurai. In Madurai almost all the national leaders stayed in his residence such as Mahatma Gandhi, CR Srinivasa Iyengar, K. Kamaraj, Subramaniam Bharti and others. In 1917, he came in contact with Smt. Annie Besant and he joined the Home Rule Movement. This project took him to England in company accompanied by Syed Husain and B. V. Narsimhan to press home the demand for the home rule for the Indians. But then the bid was foiled by the British by arresting them at Gibraltar and by sending them back to India. He was one of the leaders of the protest against the Rowlatt Act and the Jallianwala Bagh events of Amritsar. He was also one of the prominent trade union leaders of Madurai. He edited the Independent during the 1920-1921 period. Mahatma Gandhi entrusted him with the editorship of Young India in 1923 along with other leaders in 1923. He was one of the earliest members of the Syrian Christian Church from the Travancore-Cochin area to take part in the national movements for freedom.

He took keen interest in the Vaikom Satyagraha for the opening of the temple for the depressed classes. He wanted to under-take a fast for this purpose. But Mahatma Gandhi did not permit him to do so on the twin grounds that it was the problem of the Hindu community and that only a Hindu could take part in this moment and the second objection of the Mahatma was that not everybody was duly qualified to undertake a fast. This annoyed George and thereafter, he distanced himself from the Mahatma. He left the Congress.

When the Simon Commission visited the Madurai area, George was in the fore-front of the protests against the all-British Commission. They shouted Simon Go Back. He successfully defended Kamraj in the Virudh Nagar Conspiracy case in 1933. He also successfully agitated against the Criminal Tribes Act which coloured some of the tribes with criminal character without any foundation against them, such as the Pirambi Kallar and the Maravars.

Saifuddin Kitchlew (1888- 1963) He was an eminent barrister of Amritsar. His great grand-father Prakash Ram Kitchlew had converted into Islam from being a Brahmin. He obtained the degree of B. A. from the Cambridge University and Ph. D. from a German University. He started his career in the national cause with active participation in the Khilafat Movement in 1917. In 1919, he was elected as the Municipal Commissioner of Amritsar. He soon left his lucrative practice to devote his energy and time to the national cause. He was one of the leading protestors along with Mahatma Gandhi, Dr. Satyapal and fourteen others in the agitation against the Rowlatt Act which later culminated in the Jallianwala Bagh incident. Several protestors were tried and convicted with Saifuddin being sentenced to life imprisonment. He held several offices in the Congress Party such as the AICC General Secretary in 1924, Chairman Reception Committee of the Lahore Session of the Party in 1929-1930 where the Party took the historic decision of the unilateral declaration of independence as on 26. 1. 1930.

He was one of the founders of the Naujivan Bharat Sabha and also one of the founders of the Jamia Millia Islamia University, New Delhi, the Swaraj Ashram at Amritsar in 1921.

He was a champion in the promotion of the Hindu-Muslim harmony. In the various national causes, he was arrested and re-arrested time and again and in this manner, he spent a total of about 14 years in the British jails. He was one of the opponents of the partition of India and when the Indian National Congress passed the resolution to accept the division of India how-so-ever reluctantly, he described it as the surrender of nationalism before communalism. He left the Party and effected his affiliation to the CPI and then he began to work for better ties between the earstwhile USSR and India. He was awarded the Lenin Peace Prize in 1952.

Shankarlal Banker (1889-1985) Along with Indulal Yagnik, Shankarlal founded the ***Young India*** and the ***Navjivan*** publications. They later on entrusted them to Mahatma Gandhi who began thereafter to edit them. He joined hands with Mahatma in almost all the movements for freedom such as the textile mill workers strike in 1917 in Ahmedabad, the protests and agitation against the Rowlatt Act and the consequent Jallianwala Bagh massacre, the Kheda Satyagraha of 1928, the Satyagraha of 1920-21, the Salt Satyagraha of 1930 and the Quit India movement of 1942. He promoted the importance of khadi. He was the Secretary of the Bhartiya Charkha Sangh also.

But then the single event for which Shankarlal will always be remembered in the history of the independence of the country is his sentence and conviction along with Mahatma Gandhi in the famous Great Trial of Poona now Pune in 1922. Mohandas wrote a few articles in these periodicals which were found by the British Government to contain seditious material. They were tried before Justice Broomfield. Both of them admitted to their deeds, offered no defence and were convicted. Even while they were convicted by the Judge, it is remarkable that the convicting Judge became emotional while finding them guilty by their own admission

Babasaheb Gangadhar Kher (24. 8. 1888—8. 3. 1957) Babasaheb Gangadhar Kher and Manilal Nanavati started a legal firm styled as Manilal and Company. But then Babasaheb soon joined national duty in the freedom struggle. He participated in several movements. In the Civil Disobedience Movement of 1922, he was imprisoned for eight months, for a period of 2 years in 1932 for his part in the movement of 1931 and for a period of nearly 2 years for his role in the Quit India Movement of 1942 from August 1942 to July 1944.

He served as Prime Minister of the Bombay Province twice, once in 1937 and then again from March 1946 to April 1952. He was awarded the Padma Vibhushan in 1954.

Acharya Jivatram Bhagwandas Kriplani (11. 11. 1888–19. 3. 1982) He was educated in Poona now Pune and he started his career as a school teacher. He obtained the degree of M. A. in English and Economics. He taught these subjects in the L. S. College Muzaffarpur Bihar. He was also associated with the Banaras Hindu University. Here he came in contact with Sucheta whom he married. She became the Chief Minister of Uttar Pradesh later on. He worked and stayed in the Ashramas of Mahatma Gandhi and therefore, the inmates began to call him Acharya.

Kriplani was an ardent Gandhian. He wrote a well-known biography of Mahatma Gandhi which high-lights the Gandhian philosophy. He took part in almost all the freedom movements and was imprisoned several times for his parts in them. He was General Secretary of the INC for about ten years. He was the Congress President during the turbulent days of 1946-1947. He was a member of the Constituent Assembly. He was elected to the Lok Sabha in 1952, 1957, 1963 and 1967. Immediately after independence, he developed differences with the ruling Congress Party and its leaders. He left the Party and founded the Kisan Mazdoor Praja Party which later aligned with the Socialist Party of India to form the Praja Socialist Party.

He was opposed to some of the policies of Smt. Indira Gandhi. He opposed the imposition of emergency and he was one of the earliest to be arrested and detained during the Emergency period. He aligned himself with Lok Nayak Jai Prakash and this association resulted in the installation of the Janata Government at the Center.

Dr. Gopi Chand Bhargava (8. 3. 1889–26. 12. 1966) Born in Sarsa in Punjab, he obtained the degree of M. B. B. S. from Medical College Lahore in 1912. His brother Thakur Das Bhargava was also a noted freedom fighter and a member of the INC. He was active during the Jallianwala Bagh incident of 1919. He took part in movements of 1921, 1930, 1942 and was jailed for his participation in them. After independence, he was the first Chief Minister of Punjab from 15. 8. 1947 to 13. 4. 1949 and again twice later on. He was the Chairman of the Gandhi Smarak Samiti. among others.

N. R. Malkani (1890-1974) He had his education in Baroda, Karachi and Poona, now Pune. He obtained a degree in law i.e. Ll. B. in 1912. But he chose to become a teacher in a school in Karachi. But then later, he shifted to C. B. B College Muzaffarnagar Bihar where he became a faculty member with another Gandhian thinker Acharya J. B. Kripalani This was in 1913. He came in touch with Gandhian way of life by his association with Acharya Kripalani. He joined the Gujrat Vidyapeeth in 1920. Now he was a full time Congress cadre also. He took part in the Salt Satyagraha of 1930 from Poona and he was imprisoned. He was again imprisoned in 1930 and was released as a political prisoner under the terms of the Gandhi-Irwin Pact of Simla. His third incarceration was in the wake of the Quit India Movement of 1942 which was from 1942 to 1945. During these three years of jail term, he produced some jail literature. He translated the autobiography of Mahatma Gandhi My Experiments with Truth and the autobiography of Pt. Jawaharlal Nehru in the Sindhi language. He has twenty books to his credit.

After independence, he was Deputy High Commissioner for India in Pakistan. He was member Rajya Sabha from 1952 to 1962. The Government of India decorated him as Padm Bhushan in 1973.

Beohar Rajendra Singh 14. 9. 1900—2. He was one of the leading freedom fighters, Hindi activists, Gandhian philosophers and writers of Madhya Pradesh. He popularized Hindi in the South and for this purpose, he toured that part of the country several times. Hindi was declared as the Rashtra-bhasa on his 50th birth-day i.e. on 14 September. He was a member of the Harijan Sevak Sangh, Hindi Sahitya Sammelan, Rashtra Bhasha Pracharini Sabha, Akhil Bhartiya Charkha Sangh, Bhoodan Yagya Mandal, Sarvodaya Nyas (Trust) and others.

In 1933, the Congress Party held its session in Jabalpur. Many Party leaders attendedsuch as Mahatma Gandhi, Maulana Azad, Acharya Kriplani, Seth Jamnalal Bajaj, Jawaharlal Nehru, Smt. Sarojini Naidu, Veer Khurshed Framji Nariman, Mira Behn Dr. Rajendra Prasad, Sir Syed Mahmood, Dr. M. A. Ansari, Edith Alan Gray and others. Mahatma Gandhi stayed in his house. In January 1948, when the ashes of Mahatma Gandhi were immersed in the Narmada River at Tilwara Ghat, Beohar Rajendra Singh was one of the local leaders to attend along with Seth Govind Das, Pt. Ravi Shankar Shukla, Kanu Gandhi and others. He has written about 100 books in Hindi and he was awarded for many of them.

Hafiz Mohammad Ibrahim (1889-1968)He was a product of the Aligarh Muslim University. He was the Student Union Secretary in 1919. He joined the Indian National Congress and took part in various national movements. He was a delegate in the 1920 Nagpur session of the Congress. For his role in the 1942 movement, he was arrested by the British. After independence, he was a minister in the cabinet of Pt. Jawaharlal Nehru. He was instrumental in the creation of the Wakf Board Act. He was Governor of Punjab in 1966.

K. Kelappan (24. 8. 1889–7. 10. 1971) He was born in Kozhikode. He started his career as a teacher. But then, he soon joined the freedom movements. He took active part in several movements such as the Vaikom Satyagraha of 1924, the Salt Satyagraha of 1930, the Guruvayoor movement of 1932 and the Quit India movement of 1942. He edited Mathurbhumi in 1929 and again in 1936. He was jailed several times. He promoted khadi and the swadeshi movement in his state. He was popular in his state of Kerala.

Acharya Narendra Dev (30 October 1889 – 19 February 1955) Acharya Narendra Dev was educated in Faizabad, Allahabad and Benaras. He studied law also and he practiced fora while as a lawyer. Then he became a teacher before driving himself into national mainstream. He was attracted to the national cause by the philosophies of Bal Gangadhar Tilak and Aurobindo Ghose. In the initial years, he was with Mahatma Gandhi and the Indian National Congress. But then several leaders of the Party later moved away from the thinking pattern of the Congress and they went on to form another party of their own. Acharya Narendra Dev, Dr. Ram Manohar Lohia and Jai Praksh Narayan formed the Congress Socialst Party in 1934 with their philosophy of democratic socialism. Acharya was of the view that without social justice and democracy, mere political democracy was of little purpose. In other words, he strove both for social democracy and political democracy. In this manner, he was somewhat different from Dr. B. R. Ambedkar who laid more emphasis upon social justice.

Acharya was in British jail for his part in the Quit India Movement. He was elected member of the Legislative Assembly of the C. P. on a number of occasions. He was Vice Chancellor of the Banaras Hindu University during the period 1951 – 1954. Acharya was an eminent scholar who was conversant with several languages such as Sanskrit, Prakrit, Pali, German, French, English besides his mother tongue Hindi.

Hiralal Shastri (24. 11. 1889–) He left a high ranking civil service in the state of Rajasthan to serve his common people. He agitated for their civil liberties and for this purpose, he was jailed for six months. He founded the Banasthali Vidyapeeth in his state. On attainment of independence, he became the first Chief Minister of Rajasthan. He was a member of the Constituent Assembly of India.

Duggirala Gopalakrishnayya (2. 6. 1889–10. 6. 1928) Also called Andhra Ratna. After having his early education in Krishna district of Andhra Pradesh, he went to Edinburgh in 1911. There he stayed for about six years. He achieved a post graduate in Economics. On return in 1917, he took up a teaching job. But then he soon left it to join the freedom movement. He came at that time under the influence of Smt. Annee Besant and her Home Rule League movement. He attended the annual INC session held in Calcutta in 1920. By now he was under the influence of Mahatma Gandhi and his teachings of non-violence.

The service for which Gopalakrishnayya is best known and why he began to be called Andhra Ratna is his organization of a group of devoted workers known as Rama Dandu, i.e. the followers of Lord Rama. They put on bhagwa clothes, sported a vermillion tilak on their foreheads and rudraksha beads upon their chests. In this manner, they took part in the annual session of the INC which was held in Bezwada now Vijayawada. Another outstanding project of Gopalakrishnayya was an agitation which has gone down in Indian history as the **Chirala-Perala** agitation of the same period. These are the two villages adjoining each other in the Guntur district of Andhra Pradesh. The British Government of Madras Presidency joined them together in one revenue municipality with an intention of garnering more revenue tax. The Government hoped to collect Rs. 40000/- annually by this arrangement. The villagers of the two villages felt a very heavy burden upon thenselves. They resented under the leadership of Gopalakrishnayya. He settled about 15000 of them in a separate establishment namely Ramanagara. However, on the subsequent arrest of Gopalakrishnayya, the agitation could not go ahead.

Gopalkrishnayya died early. The office of the INC in Vijaywada is called Andhra Ratna Bhavan after him.

Gogineni Ranganayakulu or N. G. Ranga (7 November 1900 – 9 June 1995) N. G. Ranga obtained a degree in Economics from Oxford University. In return, he became a Professor of Economics in the Pachaiyappa College, Madras.

In 1930, he joined the freedom struggle. He played a prominent role in the Ryot agitation of 1933. In 1936, he was instrumental in the formation of the Kisan Congress Party. He participated in the Conference of the Food and Agriculture Organization in 1946 held in Copenhagen, Denmark, the Conference of the International Labor Organization held in San Francisco in 1948, the Commonwealth Parliamentary Conference held in Ottawa Canada in 1952 and the Conference of the International Peasants Union held in New York in 1954.

He left the Congress Party and founded the Swatantra Party along with C. Rajagopalachari and others. He was elected to the Indian Parliament successively from 1930 to 1991 i.e. for more than six decades which is entered in the Guiness Book of World Records

Sri Prakasa (3 August 1890 – 23 June 1971) Sri Prakash was an educationist, scholar and an eminent freedom fighter. He was the son of Dr. Bhagwan Das an eminent scholar of Indian culture and heritage and a Bharat Ratna. Sri Prakash was himself decorated with the second highest civil honor of the country i.e. the Padma Vibhushan in the year 1957 for his services to the nation.

Sri Prakash had his education in Allahabad and then he moved on to England. He had a History Tripos from Cambridge University in 1913 and then another Tripos in Law from the same University in 1914. On return, he continued in the traditions established by his illustrious father by joining the mainstream India. He became a member of AICC in 1918. He took part in almost all the freedom movements such as the Non Cooperation Movement of 1921, the Salt Satyagraha of 1930, the Individual Satyagraha of 1941 and the Quit India Movement of 1942. He was imprisoned on a number of occasions. Along with his father, he was one of the founders of the Kashi Vidyapeeth. He was elected to the Constituent Assembly of India in 1946. He worked hard during the communal fire of 1946-47 for the restoration of communal harmony.

He was appointed as the first High Commissioner of India to Pakistan where he served between 1947 to 1949. He held the posts of Governor of Madras from 1952 to 1956 and of Bombay from 1956 to 1962.

Balwantrai Mehta (19 February 1900 – 19 September 1965) He was one of the active participants in almost all the movements for freedom starting from the 1920 movement upto the Quit India Movement of 1942 also including the Bardoli movement of 1918. The Salt Satyagraha and the movements of 1930 to 1932. He was in British imprisonment for a total period of about seven years.

After independence, he was a member of the second Lok Sabha. He was one of the pioneer-founders of the Bhartiya Vidya Bhavan, a literary institution. He was also responsible for the establishment of the Panchayati Raj system in post-independence India.

He was Chief Minister of Gujarat during the Indo-Pak war of 1964. He was flying in the Beechcroft plane near the Kutch border along with his wife and his staff members when his plane was shot down accidentally by a Pakistani pilot killing all of them on board the air-craft.

Ambalal Sarabhai (1890 – 1967) Ambalal Sarabhai is one of the best known names in the Indian history of independence and philanthropy. His parents were Maganlal Karamchand Sarabhai and Godavariba Sarabhai. He inherited his family business as a Director of Karamchand Premchand Pvt Ltd. But then Ambalal took the family business to unprecedented heights which have been scaled by only a few others in the trade and business of India. The Sarabhais are pioneers in the field of chemicals and pharmaceuticals. They are one of the greatest of the philanthropists in India. They have a large number of charitable trusts and bodies to their credit such as the Ambalal Sarabhai Foundation, Ambalal Sarabhai Foundation for Health and others. M/s Sarabhai Chemicals and Piramal Sarabhai in1929, Shanti Kumar became the leading scientists of India in space science. His daughter Mridula Sarabhai has been one of the leading women freedom fighters of India. Mrinalini Sarabhai, yet another member of this family was one of the leading dancers of India.

Ambalal was the President of the Ahmedabad Mill Owners Association in the year 1918-1920. He donated a sum of

Rs. 13000/- to Mohandas Karamchand Gandhi when the nascent Sabarmati Ashram was in financial distress. He appeared before the Ashram one fine day almost unnoticed and surprised the future Mahatma with the donation of a sum which was a princely sum at that point of time. However, subsequently when the mills of Ahmedabad were encountering a big labor strike enforced by about 55 thousand workers, Mohandas stood by the side of the striking work-force with the sister of the doyen siding with the workers. The dispute was later resolved with the help of an award passed by the arbitrator Prof. Anand Shankar Dhruva. Now look at the magnanimity of Ambalal. He continued to have the same quality and quantity of admiration and respect for the Mahatma and vice versa. Ambalal continued to support the national cause with timely financial help as and when needed.

Maulana Hifzur Rahman Seoharwi (1900 - 2 August 1962) He was born in a zamindar family of Seohari in the Bijnor district of Uttar Pradesh. Hence Seoharwi to his name. He had his education in various madrassas and therefore, he was brought up in the Islamic culture. Yet he was rooted deep in the Indian heritage and in the aspirations of the Indian ethos. He fought against the British rule for a period of about 25 years and during this period, he was imprisoned several times between 1922 to 1947 for a total period of about 8 years in the British jails for his participation in different movements.

Maulana Seoharwi continued the traditions established by different divines since 1857. After the revolt of 1857, Maulana Mahmoodul Hassan established theTarbiyat in 1877 with the purpose of over-throwing the regime by an armed struggle i.e. the same as in 1857 but on a better prepared manner than it as was in 1857. Their struggle continued for several years despite crack-downs by the British. They had to change their nomenclature in 1909 to Jamaitul Ansaar and now their leader was Maulana Obaidullah Sindhi. The British still continued with their policy of purge against this body also. Now finally it is Jamiat Ulema-e-Hind. The organization of the nationalist Ulemas have been demanding complete independence even before the resolution of the Indian National Congress passed in Lahore in 1929. It is to be noted that in the early days of the previous century, there were many Indians who openly supported the British regime as beneficial to them. Then there were others who advocated the cause of dominion status within the British Commonwealth of Nations. Then Mahatma Gandhi introduced his ' purna swaraj'. Then there is a list of Maulanas who supported complete independence. They can be named like this—Maulana Waheed Ahmad Faizabadi, Maulana Aziz Gul, Hakeem Syed Nusrat Hussain, Maulana Fakhruddin, Maulana Syed Mohammad Mian Deobandi, Maulana Bashir Ahmad Bhatia, Maulana Hussain Ahmad Madni, Maulana Kifayatullah Dehlavi, Maulana Ahmad Saeed Dehlavi, Maulana Habibur Rahman Ludhianavi and others.

Potti Sreeramulu (16 March 1900–19 December 1952) Potti Sriramulu was born in the district Nellore which was in the Madras state. After having his early education in Madras upto the high school level, he moved on to Bombay from where he obtained a degree in sanitary engineering. Thereafter, he worked for a while with the Great Indian Peninsular Railways Bombay. But then he soon gave up the job. In the meanwhile, he was struck with a personal tragedy. He lost his wife and the new-born child in 1928. Soon, thereafter, he joined the Sabarmati

Ashram. Now he was full time in the independence movement and in the field of social and community service.

The first of his several imprisonments started in 1930 when he was arrested in connection with his part in the Salt Satyagraha of 1930. Next he was to be imprisoned three times in regard to his parts in the individual satyagraha and the Quit India Movement of 1942. He was an ardent promoter of khadi and worked for its popularization in the Nellore district. Removal of untouchability was yet another of his field of service. He agreed with Mahatma Gandhi that the temples should be thrown open to the dalits and the members of the depressed classes. He therefore, undertook three fasts between the period 1946 to 1948 in support of the various demands of the dalits including the temple-opening to them. He fasted for the opening of the Venu Gopala Swamy Temple in the Mollepata area of Nellore district. He fasted against the Madras govt with a charter of demands for the benefit of the dalits. He was able to secure concessions for the dalits by way of this fast.

Even Mahatma Gandhi had a word of praise for Potti for his ability to enter into fasts. Normally the Mahatma did not permit anyone to launch into a fast because he believed that not every-body was spiritually qualified to undertakes a fast. But then he had a lavish praise for Potti. He used to say that if he could have a sufficient number of fast-takers like Potti, then he could achieve anything against the British.

Potti fasted unto death in 1952 for the creation of Telugu speaking Andhra Pradesh carved out of the bigger state of Madras. The movement for a separate Andhra Pradesh was under-way since 1910. But no head-way could be made on this behalf.

After independence, this demand gathered further momentum. There were several assurances from the Union Government with Pt. Jawaharlal Nehru as the Prime Minister.

Alluri Sitaram Raju– He belonged to a rich family. But then he gave up his riches for the welfare of his community and also for the national cause. He waged a guerilla war against the British Government, something like Shivaji Maharaj did against the Mughals earlier. His region of activities was the Godavari area and some adjoining districts of Andhra Pradesh. He took up the cause of the tribals, something like Birsa Munda of Chhattisgarh and Jharkhand areas much earlier. He later achieved martyrdom in an encounter with the British police.

Sardar Goutu Lachanna–He took part in the Salt Satyagraha of 1930 and was arrested then at age 21 years. He was again arrested for his participation in the Quit India Movement of 1942 and he was again imprisoned later for his participations. He was a fearless worker, for his fearless leadership in the 1942 movement, he was called Sardar. He was an ardent admirer of Netaji Subhash Chandra Bose and also of the Azad Hind Fouz.

Kameganti Hanumanthu–He organized a protest march against the British Government for their policy of tax collection which he thought to be excessive and oppressive to his people. He was shot dead at age 30 while leading such a march.

Boorgula Ramakrishna Rao–He was one of the founders of the Hyderabad Congress Committee along with Swami Ramanand Tirtha. He took part in the Quit India Movement of 1942 and he was arrested. He took active part against the decision of the Nizam of Hyderabad not to join the Indian Union and to remain independent. He is one of the leaders instrumental in the integration of Hyderabad with the Indian Union. After independence, he became the first elected Chief Minister of Hyderabad State.

Venkatesh Kedgikar or Swami Ramanand Tirtha–He was both a revolutionary by nature and also a saint. He hailed from Latur district. He waged a war against the Nizam of Hyderabad who did not want to join the Indian Union and wanted instead to remain independent although most of his subjects were Hindus. Earlier, he was also responsible for the formation of the Hyderabad Congress Committee along with Ramakrishna Rao. The Nizam arrested him for a length of nearly four months. He took the vow of sanyas and hence he was called a sanyasi or Swami.

Garimella Satyanarayanan–He was a freedom fighter from Andhra Pradesh. He was a poet who wrote patriotic songs. He took active parts in several Civil Disobedience Movements and was jailed several times.

Kishorelal Mashruwala (5. 10. 1890—9. 9. 1952)He was one of the close associates of Mahatma Gandhi. He took part in almost all freedom movements and he was imprisoned in 1930, 1932 and 1942. He was one of the eminent social workers of Gujarat. He advocated the system of divorce to get rid of difficult alliances and the rehabilitation of widows by way of re-marriage. He edited Harijan for a period of almost nine years. He was an eminent author also. He wrote Gita Dhwani, Gita Manthan, Satyamay Jeevan and Vidya Velaye.

Gopinath Bordoloi (6. 6. 1890-5. 8. 1950)–His father was Buddheswar Bordoloi and mother Parneshwari Bordoloi. After his education, he started his career as a teacher and then after obtaining a degree in law, he practised as a lawyer in Gauhati for some time.

He started his political and nationalist career in 1921 by joining the Indian National Congress. He took part in the Civil Disobedience Movement of 1921 and following the Chauri Chaura incident, he was arrested and imprisoned for one year. In the 1936 Assembly elections, the INC secured enough seats, and Gopinath got elected. But the INC decided not to form the Government and instead, Mohammad Sadullah formed the ministry. This ministry resigned in 1938. The Governor invited Gopinath to form the govt. But his govt also resigned in 1939 in the course of the W. W. II. He was again arrested in 1942 for his involvement in the Quit India Movement and released in 1944.

In 1946, the British Cabinet Mission visited Assam during their stay in India. They recommended the constitution of three categories A, B and C wherein various states were grouped together. Assam was placed in the C category. Gopinath thought that this placement would be harmful to the interests of Assam and the Assamese people. He feared that Assam would thus go to East Pakistan. He launched an agitation and in this manner, he protected Assam for his country. After the partition of India, he worked hard for the rehabilitation of the displaced persons across the borders. For these great services, amongst others, he was decorated as Bharat Ratna posthumously in 1999.

Ganesh Shankar Vidyarthi (26 October 1890 – 25 March 1931) Ganesh Shankar passed his matriculation in 1907, but then he could not study further because he did not have financial means. So he took up a petty clerical job and then a teaching job in a high school in Kanpur. At the age of 16, he wrote a book entitled *Hamara Atmotsargart.* This proved that he had writing skill. But then his inclination was in the field of journalism. Therefore, he took up a job as a correspondent in a Hindi and Urdu daily namely **Karmayog**i and **Swarajya**. He began to write for them under the name of Vidyarthi. Pioneer of Hindi journalism Mahavir Prasad Dwivedi offered him a job as an assistant editor in his monthly journal **Saraswat**i in 1911. But then he decided to join another Hindi weekly by the name **Abhyoday**a which was a political journal of those days. In 1913, Ganesh Shankar founded **Pratap, a** weekly in Hindi which propagated revolutionary views and ideals and also the cause of the oppressed peasants of Rai Barelli and also of the workers of Kanpur. The British did not take kindly to this journalism. Several cases were launched against him, he was fined and imprisoned five times.

He came in contact with Mahatma Gandhi in 1916. He began to get involved in national movements such as in the Home Rule Movement of Smt. Annee Besant and Lokmanya Tilak. He was a prominent figure in the first textile labor strike in Kanpur. In 1920, he turned **Pratap** into a daily news-paper. He wrote an article in favor of the peasants of Rai Barelli. The govt. imprisoned him for two years. In 1922 he was released but only temporarily becausehe was again in imprisonment following his speech in Fatehgarh which the govt. thought to be seditious. He was a close associate of Sardar Bhagat Singh and Chandra Shekhar Azad. In 1929, Ganesh was elected to the C. P. Legislative Assembly until 1929 when he resigned his membership. In 1928, he founded the Mazdoor Sabha to ventilate their problems. In 1929 he was elected as the President of the C. P. Congress Committee. He was one of the crusaders of

Hindi to be the national language of the country. He attended the Hindi Sahitya Sammelan in 1930 which was held in Gorakhpur and then in New Delhi. In connection with the movement of 1930, he was again arrested and released in 9. 3. 1931 under the Gandhi-Irwin Pact.

Following the hanging of martyrs Sardar Bhagat Singh, Sukhdev and Rajguru in Lahore on 23. 3. 1931, there was a general strike in protest in Kanpur. Communal violence broke out in Kanpur. Ganesh Shankar tried to pacify the angry and violent crowd. In the violence about 400 hundred persons had lost their lives. While trying to restore peace and order in the midst of such an unruly crowd, Ganesh Shankar was badly beaten up. As a result he died.

Narhari Parikh (17. 10. 1891—15. 7. 1957) He was one of the closest and earlier associates of Mahatma Gandhi. He started his career as a lawyer along with Mahadev Desai in 1914. But then under the influence of the Mahatma, he left his work as a lawyer and joined the Mahatma in the freedom struggle. He was associated with him in the fields of campaigns against untouchability, sanitation, spread of education amongst women, drive against alcoholism etc.

He took active part in the freedom movements along with the Mahatma. But probably his main field of activity was as an author and journalist, as an editor and as an associate of the Mahatma in his movements. His fields of writing were Gandhian thought, education, politics. He wrote a large number of books influenced by Gandhian thought.

He was associated with a large number of Gandhian establishments such as the Rashtra Shala run by the Sabarmati

Ashram in 1917 and the Gujarat Vidyapeeth in 1920. He managed the Harijan Ashram from 1935 onwards. He was personal secretary of Mahatma Gandhi for sometime early in the campaign before Mahadev Desai and Pyarelal stepped in these assignments.

Indulal Kanaiyalal Yagnik (22. 2. 1892–17. 7. 1972) He was born in Nadiad, Kheda in Gujarat. He obtained the degrees of B. A. and LL.B. But then he associated himself more with journalism. He started the publication of an English magazine namely *Young India* from Bombay along with Jamnadas Dwarkadas and Shankarlal Banker. He made it over to Mahatma Gandhi in 1919. He edited *Navjiva*n a Gujrati monthly till 1919-1920. He started another Gujrati monthly Yugdharma in. 1922. He was the editor of Gujrati daily Hindustan published from Bombay from 1924 to 1928. He was in the editorial board of the *Bombay Chronicle* from 1930 to 1935. He started yet another Gujrati daily Nutan Gujrat in 1943. He was an eminent writer in Gujarati literature and he published a number of books in Gujarati. Later in his career, he entered film production by founding his company known as the Young India Pictures and he thus produced ten films in Gujarati.

In the political field, he was associated with the Servants of India Society and with the Home Rule Movement. He took part in the Kheda movement of 1918. He was one of the founders of the All India Kisan Movement. For his part in the movement, he was imprisoned from April 1923 to March 1924 and he was again imprisoned in 1940-1941 for his protests against the British decision of involving the Indian troops in the World War II against the prevalent common opinion. He is also noted for his feat of bringing the National Flag of Madam Cama from Germany.

After independence, he was one of the leaders in the movement for the creation of MahaGujarat in 1956. He was elected to Lok Sabha four times.

Kanji Dwarkadas ——-Kanji Dwarkadas is known as the author of several books which are related to the era of the freedom movements of the country. He was friendly to many of the prominent leaders of those days. He has written several books which provide a useful insight into the lives and achievements of those personalities. They are known as Kanji Dwarkadas papers. Some of them are–

1. Forty Five Years with Labor,

2. India's Fight for Freedom-1913-1937: An Eye-witnesses Story

3. Ten Years to Freedom,

4. Gandhi: through My Diary Leaves, 1915-1948

5. Ruttie Jinnah: the Story of a Great Friendship,

6. Bombays Slums: Matunga Labor Camp,

7. Plan for Labor, Indian Labor and Reconstruction,

8. Housing Indian Labor and

9. Mohammad Ali Jinnah

He was active in the struggle also. He supported the Indian Home Rule movement of Smt. Annie Besant and Lokmanya Tilak. He was General Secretary of the Indian National Congress in 1918 and a member of the Bombay Provincial Legislative Council from 1921 to 1923.

Rangnath Ramchandra Diwakar (30. 9. 1894—15. 1. 1990) It was said that R. R. Diwakar was more Gandhian than Gandhi himself. He was a member of some of the committees formed by the Mahatma to implement his Constructive Programme. He was a noted author also. He wrote My Encounter With Gandhi: Mahayogis Life (subject to correction). He also wrote Sadhna and the Teachings of Aurobindo.

He was President of the Karnataka Congress Committee from 1930 to 1942. He took part in almost all freedom movements. He was a member of the Constituent Assembly of India and Minister for Information and Broadcasting from 1949 to 1952. He was a member of Rajya Sabha also and Governor of Bihar.

P. Subbarayan (1895-1962) He hailed from the Paramasiva community of Namakkal district of Madras. He had his M. A. from the Madras University and then he studied in England in the Universities of London, Dublin and Oxford and Christ College Oxford. He obtained his law degree there also. On return, he started his legal practice in Madras High Court but then he soon joined the national cause for freedom. In 1922, he was nominated to the Madras Legislative Council and in 1926, he was again returned to the same body. The Governor invited him to form the ministry. When the Simon Commission visited his place, there were protests all over the place. His ministers were divided into two camps, one of them supported the Commission while the other group opposed the Commission. The Swaraj Party members passed a resolution to boycott the Commission. Subbarayan opposed the resolution and then he resigned. He and his colleagues accorded a warm welcome to the Commission.

In the 1930 Assembly elections, Subbarayan was again returned as an independent candidate. He was a crusader for the policy of prohibition in the state. He introduced a Bill in the assembly of the state to facilitate the entry of the depressed classes into the Hindu temples. But then the Bill had to wait for a long time to enter into the statute records when the Congress govt. came into power in the state.

Even though Subbarayan was an ardent admirer of Mahatma Gandhi from the very beginning, he formally joined the Congress only in 1933. In the 1937 ministry of C. R., Subbarayan was made the minister of Law and Education. The ministry, however, resigned office on the issue of the unilateral involvement of the Indian soldiers in the Second World War against the wishes of the Congress leaders. Subbarayan was personally also opposed to the decision of the Government.

After the independence of the country, Subbarayan was made India's ambassador to Indonesia where he served as such from 1949 to 1951. He was a member of the Rajya Sabha from 1954 to 1957. In 1957, he was elected to the Lok Sabha till 1962. He was re-elected in 1962. But then he was appointed the Governor of Maharashtra. He was a member of the first Official Language Commission of 1955. He was opposed to the installation of Hindi as the sole official language of India. He served as the Union Minister for Transport and Communication from 1959 to 1962.

Subbarayan took keen interest in sports and games particularly Hockey and Cricket. He was the founder President of the Indian Cricket Federation. He was twice President

Cricket Control Board of India once in 1937-1938 and then again in 1945-1946.

The Subbarayan family is one of the eminent families of India. The eldest son of P. Subbarayan is Mohan Kumaramangalam who was a minister in the Indira Gandhi ministry. His second son General P. Kumaramangalam has been the Chief of Army Staff of India. His third son Gopal Kumaramangalam was the head of a Public Sector Undertaking. His daughter Parvati Krishnan was a member of the Rajya Sabha on the CPI ticket from 1954 to 1957. She was also returned to the Lok Sabha.

Hiralli Chenniah Dasappa(5. 12. 1894–16. 11. 1964) – He was a lawyer by profession earlier on but then he joined the freedom struggle by becoming an active member of the INC. He was one of the founder-members of the Party unit in Mysore. For his nationalist views, he was struck off as a lawyer from the list of the State Bar Council. He took part in almost all movements such as 1920, 1930, and again in 1942. During the freedom struggle, he was active in the field of propagation of Hindi in his part of the country. After independence, he was member of Rajya Sabha from 1954 to 1957 and member Lok Sabha from 1957 to 1962. He was Railway Minister from 1963 to 1964 in the Nehru Cabinet.

Shankar Rao Deo (1895–1974) He was educated in Bombay, now Mumbai. He came under the influence of Mahatma Gandhi early in his career. He participated in almost all movements for freedom such his protest against the Simon Commission of 1928, Salt Satyagraha of 1930, Civil Disobedience and Non-Co-operation Movements of 1922 and 1931 and the Quit India Movement of 1942. He was incarcerated by the British

Government. He was General Secretary of the INC from 1946 to 1950. He was elected to the Constituent Assembly of India. He was also the President of the Gandhi Smarak Samiti. He was a follower of the Sarvodya movement and the Bhoodan drive of Sant Vinoba Bhave.

Narhari Vishnu Gadgil or Kakasaheb (10. 1. 1896-12. 12. 1. 1966) He was a lawyer by profession, but then he soon joined the Indian National Congress and took part in the freedom movements. He was imprisoned a number of times. In1934, he was elected to the Central Legislative Assembly. He was the President of the Maharashtra Pradesh Congress Committee from 1937 to 1945. After independence, he was a minister in the first cabinet of Pt. Jawaharlal Nehru from 1947 to 1952. He was Governor of Punjab from 1958 to 1962 and Vice Chancellor of Poona University in 1962. He was an eminent writer in Marathi and English languages.

His son Vithalrao was also a Congress leader. He was a member of both the Rajya Sabha and Lok Sabha and a Union Minister in the Rajiv Gandhi ministry.

Brijlal Biyani 1896-1968– He was active in the political scene of C. P. & Berar, Madhya Pradesh and Maharashtra. He was an active freedom fighter who took part in the Civil Disobedience, Non-Co-operation and Quit India Movements of 19220, 1930 and 1942 respectively and was imprisoned a number of times by the British. He was an MLC in the C. P. & Berar Legislative Council from 1927 to 1930 and member Bombay now Mumbai Legislative Assembly in 1957. The Brijlal Biyani Science College, Amravati commemorates his memory. The Government of India issued a postal ticket in his honor in 2005.

Samaldas Gandhi (1897–1953) Mahatma Gandhi was his paternal uncle. His father Laxmidas was his elder brother. Earlier on, Samaldas edited Gujrati evening paper **Janmabhoomi** for sometime. Thereafter, he started his own **Vande Matram.** Samaldas is best known for his role in the integration of Junagarh in the Union of India. The Nawab of the Princely State acceded to Pakistan against the popular wishes. Samaldas established a Government in exile. Later Junagarh acceded to India thanks to the efforts of the Iron Man of India Sardar Vallabh Bhai Patel. He was elected as a Member of the Constituent Assembly of India in 1946. Princess Street in Mumbai has been re-named as Samaldas Marg in his honor.

Meher Chand Khanna (9 1. 6. 1897–10. 7. 1970) He had his education in Peshawar now in Pakistan. He practised as a lawyer for sometime before joining the freedom movement. He was influenced by the philosophy of the Hindu Mahasabha and therefore, he was active in this movement also. In 1932, he was elected to the NWFP Assembly and he was returned again as such in the 1937 elections. This time, he was a member in the cabinet of Khan Abdul Jabbar Khan as Minister of Finance from 1937 to 1939. He was again a minister in the NWFP ministry from 1945 to 1947. In 1948, he was arrested along with Khan Abdul Jabbar Khan on the charges of possessing illegal arms and he was detained in the Peshawar jail. The noted lawyer Frank Anthonty defended him in the trial. He decided to come over to India thereafter. He was elected to the Lok Sabha in 1952 and he was made a minister for Rehabilitation from then upto 1962. He did remarkable service in this responsibility. From 1954 to 1957, he was Union Minister for Law.

Shripad Amrit Dange (10. 10. 1899–22. 05. 1992) He was born in the Nasik district of Maharashtra. He had his education in Pune. He was enthused with revolutionary views even while he was in college. He protested against the compulsory teaching of Bible and, therefore, he was expelled from the college.

In 1917, the Socialist Republics of the Soviet Union (USSR) under the leadership of Vladimir Leniin was established in Russia. The movement spread like wildfire in Europe and in some other parts of the world. Many leaders in India were also influenced by the Communist philosophy. Therefore, they decided to overthrow the British regime by Bolshevik means and methods. They are M. N. Roy, Muzaffar Ali, P. C. Joshi, Shaukat Ali Usmani, Nalini Gupta, Ghulam Hussain, Singaravelu Chettiar, Hari Kishan Surjeet and others. S. A.. Dange was one of them. They were involved in several conspiracy cases such as the Kanpur Conspiracy Case of 1922 and the Meerut Conspiracy Case of 1929 along with 32 others. In the earlier case, he was sentenced and released in 1925.. In the second case, he was initially convicted and sentenced for twelve years. But the sentence was reduced to three years in appeal.

In 1922, he started an English weekly by name Socialist which was the first socialist journal to be launched in India. He is one of the founders of the trade union movement namely the All India Trade Union Congress ((AITUC) and of the Communist Party of India. The Socialists viewed the movement for independence launched by the Indian National Congress as a struggle of the bourgeoisie against the Capitalist British Government. They, on the other hand, believed in Bolshevik means and methods to achieve the same objective with a proviso that they also wanted to establish the dictatorship of the proletariat followed by the rule of a class society. As a result, they found themselves aloof in the eyes of the general public at large.

Dange suffered incarceration in the British jails for a total period of thirteen years. Some of them were in relation to trade union activities also. The British Government had banned the CPI for sometime. But then the USSR was an Allied Power in the Second World War. Therefore, the Government removed the ban upon the CPI. The representative career of S. A. Dange started in 1946 when he was elected to the Bombay Legislative Assembly. After independence, he was a Member of the Second Lok Sabha in 1957 and also of the Fourth Lok Sabha in 1967. The Chinese war of 1962 had an adverse impact upon the Socialist movement in India. The Party split into two entities, one the initial CPI and the other the Communist Party of India (Marxist).

Harekrushna Mehtab (21. 11. 1899—2. 1. 1987) He hailed from the village Agarpada of Bhadrak district of Orissa. He left his studies mid-way to join the freedom movements. He took part in almost all of them starting from the Civil Disobedience Movements of 1922 and 1930, the Salt Satyagraha of 1930 and the Quit India Movement of 1942. He was imprisoned in 1922, 1930, 1932 and 1942. He was President of the Utkal Pradesh Congress Committee in 1930 and 1937. He was nominated to the Congress Working Committee in 1938 and from 1946 to 1950.

He participated actively in the movement against untouchability and he threw open his family temple to the harijans in answer to the call of Mahatma Gandhi.

He was the first Chief Minister of Orissa from 1946 to 1950 and again from 1956 to 1960. He is also responsible for the integration of a unified Orissa which included the former Princely states into Orissa and also for the construction of the Hirakud Dam in his state. He was elected to the Lok Sabha in 1962. But then he resigned as a Congress member and he founded the Orissa Jan Congress. On this ticket, he was elected to the Lok Sabha in 1967, 1971 and 1974. He was imprisoned in the Emergency days in 1976. Harekrushna Mahtab is one of the architects of modern Orissa.

Shreedhar Mahadev Joshi (1904-1989) He was one of the founders of the socialist movement in India along with such stalwarts as Acharya Narendra Dev, Dr. Ram Manohar Lohia, S. M. Bagri in the early thirties and others and later of the Janata Party in association with Jai Prakash Narayan 1977. He was attracted towards the freedom struggle while still in college. He joined the Forward Bloc of Netaji Subhash Chandra Bose. He was arrested and jailed twice for his part in the movements for freedom.

Yashodhara Dasappa (1905-1980)-She was a noted Gandhian philosopher from her state of Mysore. She was active in the freedom movements despite hailing from a rich family. She was a minister in the S. R. Kranti ministry in 1962 of her state. She married H. C. Dasappa. She was imprisoned in 1938 with regard to the Vidurashwatha incident. She was awarded the Padma Bhushan in 1972.

Hari Vishnu Kamath (1907-1982) He was born in Mangalore, studied in Mangalore and Madras and then in the celebrated London School of Economics, London. He was an I.

C. S. officer who resigned after sometimes joining the freedom movement of the country by aligning with the Forward Bloc of Netaji Subhash Chandra Bose. He was arrested by the British Government for his opposition to their decision of involving the Indian troops in the Second World War despite protests from the various nationalist parties. He was a member of the Constituent Assembly of India who was known for his debating skills. He was twice a member of the Lok Sabha.. He passed away in 1982

Minjur Bhaktavatsalam or Minjur Kanakasabapathi Bakthavatsalam Mudaliar (9 October 1897 – 13 February 1987) His parents were Kanak Sabhapati and mother Mallika. He had his early education in Madras and his legal degree was obtained from the Madras Law College, Madras. He started his law practice in the Madras High Court. He was successful as a lawyer. But then he was drawn into the freedom movements. In 1922, he became a primary member of the Indian National Congress. He soon rose to become a member of the Congress Working Committee in 1926.

He founded a daily newspaper namely **India** which he managed till 1933. He took part in the Salt Satyagraha of 1930 and was imprisoned for six months. In 1936, he won the elections for the Madras City Corporation and he was Deputy Mayor of Madras. In 1937, he was elected to the Madras Legislative Assembly. But the ministry had to resign in 1939 as a protest against the govt decision to involve the Indian soldiers in the World War II unilaterally. In 1942, he took part in the Quit India Movement and he was imprisoned between 1942 to 1944. He was elected to the Constituent Assembly of India in the 1946 elections. He was elected to the Madras State Assemblyin 1957 from Sriperumbudur constituency.

In 1963, he was chosen as the Chief Minister of Madras. This is the last Congress ministry of Madras now Tamil Nadu since then. His ministry is recalled even today for the anti-Hindi protests of 1965 following the end of the 15 years waiting period as stipulated by the Constitution for Hindi thereafter to take over as the national language of the country. The protests were being staged against the alleged imposition of Hindi upon the Tamil language. A number of protestors self-immolated themselves. Public property worth countless crores was destroyed. Finally the Central govt. decided to roll back the policy. Bhaktavatsalam was opposed to these protests. He evolved anew scheme of his own which is known as the three-language formula, i.e. there should be three languages to be learnt and to operate as media of communication, i.e. Hindi, English and one of the other national languages from the list in the Constitution, Tamil in this case.

Gulzarilal Nanda (4 July 1898 – 15 January 1998) It is with great amount of difficulty that this illustrious name has to be included in this list, but simply with the intention to recollect some of the legends associated with his name. Guljarilal Nanda was known for his simplicity, honesty and integrity. He achieved the highest without any sophisticated efforts sheer on the dint of his merits. He was born in Sialkot now in Pakistan. He had his early education in Lahore, Amritsar, Agra and Allahabad. He became a professor of Economics in 1921 in the National College, Bombay. Next year, he joined the Indian National Congress. His main field of activity was, however, the labor problems. In 1922, he became the Secretary of the Ahmedabad Textile Labor Association. He participated in almost all the movements for freedom such as the Civil Disobedience Movement of 1931 and the Quit India Movement of 1942. On both occasions, he was imprisoned. Earlier in 1937, he was elected to the Bombay Legislative Assembly. He was one of the trustees of the Kasturba Memorial Trust. In 1947, he was a member of the Indian delegation to the conference of the International Labor Organization which was held in Geneva Switzerland. After independence, he held several important positions under the Union govt, such as Vice President of the Planning Commission of India in 1950, Union Minister for Labour, Employment and Planning and Minister for Home Affairs between 1963 to 1967. He was elected to the Lok Sabha on five occasions i.e. in 1952, 1957, 1962, 1967 and 1971. He had the honour of being the interim Prime Minister of India on two occasions, once in 1964 following the death of Pt. Jawaharlal Nehru and secondly in 1966 a following the death of Lal Bahadur Shastri. In 1997, he was decorated with the Bharat Ratna. He passed away at the age 99 years in 1998.

Dr Sampurnanand (1 January 1891 – 10 January 1969) Born in a scholastic family of Benaras. He had B. Sc and L. T. degrees, took up a few teaching jobs before he resigned to join Mahatma Gandhi and the national movement. He was very proficient in Hindi, Sanskrit and Pharsi. He was a journalist for a while by editing **Maryada** in Hindi and **Today** in English. He regularly contributed articles in several periodicals also. It is to his credit that he continued his literary interests alongside his national duties. He has to his credit 45 books in Hindi. He was a keen scholar of ancient Hindu culture and heritage. He followed them his entire life by living a traditional way of Hindu life and culture. He joined the Indian National Congress as a primary member. He went on to become a member of the AICC in 1922. He was a member in the 1937 ministry of Pt. Govind Vallabh Pant which had to resign on the issue of the decision of the British to engage the Indian soldiers in the second World War. He participated in almost all the movements and was jailed several times. He held the office of the Chief Minister of Uttar Pradesh from December 1954 to 1960 i.e. for about 6 years which should be a record in the strife-dominated politics of Uttar Pradesh. He was the Governor of Rajasthan from 1962 to 1967. While being the Governor of Rajasthan, he initiated jail reforms. He believed in the reformative theory of rehabilitation of the criminal offenders. He believed that crime was a mental and psychological issue which could be cured by reformative therapy. He experimented successfully with the system of allowing the jail-inmates to come out in the open even as they were serving their sentences and convictions. This is an open-jail system. The Rajasthan Government has launched and named the scheme as the Dr. Sampurnanand Khula Bandi Shivir (open jail). As Governor of Rajasthan, he started the Old Age Pension Scheme.

Kumarappa Brothers –Joseph Chelladurai Cornelius Kumarappa (4. 1. 1892-30. 1. 1960)

Born in Tanjore in Tamil Nadu, he was educated in Madras and later in England where he obtained degrees in Economics and Chartered Accountancy and then he obtained further degrees in Economics and Business Management from Syracuse and Columbia Universities of America. On return to India, he taught Economics in the Gujarat Vidyapith Ahmedabad. It was not long when he joined the national struggle under Mahatma Gandhi. During the course of the Salt Satyagraha of 1930, he edited the Young India for sometime. He was imprisoned for nearly two years in 1942 for his part in the Quit India Movement of 1942. Joseph is, however, primarily noted for his contribution in the field of Gandhian economics. He believed that Indian economics could be improved not by the Western means and principles, but by indigenouus means and methods which were suitable to the local conditions and requirements. He did not believe in free market economics of the West. He was a moderate socialist of a different color. He did not subscribe to the proletarian means and methods of Karl Marx primarily because that philosophy necessitated resorting to proletarian violence and class war. He was also an environmentalist and conservationist of note. He wrote and authored the following books–

1. The Public Finance and Our Poverty, 1930
2. Christianity: Its Economy and Way of Life, 1945
3. Grinding of Cereals, 1947
4. Village Industries, 1947
5. Clive to Keynes, 1947
6. Swaraj for the Masses, 1948
7. Europe through Gandhian Eyes, 1948
8. Peace and Prosperity, 1948
9. Economics of Permanence, 1948
10. Stone Walls and Iron Walls, 1949
11. Present Economic Situation, 1949
12. The Gandhian Economics and other Essays, 1949

13. An Economic Survey of Matar Taluka, 1952 and

14. Lessons from Europe, 1954.

Some other books written by him were published after his death.

Dr. Bharatan Kumarappa: He was a younger brother of J. C. Kumarappa. He was also highly educated in the subject of Economics with two Ph. Ds to his credit. He was also influenced by Gandhian economics and thought just like his elder brother. There was not much to choose between the thought process of these two eminent brothers. Bharatan also believed that the economical condition of Indiacould better be solved and improved by resorting to means and methods which were more applicable to the local conditions and requirements. The brothers noted that India was an agriculture-based country where only those methods could be useful which could advance agriculture and other local and cottage industries such as spinning and weaving. He wrote and authored the following books–

1. Gandhi's Autobiography

2. Darubandi Sha Saru

3. Ishuna Acharan Ane Updesh

4. Realism and Illusionism in Hinduism

5. My Student Days in America

6. The Hindu Conception of Deity as Culminating in Ramrajya

7. Capitalism, Socialism, Villagism?

Like his elder brother J. C. Bharatan also spent sufficient time in the Maganwadi of Wardha and in the Ashram. Bharatan believed that the object of economics should not merely be to advance material wealth, but also to increase spiritual and moral wealth of an individual. He had a good knowledge of the Hindu religion. He was more influenced by the teachings of Ramanujam than by the teachings of Adi Guru Shankaracharya.

Mahadev Desai (1892—1942) Mahadev Desai was the personal secretary of Mahatma Gandhi for nearly 25 years and in this manner he became indispensable for him. The Mahatma was in the habit of taking the passing away of some-one close very stoically. But he grieved when Mahadev passed away in his presence in the Agha Khan confinement. Mahadev met the Mahatma in 1915 immediately after his return from South Africa. He accompanied him in 1917 in his Champaran campaign. Mahadev himself became a devoted freedom fighter and he took part in almost all movements starting from the Civil Disobedience Movement of 1920 when he was imprisoned for one year. He took part in the Bardoli satyagraha and the Salt Satyagraha. He was imprisoned and he was released under the Gandhi-Irwin Pact. He accompanied the Mahatma in the Second Round Table Conference held in London and he was the sole company of the Mahatma before the King of England. Mahadev suffered two more quick imprisonments in 1932 and 1933. During his confinement in the Belgaum jail, he wrote Gita According to Gandhi. However, the book could not be published during his life-time. It was published in 1946. He took part in the agitations that took place in the princely states of Rajkot and Mysore. For his role in the 1942 movement, he was arrested and kept in the Aga Khan Palace along with the Mahatma and Kasturba Gandhi. It is here that he passed away on 15. 8. 1942 aged 51 years. He was laid to rest under a peepal tree where the Mahatma sat silently for hours. Mahadev wrote a diary of Mahatma regularly from 1917 till 1942. Pt. Motilal Nehru requisitioned his services from the Mahatma to edit his paper **Independent** which was published from Allahabad. The British Government closed the news-paper. Mahadev brought out a hand-written and cyclostyled edition so as to keep it under circulation. He was an outstanding translator. He translated John Morleys On Compromise from English into Gujarati, Sharat Chandra's short stories and novel Biraj Bahu in Gujarati, Jawaharlal Nehru's auto-biography and Mahatma Gandhis My Experiments With Truth from Gujarati in English. He contributed regularly to Young India, Harijan Bandhu and Navjivan and to leading English news-papers such as Bombay Chronicle, Hindustan Times, the Hindu and Amrit Bazar Patrika. He wrote several other books also such as Gandhi in Indian Villages 1927, With Gandhi in Ceylon in 1928, the Story of Bardoli 1929, Unworthy of Wardha published in 1943, Eclipse of Faith published in 1943 and A Righteous Struggle published in 1951.

Ranjit Sitaram Pandit (1893 – 14 January 1944) Ranjit hailed from a family of lawyers. He was also called to the Middle Temple in England. On return, he started his practice in Calcutta with Sir B. L. Mitter. But then after his marriage with Vijaylaxmi Pandit sister of Jawaharlal Nehru on 10. 5. 1921, he moved on to Allahabad where he joined the same work with Motilal Nehru and Jawaharlal Nehru his brother-in-law.

He was drawn into the national struggle along with the Nehrus in almost all the movements such as the Non co-operation Movement of 1921 and 1930. He was jailed five times for his role in the movements. He shared jail terms with Jawaharlal on two occasions, once in Naini Central Jail Allahabad and then in the Dehradun jail. He produced some significant jail literature. He translated Kalhana's Sanskrit classics Rajatrangini, Mudrarakshas and Ritusamhara from Sanskrit into English. Another notable aspect of Ranjit was that he was proficient in eleven languages such as French, Germany, Persian, Bengali, Persian besides Hindi. He was a versatile personality. Unfortunately Ranjit passed away very early aged 51 years.

Rafi Ahmad Kidwai (1894-1954) Rafi Ahmad Kidwai entered the national scene by joining the Khilafat Movement of 1917. In the 1926 elections to the C. P. Legislative Assembly, he was elected from the Oudh constituency. He became the Chief Whip in the Assembly. He was very friendly to Pt. Motilal Nehru. He also participated in the Movement of 1920 and he was imprisoned for his role. He was made a minister in the G. B. Pant ministry of C. P. which had to resign in 1939. He was a member of the Party launched by Pt. Motilal Nehru. He is also known for his outstanding contributions in the field of agriculture. In 1956, the Indian Council of Agricultural Research instituted an award in his memory namely the Rafi Ahmed Kidwai Award to promote research in the field of agriculture.

Bhimsen Sachar (1. 12. 1894—18. 1. 1978) He was one of the leading freedom-fighters and politicians from the undivided Punjab before partition and after partition, he shifted his services in India. After obtaining B. A. and LL. B. from Gujranwala which is now in Pakistan. He practiced as a lawyer there for some time. He joined the Indian National Congress early at age 20 or so. He took part in almost all the freedom-movements and he was imprisoned for his role in 1930 and again in 1940.

In 1945, he was elected to the Punjab Legislative Assembly and then in 1946, he was elected to the Constituent Assembly of India. But then his constituency of West Punjab fell into that part of India which is now Pakistan. Therefore, technically, he was elected to the Constituent Assembly of Pakistan. But then he chose to join the Indian main-stream. He was elected as the Chief Minister of Punjab twice, once in 1949 and then again in 1957. He was Governor of Andhra Pradesh from 1959 to 1962 and High Commissioner of India in Ceylon for some-time. He was arrested and detained during the emergency of 1975-1976. His son Shri Rajinder Sachar was the Chief Justice of the Delhi High Court and the well-known journalist Shri Kuldip Nayar was his son-in-law.

Pyarelal Nayyar (1899—1982) He was personal secretary of Mahatma Gandhi in the later part of Mahatma's life i.e. after the death of Mahadev Desai in 1942. He was brother of Dr. Sushila Nayyar who was the personal physician of both the Mahatma and Kasturba Gandhi. He took part in the Salt March of 1930. He wrote ten books on the Mahatma.

Shankar Trimbak Dharmadhikari (18 June 1899 – 1 December 1985) Born in Betul Madhya Pradesh in an illustrious family with a record of service to the society and impeccable honesty. He left his studies early in 1920 and joined mainstream India and the Gandhian movements. His intellect and wisdom were of the highest caliber. His advice was sought by almost all the leaders of the era such as Mahatma Gandhi, Sant Vinoba Bhave, Jai Prakash Narayan and others. He was a powerful orator and a motivational speaker. He lived a life free from any ostentatious display. He never went for name and fame, office or awards or rewards. He even refused highest possible national recognitions simply because he did not want any decorations added to his name. He was the best possible interpreter of Gandhian philosophy and the Gandhian way of life. He was proficient in several languages such as Hindi, English, Gujarati, Bengali, Sanskrit besides his mother-tongue Marathi. He wrote and/or translated about 18 books, mostly in Marathi. He was married to Damayantibai who turned out to be an equally devoted life partner with a similar way of living. She also participated in the Quit India Movement of 1942 along with her husband. One of their sons was Y. S. Dharmadhikari an Advocate General in the High Court of Madhya Pradesh and the other son Chandra Shekhar Dharmadhikari a Judge in the High Court of Mumbai. Another member of this distinguished family Devdatt Dharmadhikari was elevated as a Judge of the Supreme Court of India and yet another member from this family is Justice S. Dharmadhikari in the High Court of Madhya Pradesh.

Dada, as he was popular amongst the public at large, took part in almost all the movements for independence. He was imprisoned in 1930, 1932 and 1934. Dada joined Sant Vinoba Bhave in his Bhoodan Andolan.

Kumaraswami Kamaraj (15. 7. 1903—2. 10. 1975) Kamraj Nadar should rank as one of the stalwarts in the history of the Indian National Congress for his contributions both pre and post independence eras. Let us recall some of the legends associated with his name. He was born in Virudhunagar in Madras, now Tamil Nadu. His father passed away when he was hardly six years of age. So his mother Shivakami Ammal had to look after him and his younger sister. Under these circumstances, he had to leave his studies when he was just eleven years old. Kamraj Nadar is one of the known names, but then there are several legends about him which need to be refreshed in our minds. He joined the Indian National Congress in 1920 following his disenchantment with the British govt in the wake of the Jallianwala Bagh massacre. He met Mahatma Gandhi for the first time when he visited Madras in 1921. He took part in the Non Cooperation Movement of 1922 and was a part of the agitation against the Simon Commission when it visited Madras in 1928. He was jailed twice in connection with his part in the Salt Satyagraha which was led by C. Rajagopalachari in Madras in 1930 and he was released as a political prisoner under the general amnesty of the Gandhi-Irwin Pact. He was arrested again in 1932 when he was taking part in a procession in protest against the arrest of Gandhiji. This time he was sentenced to one year in jail. He was falsely implicated in the Virudhunagar Bomb Case. He was successfully defended by Grorge Joseph. In 1937, he was elected to the Madras Legislative Assembly from the Sattur seat. The ministry was led by C. R. But it had to resign in 1939 as a protest of the unilateral decision of the British Government to take India in World War II without taking the INC leaders in confidence. He was again arrested in 1939 for making speeches against the unilateral involvement of India in WW 2. The Defence of India Rules were used for his detention which lasted nine months. In 1942, he was again arrested for his part in the Quit India Movement and he was released in 1945. In all, Kamraj was imprisoned six times for a total period of 8 years and 219 days.

After independence, Kamrai was chosen to be the Chief Minister of Madras state three times from 1954 to 1957 for about three years, from 1957 to 1962 full term and then from 1962 to 1963 i.e. one year and ten months. His terms as Chief Minister are remarkable for the all-round development that was witnessed in Madras state. He started a mid-day meals scheme in the primary schools and he provided school uniforms to the school going children across the state. These schemes were carried forward by the ministries later on in the state and they are even copied in other states also thereafter. He opened schools through-out the state of Madras with the result that the literacy level in the school education rose upto 37% in Madras. He brought about several schemes for the benefit of the agrarian sector. He provided easy loans to the farmers. He built up canals and dams across the state for example the Lower Bhavani Dam near Erode. In the industrial sector, he established Neyveli Lignite Corporation, BHEL at Trichy, Manali Refinery Hindustan Factory at Ooty, Railway Coach Factory at Chennai and other projects such as sugar and paper factories.

Kamraj contested nine elections, seven times for the Legislative Assembly of Madras out of which he lost only once and twice for the Parliament successfully.

Kamraj Nadar will always be known for **the Kamraj Plan of 1964**. He was President of the Indian National Congress at that time. According to his Plan, an age limit of 65 years was fixed as a ceiling for the politicians beyond which they could not remain in office. That means that they had to retire from active politics just like in Government jobs on attaining the age 65 years. In the follow-up of this Plan, a number of important leaders had to relinquish their offices and seats. The idea under-lying this scheme was to enthuse young blood and better efficiency in the domain of the public services. However, this Plan could not go any distance and soon thereafter, age could no longer remain as a criterion of remaining in public offices. Another important legacy left behind by Kamraj is his simple way of life and living. He was decorated Bharat Ratna posthumously in 1976.

Dahyabhai Patel (1906–1973) —He was the son of Sardar Vallabh Bhai Patel the Iron Man of India and a nephew of Vitthal Bhai Patel, another name in Indian history. Dahya Bhai was educated in Bombay and in the Gujarat Vidyapeeth. He started his career in the insurance business. But then the national duty soon attracted him like the family tradition before him. He entered the Bombay Municipal Corporation in 1939 and went on to remain there for the next 18 years. In between, he had the honor to be their Mayor also. He was in the INC. But then he had to distance himself from the Party of his father because he subjectively felt that his father's contribution to the nation-building project was not getting the due which he deserved. But then it could only be a physical distance because conscientiously he still remained a Congressman. In 1958, he joined the MahaGujarat Janta Parishad founded by Indulal Yagnik, went on to become its Vice President and a Rajya Sabha member on this ticket since 1958 till 1973. In between, he was a Lok Sabha member in 1962. Dahya Bhai was very active in the freedom movements in the foot-steps of his father and uncle. For his role in the Quit India Movement of 1942, he was impisoned from 1942 to 1944. His sister Maniben Patelwon the Lo Sabha election in 1952 from the Kheda South constituency a a Congress candidate. She won again for the Lok Sabha this time from the Anand constituency again as a Congress candidate. Although she lost the 1962 election for Lok Sabha, she joined the Rajya Sabha in 1964 as a Congress member. She remained so till 1970. In 1977, she won from Mehsana seat as a Congress contestant. In this manner, she had a career as an M. P. for about thirty years.

The sons of Mahatma Gandhi

Harilal Mohandas Gandhi 23 August 1888 – 18 June 1948

Manilal Mohandas Gandhi 28 October 1892 – 5 April 1956

Ramdas Mohandas Gandhi 2 January 1897 – 14 April 1969

Devdas Mohandas Gandhi 22 May 1900 – 3 August 1957

Mohandas Karamchand Gandhi and Kasturba Gandhi had four sons, namely Harilal, Manilal, Ramdas and Devdas. Of them, Harilal was born in India shortly before Mohandas left for the studies of law in England. The remaining three brothers were born in South Africa.

Of the four brothers, Harilal had the tendency to take independent decisions. For example, he married Chanchal or Gulab in Rajkot when his parents were in South Africa. He wanted to become a barrister. But then his illustrious father did not permit him to do so. This is how Harilal embarked upon the path of estrangement from his father. In 1911, he separated himself from his father if not from his mother for whom he reserved nothing but the highest possible respect. He used to tell his father that Ba was the reason behind his name and fame. On his part, Mohandas tried to rehabilitate Harilal the best way he could. But he could not succeed in doing so. Mohandas is said to have only two regrets in his life, one; he could not convince his eldest son the way where virtue lay and secondly; he could not convince Mohammad Ali Jinnah that the two communities were one and the same. The life and career of Harilal can be easily divided into two parts, one in South Africa and the other in India. In South Africa, he took part in the passive/active resistance movements against the South African Government for the civil rights of the British Indian contract-laborers and workers. He suffered gaol-imprisonments six times. As a result, he became a popular leader as Chhota-Gandhi. But then here in India, he could not quite repeat the same feat as in South Africa. He lost his wife Gulab in the 1918 pandemic of cholera. Thereafter, his deterioration started more precipitiously. He even converted into Islam in 1936, but only to return to his old religion some time thereafter. He could not redeem himself and his father also could not reclaim him in the national mainstream. There are all the reasons to believe that Harilal could have shone in the Indian freedom movement if perhaps he had his ways and methods. In South Africa, he was called junior Gandhi. That is why Neelam Parikh has called him as Gandhiji's Lost Jewel.

The second son Manilal had the reputation of being the most obedient of the four brothers. He went to South Africa in 1897 to live with his parents there. He lived with them in the Phoenix Settlement and also in the Tolstoy Farm. He looked after the managerial and the editorship work in South Africa of *the Indian Opinion* started by his father. He wanted to transfer the paper from the village into a town for better circulation. But he was not allowed by Mohandas. Manilal was further prohibited from soliciting commercial advertisements for the paper simply because his father did not want the paper to survive in this manner. During the time of the last illness of his mother, Manilal wanted to come to India. Even one of their friends and well-wishers had offered to meet his expenses. But Mohandas counselled him that his duties were of first priority. Obedient son stayed back not only at that time, but even after India achieved independence. He carried forward from where his father had left. He continued the agitation for the demands which the Mahatma had initiated there. He continued with the publication of *the Indian Opinion* right up to 1956 when he passed away. Manilal had one opportunity to show his mantle here in India. He participated in the Salt Satyagraha of 1930. He was one of the marchers who set out from the Sabarmati Ashram in a historical march that ended in the fabled Dandi. He was imprisoned for his contribution in the freedom movement in India.

The third son, Ramdas participated in the freedom struggle of India. He was jailed several times in the British Indian jails. Ramdas performed the last rites of his saintly father in the Rajghat on 30th of January 1948. It was the desire of the Mahatma also.

Devdas took part in several freedom movements. He was jailed a number of times also. He was sent by his father into Madras, now Tamil Nadu in 1918 to popularize Hindi there. He was a member of the Dakshin Bharat Hindi Prachar Sabha. There he came in contact with Laxmi the daughter of C. Rajagopalachari. He wanted to marry her. The Mahatma asked him to wait for five years, never meeting her in between. Dutiful Devdas complied with this requirement. Thereafter, they were married in a simple ceremony. He distinguished himself as an editor of the Hindustan Times.

In his autobiography, Mahatma Gandhi has described why the sons could not get proper education. " These experiments were all inadequate. I could not devote all the time I had wanted to give them. My inability to give them enough attention and other unavoidable causes prevented me from providing them with the literary education I had desired and all my sons have had complaints to make against me in this matter. Whenever they come across an M. A. or even a B. A. or even a matriculate, they seem to feel the handicap of a want of school education. "1 An Autobiography or The Story of My Experiments With Truth, M. K. Gandhi page 167, 2007 edition.

However, he justifies his inability in these words—"... Therefore, though I have not been able to give them a literary education either to their or to my satisfaction, I am not quite sure, as I look back on my past years, that I have not done my duty to the best of my capacity. Nor do I regret not having sent them to public schools. I have always felt that the undesirable traits I see today in my eldest son are an echo of my own undisciplined and unformulated early life. I regard that time as a period of half-baked knowledge and indulgence..." 2 An Autobiography as above.

Sitaram Patwardhan Appasaheb (4. 11. 1894–10. 3. 1971)– He obtained the degree of M. A. from the Bombay University. But he soon engaged himself in social work and the national cause of freedom. He came under the influence of Mahatma Gandhi in 1916 during a meeting of the INC in Bombay. He took part in all the freedom movements and was jailed a number of times such as in 1930 and 1931. While he was incarcerated in the Ratnagiri jail, he was not permitted by the jail authorities to do bhangi work. He fasted in the Ratnagiri jail in 1931 for this purpose. Mahatma Gandhi wrote a letter to Superintendent Major E. E. Doyle dated 28. 11. 1932. Earlier also, he was not allowed by the jail authorities to do spinning work. Mahatma Gandhi had written a letter dated 19. 1. 1931 to the same officer that Appasaheb was not allowed to do so. Later Appasaheb was allowed to spin during his term injail. He was popularly known as Konkan Gandhi.

Seth Govind Das (16. 10. 1896—18. 6. 1974)—Seth Govind Das hailed from the rich family of Seth Gokul Das of Jabalpur, Madhya Pradesh. He was the only son of Diwan Bahadur Seth Jiwan Das and Parwati Devi. But still then, he adopted a simple way of living and he dedicated his life to the cause of the freedom of the country and also for the propagation of Hindi. He was the President of the Hindi Sahitya Sammelan. He was also instrumental in the establishment of Hindi as the national language. He joined the Indian National Congress in 1920 at the age of twenty and he was elected to the Central Legislative Assembly in 1923. Thereafter, he went on to be elected to the Indian Parliament successively for a record period of more than fifty years as a parliamentarian. He was a member of the Indian Constituent Assembly. He was a part of the Indian delegation of Parliamentarians to New Zealand in 1950. He married Godavari Bai of Sikar Rajasthan. She also took part in the freedom movement. Although he hailed from a very rich family, yet he renounced his claim to his ancestral property He received a letter of congratulations dated 3. 4. of September 1939 from Mahatma Gandhi. Sardar Vallabh Bhai Patel and Mahadev Desai also felicitated him on this behalf. In 1942, the Congress Party constituted a Committee comprising of Motilal Nehru, Dr. M. A. Ansari, Vithabhai Patel, Rajgopalacharya,

Kasturi Ranga Iyengar, Hakim Ajmal Khan and others to find out if the country was fit to enter into another satyagraha. When the Committee came to Jabalpur, Seth Govind Das offered them to stay in his residence at Govind Bhavan, Civil Lines. His father was friendly with the British Government. So he was not willing to offer hospitality to the Committee. But finally, Seth Govind Das had his say and the Committee members were his guests. The Committee decided that the country was not fit at that point of time to stage another satyagraha. So the Mahatma decided to under-take individual satyagraha instead of mass satyagrahas of earlier dimensions.

Mahavir Tyagi (31. 12. 1899-22. 5. 1988) Mahavir Tyagi was one of the leading freedom fighters and parliamentarians from the Dehradun region. After his education in Meerut, he joined the British Indian army and was posted in Persia on war duty. But he resigned following the Jallianwala Bagh atrocities. He was court-martialled in Quetta and he was released from the service but without any benefits. He joined the freedom struggle of the country as a Congress soldier and took part in almost all national movements. He was jailed no less than eleven times for his participation in them. Following the disturbances in the wake of the partition in 1947, he worked hard for the rehabilitation of the disturbed persons across the borders. He was a member of the Constituent Assembly of India and also of the Provisional Parliament between 1950-1952 and Member Lok Sabha from 1952 to 1957. He was a Union Minister in the Ministry of Pt Jawahar Lal Nehru. He was a Member of the Fifth Finance Commission. and finally Member Rajya Sabha from 1970-1977.

Sugarmal Gope–(3. 11. 1900-4. 4. 1946) He hailed from Jaisalmer Rajasthan. He took partin the CD Movement of 1921. He was arrested for yet another part in the movement, arrested on 25. 5. 1941. As a result of torture in jail, , he died on 4. 4. 1946. A commemorative stamp was issued by the Government of India in his honour on 29. 12. 1986.

Pandit Dwarka Prasad Mishra— He participated in various freedom movements under the banner of the Indian National Congress and Mahatma Gandhi and he was imprisoned a number of times. He was an eminent writer/author who wrote the Krishnayan. He edited Lokmat, Sharda and Saarthi. In 1937, he was elected to the Legislative Assembly of the Old C. P. and Berar and he was a minister in the cabinet of Dr. N. B. Khare. But then the ministry had to resign in 1939 on a policy decision of the INC with regard to the involvement of the country in the W. W. II. After independence, he was the Chief Minister of Madhya Pradesh twice. He was also a Union Minister in the Nehru cabinet. He was one of the founders of the new Madhya Pradesh. Eminent diplomat Brijesh Mishra was his son.

Yusuf Meherally (23. 9. 1903—2. 7. 1950) He was elected as Mayor of Bombay at an early age. He participated in the 1942 Movement and was imprisoned in the Yerwada Jail. He coined the terms **Simon Go Back** and **Quit India.**

T. V. S. Avinashilingam Chettiar (5. 5. 1903–21. 11. 1991) He was a lawyer by profession. But then under the influence of Gandhian philosophy, he joined the freedom movement. He took active part in almost all of them such as the Civil Disobedience and Non-Co-operation Movements of 1930, 1932, 1941 and 1942. He was arrested and jailed for his roles in them. He was a member of the Imperial Legislative Council from 1935 to 1945. He was elected as a member of the State Legislative Council in 1946. As a minister in the Tamil Nadu Government in 1946-1949, he made Tamil as the medium of instruction in the State. He was a member of the Lok Sabha from 1952 to 1957 and Rajya Sabha from 1958 to 1964. In the field of education, he established the Avinashilingam College of Home Science for Women in 1957 which was later converted into the Avinashilingam University for Women in 1988. He was decorated as Padma Bhushan in 1970 and was awarded the Jamnalal Bajaj Award in 1985.

Achyut Patwardhan (5. 2. 1905—5. 8. 1992) His father Hari Krishna Patwardhan was one of the leading lawyers of Ahmednagar. Achyut is, however, more connected with Benaras. He obtained his M. A. in Economics from the Central Hindu College, Benaras and he taught there till 1932 again to join the same institution in 1966 perhaps because the teaching job was close to his choice. He joined the Indian National Congress and took part in almost all the movements for freedom under the Congress banner. But then some differences developed with the Congress leaders somewhere in 1934 and he founded the Congress Socialist Party along with J. P Narayan, Acharya Narendra Dev, Ashok Mehta, Dr. Ram Manohar Lohia, Madhu Dandawate and others. He took active part in the 1942 Movement. But then he went under-ground like Smt. Aruna Asaf Ali. They formed a parallel Government. He was imprisoned several times for his involvement in the movements. He led a secluded life in the later stages in his life.

Minocher Rustom Minoo Masani (20 November 1905 – 27 May 1998) Minoo had his early education in Bombay and then he moved on to England from where he obtained a degree in Economics from the London School of Economics. After getting a degree in law, he was called to the Lincolns Inn in 1928. On return, he practised in the Bombay High Court before joining the freedom movement thereafter. He was imprisoned several times for his participation in the freedom movements. While he was imprisoned in the Nasik jail in 1932, he came in touch with Jai Prakash Narayan and they founded the Congress Socialist Party along with other like-minded leaders in the year 1934. In the beginning, he had an understanding with the Commintorn International, but then he moved away from the Soviet policies on account of the purge- policies of Joseph Stalin. Now he became a follower of the free-market economy and of democratic socialism. In 1946, he was elected to the Constituent Assembly of India. After a brief respite from active politics, he had another spell as a Parliamentarian, being returned to the Lok Sabha in 1957 from Ranchi Bihar as an independent candidate. In 1959, he founded the Swatantra Party along with C. Rajagopalachari and others. By that time, he was again elected to the Lok Sabha on a Swatantra Party ticket and he continued to be a member till 1971. He was one of the few opponents of the policy of the nationalisation of Banks of 1970 started by Smt. Indira Gandhi. He represented India in the UN Sub Commission on Minorities and he was India's Ambassador to Brazil for about one year in 1948.

Puran Chand Joshi (14. 4. 1907–9. 11. 1988) He was one of the leading forces in the peasants and the working-class movement in India during the era of the freedom movement. He was a radical by nature. He was arrested and tried in the Meerut Conspiracy case along with Shaukat Usmani, Muzaffar

Ahmad, S. A. Dange and G. V. Gupta. He was awarded six years imprisonment. But the term was later reduced to three years. He was released in 1933. He was elected as the first General Secretary of the Communist Party of India in 1935 and he continued as such till 1947. He was the editor of the CPI mouth-piece the National Front in 1938. He married Kalpana Datta who was involved in the Chittagong armory case.

Anand T. Hingorani 1907– He was hardly thirteen years of age when he came to know of Mahatma Gandhi and his philosophy. But then he actually joined him in 1929 at age 22 in the Sabarmati Ashram. The Mahatma was visiting Sindh now in Pakistan. He gave up his studies of law to join whole-time the national movements. Before that, he had obtained a graduate degree from the Bombay University. Anand participated in all the Civil Disobedience Movements launched by Mahatma Gandhi. He was imprisoned no less than five times. He was one of the marchers and the only one from Sindh in the Dandi March of 1930. He was almost a personal secretary of the Mahatma. He started writing the philosophy of the Mahatma regularly from 1941 which continued right up to 1948. These thoughts are available in the Collected Works of Mahatma Gandhi published by the Publication Division of India, New Delhi. They are also in the shape of a separate book by the same name authored and compiled by him. Anand has written other books also– The Law of Continence:Gandhi for the 21st Century and Gandhi on Nehru.

Frank Anthony- (25. 9. 1908–3. 12. 1993)He was born in Jabalpur and educated in the well-known Robertson College of this town and then in Nagpur. He then went to England for the study of law. He was called to the Inner Temple of London and thus he became a barrister. Back in India, he was a successful barrister. But then he devoted his efforts and time for the safe-guard of the rights of the members of his Anglo-Indian community which were in considerable numbers even by the dawn of independence. Many of them migrated to other countries such as England, New Zealand, Canada, Australia and America. He founded the All-India Anglo-Indians Association which catered after their interests. He was a member of the Provisional Parliament from 1950 to 1952. By now he was definitely the most prominent member of his community. So he was nominated to the Lok Sabha continuously from the first Lok Sabha to the tenth Lok Sabha except for the 6th and the 9th Lok Sabhas. It is largely because of his efforts that a provision for reservations for his community was inserted in the Constitution of India which has since then lapsed in 2020.

He defended Meher Chand Khanna successfully in a criminal case in Peshawar. He represented India in the UNO in 1946 and in the Commonwealth Parliamentary Conferences of 1948 and 1957. He was an eminent educationist also. He founded the All-India Anglo-Indian Educational Trust which owns and manages the following institutions–

1. The Frank Anthony Public School, New Delhi

2. The Frank Anthony Public School, Bengaluru,

3. The Frank Anthony Junior School, Bengaluru,

4. The Frank Anthony School, Kolkata,

5. The Frank Anthony Junior School, New Delhi and

6. The Frank Anthony Public School, Kolkata.

Dr. Ram Manohar Lohia (23 March 1910 – 12 October 1967)–
After having his college education in Banaras Hindu University
and in Calcutta, Ram Manohar went to Germany for specialised
studies. He studied at Frederick William University Berlin which
is today Humboldt, University Berlin. His subject for Ph. D.
was Salt Taxation in India.

Back home, he involved himself soon in the national struggle
for independence. In the early stages, he was with the Indian
National Congress. But then there was a division in the ranks and
file of the Party on ideological basis. Many of the old Congress
members like him and Acharya Narendra Dev, Jai Prakash
Narayan and others thought that the Congress Party policies
could not deliver socialistic goods to the common masses of
India because they also thought that under Mahatma Gandhi
the Party was something like a social-welfare Party. So they broke
away at least physically if not mentally. They formed a new party
within the Congress vicinity in 1934 namely Congress Socialist
Party. Dr Lohia was one of them. They began to be called the
Lohia Group or the Lohiaites. After independence, they further
entered into another alliance, this time with the Kisan Mazdoor
Praja Party in 1952. So this in brief is the contribution of Dr.
Ram Manohar Lohia in the socialist movement of India. When
the first general elections took place in India, there were two
social-group parties in the electoral fray, Socialist Party and the
Praja Socialiist Party. He lost an election to the Lok Sabha in
1962 to Jawaharlal Nehru. But then he won a by-election the
same year and he entered Lok Sabha in this manner. He was
re-elected to Lok Sabha in 1967. In the early stages, he was on
friendly terms with Jawaharlal Nehru which is clear from the
fact that he was appointed the Secretary of the foreign wing of

the Congress Party in 1936 by Jawaharlal himself. But then he contested a Lok Sabha election against him in later years. During the debates in Lok Sabha, he used to ask difficult questions to the ruling party headed by Jawaharlal Nehru.

Dr. Lohia was arrested in1940 for making inflammatory and anti-war speeches and he was sentenced to two years imprisonment. He was released in 1941. For his part in the Quit India Movement 1942, he was again imprisoned and kept in the high-security jail Lahore Fort in Lahore. There he had the company of Jai Prakash Narayan. He was released in April 1946. Dr Lohia played an important part against the Portuguese rule on Goa in 1946. He will be recorded in history as one of principal volunteers in the movement for the liberation of Goa.

Ashok Mehta (1911–1984) He had his early education in Ahmedabad and Sholapur. He graduated from Bombay University. He participated in almost all the freedom movements from the Civil Disobedience Movement of 1930 to the Quit India movement of 1942. He suffered five imprisonments in the British jails. He was an active member of the Indian National Congress. But then ideological differences arose between a set of the Congress members on the one hand and Mahatma Gandhi and other leaders on the other hand. As a result, Ashok Mehta and his like-minded colleagues established the Congress Socialist Party. This party had a chequered career after independence. It merged in 1952 with the Kisan Mazdoor Sabha to form a new entity namely Praja Socialist Party. Ashok Mehta was elected to the Lok Sabha from 1952 to 1962 and then again in the fourth Lok Sabha. He was Deputy Chairman of the Planning Commission in 1962 and Union Minister for Finance in 1964.

Differences arose between him and Smt. Indira Gandhi when she was the Prime Minister of India. He was jailed during the Emergency of 1977.

Shriman Narayan (1912–1978) He was a prominent Gandhian. He drafted the Gandhian Constitution for Free India based upon the Gandhi philosophy. He was Governor of Gujarat in 1946.

M. C. Perumal (3. 9. 1912-24. 2. 1992) He was one of the most prominent members of the Mysore state Congress ever since his association with the INC in 1935 being one of its founders along with K. T. Bhashyam. He was prominent in the trade union activities in Mysore along with Shri V. V. Giri the former President of India. He held various offices in the state Party both pre and post independence.

Feroze Jehangir Ghandy—(12 September 1912 – 8 September 1960)– Feroze Gandhi was born to Jehangir Faredoon Gandhi and Ratimai. In 1920, Feroze and his widow mother moved to Allahabad where Feroze could live with his sister. Kamla, Jawaharlals daughter Indira Priyadarshini had already founded the Vanar Sena. Feroze joined this young brigade and this is how he came in contact with her and with the Nehru family. He abandoned his studies and he involved himself in the national struggles of course influenced by the Nehru family. In connection to the various movements with which Feroze involved himself with, he had to suffer imprisonments several times such as in 1930, 1932 and again in 1933. He came in close contact with Smt. Kamla Nehru. He helped her with her illness. He went to meet her in Badenweiler Germany and Lausanne Switzerland sanatoria. But unfortunately, she could not be saved. Feroze proposed matrimony to Indira who was hardly sixteen at that time. Jawaharlal was opposed to this alliance. He even approached Mahatma Gandhi with a request that he should advise and influence Indira against this relationship. But the Mahatma did not intervene. He was opposed to inter-religion marriages. He supported inter-caste marriages. But this time for some reason or other, the Mahatma did not oppose an inter-religion marriage. So finally, Feroze and Indira were man and wife in March 1942. Barely six months into their marriage, Feroze was again imprisoned for his part in the Quit India Movement of 1942 for one year. -They had two sons, Rajiv and Sanjay. It is well known that the younger of the two Sanjay lost his life in an unfortunate air-crash. The elder of the two, Rajiv went on to become Prime Minister of India. After independence, Feroze continued with his career as a parliamentarian. He was elected from the Rae Bareli constituency in Uttar Pradesh in 1952 and again in 1957. In the Lok Sabha debates, he was a fiery critic of Pt. Jawaharlal Nehru. He brought in open few scandals such as Ram Krishna Dalmia take-over of Banett Coleman and the Mundhra scandal of LIC which also implicated T. T. Krishnamachari. Feroze passed away in September 1960.

Dr. M. C. Davar (24. 4. 1913-9. 11. 1977) He was a successful homeopathic doctor and he gave it up at the altar of national duty. He joined the Indian National Congress after attending the Lahore session of 1929 where Pt. Jawaharlal Nehru was the President. He was imprisoned for his participation in the Salt Satyagraha of 1930. He was opposed to the partition of India and for this propagation, he founded the United Party of India. He advocated that there should be a confederation of India and Pakistan once Pakistan was created. He promoted peaceful co-existence between the two nations. He also favoured a no-war pact between them. He visited Pakistan in 1955 on a friendly mission. He worked for the rehabilitation of the refugees in some areas in Delhi and some of which are now parts of Haryana. He was a friend of the Nehru family.

Mahesh Datt Mishra (1913—2006) He was one of the close associates of Mahatma Gandhi and a keen Gandhian thinker. He took part in the freedom movements from 1930 to 1942. He was elected as an M. L. A. from the Harda constituency in 1952 and as a member of the Lok Sabha in 1962 from the Khandwa seat. He was the Head of the Department of Political Science in the University of Jabalpur from 1956 to 1973.

Kaloji Narayan Rao 1914–He was associated with the Arya Samaj.. He was also a poet. He led the rebellion against the Nizam of Hyderabad in the liberation and its integration in the Indian Union. He was decorated with the Padma Vibhushan.

Hitendra Kanhaiyalal Desai (1915-1993) He suffered one year jail term for his part in the Quit India Movement of 1942.

Bijayananda ' Biju ' Patnaik (5. 3. 1916–17. 4. 1997) Born to Lakshminarayan and Ashalata Patnaik in the Ganjam district of Orisssa, Biju started his career with a private airline as a flying pilot. But then he joined the British Royal Air Force as a combat fighter pilot in the wake of World War II. He flew British Indian troops into the Burmese war zone during the War. He also dropped political leaflets and pamphlets there for the benefit of the Indian soldiers who were fighting for the Allied forces. The British imprisoned him for this act from 1942 to 1946. When the Pakistani razakars invaded the Kashmir Valley in 1947, he carried the troops in his air-craft to and fro Shri Nagar and New Delhi.

In this manner, he was instrumental in saving Srinagar airport for India. In July 1947, Pt. Jawaharlal Nehru planned to host an Asian conference in New Delhi. He wanted a representative from Indonesia to attend the conference. President Sukarno also wanted to send a delegation. But he was unable to do so because of the control of the Dutch over all the Indonesian outlets. At that point of time, Pt. Nehru called upon Bijayananda to fly to Jakarta and try to bring a delegation from there. Bijayananda daringly flew out Douglas C-47 (Dakota) plane accompanied by his wife Gyanwati who herself was a trained pilot. She has the credit of being the first Indian lady to get the license as a commercial pilot. They succeeded in their mission by flying Sultan Sjahrir their former Prime Minister and Achmad Sukarno to New Delhi. The Indonesian Government decorated him with two of their highest civilian honours- Bhumi Putra and Bitang Jasa Utama, the later being similar to our Bharat Ratna. This is the reason, amongst others post independence, why there has been a demand in India to confer the highest civilian honour that is the Bharat Ratna upon him.

He is an architect of modern Orissa. He built it up anew by being instrumental in establishing Kalinga Airlines, Kalinga Tubes, Kalinga Iron Works, Port of Paradeep, Bhubaneswar Air Port, various schools and colleges and the University for Agriculture and Research in Bhubaneswar. Chief Minister Naveen Patnaik is their younger son. The elder Prem Patnaik is a successful industrialist in New Delhi. Daughter Gita Mehta is an author in English language.

Dr. Khan Abdul Wali Khan (1917-2006) He was the son of Khan Abdul Gaffar Khan the Frontier Gandhi. He took active part in the Quit India movement of 1942 and was imprisoned. After the creation of Pakistan, he opted for the new state. He was active in their politics. But he could not mend fences with the establishment of Pakistan and he was jailed by them several times.

Shambhu Dutt Sharma- (1918-2016-) At the age of 24 years, he resigned from the British Army as a civilian gazetted officer and joined the national movement. He took part in the Quit India Movement of 1942 and he was jailed.

Members Drafting Committee of the Constitution of India–

Dr. B. R. Ambedkar was the Chairman of the Drafting Committee. Other members were Sir Alladi Krishnaswami Iyer and K. M. Munshi. Besides them, the following members were also a part of the Drafting Committee–Sir Muhammad Sadulla- who was elected as the Prime Minister of Assam after the elections of 1937 and he was later elected to the Constituent Assembly of India, Sir Gopalaswami Ayyangar–he was an expert in the Kashmir affairs, he represented India in the UNO. He was also instrumental in the insertion of Article 370 which has since been abrogated. D. P. Khaitan– He was the founder of the eminent law firm of Calcutta now Kolkata known as D. P. Khaitan & Company which was established in 1911. B. L. Mitter– He hailed from Baroda. He played a significant role in the integration of Baroda Princely State into the Indian Union in 1947.

Sudhir Ghosh– When India was on the verge of independence in 1945-1946, Mahatma Gandhi chose Sudhir Ghosh as his and

Indias emissary to communicate with the British Government to deal out the details of the transfer of power and the other related subjects. He won the confidence of the British Prime Minister Clement Atlee, Sir Stafford Cripps, Lord Penthick Lawrence and Mr. Alexander and others.

Haridas T. Mazumdar: He is primarily known as a Gandhian thinker and author of the following books– Gandhi the Apostle 1923, Gandhi versus the Empire 1932, Gandhi Triumphant 1939, Mahatma Gandhi: Peaceful Revolutionary 1952, Mahatma Gandhi: A Prophetic Voice 1963 and The Grammar of Sociology 1966. He attended the Congress session of 1929 held at Lahore and thereafter, he stayed with Mahatma Gandhi in the Sabarmati Ashram from January to March 1930. He took part in the Dandi March and attended the Round Table Conference with him in London 1931.

Dattopant Bapurao Thengadi (1920–2004) Early in his career, he was a lawyer by profession. But then he joined the freedom struggle by being a member of the Hindustan Socialist Republican Association HRA. He is primarily known as a leading Hindu ideologue. He was influenced by the philosophy of Guru Golwalkar, he became a member of the Rashtriya Swayam Sevak Sangh RSS in short and remained a Sangh pracharak all throughout his life. He was a leading trade unionist also who was a founder member of Bharatiya Mazdoor Sangh, Bhartiya Kisan Sangh and some railway unions. He was also instrumental in the founding of Akhil Bhartiya Vidyarathi Parishad, Akhil Bhartiya Adhivakta Parishad and Bhartiya Vicharan Kendra. For the freedom of the country, he held revolutionary views, as a trade unionist, he was almost a communist, but as a Hindu ideologue, he advocated the Hindu way of Sanatan Dharma for the economic upliftment of his countrymen. He was a widely traveled person. He visited several countries all over the world as a member of various Indian delegations. He refused the decoration as a Padma Bhushan.

V. Kalyanam (born 15. 8. 1922— He was one the personal secretaries of Mahatma Gandhi during 19443—1948. He was with him when he was assassinated on 30. 1. 1948.

Ammembala Balappa-23. 2. 1922–15. 4. 2014– At the age of 20 years, he joined the freedom movement. He took active part in the Quit India Movement of 1942. He had revolutionary ideas also, so he planted a bomb in the District Court Comple in Mangalore. He was arrested and jailed in the Vellore Central Jail where he had the company of P. V. Narsimha Rao.

The triumvirate of the Chapekar Brothers–

Damodar Hari Chapekar (25. 6. 1869-18. 4. 1898), Balkrishna Hari Chapekar (1873-12. 5. 1899) and Vasudev Hari Chapekar (1880-8. 5. 1899)

The lives of these patriot martyrs coincided with the resurgence of the cultural, social and religious renaissance started by LokManya Bal GangaDhar Tilak in Poona now Pune. Just then the deadly epidemic Plague broke out in Maharashtra which caused the death of thousands. The British Government came out with the draconian Epidemic Diseases Act 1897 which empowered the police to carry out searches in any dwelling place. A large number of women were molested. This caused wide-spread resentment everywhere. The Chapekar Brothers decided to take revenge. They killed the oppressive ICS officer

W. C. Rand.. They were caught due to an act of betrayal. Damodar was hanged on 18. 4. 1898, Balkrishna on 12. 5. 1898 and finally Vasudev and Mahadev Ranade were hanged on 8. 5. 1898 and 10. 5. 1898 respectively. Swami Vivekananda's disciple Sister Nivedita went to their houseto offer condolences. She found their mother not showing any signs of sorrow, but she was putting on a brave face.

Damodar was 27 years of age, Balkrishna 24 and Vasudev was only 18 years at the time of their martyrdoms. This should be the only case of three brothers of one family offering supreme sacrifice at the altar of their motherland in any part of the world.

Chapter Thirteen
Lawyers in the Struggle

Here are some of the lawyers who participated in India's independence movement. They played very prominent roles in the movements. But they are more or less forgotten today. Some of the lawyers mentioned here are still remembered. But their main contributions are more or less forgotten. Therefore, their names have been included here. It is also to be noted that in some of the other chapters of this book, there is a mention of a number of freedom-fighters who were lawyers. They are besides the lawyers who are being mentioned below.

Shyamji Krishna Varma (4 October, 1857 – 30 March, 1930) was an Indian revolutionary fighter, lawyer and journalist who founded the Indian Home Rule Society, India House and *The Indian Sociologist* in London. A graduate of Balliol College, Krishna Varma was a noted scholar in Sanskrit and other Indian languages. He pursued a brief legal career in India and served as the *Divan* of a number of Indian princely states in India. He had, however, differences with Crown authority, was dismissed following a supposed conspiracy of local British officials at Junagadh and chose to return to England. An admirer of Dayanand Saraswati's approach to cultural nationalism, and of Herbert Spencer, Krishna Varma believed in Spencer's dictum: "Resistance to aggression is not simply justified, but imperative".

In 1905 he founded the India House and *The Indian Sociologist*, which rapidly developed as an organised meeting point for radical nationalists among Indian students in Britain at the time and one of the most prominent centers for revolutionary Indian nationalism outside India. Most famous among the members of this organisation was Veer Savarkar. He was greatly influenced by the teachings of Swami Dayananda Saraswati, a radical reformer and an exponent of the Vedas, who had founded the Arya Samaj. He became his disciple and was soon conducting lectures on Vedic philosophy and religion. In 1877, a public speaking tour secured him great public recognition. He became the first non-Brahmin to receive the prestigious title of Pandit by the Pandits of Kashi in 1877. He came to the attention of Monier Williams, an Oxford professor of Sanskrit who offered Shyamji a job as his assistant. This is how he moved to the West from where he conducted his patriotic activities.

Later in 1905, Shyamji attended the United Congress of Democrats held at Holborn Town Hall as a delegate of the India Home Rule Society. His resolution on India received an enthusiastic ovation from the entire conference. Shyamji's activities in England aroused the concern of the British Government: He was debarred from Inner Temple and removed from the membership list on 30 April 1909 for writing anti-British articles in *The Indian Sociologist*. Most of the British press was highly critical of the writings of Shyamji. *The Times* referred to him as the Notorious Krishnavaram. His movements were closely watched by British Secret Services. He apprehended his arrest any time. So he decided to shift his headquarters to Paris, leaving India House in charge of Vir Savarkar. He arrived in Paris in early 1907 to continue his work. The British Government tried to have him extradited from France without success as he gained the support of many leading French politicians.. Shyamji's work in Paris helped gain support for Indian independence from European countries. He agitated for the release of Savarker and acquired great support all over Europe and Russia. He died in 1930.

Dr. Pranjivan Mehta barrister. One of the closest well wishers of Mohandas since the earliest days till his death in Rangoon on 3. 8. 1932. It seems that he did not practise law regularly. He had a flourishing business and a lot of property both in India and in Burma. He was a tower of strength and constant counseling to Mohandas. He was a gold medalist of the Grant Medical College, Bombay and also a barrister. He was Gandhiji's ' oldest friend '. From the time he received him in England from 1888 till his death in August 1932 in Rangoon, he was a constant help to Mohandas, both spiritually and financially. He was a philanthropist who helped almost everybody. He helped Mohandas in establishing the Phoenix Settlement of Durban. He wrote *M. K. Gandhi and the South African Problem.*

Badruddin Tyabji (1844-1906) He became a barrister and joined the Middle Temple in 1867. He was one of the first barristers from Bombay. He soon made a mark for himself in the profession. He was elevated as a judge in the Bombay High Court. As a judge, he was fearless. He granted bail to Lokmanya Bal Ganga dhar Tilak in the sedition case while his bail application had been turned down twice earlier. He acted as the Chief Justice of the Bombay High Court. In public life, Tyabji was a part of the famous triumvirate, the other two being Sir Pherozeshah Mehta and Kashinath Telang. He was the President of the Indian National Congress in 1887 at the Madras session. He was one of the pioneers of the Indian National Congress and also one of the members of the Naoroji school of patriotism, the others being Dada Bhai Naoroji, W. C. Bonnerjee and Sir Pherozeshah Mehta.

Abbas Tyabji(1853-1936). He was a nationalist Muslim who took very active part in the constitutional development of India. He was a judge of the Baroda High Court. He was one of the five Commissioners appointed by the Punjab sub-committee of the Congress to report on the Punjab disturbances of 1919-1920.

Sir Pherozeshah Merwanji Mehta. (1845–1915). He was one of the founder members of the Indian National Congress and its President in 1890 and 1909. He was one of the doyens of the Bar of Ahmedabad and Bombay. He had a very distinguished career as a counselor and as a legislator of the Bombay Legislative Assembly. He presided over the meeting to accord a reception of welcome to Mohandas Karamchand Gandhi and Kasturba Gandhi at a meeting held on 12. 1. 1915 at Mount Petit Bombay when they returned from South Africa. Mohandas recalled that Sir Pherozeshah had encouraged him with his timely advice when he was struggling with his legal practice in Bombay. Sir Pherozeshah was an admirer of Mohandas for his work in South Africa and just like Gopal Krishna Gokhale, he also advised him to return to India where his services were required. Sir Pherozwshah was known for his powerful presentation of his cases because of his thundering voice. He was a member of the Bombay Municipal Corporation for a record thirty years. Sir Pherozeshah was a moderate liberal in the political field. He did not oppose the British rule in India and did not demand complete independence for India. He demanded more autonomy for the Indians. He became a barrister and joined the Lincolns Inn in 1867 and in 1868, he started his practice in Bombay. He soon made a mark for himself at the bar. In 1910, he started the *Bombay Chronicle*, an English language news paper of weekly circulation, which became an important vehicle of the sentiments of the political aspirations of India in the subsequent decades. Benjamin Horniman was one of the eminent editors of this news-paper. He was called 'the Uncrowned King of Bombay' who roared like a lion in the law courts '. He worked in the organizational work of the Congress particularly in connection with the protest against the recommendations of the Public Service Commission in 1892. He was a member of the deputation to England in 1894 which waited upon Lord Elgin. In 1896, he met Gandhiji for the first time '' as a loving father would meet his grown up son '. In 1901, he advised Mohandas not to go to South Africa and instead devote his energies to work here in India. He was skeptical of the success of the method of satyagraha.

Sir Narayan Ganesh Chandavarkar (1855-1923): Was a judge of the Bombay High Court and thereafter, a liberal leader of Bombay. After a very successful career as a lawyer, he was appointed a judge of the Bombay High Court in 1901. He was appointed as the first unofficial President of the Bombay Legislative Council. At that time, the Congress Party and the Congress leaders were of moderate views. They were not hostile to the British Government. So Sir Chandavarkar held the office of the President of the INC at one time and the judgeship of the Bombay High Court at another time. When Mohandas returned to India from South Africa in January 1915, the INC was divided into two parts, and as a result of these differences, a wing of the Party known as the All India Moderates Conference was established. The other two prominent leaders of this Conference were Sir Surendra Nath Banerji and Sir Dinshaw Wacha. In1920, he presided over a public meeting held at Bombay to protest the Report of the Hunter Committee over the Jallianwala Bagh massacre.

S. Srinivasa Iyengar (1874-1941) An eminent lawyer of Madras. Presided over the Gauhati session of the Congress in 1926. Elected to the Central Assembly in 1926. He started his practice in 1898 and he soon made a mark for himself at the Bar. He was appointed as the Advocate General of Madras High Court, but then he resigned this post in 1920 and he even gave up his lucrative practice to devote all time to active politics for the emancipation of the country. He presided over the Madras Provincial Conference of the Congress Party which was held in Tirunelveli. He also resigned his membership of the Madras Legislative Council and returned the decoration of C.I. e. to the British Government. In 1926 he was elected to the Central Legislative Council from Madras and the same year, he presided over the session of the Congress Party which was held in Gauhati. He was a champion of the Hindu Muslim unity. His resolution for this unity was accepted in the Madras session of the Party in 1927. The All Party Report better known as the Nehru Report was published in 1928. Perhaps Shriniwas did not so much subscribe to the idea of dominion status for India. He favored complete independence for India. Therefore, he organised a party of his own, namely the Independence League along with Jawaharlal Nehru and Netaji Subhash Chandra Bose as other prominent members. His efforts bore immediate fruits. The Congress adopted the programme of complete independence in the December 1929 session held at Lahore. He was definitely the most important Congress leader from that part of the country between the years 1919 to 1940.

Vithalbhai J. Patel (1873-1933) —It is difficult to place Vithalbhai Patel in this category because his services to the nation are no less significant than those of his more oftenly remembered younger brother Sardar Vallabh Bhai Patel. But his services need to be refreshed in our memory and several legends about him need to be refreshed. Hence his name.

Vithalbhai was an eminent lawyer of Ahmedabad. He was a member of the Bombay Legislative Council, its president and the first elected president of the Central Legislative Assembly, Delhi. He played an important role in resolving the issue between Mohandas on the one hand and Motilal and C. R. Das on the other hand on the question of council entry. On 22. 12. 1924, Vithalbhai told Mohandas that he was playing a fatal ga me by insisting that only those Congressmen could be given the right of franchise who adopted spinning as a part of their daily routine because 90 per cent of the Congressmen were against the existing franchise rules. When Vithalbhai accepted the office of the President of the Legislative Assembly, he had made a resolution with himself that he would devote a part of his salary towards a cause which would promote some national welfare scheme. In the earlier days of his office, he was not able to do so. But after some time, he was able to contribute a part of his salary towards such a project. He required a total amount of Rs. 2000 per month for his personal needs. He set apart an amount of Rs. 1625 per month from his gross salary beginning from the previous month of April 1926 to be utilized for such national purposes that the Mahatma deemed fit and necessary. This contribution continued thereafter regularly. But Vithalbhai did not want any publicity for his deeds of charity. He disclosed his intention to seek re-election to the State Assembly. But he did not want his correspondence with Mohandas with respect to his charity to be published so that the voters were not influenced in any manner. When Gujarat was ravaged by floods, Vithalbhai came to Nadiad and supervised the relief work. He was speaker of the state Assembly at that time in August 1927.

Madhusudan Das:– He was a brilliant lawyer of Orissa. Mohandas writes that the poverty of Orissa woke him up from his slumber and it made him realise that there should be carried out large scale reforms in the field of agriculture in his state. Thereafter, he devoted his energies in this field along with his patriotic duties.

Jivanlal Desai, barrister of Ahmedabad He helped Mohandas in establishing the Kochrab Ashram in Ahmedabad which was later on known as the Sabarmati Ashram.

S. Satyamurti (1887-1943) a lawyer of Madras.. His father Surendra Sastriar was a lawyer. He had his schooling in Madras. After completing his law degree from the Madras Law College, he started his legal practice firstly under V. V. Srinivas Iyengar and then later, he took his apprenticeship under S. Srinivasa Iyengar who was formerly the President of the Indian National Congress from whom he not only learnt the finer points of a lawyer, but he got initiated into the freedom movement. In 1919, he was made the secretary of the Indian delegation of the Joint Parliamentary Committee that went to England to protest the Montagu – Chelmsford Reforms and also against the

Rowlatt Act. In 1926, he again went to England to present the Congress point of view. During this period, he worked there as a correspondent of *the Hindu* newspaper. He took part in all the freedom movements and was imprisoned a number of times. For example, in 1930 he was arrested for unfurling the Indian flag atop the Parthasarathi Temple in Madras in defiance of British rule. The Congress won many seats in the assembly elections in 1939 in Madras. Satyamurti was the Mayor of Madras in 1939. During his tenure, he succeeded in getting a water reservoir constructed in Madras namely the Poondi Reservoir which is today known as Satyamurti Sagar. In 1940, he was arrested and sentenced to six months for his offering of individual satyagraha in Madras. He was again arrested for his participation in the Quit India Movement of 1942. Kumaraswami Kamraj Nadar was one of his disciples.

T. Prakasam (1872 – 1957) He had his schooling in Madras from where he obtained his legal degree. Earlier, he worked as a second grade pleader according to the rules of the bar council of that state and later, he became a full fledged lawyer. Soon he was a successful lawyer. Along with his legal practice, he joined local and national politics. He was elected as Municipal Chairman of Rajahmundry in 1904 when he was hardly 31 years of age. After some time, he went to England to become a barrister. At that time, it was a taboo to cross the seven seas. Just like Mohandas before him, Prakasam promised to his mother that he would not touch the forbidden wines and meat. After his return to India, he appeared in a number of head-line cases such as the Ash case of murder. By 1916, Prakasam was in active public field of duty. He began to attend the Congress sessions regularly and took the satyagraha pledge in 1921.

He founded the Swarajya newspaper which was published in three languages, English, Tamil and Telugu. The paper wrote on patriotic themes. He was elected the general secretary of the Congress Party in the Ahmedabad session of 1921. He actively participated in the Non Cooperation Movement of 1922 and was arrested. He worked hard for the propagation of khadi and spinning in his area. He greeted the Simon Commission with a patriotic fervor when the Commission visited Madras. The police opened fire to dispel the agitators. In the firing, one young man Pardha Saradhi was shot dead on the spot. This enraged Prakasam. He tore open his shirt and showed his bare chest before the police and dared to shoot him. The police did not have the courage to shoot him and they melted away from the scene of agitation. After this daredevil incident, Prakasam was called ***Andhra Kesari.***

In 1926, he was elected to the Central Legislative Assembly on the Congress ticket. But when the Party gave a call to all the members to resign, he resigned his membership. But since he was not fully satisfied with the policy of resignation, he contested the by-election to the seat and was duly returned as a member. But he continued his affection and respect for Mahatma Gandhi which was evident in his active participation in the salt movement in the Madras region. Due to several reasons, Prakasam had to suspend the publication of the *Swarajya*. In 1937, the Congress Party won the provincial elections in Madras and Prakasam was returned. He was in the running for the seat of Chief Minister. But in the Party interest, he made way for Rajaji for the post of CM. He was made the revenue minister. In that capacity, he worked in the abolition of the zamindari system. He offered individual satyagraha in 1941 against the mobilisation of the

Indian man –force in the War and again he was an individual satyagrahi in the 1942 Movement. He was sentenced to three years imprisonment and he was released in 1945. In 1946, the Congress won the elections in the Madras Presidency and now this time, he was made the Chief Minister of Madras. It is another matter that the ministry lasted for about one year only. After the independence of the country, Praksam was active in state politics. The state of Andhra Pradesh was carved out of the old Hyderabad following the sacrifice of Potti Sriramulu in a fast for this cause. T. Prakasam was elected as the Chief Minister of the newly formed Andhra Pradesh. He died following a severe sun- stroke on 20. 5. 1957.

Abdul Majeed Khwaja (1885 – 1962)Abdul Majeed was the son of Khwaja Muhammad Yusuf who himself was an eminent lawyer. Like his father, Abdul believed that the Indian Muslims needed the western type of lifestyle and English medium education. He had his early studies at home where he learnt Arabic, Pharsi and Urdu. But later, he was sent to England for higher studies in 1906. He was admitted to Christ College at Cambridge. He studied law also and in 1910, he was called to the Bar. Jawaharlal Nehru, Sir Iqbal and Sir Shah Sulaiman were his contemporaries at Cambridge. He returned to India in 1910. He started practice in the District Court at Aligarh. But then he shifted to Patna where he soon set up a good practice in the Patna High Court.

Abdul Majeed gave up his lucrative practice in 1919 under the influence of Mohandas for the national cause. He participated in the Khilafat Movement and the Civil Disobedience Movement of 1922. He suffered imprisonment of six months. Abdul

Majeed was closely associated with the Mohammedan Anglo Oriental College, now the A. M. U of Aligarh and also with the Jamia Millia of New Delhi. The Jamia Millia was the creation of Maulana Mohammad Ali, Dr. M. A. Ansari, Hakim Ajmal Khan, Shaffiqur Rahman Kidwai, Kalat Sahab and Aqil Sahab. Dr. Zakir Hussain was a teacher here. Maulana Mohammad Ali requested Abdul Majeed to look after the management of the Jamia Millia because he could not find enough time from his political commitments. In 1925, Abdul Majeed shifted the Jamia Millia from Aligarh to Karol Bagh with the concurrence of Mahatma Gandhi and Hakim Ajmal Khan. He remained associated with the Jamia Millia till his death in 1962.

Abdul Majeed was an ardent nationalist Muslim. He opposed the two –nation theory of Jinnah. He founded the All India Muslim Majlis to counter the divisive theory. He toured India extensively in 1945-46 to educate the Muslim opinion against the partition of India.

Govindrao Appaji Patil—He was one of the leading lawyers of Ahmedabad, a social worker and a freedom-fighter. He passed away early. Mahatma Gandhi condoled his passing away.

Lala Harkishan Lal: He was a contemporary of Lala Lajpatrai. He was a Cambridge scholar who excelled in mathematics. He qualified as a barrister. On return to India, he established a successful law practice. But like the Lala, his mind was in the other fields of social service and in the Arya Samaj.

The lawyers of Lyallpur

The seeds of discontent against the British Raj had been sown in Punjab by Lala Lajpatrai and his Arya Samaj colleagues such as Ajit Singh the ' Bharat Mata ' fire-brand and Kishan Singh the father of Sardar Bhagat Singh. There were some prominent lawyers of Lyallpur also who ignited the fire of revoltsuch as Hans Raj Sawhney and his brother **Gurdas Ram Sawhney** both distinguished members of the Lyallpur bar. They were active members of the Arya Samaj also. They were the guarantors of the leading newspaper of the day namely *The Punjabee.* These were the days of 1907 when there was discontentment against the revenue law of Punjab. There was an agitation going on against this Act. A meeting was organised in Lyallpur to protest against this revenue law. The aforesaid lawyers addressed the meeting. The District Magistrate Lyallpur took precautionary measures against them and asked them to show cause why they should not be debarred from participating in the meeting. There were three other members of the bar who were similarly given the show-cause notice, namely Janki Nath Kaul, Khazan Singh and Amolak Ram. The show-cause notice caused a tremendous stir in Punjab because they were greatly respected in Punjab. The administration had to deploy a large force to quieten the agitators. The lawyers were detained. Their bail applications were rejected. They were released much later.

The Champaran lawyers

Babu Brijraj Kishore Prasad. He was one of the leading lawyers of Darbhanga at the time when Mohandas launched his agitational movement in Champaran which brought him national importance. When one peasant of Champaran namely Rajkumar Shukla brought Mohandas to Champaran to lead the indigo planters of Bihar in their fight against the exploitation by the British owners of the fields. Mohandas stayed with Babu

Brijkishore Prasad. His daughter Prabhavati married Babu Jaiprakash Narayan.

Similarly, another lawyer namely Gorakh Prasad (1869-1962) a leader of Motihari hosted Mohandas when he visited Motihari during his Champaran sojourn. Mohandas chalked out a programme as to how to highlight the grievances of the peasants of Champaran. A part of this programme was to record the evidence of the lawyers of the area who had anything to do with the case of the ryots and that the procedure should be on the lines as suggested by Gorakh Prasad.

Some other lawyers of the area helped Mohandas considerably. They are, Babu Dharnidhara pleader and Congressman of Darbhanga, Babu Ram Navami Prasad a lawyer from Muzaffarnagar who took up the cases against the Bihar indigo planters and who later joined the Champaran agitation and the Non-Co-operation Movement and, therefore, courted arrest, Babu Shambhu Sharan (1892-1930) a lawyer and eminent Congressman of Bihar who took part in the Champaran agitation, Non-Co-operation and Khilafat movements and **B**abu Anugraha Narain Sinha (1889-1957) lawyer, legislator of Bihar who took active part in the freedom movement and who was a minister in the Ministry of Bihar from 1946 to 1957.

The Gujarat Sabha lawyers

Some of the Gujarat Sabha lawyers who helped Mohandas in the national cause are **S**hivbhai Motibhai Patel and Kishanlal N. Desai. G. V. Mavlankar was another member of the Sabha. Mr. Montagu was to visit India in October 1917 in consultation for his Reforms Act. The Sabha decided to file a petition with him to highlight their suggestions. Narhari Parikh and Kishorelal Mashruwalal are also referred to as LL. B. and, therefore, as lawyers. They are two of the most trusted associates of Mohandas. **Barrister Popatlal Chudgar** of Rajkot was for long associated with the State's People's Movement and he later retired as Judge of the Saurashtra High Court.

The Lawyers of Punjab who deposed with respect to the Jallianwala Bagh massacre

Barrister Labh Singh and Sardar Sant Singh a vakil from Lyalpur were deputed by the Indian National Congress to collect evidence as to how soldiers were recruited by the British Government for war efforts and how the loans for war effort were disbursed.

Labh Singh, barrister. He took an active part in the inception of the agitation against the Rowlatt Act and he was present at the site of the meeting which took place in the fateful days of the 12th and the 13th of April, 1919. The police alleged that initially he was not actively participating in the agitation, but later he became an active participant in the disturbances. He was convicted for life imprisonment.

Dr. Saif-ud-din Kitchlew, barrister, had a large practice in Amritsar. He held a degree of Doctor of Philosophy from Munster and he was a graduate from the Cambridge University. He had earlier studied in the Aligarh Muslim University. He was actively involved in the promotion of Hindu –Muslim unity. He organised the *Ram Navami* festival along with Dr. Satpal which was held on the 9th of April that year. Both Hindus and Muslims participated in the baisakhi and Ram Navami festivals in an atmosphere of complete cordiality. He was a nationalist Muslim leader of Brahmanic roots from Kashmir. He became the Secretary of the AICC in 1924. He earned national recognition following his protests against the Rowlatt Act of 1919. He also protested against the Jallainwala killings. He was awarded the Lenin Peace Prize by the former Soviet Union in1952.

Badrul Islam Khan, barrister of Amritsar presided over a meeting which was held in Amritsar to agitate the restrictions of movement and freedom of speech and expression that were imposed upon Dr. Satpal by an order passed by Sir Michael O'Dwyer and also to demand the repeal of the Rowlatt Act. He called upon the meeting to be peaceful in their method and that they would not suffer any hardship if they agitated calmly. Later he was arrested also for an offence of breach of peace and order. His arrest generated a feeling in Amritsar that every one who was associated with the INC and the movement would be arrested. He was arrested on the 19th of April from inside his bedroom. He described the pathetic conditions of detention places and the humiliations that the arrested persons had to face in police custody.

Maqbool Mahmood, **a** vakil of the High Court tried to restore orderly behavior of the crowd who had collected in the Bagh and to call upon them to go back to their places. He called upon the Deputy Commissioner not to open fire upon the crowd because they still hoped that the meeting would disperse peacefully. Maqbool Mahmood was helped in these efforts by another lawyer of Amritsar namely Salaria. The Deputy Commissioner, however, did not listen to their requests, he ordered firing upon the assembly killing about 25 persons and injuring many more. He risked his life on the 10th of April by trying to turn away the crowd near the bridge. He was later arrested, taken to the police station and he was made to state that he could identify the murderers of Robinson and Rowland.

Mohammad Sadiq Barrister deposed before the inquiry committee of the INC that he tried to help the authorities in the disposal of the dead bodies and to provide medical help to the injured persons after the fateful firing was carried out. He deposed that the authorities wanted to avenge the deaths of some Europeans who had been killed prior to the incident in the Jallianwala Bagh.

Lala Balmokand Bhatia, High Court vakil pointed out that several members of the Bar were enrolled as constables. He said that two common citizens were flogged before them. Pandit Rajendra Mishra and other lawyers supported the statement of vakil Bhatia.

Gurdial Singh Salaria barrister was arrested while he was trying to pacify the crowd who had assembled in the Bagh. He was in police custody from 23rd of May to 5th of July 1919.

Dr. Gokul Chand Narang barrister. He was an eminent barrister of Lahore. He said that perfect communal harmony was established between the two communities. The police had issued orders for not taking out processions in April 1919. But in Lahore a large gathering had been held. Narang apprehended some disturbances. So he succeeded in preventing the crowd from proceeding towards the Mall and in this manner he was able to restore peace and order.

Manohar Lal –– He was a prominent lawyer of Lahore. He was the Vice President of the Lahore Bar Association. He was known for his loyalty to the Government. But still then he was harassed and arrested for no reason and for no charges against him. He was put in the Central Jail in Lahore where he described that the conditions were very unhygienic. He was a trustee of the popular newspaper *The Tribune*. It might have been the main reason behind his arrest. The Government must have desired to stifle the voice of public opinion via a widely circulated newspaper.

Santaram barrister. He was a barrister for about ten years standing in Lahore. He has given a detailed account of the trials of the agitators which in his opinion were merely a farce.

Sardar Boota Singh a lawyer of Lahore. He was a member of the District War League who had assisted in the recruitment of soldiers in the army and he had received a certificate for his services. He did not take part in the hartal, but he was arrested along with other lawyers without being assigned any reasons. Similarly, some other pleaders and lawyers such as Gosai Maya Ramand Sardar Pritam Singh of Sheikhupura described how several uncalled for arrests had taken place and the arrested persons harrassed for no reason.

Lala Ushnak Rai a lawyer of Lahore. He had a standing of nearly nine years at the Bar. He was a hereditary lambardar of Lahore and held extensive lands there. He had donated generously to the war funds. He also narrated the plight of the arrested persons.

Sardar Sant Singh avakil and Ram Das Chokhraa barrister, both of Lyallpur, now in Pakistan, have given an account of the farcical trials of the lawyers who were arrested in connection with the allegations of breach of peace and order.

Har Gopal, a barrister of Gujrat was arrested and kept in detention for a long period of time. He was tried along with others under martial law. But the Martial Law Tribunal acquitted them all.

Some Other Eminent Lawyers

Ganesh Vasudev Mavalankar (1888-1956) —He was also called Dadasaheb. He started his career as a lawyer but after a successful practice, he dedicated his time to the national cause by joining freedom movements of the Indian National Congress. He was elected to the Ahmedabad Municipality in 1919-22, 1924-27, 1930-33 and 1935-1937. He was elected to the Bombay Provincial Legislative Assembly and then as its Speaker in 1937 and worked as such till 1946. The same year, he was elected to the Central Legislative Assembly which soon transformed into the Constituent Assembly of India w. e. f. the midnight of 14/15 August 1947 and which again became the Provisional Parliament of India with the Republic Day 1950. He was elected as the Speaker of the Constituent Assembly 17. 11. 1947 and after the first general elections of free India as the Speaker of the Lok Sabha. He passed away on 27. 2. 1956. In the by-election that followed, his wife Smt. Sushila Mavlankar was elected to the Lok Sabha. Their son Purushottam was elected to the Lok Sabha in 1972.

Hassan Imam (1871 -1933)—He was an eminent lawyer of Patna and was later elevated as a judge of the Calcutta High Court. In 1916, he resigned his post as a judge and began his practice as a lawyer again. He presided over the annual session of the INC in September 1918. He led the Muslim deputation to England for revision of the Treaty of Sevres with Turkey. It seems that he had some initial reservations about the concept of Non-Co-operation Movement. But when later he understood the meaning of this movement, he assured his cooperation to the Mahatma. He was imprisoned in 1921 for his writings. He was one of the founders of the Bihar Vidyapith.

Mazharul Haq (1866-1930) He was a prominent barrister of Patna. He was with Mohandas in England when they were studying there for law. He opposed the system of separate electorates for the Muslims which was contemplated under the Morley Minto Reforms. He helped Mohandas in his work during the Champaran movement. He was actively associated with Mohandas in the Non-Co-operation Movement of 1921-1922. A meeting was held in his house which was presided over by Babu Rajendra Prasad during the Champaran days. When the Swaraj Sabha was organised in Patna in 1919, Haq worked as its president and Babu Rajendra Prasad was its secretary. Maulana Mazharul Haq was instrumental in the opening of the Bihar National University and National College Patna in February 1921. In the opening ceremony, Mohandas was present as a guest. Mazharul Haq was selected for the post of the Chancellor, Babu Braj Kishore Prasad as Vice Chancellor and Babu Rajendra Prasad as Principal and Registrar of the University. He founded in 1888 the ' Anjuman Islamia ' an association of Muslims in England where he had gone for the studies of law. He was appointed a munsif of Audh in 1893. He was one of the founders of the Indian Muslim League in 1906. He became its Secretary and he presided over its session of 1915 in Bombay. He was elected to the Central Legislative Council in 1910 under the scheme of separate electorates. He was a member of the 1914 Congress delegation to England. In 1916, he helped in bringing about the Congress – Muslim League accord at Lucknow. He founded *the Motherland* and theSadaqat Ashram in Patna. He was one of the nationalist Muslims in the freedom struggle.

M. R. Jayakar (1873-1959) He was a prominent lawyer of Bombay and a liberal leader. He was called to the Bar at Lincoln's Inn in 1905. He was a very good negotiator. He was involved in negotiations between the Congress and the British Government in 1930 and also during the early thirties following the Salt movement and preparatory to the First Round Table Conference in London. His negotiations are said to be responsible for the bilateral dialogue between Lord Irwin the Viceroy and Mohandas which were held in Simla in 1931 which created the famous Simla Pact whereby all the political prisoners were released in return for discontinuation of the Non Cooperation Movement of the Congress. He was a member of the All India Home Rule League, but later when Mohandas converted it into the Swarajya Sabha in 1920, he resigned along with Jinnah and 18 others over the means to be adopted to achieve swaraj. Following the disturbances in Punjab in 1919, the INC appointed a sub-committee to enquire into the disorders of April 1919. C. R. Das, Pandit Madan Mohan Malviya, Motilal Nehru, Lala Harkishan, Lala Girdhari Lal and M. R. Jayakar were some of the eminent members of this committee.

He was also a judge of the Federal Court of India in 1937 and Vice Chancellor Pune University. He stood for the ratification of the Nehru Report and that some necessary inclusions into its recommendations could be carried out before the All Party Conference later on. He also thought that most of their demands four out of six had been accepted by the members of the Committee and that it was not desirable to agree to all the demands of Jinnah. There could be no end to the ever increasing demands of Jinnah, as for example he was insisting on the separation of Sind irrespective of whatever may be the terms of the Constitution.

C. Vijayaraghavachariar (1852 – 1943) was elected as the president of the INC when the Party held its annual session in Nagpur in December 1920. He was an eminent lawyer of Karnataka. He developed some sort of difference of opinion with Mahatma Gandhi on the question of eradication of untouchability. He seemed to believe that the Congress had not done enough in the matter of the removal of this social evil.

George Joseph was a prominent barrister of Madurai. He was a journalist also. He was on the staff of the *Independent* as an editor. He was arrested when the Government took action against that newspaper for publishing allegedly disturbing writings. He edited *Young India* also for some time. George Joseph wanted to take an active part in the opening of the Vaikom Temple to the untouchables. Indeed he was very active in this movement upto a time. The Mahatma did not want George to be associated with the satyagraha as a field satyagrahi. He wrote to him that he should let the Hindus do the work because it is they who had to purify themselves and that he could help by his sympathy and by his pen, but not by organising the satyagraha: and certainly not by offering satyagraha. The Mahatma did not permit George even to fast for the cause of removal of untouchability. Needless to say, George must have been greatly disappointed by this counselling from the Mahatma.

He had edited *Young India* for some time and was also *Independent*for some time. George published an article in one of the newspapers outlining his future policy and line of action

The lawyers of Multan– When Mohandas visited Multan in March 1921, he found that no lawyer had given up his legal practice. He reminded them that several prominent lawyers had given up their practice for the national cause, two lawyers, namely Bodhraj and Keval Krishen announced that they were suspending their practice for one year.

V. V. S. Garu of Nellore gave up his legal practice at the altar of national cause. Garu opened theTilak JatiyaVidyalaya in Nellore. It was inaugurated in April 1921 by the Mahatma.

Gopabandhu Das was a lawyer of Sakhigopal which was twelve miles away from Puri. He practised law for a few years. But then he gave up his practice for national cause. He opened a school in Sakhigopal where the children were imparted education in craft and vocation in an open area so that his school was called a garden school. He did not seek any help from the Government for his school and collected funds for his school from voluntary donors. The Mahatma visited this school in April 1921 during his visit to Orissa in 1921. He was an M. L. C. also. He died in June 1928 at Sakhigopal, Puri. Mohandas eulogised him as one of the noblest among the sons of Orissa, the land of sorrows and tears.

When Lala Lajpat Rai founded his Servants of the People Society in 1924 for his various philanthropic works such as opening a mahavidyalaya, a hospital and running a newspaper, he inducted Das as a member. A branch of the Society was opened in Orissa also with Das as its Vice-President. He attended the anniversary of the Society in Lahore in 1928 and he fell ill soon after his return to Puri. He died soon after.

Mulchand of Sukur. Lawyer Mulcahnd renounced his practice during the tour of Mahatma Gandhi in Sindh, Hyderabad, Karachi, Larkhana, Shikarpur, Rohri, Kotri and Mirpur Khas in May 1921. He announced that now onwards, he was devoting himself completely to the national cause of freedom of the country.

Konda Venkatappayya and the **other lawyers of Andhra Pradesh**

Konda Venkatappayya was one of the leading lawyers of Andhra Pradesh. He suspended his practice for national duty. He took part in the Civil Disobedience Movement of 1920 and he was arrested. He was called Deshbhakta. Konda was active in the movement to get the temples opened to the harijans also. On the lines of the Sabarmati Ashram, Konda opened the Pallipadu Ashram at Guntur in Madras. A referendum was held in 1932 whether the Guruvayur Temple should be opened for the untouchables. Majority of the temple goers said that it should be opened. Konda was one of the active workers in this referendum. Later he suggested that it was of no use to have legislation for the temple entry.

Sankara Menon, a lawyer of Quilon, was the president ofthe Quilon Congress Committee. He worked for the freedom cause devotedly.

The lawyers of Nagpur suspended their work in obedience to the call for non co-operation. A note in the *Young India* dated 1. 9. 1921 stated that the pleaders of Nagpur have done well through the ordeal to which the Sessions Judge subjected them.

He required the non co-operating lawyers to show the consistency between their suspension and their oath as lawyers. All of them said that they had suspended obedience to the Congress call. Narayan Rao T. Vaidya said that times had changed very much, that the oath of allegiance would have to be changed to suit the circumstances and that otherwise no self respecting lawyer would care to practise in any British Court. The lawyers deserve congratulations on their fearless attitude. Times are indeed gone when people could be frightened into slavish submission. Man does not live by bread alone. He has at his disposal a sustenance far richer than the richest bread can afford.

Babu Kamini kumar Chanda was an eminent lawyer of Silchar. In September 1921 when Mohandas visited Assam, he stayed in his house. He gave up his practice as a lawyer to join the Non Cooperation Movement. He was a member of the Imperial Council. He boycotted the legislature also. His wife and his daughters also joined the freedom movement. They took up spinning the khadi and made all possible efforts to propagate the cause of khadi.

Maulvi Mahomed Abdulla was a lawyer of Sylhet. He collected funds for the Khilafat Movement and Smyrna Funds.

Bhupati Babu of Barisal gave up his practice to join the Non Cooperation Movement. Ramaswami Iyengar was a leading leader of Coimbatore. He was arrested in November 1921 for writing a spirited letter to *the Hindu* which the authorities thought incited violence.

K. Santhanam a prominent lawyer and politician who was appointed as the Secretary of the Sub Committee by the Congress Party to report on the Punjab disorders of 1919. He was a keen khadi worker also. He propagated the cause of khadi in Madras being the Secretary of the Tamil Nadu Khaddar Board.

J. V. Vaidya a lawyer of Devrukh, Ratnagiri appeared in the court with a khadi cap on, which is popularly knownas Gandhi cap. The District Judge, Ratnagiri served Vaidya with an order to the effect that the Chief Justice of the Bombay High Court had issued an order to all the District Judges that no lawyer should be permitted to appear in a court of law with a Gandhi cap on his head and further that in case any lawyer acted contrary to these directions, then proceedings of contempt of court should be drawn up against him. Lawyer Vaidya gave up his practice as a lawyer and he refused to appear in the court of Sub Judge without his Gandhi cap on.

Babu Prasanna Kumar Sen was a prominent lawyer of Chittagong. He was arrested in November 1921 offering non co-operative resistance. He was Secretary of the District Congress Committee.

T. A. K. Sherwani a prominent lawyer of Aligarh. He was in charge of the National Muslim University when he was arrested for offences under Section 153 A IPC. He was served with a notice by the High Court to show cause why his sanad should not be cancelled or why he should not be allowed to practise for a period of two years. He had already suspended his practice earlier for national cause.

Lala Hansa Raj barrister of Jalandhar belonged to an old noble family of Jalandhar which had rendered many valuable services to the Government. Lala Hnsaraj dared like Lala Dunichand of Ambala personally to picket the liquor licence auction which was to be held in Jalandhar. He was arrested.

Bhupati Babu, a lawyer of Silhat. He joined the Non Cooperation Movement. He also worked in the field of the rehabilitation of the fallen women

Mangaldas Pakvasa–In October 1945, Mohndas entrusted to him the responsibility of finding out ways and means to promote the sale of the khadi products in view of the executive orders of the C. P. Government issued at that time and which could be an obstacle to the sale of khadi. Mahatma opined with Mangaldas Pakvasa that the sale of khadi could not be classed as because there was no element of earning a profit like so many mill owners and that the khadi workers were merely trying to win their bare sustenance through khadi.

Sita Ram, a pleader of Kheri. He was a member of the Legislative Council of the United Provinces. He resigned this membership in the wake of arrests all over the country.

Babu Bimalanand Das Gupta of Dacca. A pleader of Dacca, Das Gupta was arrested on 23. 1. 1922 in connection with a meeting that was held in Dacca which was in contravention of a prohibitory order passed by the District Magistrate of Dacca. He was tried for various offences, but then he was acquitted.

Maulvi Nurul Haq a vakil of Feni, Noakhali. He was beaten up by the police because he stood as a candidate for election for the Legislative Council and for being a non co-operator.

Shah Abutorab Wazi Ahmad a vakil in the High Court of Allahabad was arrested for being a non co-operator. He was transferred from the Central Jail Buxar to the Hazaribagh Jail. He was arrested sometime in March 1922.

Karnad Sadashiv Rao (1881- 1937). Sadashiv was born in a rich family. His father Ramachandra was a successful lawyer of

Mangalore. His mother was Radhabai. He was their only child and, therefore, he received extra parental care and affection. He studied in the Presidency College, Madras and later studied law in Bombay. In Mangalore, he was able to set up a good practice quite soon. But then, he joined the freedom struggle early in his career as a lawyer. But soon he almost gave up his practice.

In 1919, he was one of the first to join the satyagraha movement in Karnataka and he was also one of the first in Karnataka to take the pledge of a volunteer in the independence movement. In the wake of the First World War, almost famine conditions prevailed in Karnataka. Sadashiv Rao purchased edibles from his personal funds and sold them to the poor at the minimum of the costs. To the extreme poors, he distributed the food free of cost.

He was an eminent lawyer, social worker and Congress leader from South Kanara, Mysore. He organized the Congress Party in Karnataka. He was four times the president of Karnataka Provincial Congress Committee. Soon his house became the hub of political activity in Karnataka. Almost all the important leaders stayed in his house even though the house did not have enough facilities. Mahatma Gandhi, Kasturba, Rajaji, C. R. Das, Sarojini Naidu, Jawaharlal Nehru, the Ali Brothers and others all stayed or waited in his house. As a volunteer in the movement, he was jailed three times and each time, he acted as an ideal prisoner in the Gandhian definition. At one time, he refused to have for himself those facilities which were denied to other inmates, such as he refused to have mosquito nets because other inmates were not given these nets. By now he was not earning as a lawyer. So gradually all his immovable assets were sold out, such as his ancestral house. His old mother and his daughters had to live in a small rented house.

In 1923, he lost his youngest daughter, his son and also his wife Shantabai who had actively supported him in his national duties. But still, he continued with his patriotic and social service activities. For some time for solace, he went to the Sabarmati Ashram. But he could not wait there for a long period because he had to return to Mangalore because of a flash flood there. He was no less a leading social worker than a patriot of the highest order. With the help of his wife Shantabai, he founded an organisation called Mahila Sabha which looked after the welfare of the child-widows and the neglected women. For their betterment, Sadashiv spent freely from his personal funds. He organised several marriages of child –widows. He worked in the field of the welfare of the harijans by being an active member of the Mission for the Depressed Classes NGO and he finally served as its president. He opened a school namely, Tilak Vidyalaya in his premises which was open to the children of all the communities. In this school, Hindi was propagated and taught, besides weaving, spinning and other handi-crafts were also taught. Sadashiv Rao prevailed upon the devotees not to offer animal sacrifices in the temples during the Puja festival. He was an active participant in the Salt Satyagraha of 1930.

He attended the Faizpur Congress session of 1936. He was soaked in the hut in which he was staying, he caught fever. But he traveled to Bombay on Congress work without caring for his health. He could not regain his health and he died at age 56 on 9. 1. 1937 leaving behind his old mother and daughters. He was born in the riches, but he died almost penniless, all in the cause of the poor and in the cause of the nation. Mahatma Gandhi traveled to Mangalore to offer his tributes to her: '' Blessed are you mother for having borne a son such as he ''.

Sadashiv Rao was called the Second Gandhi of Karnataka and also as the Dharmaraj. A locality in Bangalore today is known as Sadashivnagar in his memory. Dr. Shivram Karanth has based his famous novel *Adarayada Uralkali*; embodiment of charity, upon the character of Sadashiv Rao.

S. Srinivas Iyengar (1874-1941) Lawyer and Congress leader of Madras, presided over the Congress session of Gauhati 1926 and was elected to the Central Assembly in 1926.

T. R. Krishnaswamy Iyer, a lawyer from Vaikom. He took active part in the Vaikom movement.

Khan Bahadur Khuda Bux a vakil from Patna. He established the well known and famous **Khuda Bux** Library at Patna. He collected rare manuscripts and Perian and Arabic books from abroad. He brought some rare hand –written Quran with beautiful decorations.

Raizada Bhagat Ram barrister, Jalandhar City. He took active part in the national movements.

Vinayak Vasudev Dastane: He was a leading lawyer of Bhusawal. He gave up his practice for national duty. He performed the marriage of his daughter in a simple manner. He found himself in financial straits. Therefore, Mohandas advised him to enter again into *grihastha-ashram*.

S. V. Visvanatha Iyer, a vakil from Tuticorin. Took an active part in the freedom struggle.

Richard B. Gregg an American lawyer: Hecame to India in 1926 and he studied India's struggle for freedom. His specialization was in the field of the economics of khadi, spinning and weaving. He wrote a book on the freedom movement with a chapter on khadi entitled *Economics of Khaddar*. A part of his thesis on khadi is as under: "… We do not usually think of charkha as a machine, but it really is so. It uses the available mechanical energy of a man, woman or child for producing material goods. The handloom does the same. The mechanical energy is derived from the food eaten by the person. Though in different degrees, manner and mode, the process is the same as that occurring in a steam engine or hydraulic power plant, namely, the transformation of solar energy into mechanical motion. There are today great number of unemployed Indians today. They are, in effect, engines kept running by fuel (food), but not attached to any machines or devices for producing goods. Mr. Gandhi proposes to hitch them to charkhas and thus save a vast existing waste of solar energy…"1. Page 215 Vol. 36 CWMG

A. Shankara Poduval: A lawyer from Trivendram who moved a resolution in March 1929 for the propagation of Hindi in the South expressing deep sense of gratitude to Gandhiji and Seth Jamnalal Bajaj for their untiring efforts in pushing on the Hindi movement in South India and trying to make Hindi the national language of India.

Pandit Durgashankar Mehta of Seoni M. P. He was an active participant in the movements for freedom. He put on khadi clothes. He was chairman of the District Council Seoni.

K. Ganesan: He was a vakil in the High Court of Orissa and he used to practise in Dindigul. He was a khadi worker. He presented thirty thousand yards of khadi to Gandhiji as a gift on his birthday.

B. S. Gopala Rowan advocate from Rajahmundry. He had opened a Hydro Chromopathic and Nature CureAcademy at Rajahmundry.

Sayaji Lakshman Silam is an advocate from Amravati. He was a member of the local Corporation and also of the Anti-untouchability Committee. He presided over the last meeting of the Committee. The Committee decided that the temples belonging to the Telugu Munivar community should be thrown open to the untouchables. This community owned eight temples in Amravati. They were thrown open to the untouchables.

Lala Shyamlal of Rohtak: He gave up his practice of law at the time of the Non Cooperation Movement of 1921. But then due to some financial difficulties in the family, he re-started his practice again. But after the Lahore Congress, he left his practice for all time to become an active Congress worker. He joined the Sabarmati Ashram and he expressed his desire to join the Dandi March also. He was arrested for an offence under Section 124 A of the IPC for sedition on the allegation that he made a fiery speech which had the effect of sowing disaffection against the Government.

Lala Duni Chand, pleader Lahore, Barrister. He was the President of Punjab Congress Committee. He served Congress for forty years, But then he could not any further subscribe to the policy of non-violence under all circumstances. He, therefore, gave up all responsible positions in Congress in July 1941.

U. Gopala Menon, lawyer from Calicut. He endeavoured to get the release of Narayan Menon who was detained for his non operating activities.

D. N. Bahadurji lawyer. He was an eminent lawyer of Bombay. He was Advocate General also. He was the Chairman of the Committee appointed by the Congress to look into the obligations between the British Government and India. In July and August, 1937 there was a lot of repression going on in the Frontier areas such as Akbarpura, Dera Ismail Khan and other places. The Congress requested him to go there and find out and submit a report.

Bhulabhai J. Desai (1877-1946) An eminent lawyer of Bombay. He was an Advocate General also. He was the leader of the Congress Party in the Central Assembly. In 1917, the Indian National Congress passed a resolution to de-recognise and to abolish the evil of untouchability. The resolution was moved by T. Natesan and Bhulabhai J. Desai supported the resolution. In 1944-45, he tried to negotiate the deadlock between Congress and the Muslim League with respect to the formation of a national Government at the centre while holding talks with Liaqat Ali Khan, the Deputy leader of the Muslim League in the Central Assembly. The negotiations failed. As a result of Bhulabhai efforts, Liaqat Ali agreed to what is now called the Desai-Liaqat Pact of 1945. The terms are as under: The Congress and the League agree that they will join in forming an Interim Government at the center on the lines that they will nominate an equal number of persons in the Central Executive, there will be representatives of the minorities particularly the Scheduled Castes and the Sikhs and that the Government will function under the present constitution, i.e. the Government of India Act, 1935.

Subsequently an interim Government was formed at the center. But then it did not work smoothly. After some time, it collapsed. In May 1945, the Communist Party of India had to face several charges from the public at large with respect to their patriotic integrity. The Communists suggested that their charges should be heard and decided by a tribunal. Bhulabhai Desai was one of them in the tribunal. Desai gave his opinion on 9. 8. 1945. Comrade P. C. Joshi admitted before the tribunal that the War which had just ended, was a people's war. He also admitted that the policies of the C. P. I. were opposed to those of the Congress Party.

In September 1945, the A. I. C. C. adopted a resolution to the effect that the soldiers of the Indian Army of Netaji Subhash Chandra Bose should be extended expert legal assistance who were facing trials on several charges. Barrister Jawaharlal Nehru, Barrister Asaf Ali and Dr. Katju and Bhulabhai Desai defended the soldiers of the INA in the trial in the Red Fort.

Kashinath N. Kelkar–A lawyer of Satara City. He was actively involved in the movement for the opening of temples for the untouchables. He wrote a book on the Hindu Law.

R. L. Biswas, a lawyer of Calcutta. –He was associated with the movement for the opening of temples. He was Secretary of the All India Depressed Classes Federation.

C. V. Vaidya an advocate of Bombay. He put up the views of the orthodox Hindus with regard to the issue of temple entry. He wrote a letter to the Prime Minister Mr. Ramsay Mc Donald suggesting to him that the subject of temple entry should not be hastened by legislation to that effect.

Lala Mohanlal an advocate of Simla. He was an M. L. C. also. He was an Arya Samaji. He was involved in the movement in Punjab against untouchability.

Mukundi Lala barrister of Lansdowne U. P. He was actively involved in the movement against untouchability. He wanted to open an orphanage in Garhwal for the children of the depressed classes and he also wanted to provide scholarships to these children. He was a close associate of Pandit Govind Ballabh Pant. He attended the Congress session of Nagpur in 1920 along with Pant.

M. R. Ramaswami a lawyer of Trichur. A temple entry worker.

R. Somasundaram Aiyar an advocate from Madras. He worked for the economic betterment of the poor persons in his own individual manner.

S. Krishna Iyer High Court vakil from Trivandrum. Actively involved in the temple entry agitation. B. *N.* Samsala barrister from Midnapore took part in the freedom movement.

Vishvanath Prasad Sinha, pleader from Chhapra. An active worker in the movement against untouchability.

Loknath Mishra a lawyer from Puri. He was Secretary of the Anti Untouchability Committee, Puri. A. Kaleshwar Rao, a pleader of Bezwada. Took active part in the freedom movement by helping the prisoners.

K. R. Chhapkhane, pleader of Sangli. He helped in collection of funds for the state subjects during the 1920 movement.

Harilal Govindji, a lawyer of Amreli. He worked for the removal of untouchability. He helped in creating a congenial atmosphere for both the proponents and opponent-satanists.

P. N. Gadre, a lawyer of Nasik. He worked for the improvement of the conditions of the Bhangis and Mahars of Nasik.

Parasuram Gopal Masurekar, lawyer of Rajkot. He worked for harijan welfare in Rajkot. The residents of Rajkot decided to build a new temple for all communities, the priest would be a harijan who did not believe in untouchability, there would be a public library, a free dispensary and a night school for the adults.

Bipin Bihari Verma, a lawyer of Champaran: He was a close associate of Babu Brijkishore Prasad.

Lalchand Navanrai, a lawyer of Larkana Sindh, now in Pakistan. An active worker in the cause of harijans. He helped in the collection of funds for them.

K. Rama Menon an advocate of Chalapuram, Calicut. He was an active worker in the cause of the harijans

G. B. Pradhan a lawyer of Bombay. He was actively involved in the work of the education of women. S. S. Pande, a lawyer of Khandwa, his field of interest was the preservation of the village industries. Rajendra Nath Barua a lawyer of Golaghat Assam. He was a khadi worker. He tried to popularize spinning and khadi in his place.

Damodar M. Damle, a lawyer of Berar. He was interested in the improvement of a lot of poor agriculturists. He wrote an article on his means and methods which he wanted to be published in the *Harijan*.

P. Narayana Reddy a lawyer of Peddathippa Sumudram, Chittor. He was a worker in the field of harijan welfare and village industry.

Justice Sir Govindrao Madgaonkar. He was a judge of the Bombay High Court. He was interested in the reforms in the caste system. He called upon Mahatma Gandhi, Pt. Mdan Mohan Malviya and N. C. Kelkar to give a positive leadership in the reform of the caste system.

Munnalal G. Shah a lawyer of Gujarat. He gave up practice to educate the poor villagers of Seagon.

Sir C. P. Ramaswami Aiyar. An eminent lawyer of Travancore Cochin. He was Dewan of this place. His handling of the situation in Travancore Cochin during the temple agitation raised many eye–brows. He was accused of not allowing the popular Government to take root in Travancore. When in August 1942 Mahatma offered that the Muslim League could take over the administration of the whole of India ''including the so called Indian India, ''provided the Muslim League agreed to the independence of India, Sir Aiyar was quick to file his objection to such a scheme. Travancore Cochin was one of the 642 or so- called 'Indian India ' whom the British Government had given some sort of autonomy in several spheres. With the lapse of British paramountcy, these States would have been free to exercise an offer whether to remain free or to join the Indian federation or the newly formed Pakistan. Sir C. P. being the Dewan of Travancore, Cochin immediately objected. After independence, Sir CP was involved in the framing of the Constitution of India as a member of the Constituent Assembly.

T. S. Subrahmanyan of Bellary, **a** lawyer. He was a worker in the field of khadi, village industries, harijan service and communal harmony.

T. M. Verghese, a lawyer of Travancore Cochin. He was an eminent lawyer who was active in the movement for the integration of the Travancore and Cochin. He was elected to the Travancore Legislative Assembly and was made the Deputy Speaker. He was responsible for the establishment of the Congress in Kerala. During the period between 1930 to 1943, he participated in all the movements and was imprisoned several times. While taking part in the movement for the temple entry for the harijans, the police resorted to repression of the satyagrahis. Verghese was assaulted and beaten up. After independence he was again returned to the Travancore Assembly and became its Speaker.

K. Madhavan Nair: He took his law degree in 1909 from the Trivandrum Law College and he started his practice in Manjeri. But he later shifted to Calicut in 1915. By this time, he had already begun to take active part in the freedom movement. He was drawn in the Home Rule movement. He was imprisoned during the Non Cooperation Movement of 1920-21. After the Moplah disturbances, he organised relief work for the victims. He was elected as the Secretary of the Kerala Congress Committee and in 1925, he was chosen as the President. He took active part in all the agitations, such as the Civil Disobedience Movement, boycott of the foreign clothes, prohibition and against the Simon Commision. He was active in the Vaikom temple entry agitation and also in the Guruvayur Satyagraha. He served as the director of the referendum committee in the Vaikom movement. He founded the *Mathrubhumi* newspaper and served as its managing director.

K. P. Kesavan Menon, barrister: He took his B. A. degree from the Madras University and Bar-at-law from the Middle Temple, London. He started his legal practice in Calicut and soon made a mark. At the same time, he began to take active part in the freedom movement such as in the Home Rule movement. He was a member of the Home Rule deputation under Mrs. Annie Besant which went to London to present a memorandum to the Secretary of State for India in 1917. In 1921, he took part in the Non Co-operation Movement and was jailed. He took active part in the Vaikom satyagraha of 1924 and was imprisoned for six months. He faced acute financial difficulties and, therefore, he went to Malaya to set up his legal practice there. There too, he could not sit idle and worked his best for the betterment of the indenture laborers of Indian origin working there. Kesava Menon joined the Indian Independence League which was established by Ras Bihari Bose. But after Netaji Subhash Chandra Bose took over the leadership of the League and the Indian National Army and then formed the Azad Hind, he parted ways with Netaji because of certain differences of opinion with Netaji. He was a combatant against the Japanese in Malaya at Singapore, he was caught by the Japanese and detained and was released after the W. W. II ended in1945. In 1946 he returned to India and took over the editorship of the *Mathurbhumi*. He was appointed as High Commissioner of India to Sri Lanka. He was an eminent writer of Malayali literature and was awarded the Kerala Sahitya Akademi. He was highly respected in Kerala. The Government of India decorated him with the second highest civil honor Padma Vibhushan. He died in November 1978.

C. Kesavan (1891 TO 1969). He took his law degree from the Trivandrum Law College and he started his legal practice in Quilon. He was an active worker in the field of the eradication of untouchability in the Kerala province. He was an active participant in the Abstention Movement of Travancore. He made a fiery speech in July 1935 and was charged with the offence of sedition and he was sentenced for two years. In the Quit India Movement of 1942, he was sentenced for one year and he was released in July 1943. He was the Chief Minister of Travancore Cochin in 1951. He died in July 1969

E. Ikkanda Varier: While studying for law in the Madras Law College, Varier came in contact with Mahatma Gandhi which turned out to be the turning point of his career. He not only started his legal practice in Trichur, but at the same timehe began to take part in the national movements. He was elected to the Trichur Municipal Council. He was elected to the Cochin Legislative Council for four terms. He was President of the Cochin Prajamandal and in this capacity, he worked for the establishment of the responsible Government in Travancore Cochin. He was an exponent of khadi and worked for its promotion in Trichur. He took active part in the Quit India Movement of 1942 and was sentenced for one year. After independence, he was appointed as the Prime Minister of Cochin. He died in June 1977

Popatlal Purushottam Ananda and Gajanan Bhavanishankar Joshi, two well-known lawyers of Kathiawar who took active part in the Rajkot agitation. They were two of the members of the Committee which was formed to resolve the issues involved in the agitation. Advocate Ananda was a member of the Praja Pratinidhi Samiti, Kathiawar and advocate Joshi was Secretary of the local Ramkrishna Mission.

Lala Kewal Krishna and Lala Bodhraj of Multan. Two well known lawyers of Multan, now in Pakistan. They gave up their established practices to join the freedom struggle by being part of the Non Cooperation Movement of 1920.

U. N. Dhebar (1905 -1977)A lawyer of Rajkot, who took active part in the Rajkot agitation. He organised the Rajkot Mill Kamdar Mazdoor Sangh; he was a minister in the Saurashtra Government in 1948. He was closely associated with the Kathiawad Political Conference. He was the President of the INC 1955-59. He was Chairman of the Scheduled Tribes Area Commission and President of the Bhartiya Adim Jati Sangh 1962-1964. He was elected to the Lok Sabha in 1962. He was Chairman of Khadi and Village Industries Commission 1963 and Chairman of the Primary Education Commission after independence. During the communal carnage of 1947, Kathiawad was under fire. Dhebar worked hard to quell the disturbances.

Devchand Bhai Parekh, a barrister of Gujrat. He was a fellow student of Mahatma since school days and a life-long friend. He helped him in collecting funds for the Sabarmati Ashram when there was such a need in 1917.

Chaudhari Abdul Majid of Punjab. He was anxious about the participation of the Muslims under the Congress banner in the freedom movement.

H. C. Dasappa, a lawyer of Mysore. He was an active participant in the satyagrahas that were staged in Mysore from time to time. The District Magistrate of Mysore issued prohibitory orders that nobody will take out processions and nobody will address public meetings. H. C. Dasappa did just the opposite. He addressed a meeting which was prohibited in this manner. The Chief Justice of the Mysore High Court took disciplinary action against him. He debarred Dasappa from practising as a lawyer for life. This case was reported by the

Hindu. H. C. Dasappa had put in twenty years of practice at the Bar.

Justice Changanacherry K. Parameswaran Pillai. He retired as a judge of the Travancore High Court. He was a member of the Executive Council of Harijan Sevak Sangh.

Sir B. N. Rau. He was the Chairman of the Hindu Law Committee which was appointed in January 1941 ''to examine the Hindu Women's Rights to Property Act of 1937 with special reference to five private bills 'The report which was published from Delhi on 26. 7. 1941 advocated immediate admission of the daughter to an equal share with the daughter-in-law. It suggested legislation for agricultural land with retrospective effect in order to give widows the full measure of the multiplicity of rules of succession. The Committee had recommended ' preparation, gradual stages of a complete code of Hindu law beginning with the law of succession instead of piecemeal legislation. The task of the codification of the Hindu law was completed by the Committee on 4. 8. 1941.

He was a member of the Conciliation Committee which was appointed by the Standing Committee of the Non Party Conference in November 1944 following the failure of the talks between Gandhiji and M. A. Jinnah with regard to the communal problems between the Hindus and the Muslims.

L. Krishnaswami Bharati, a lawyer and an MLA from Madura. He was listed as a satyagrahi and was imprisoned.

R. K. Nandkeolyar, barrister of Gaya. He took part in the satyagraha movement. He was ordered not to enter the United Provinces. He defied the order of externment.

Dr. T. R. Kedar, advocate of Nagpur. He helped the accused persons in the Ashti and Chimur trials.

Devraj Sethi, lawyer of Jhang City. He was involved in the work of Nayee Talim.

V. Bhashyam Ayyangar. He was a judge of the Madras High Court. Later, he joined the freedom movement. He was instrumental in the opening of the Harijan Industrial School, Kodambakkam, Madras.

Ali Hussain, a barrister of Patna. During the partition carnage in 1946-47, he worked hard to restore communal harmony in Patna.

Abdul Aziz, a barrister of Patna. He was a member of the Muslim League of Patna, Bihar. During the carnage of March 1947, he worked for the restoration of peace. Affected persons had abandoned their places. Abdul Aziz suggested that there should be pockets of residences for the victims of riots.

Ganesh Krishna Khaparde (1854 – 1938); lawyer, orator and public worker of Amravati; member of the Council of State under the Montague – Chelmsford Reforms. He did not favour the Non- Co –operation Movement of the Mahatma.

Yadwarkar Patwardhan of Amravati:He was a graduate of law from the Bombay University, but he never practised law. He met Mohandas in 1915 and lived in the Sabarmati Ashram. He worked as sub- editor of *Young India* for about one year without any payment. He attended the Congress session of 1920. He died soon thereafter of an illness on Ekadashi day. He was a silent worker, shy of publicity and devoted to his duty.

Sir Ras Behari Ghosh (23.12.1845–28.2.1921) – After obtaining the degree of Bachelor of Law in 1867, Ras Behari Ghosh started his practice in Calcutta High Court as a vakil. He soon developed a successful practice at the Bar of Calcutta. In 1871, he was awarded the prestigious Doctor of Laws degree. Simultaneous to his practice as a lawyer,he began to take active part in the freedom movement of India by joining the Indian National Congress. In this field also, he soon created a distinct place for himself. He presided over the annual sessions of the INC in the years 1907 at Surat and 1908 at Madras. He was elected as a member of the Bengal Legislative Council in the years 1891 to 1894 and 1906 to 1909.He earned the reputation of an authority in the civil side of law. The British Government knighted him in the year 1915.He was a great philanthropist. He donated generously in the field of education. Ras Behari Ghosh Avenue in Calcutta now Kolkata and Sir Ras Behari Ghosh Mahavidyalaya in Ukhrid affiliated to the University of Burdwan perpetuate his memory.

Chapter Fourteen

Some of the Foreigners Who Espoused the Cause of India's Freedom but Are Almost Forgotten Today

Allan Octavian Hume ICS (4 June 1829)–

He was one of the founders of the Indian National Congress which was founded on 28 December 1885 at the Gokuldas Tejpal Sanskrit College in Bombay, with 72 initial delegates. Hume assumed the General Secretary position with Womesh Chunder Bonnerjee of Calcutta as the first President. Along with him, two other British members were members of the founding group i.e. Sir William Wedderburn and Justice Sir John Jardine. The other members were mostly Hindus drawn from Bombay and Calcutta.

He had worked as District Collector and Magistrate of Etawah which is now in U. P. from 1856 to 1857. He was a very successful and popular officer of the ICS. In 1867 Hume became Commissioner of Customs for the North West Province, and in 1870 he became attached to the central Government as Director-General of Agriculture. In 1879 he returned to provincial Government at Allahabad Secretary to the Department of Revenue, Agriculture and Commerce (1871–1879).

He brought the situation in Etawah under control earlier than many other places following the up-risings of 1857. He had closely watched the events of 1857, he drew out his conclusions as to why there was a revolt and he decided that there was something wrong with the British policies towards their subjects and also inthere implementations. He decided that the Indians deserved better treatment and more involvement and participation in their political and constitutional affairs. He also believed that the Indians also required a representative body to express their demands before the British Government. He worked along with other pioneers/founders on this behalf and this is how the Indian National Congress came into existence. Allan Octavio Hume has been considered to be the pioneer of Ornithology in India. He was a keen bird-watcher. He had a large collection of birds in Simla.

Sir Henry John Stedman Cotton, KCSI (13 September 1845 – 22 October 1915)–He arrived in India in 1867 as an ICS officer with his first posting in Midnapore. He served in various capacities such as Assistant Secretary to the Government of Bengal, Magistrate and Collector Chittagong, Senior Secretary to the Board of Revenue Government of Bengal, Revenue Secretary to the Government of Bengal and finally as Chief Commissioner to the Government of Bengal.

Sir Cotton was sympathetic to the aspirations of the Indians. He advocated that the Indians should be involved in their administration. He supported Home Rule for them in his book *New India or India in Transition* 1885 revised in 1907. The book raised controversy as it was not taken properly by the British Government. Sir Cotton was elected as the President of the INC in 1904. He died in October 1915.

George Yule (1829-1892) George Yule was a British Scottish merchant, founder of the George and Yule Company of London and head of the Andrew Yule and Company of Calcutta. He served as the fourth President of the Indian National Congress held in 1888 at Allahabad. He was also the sheriff of Calcutta and President of the Indian Chamber of Commerce.

Alfred John Webb (1834–1908) Alfred was an Irish nationalist who stood against imperialist empires all over the world, including the United Kingdom. However, he disagreed with other Irish nationalists who believed that Irish independence could be achieved only through violent means. He stood for peaceful and constitutional methods for achieving independence. He also stood for universal suffrage and abolition of slavery system besides being an active anti-imperialist. He was a Member of British Parliament a number of times.

He was a close friend of Dada Bhai Naoroji who invited him to preside over the Indian National Congress. He did this job in 1894 and thus became the third foreigner after George Yule and William Waddenburn to hold this important assignment.

Sir William Wedderburn (25 March 1838 – 25 January 1918)–He was posted at Dharwad as an ICS officer as an Assistant Collector. He went on to hold several posts such as Judicial Commissioner in Sindh, District and Sessions Judge Poona in 1887 and finally the Chief Secretary to the Government of Bombay in 1887 at the time of his retirement.

Like some of his other colleagues in the ICS, Sir Waddenburn had the occasion to witness the happenings of 1857. He would like them to appreciate the reasons behind the dis-satisfaction against the British Raj. But unlike many of them. Sir Waddenburn set about the path of their redressal. He noticed that the field of agriculture and the condition of indebtedness of the poor farmers needed immediate reforms. He also wanted to revive the traditions of the ancient village system such as their local self governance since ages. Sir Waddenburn found a platform in the shape of the newly created Indian National Congress which he went on to preside over in its 20th session held at Bombay In 1889. He repeated the same responsibility in the 25th session in 1910.

During his service in India, Wedderburn's attention was focussed on famine, the poverty of the Indian peasantry, the problem of agricultural indebtedness and the question of reviving the ancient village system. In 1895 Sir Wedderburn espoused the cause of Indian finance before the Welby Commission i.e. Royal Commission on Indian Expenditure. He was also associated with the activities of the Indian Famine Union which was set up in June 1901 to investigate the causes of the famines and also for proposing preventive measures. Many of his colleagues criticized him for his inclination towards Indian affairs, for his support for constitutional reforms for India and for his recommendation of greater participation of Indians in their local governance. He was elected as a Member of Parliament as a Liberal in 1983. He continued his support for the Indian cause from that platform also. He entered Parliament in 1893 as a Liberal member and sought to voice India's grievances in the House. He formed the Indian Parliamentary Committee with which he was associated as Chairman from 1893 to 1900.

Smt. Annie Besant Wood (1 October 1847 – 20 September 1933) Annee Besant was a person of multi-talents with versatile interests ranging from the field of social service extending upto the other fields of education, philanthropy, writing and activism in the field of women's rights. She supported self rule for her Irish countrymen and also for the Indians. Annee married Frank Besant at age 20 in 1867. The Besants had two children. But the marriage did not last long. It terminated in a judicial separation in 1873 because of incompatibility arising out of unconventional views of Annee in the religious issues. By about this time, Annee came in contact with Charles Bradlaugh and Helena Blavatsky who held secular and theosophical views. She joined the Theosophical Society of Helena Blavatsky in this capacity, she visited India sometimes in 1887or so. She founded the Theosophical Society of India. In 1898, she helped in the establishment of the Central Hindu School in Benaras which later on blossomed into the Banaras Hindu University. In 1907, she became the President of the Theosophical Society of India. Annee was a person of open mind and, therefore, she felt liberated by the judicial separation with her husband. She could now on wards give more flight to her secular and liberal views. She did not subscribe to the orthodox Christian doctrines and she began to dispute the authority of the organized religion as embodied by the Church of England as the repository of Christianity as the state-sponsored religion. She joined the Indian National Congress. In 1914, she founded the Home Rule League along with Lokmanya Balgangadhar Tilak and began to propagate the idea of Home Rule and dominion status for the Indians within the British Empire. She was elected as the President of the Indian National Congress in 1917. She treated Jiddu Krishnamurthi as her adopted son along with whom she traveled to the United States in 1920. He took over from here to stay further there and he went on to become one of the leading philosophers of the age. In 1893, she was the representative of The Theosophical

Society at the World Parliament of Religions in Chicago. Here she came in acquaintance with Swami Vivekanand and this relationship was to last till the untimely death of the Swami. In her memory, there is a locality in Chennai by the name Besant Nagar. Starting her campaign for home-rule for the Indians, she went on to advance the cause of independence for them. She was detained and arrested for her participation in the freedom movement. Both Mahatma Gandhi and Mohammad Ali Jinnah voiced for her release. She was a brilliant speaker and a prolific writer. She wrote more than three hundred books and papers on subjects of contemporary interests. She died in Adyar Madras now Chennai on 20. 9. 1933 at age 85.

Sir Alexander McRoberts (1854—1922)–He was a British entrepreneur who came to India in 1884. He became the manager of the sick Cawnpore Woolen Mill. By sheer hard work and skill, Sir Alexander changed the fortunes of the ailing company into a prosperous company. He acquired a few other companies also. In 1920, he established the British India Corporation as a public limited company which manufactured **Lal Imli** and **Dhariwal** woolens for the civilians and also for the defence forces. The Company was nationalized in 1981 and it was taken over by the Government of India.

Romain Rolland (29 January 1866 – 30 December 1944)–He was a French author, writer, idealist and philosopher who won the Nobel Prize for literature in 1915. He was sympathetic to the aspirations of the Indians in their struggle for independence and also a great admirer of Mahatma Gandhi. He advised Madeleine Slade to go to India and join the life of the ashram of Mahatma Gandhi.

Margaret Elizabeth Noble or Sister Nivedita (28 October 1867 – 13 October 1911)– Margarete Elizabeth Noble met Swami Vivekanand for the first time in England in 1895 when he was staying there for a period of three months. The Swami was explaining the Hindu way of life and Vedanta philosophy to the hosts there. Margaret was immediately impressed. She was herself of religious bent of mind. So she decided to pursue a life of asceticism. She came to India in 1898 much to the displeasure of her family members. In Calcutta, she joined the Ramakrishna Mission and the Dakshineshwar Temple where Swami Ramakrishna and Sarda Devi used to spiritualise. Swami Vivekanand introduced her to the Calcutta audience in a public meeting and he gave her the name Sister Nivedita. The Swami had invited her to India to spread education to the girls and women of Bengal. Besides this project, Sister Nivedita engaged herself in social service works such as she worked during the spread of famine, plague and floods in Bengal. Sister Nivedita soon engaged herself in the national cause of independence. The partition of Bengal in 1905 agitated her into active participation. She publicly challenged the policy of Lord Curzon who was responsible for the partition. She affiliated herself with the Anushilan Samiti which bred most of the revolutionaries of Bengal like Sri Arubindo. She edited *Karma Yogi* journal of Sri Arubindo. She also influenced the patriotic and nationalistic writings of the great Tamil poet Subramania Bharti. In her school, she asked her students to sing Vande Mataram. She died young aged 44 on 13 October 1911 in Calcutta.

Charles Freer Andrews (12 February 1871 – 5 April 1940)– He arrived in India in 1904 as a priest of the Church of England. India was soon to become his permanent home and the main theater of hissocial activities. He had come here primarily on missionary work, but then he ended up doing almost everything else except evangelical proselytization. Mahatma Gandhi used to quote his example as a model Christian. The Mahatma used to call him as the Christ's Faithful Apostle. He was popular amongst the masses as Deenbandhu. Along with Gopal Krishna Gokhale, he was instrumental in recalling Mahatma from South Africa on the ground that his next sphere of activity was India. It is therefore, natural that C. F. himself got involved in the freedom movement of India. His gospel taught him to take up the cause of the oppressed people all over the world. So he felt some division of loyalty between the Church of England and his social philosophy. This Church soon divested him of these responsibilities. Andrew visited South Africa in 1914. There he came in personal contact with Mohandas. He was immediately impressed by the non-violent and peaceful means of Mohandas there which he believed to be in alignment with the Christian teachings. Back in India, he was soon to be drawn in the freedom struggle with him. Andrews served as an intermediary between General Smuts and Mohandas and it can be said that he was instrumental to some extent in the creation of the final settlement between the South African Government and the British Indians there. Andrew visited Fiji a number of times to help resolve the problems of indentured Indian workers there. He helped resolve the labour problems in Madras now Chennai in 1913. When Mohandas actively worked for the enrolment of the Indian soldiers in 1919 to help the British Government in their involvement in the First World War, Andrew disagreed with him in the conscientious objection that the war could not be compatible with the teachings of ahimsa. The two perhaps resolved their differences later on when the Deenbandhu realised that Mohandas was hopeful of eliciting greater self governance for the Indians from the British Government. It is another matter that the hopes of the future Mahatma were later unfulfilled. He was very close to the Poet Tagore also. He visited Shanti Niketan and spent a lot of time with the Poet.

Andrews agitated for the removal of untouchability. He participated in the Vaikom Satyagraha. He joined hands with Dr. B. R. Ambedkar in formulating the demands of the dalits. He accompanied the Mahatma in the Second Round Table Conference in 1931. Even though he was one of his closest friends, there were some irreconcilable differences between them. For example, Mohandas asked him to leave the issue of the freedom of India to the Indians themselves. So after 1935, C. F. began to spend more time in England from where he continued to espouse the Indian cause. C. F. died on 5. 4. 1940 in Calcutta now Kolkata during his visit to India. He rests in perpetual peace in the Lower Circular Road Cemetery there.

Dinabandhu Andrews College Calcutta, Dinabandhu Institution Calcutta, High School Salimpur South Calcutta and Deenabandhu Hospital Thachampara Palakkad Kerala are some of the monuments which remember him to us.

Josiah Clement Wedgwood (1872-1943)–He was British Member of Parliament on Labour ticket from 1919 to 1942. He was sympathetic with the Indian cause. He attended the INC session of 1920 which was held in Nagpur. His wife Florence was in correspondence with Mahatma Gandhi.

Henry Soloman Leon Pollock –He was an English Jew who was a very close associate of Mahatma Gandhi in South

Africa since 1903 in his passive/active resistance against racial discrimination against the British Indians. His wife Milli was also associated in these movements.

The South African British Indians Congress sent Pollock a couple of times to India to express the conditions of the British Indians there with an intention to seek popular support from here. He addressed the Calcutta session of the Indian National Congress in 1909. He toured many cities here and addressed several meetings. After the return of Mahatma Gandhi to India in January 1915, Pollock retained his association with the cause of India. He was the editor of the journal namely *India*, the journal of the British Committee of the Indian National Congress. He was deeply worried about the division of the Congress Party into two factions, moderates and the extremists. He, therefore, wrote to G. A. Natesan the editor to use his good offices to see to it that the Party remained united. In April 1919, a delegation of the Congress Party arrived in London to take stock of the situation there. The delegation concluded that the journal *India* under the editorship of Pollock was too simple and it did not reflect the views of the Indian National Congress in an effective way even though it was founded by the Indian National Congress. In July 1919, mainly due to the efforts of Lokmanya Bal Gangadhar Tilak and Vithalbhai Patel, the London branch was brought under effective and complete control of the INC with a new constitution. He was a regular subscriber to the *Young India*.

Samuel or Sam Higginbottom (27 October 1874 – 11 June 1958)– He was an English Christian missionary who visited India on evangelical work. But he soon engaged himself in social service projects mainly in the scientification of agriculture and farming. He was primarily based in Allahabad. He went to the United States, stayed there for a period of three years, learnt modern technology of agriculture in the Ohio University, returned to India and revolutionized agriculture here. By his efforts, the Allahabad Institute of Agriculture was founded in 1919. The Institute has been re-named as the Sam Higginbottom University of Agriculture, Technology and Sciences (SHAUTS). Sam sympathized with the nationalistic aspirations of the Indians. He admired Mahatma Gandhi and Jawaharlal Nehru.

Samuel Evans Stokes or Satyananda Stokes (16 August 1882 – 14 May 1946)–Samuel arrived in India in 1904 at age 22 because he was interested in doing social service work in a place like India. His father was opposed to this plan because he had a large business and he naturally wanted that his son should step into his shoes in the days to come. Young Samuel settled down in Shimla where he began to work in a lepers colony. He soon became very popular with the lepers. In 1922, he married a Rajput girl by name Agnes who was a Christian. His father later turned on to help him financially once the senior realized that his son was doing admirable work in India. Samuel purchased a piece of land in Shimla and he began to cultivate a new variety of apples here. The enterprise soon became successful and he earned a reputation as a pioneer in this field. Samuel came under the influence of Hindu way of life Hindu philosophy and religion and he embraced Hinduism with a new name as Satyananda. Agness also changed her name to Priyadevi. Samuel or Satyananda took an active part in the freedom struggle of India. He was made a member of the All India Congress Committee (AICC). He had the rare honour of signing the

Congress manifesto in 1921. He took active part in the Civil Disobedience Movement of 1922 and he was imprisoned for an offence of sedition. He passed away on 14. 5. 1946.

Muriel Lester (9 December 1883 – 11 February 1968)– Nobody knows when the fire of devoting one's life to the service of the more deserving may ignite in one's conscience. In the case of nineteen year old Lester this turning point arrived during a visit with her father in 1902 to a destitute place Bow London. Her impressionable mind was disturbed by the needs of the destitutes. She began to visit them regularly and did her best for them. The loss of her brother at age 26 must have created another impact upon her psyche. She decided to open up a community hall from where the needy persons of the locality could arrange their community requirements such as community meetings, community ceremonies and other charitable activities. She and her sister Doris bought a premise namely Zion Chapel in Bow in 1914 She named it to commemorate her brother who had the name Kingsley Hall. Hence the name Kingsley Hall to her venture. It was a place for those who had no place anywhere else. It is remarkable that Mahatma Gandhi stayed here for a period of three months during his visit to London for the Round Table Conference. Mohandas invited Lester to visit India which she did subsequently in1934. She stayed with the Saint for about three months in the Ashram and toured the length and breadth of India along with him. A born pacifist, she was immediately attracted by the aspirations of the Indians in their struggle for freedom from her own country. She lent her moral support to this cause. She worked along with the Mahatma during her stay in India towards the efforts to eradicate the curse of untouchability. It is about this time that she took over the management of the

Kingsley Hall to her equally devoted sister Dorothy in order to devote her greater time in her pacifist activities as an Ambassador-at-large for the International Fellowship for Reconciliation (IFOR). She lent her powerful voice against the happenings in the Spanish War of 1936, against World War II and in any other place the world over where there were such events taking place. She became a world celebrity. She was twice nominated for the Nobel Prize for Peace. But she could not climb the last ladder up to the pinnacle. She died on 11. 2. 1968.

Agatha Mary Harrison (1885–1954)–She visited India in 1929 and then she had extended stays here with Mahatma Gandhi. Like so many of the British citizens, she was sympathetic of the aspirations of the Indians. She, therefore, acted as a siphon between the British Government and the Indian National Congress which otherwise meant Mohandas Along with Horace Alexander, she prepared Mohandas mentally to attend the Round Table Conference in London in 1931-32 which was slated to define the future constitutional frame of the Indians. She spent sufficient time in the Sevagram Ashram with Gandhiji. She came in close proximity with him. During the hunger strikes or fasts of the Mahatma, she acted as a conduit of his views to the world outside. She visited India again alongside the visit of the Cabinet Mission in 1946 to draw out the final plan of India towards independence and towards the creation of Pakistan. She had an understanding with the leaders of the Muslim League also so that she was able to restore rapproachment between the two communities when-ever communal problems arose. She worked along with women's groups in India also and she participated in the Women's Conference of 1949.

Nellie Sengupta or Edith Ellen Gray (12 January 1886– 23 October 1973)–Edith Ellen Gray the daughter of Fredrick and Henrietta Gray of Cambridge fell in love with Jatindra Mohan Sengupta when he was studying in Cambridge University. She defied the opposition of her parents to marry Jatindra who went on to become a well-known freedom-fighter of Bengal.

On return to India, Jatindra launched a successful career as a lawyer soon to enter into the movement for freedom. He was the mayor of Calcutta three times and member of the Legislative Assembly of Bengal. She joined her husband in the Non-Co-operation Movement of 1921. Jatindra was imprisoned for his role in the Assam-Bengal Railways strike. She made several public speeches in support of the freedom movement and she was imprisonment. She was again imprisoned for four months in 1931 for addressing a public meeting which the authorities deemed to be unlawful. She was an active khadi-worker also and she promoted its sale. She participated in the Salt Satyagraha of 1930. When several senior Congress leaders were arrested in the wake of this movement, Nellie was elected as the President. In this manner, she became only the third woman to hold this important post. She became the second foreign woman to get this honour. She was also elected as an MLA of Bengal in 1940 and 1946. After the independence of India and the birth of Pakistan, she chose to reside in East Pakistan in Chittagong with the intention of looking after the interests of the minorities there. There also she was equally active. She was elected to the Legislative Assembly there unopposed in 1954. She held several important posts there. She died in 1973 the same year she was decorated with the second highest civilian honour of Padma Vibhushan by the Government of India.

Horace Gundry Alexander (18 April 1889 – 30 September 1989) –Horace Alexander was sent to India in 1928 by the Quaker committee of the British to try to mend fences between Lord Irwin the Viceroy and Mahatma Gandhi. There was a feeling prevalent there at that point of time that the Indians were not yet fit for self rule. This is the first time in 1928 that Horace met the Mahatma; he went on to become one of the best friends of Mohandas. He developed an understanding of the problems and aspirations of the Indians and thereafter, he sought every possible occasion and every possible forum to espouse the cause of Indian freedom either here in India or in England. He was instrumental in the meeting between the Viceroy and the Saint in 1931. He also facilitated the visit of Mohandas to the RTC in London in 1931-32. After the conference was over Horace founded the India Conciliation Group along with Agatha Harrison and Carl Heath. The two were also in India for a long period and they were also associated with Mahatma Gandhi. Horace did not fully support the Quit India movement of 1942. He advised Mohandas not to embark upon this movement when the British Government was facing the crisis of World War II. Horace also worked along with Mahatma in trying to restore communal harmony between the two communities.

Horace was with Mohandas in Calcutta when India was ushering into the era of independence. He witnessed Noakhali and other incidents during those fateful days. He has described these events and his experiences with him in his auto-biography *Gandhi- Through the Western Eyes*. The Government of India decorated him with the second highest civilian award –Padma Vibhushan in 1984.

Madeleine Slade also known as Mirabehn or Meera Behn (November 22, 1892- July 20, 1982)–Her father was Sir Edmond Slade Commander-in-chief of the East Indies Squadron and then he became Director of the Intelligence Division.

The music of Ludwig van Beethoven was one of the main driving forces of Madeline. She visited Vienna and Berlin to see the places where Beethoven had lived and composed his symphanees. She was also interested in the works of Romain Rolland on Beethoven and this passion took her to Villeneuve France where she met the French philosopher. He advised her to go to India and meet Mahatma Gandhi whom he described as the incarnation of Jesus Christ and as the greatest living person of the century. Madeline wrote a letter to the Mahatma asking whether she could join him in his Ashram. Mohandas wrote back to inform her of the discipline of the Ashram. She agreed to abide by these stringent rules of asceticism, vegetarianism and spinning. She came to India on 7. 11. 1925. Mahadev Desai, a long time secretary of the Mahatma, Sardar Vallabh Bhai Patel and Swami Anand welcomed her into the Ashram. Soon she learnt Hindi in the Gurukul Kangri and she soon initiated herself in the spirituality of India by joining the Bhagwat Bhakti Ashram in Rewari of Swami Parmanad Maharaj.

It was a smooth transition for her from spirituality to mainstream nationalism of the freedom struggle of India. She actively participated in all the movements for freedom which were launched by the Mahatma. She accompanied him to London in 1931 during the Round Table Conference. For her participation in the Non Cooperation Movement, she was imprisoned by the British Government in 1932-1933. While in

England, she pleaded the cause of Indian freedom with David Lloyd George, Sir Winston Churchil and other prominent British politicians. She also went to the USA where she met Mrs. Eleanor Roosevelt, the wife of the President of the USA. She even wanted to convert herself into Hinduism. But she was dissuaded from doing so by Mohandas on the plea that she could still be a better Christian. He gave her a new name Mirabehn. When in 1936, Mohandas decided to wind up the Sabarmati Ashram and instead establish another ashram in Sevagram Wardha, she helped him in the change over. During the World War II, there was a threat of the Japanese invasion of India following their rapid march into Burma. Mirabehn toured Orissa extensively to allay the fear of the people against this threat. She took active interest in the Quit India Movement of 1942 although it was confined to only two volunteers i.e. Jawaharlal Nehru and Sant Vinoba Bhave. She aroused the sentiments of the people in favor of this historic event. She was arrested by the British and incarcerated for a period from August 1942 to May 1944 in the Aga Khan Palace confinement along with Mahatma Gandhi, Kasturba Gandhi, Mahadev Desai and others. It is here that she witnessed the passing away of Mahadev Desai and Kasturba. She took the permission of the Saint to set up Kisan Ashram at a village namely Muldaspur Majra near Roorkee. Then she set up an ashram namely Pashulok Ashram near Rishikesh, another ashram namely Bapu Gram and Gopal Ashram in Bhilangana in 1952. The ruthless deforestation in Kumaon and Garhwal pained her a great deal and she went there to prevent the destruction as much as she could help in this behalf.

She was also a witness to all the historic moments such as the Simla Conference, the Cabinet Mission visit of 1946, the elections to the Constituent Assembly of India, the earlier Direct Action of the Muslim League, the holocaust preceding the independence of India and the birth of Pakistan and the actual events of 14 and 15 August of 1947 and finally the assassination of the Mahatma. Perhaps her life's mission achieved in India, Mirabehn devoted the rest of her remaining days in the pursuit of her other motivating passion i.e. the music of Beethoven. She moved on to England and Vienna in 1959 thereafter to be with the beauties of the master composer. The Government of India recognized her services to the nation by decorating her with the second highest civil honour i.e. the Padma Vibhushan in 1981. She passed away in 1982.

Maurice Frydman (1894—1976)–Maurice came to India in late 1930s as a Jew refugee from Warsaw Poland in the wake of the World War II. He was an electrical engineer and he worked as a Managing Director in the employment of the Government of Mysore princely state. He began to take active part in the princely affairs immediately on his arrival here. He motivated the Maharaja of Mysore to frame a democratic constitution for the state of Aundh which was a part of Mysore. This was in 1938-1939. In those days many of the princely states were not ruling over their subjects in a democratic manner. So in this way, the state of Aundh became the first princely state to become democratic even before the achievement of independence. He lived in the Sevagram Ashram with Mahatma Gandhi and he invented a special charkha which was notable for its efficiency and performance. He was influenced by the doctrines of Maharshi Ramanna, philosopher Jiddu Krishnamurthi and advaita Guru Nisargadatta Maharaj. He converted into Hinduism and he put on the name Swami Bharatanand.

Another Polish national Wanda Dnynoskwa visited India about the same time. Wanda and Maurice established a library which kept Indo-Polish literature. They helped in the rehabilitation of the Polish refugees in India, Kenya and New Zealand in other places. In 1959, they also helped the Tibetan to settle down in India. Maurice translated the spiritual classic *I Am That* written by Guru in English.

Louis Fischer (29 February 1896 – 15 January 1970) — Louis Fischer was an eminent journalist who worked as an European correspondent for *New York Evening Post* and *the Nation* during the cold-war period. He wrote about eleven classic works such as Oil Imperialism: The International Struggle for Petroleum 1926, The Soviets in World Affairs 1930, Gandhi and Stalin 1947, The God That Failed 1949, The Life of Mahatma Gandhi 1950, The Life of Lenin and others. Louis visited Wardha in May-June 1942 and stayed with Mohandas for seven days in the Sevagram Ashram. Gandhi gave him one hour each for seven days walk-and-talk. This resulted in yet another classic Seven Days with the Mahatma. Louis was sympathetic with the cause of the freedom movements of the Indians. This trait is evident from his writings.

Easther Ferring Menon, Miss Peterson and Mrs. Helen Horup—These are the three women from the Nordic country Denmark who had come to India on missionary evangelization or the spread of the Christian gospel. They were members of the Danish Missionary Society. The British Government imposed several restrictions upon the activities of several missions in India. They expected them to inculcate the culture of understanding towards the British Government in the minds of the Indians.

These three ladies did not appreciate these restrictions. So they resigned from the Society.

Miss Peterson and Easther Ferring –(later Mrs. Easther Ferring Menon following her marriage to an Indian by name Menon) were orthodox in their religious affiliations while the third of them Mrs. Ellen Horup was not so stead-fast with her religious assignments. On the other hand, Mahatma had entirely different lines on matters of religion. He did not support conversion as such unless it was for genuine and conscientious reasons. Gandhiji stood for adherence to one's religion of birth and he advocated that one should remain in his or her religion of birth by trying to become a better person there. These views were at odds with the views of Easter Menon and Miss Peterson in particular with the result that there were some differences of opinion between them. Miss Petersen or Sister Maria fervently hoped that the entire India should accept Christianity. She engaged herself in social service projects also. She set up a girls' school in 1921 despite opposition by the DMS and disapproval from the British authorities. She took interest in the Civil Disobedience Movement in 1930 and went on to provide shelters to the families of the volunteers who were imprisoned. But she could not be restrained from appreciating the Constructive Programme of the Ashram. Mrs. Ellen Hørup was not so much orthodox in religion. She was initiated in Indian affairs in about 1927 or so by Easther Menon. She was more expressive in her appreciation of the aspirations of the Indians. She collected better understanding of the struggle of the Indians in her home country Denmark. She established an International Committee for India in Geneva.

Margaret Spiegel —She was a German lady who visited India and she spent some time in the Sevagram Ashram. She also spent some time in the Shanti Niketan with the Poet who called her Amla. She was very sympathetic to the national cause for independence.

Catherine Mary Heilman Sarla Behn (1901-1982)– Catherine was born in England in 1901 to a German soldier and an English mother. She came in contact with some Indian students in 1920 who introduced her to Gandhian thought and action. She was immediately impressed. She, therefore, came to India in January 1932 and joined a school staff in Udaipur Rajasthan. She met Mohandas two years later. She joined him in the Sevagram Ashram where she went on to spend the next two years in close proximity of Mohandas. He gave her the name Sarla Behn. She took active part in the freedom movements under the Mahatma and she was imprisoned for two years for her role in the Quit India Movement of 1942. Sarla Behn was keenly interested in the *Nayee Talim* of Mahatma Gandhi. She supervised the success of this project in the Sevagram Ashram. Sarla Behn was keenly interested in the protection of the forests which were being ruthlessly cut in the Kumaon area of Himachal Pradesh. She set up the Kasturba Mahila Utthan Mandal or the Lakshmi Ashram in a village namely Kausani in 1946 which is near Garhwal region. Sarla Behn worked along with Mirabehn for the social upliftment of the women of the Kumaon area by instilling in them a sense of self-respect. These women had suffered during the confinement of their husbands while agitating for independence. She also called upon the residents of these areas to protect their forests and trees. In fact, her activism was a precursor of the future chipko aandolan of Sundarlal

Bahugana, Vimla Bahugana, Chandi Prasad Bhatt and others. In fact, Sarla Behn had the management of the Sevagram as one of her responsibilities which she handed over to another Gandhian worker Radha Bhatt. After independence, she associated herself with the Bhoodan Andolan of Sant Vinoba Bhave and the Sarvodaya Andolan of Jai Prakash Narayan. She also helped Jai Prakash Narayan in facilitating the surrender of the dacoits of Chambal Valley in the 1970s. She was also instrumental in the establishment of the Uttarakhand Sarvodaya Mandal in 1961 with the avowed purpose of channelizing the women power against such evils as alcoholism and also for promoting small scale industries in the Uttarakhand vicinity. Sarla Behn was a prolific writer. She authored twenty two books in Hindi and in English such as Reviving Our Dying Planet, A Blueprint for Survival of the Hills, her auto-bio-graphy A Life in the Woods: Autobiography of Mahatma Gandhi's English Disciple and others. She died in July 1982. She was awarded the Jamnalal Bajaj Award for excellence in social service.

Verrier Elwin (29 August 1902– 22 February 1964)–Harry Verrier Holman Elwin was born on 29 August 1902. He is the son of Edmund Henry Elwin who was the Bishop of Sierra Leone. He received his education at the Dean Close School and Merton College Oxford from wherehe received his degrees of BAin English Language and Literature and then an MA. After a bright academic career at Oxford, Verrier was ordained a priest in the Church of England. He came to India in 1927 for evangelical work along with Christ Seva Sangh of Poona. He had by now come under the spell of Mahatma Gandhi. He developed keen interest towards the aspirations of the Indians for their freedom. He stayed with Mohandas and actively supported the freedom movements of the Mahatma such as the movement of 1930. However, his main interest was always the welfare of the tribal communities all over the country. Like some other clergies, Verrier also gave up gospel work to devote for their cause along with his interest in the freedom movements. He stayed in the Sabarmati Ashram with the Saint in 1935 and he adopted Hinduism as his religion. He was later to acquire Indian nationality also. His acquaintance in the early part of his arrival in India with one young man of Poona now Pune namely Shamrao Havale turned out to be one of the defining moments of his life and career. Havale took him around several tribal areas in the Central Provinces now Madhya Pradesh, Maharashtra and that part of Madhya Pradesh which is now Chhattisgarh. He spent a lot of time with the tribals of Mandla and Dindori and some other adjoining places. Under their spell, he decided to devote his life for the rights of the tribal peoples of India. Havale and Verrier worked together for their upliftment for the next twenty years Later he also worked in Orissa and in the Eastern states which are called as the North Eastern Frontier Agency NEFA in short. He finally settled in Shillong which is the capital of Meghalaya. In this manner, it can be said that Verrier had accumulated a treasure of the knowledge of the culture of the tribes all over India. When the Anthropological Survey of India was established in 1945, he was appointed as its Deputy Director. After independence, he was appointed as an advisor to the Government of India on tribal affairs. He was also appointed by the Government of Arunachalam as the Anthropological Advisor to them. His auto-biography *The Tribal World of Verrier Elwin* won him the prestigious Sahitya Academy Award in 1965 in the English language. In personal life, Elwin married a tribal woman namely Kosi hailing from the Raithwar place of Dindori. The marriage resulted in a divorce later. Elwin married the second time again to another tribal woman namely Lila belonging to the Pradhan community. Elwin died on 22. 2. 1964 in Delhi. The Government of India decorated him with the Padma Bhushan in 1961. The eminent historian Ramachandra Guha's biography *Savaging the Civilized: Verrier Elwin, His Tribals, and India* (1999) brought renewed attention in India to Elwins life and career.

Savitri Devi Mukherji or Maximiani Portas(30 September 1905-22 October 1982)–During World War II, she was a spy for the Axis power as against the Allied powers. Her philosophy was a blend of Hinduism and Nazism. She believed in the Nazi doctrine of the supremacy of the Aryan race. She believed that Adolf Hitler would deliver the rest of humanity to the evil forces identified by the Jews and, therefore, he would end the kaliyuga and usher humanity into a better period in human history. In 1932, she visited India. She wrote an article entitled A Warning to the Hindus wherein she lent her support to the Hindu nationalism and movement for independence and also to warn them against proselytization and evangelization of other religions. She adopted the Hindu name of Savitri Devi and later on married a Hindu by name Asit Kumar Mukherji in 1940. She is also believed to be a help between Netaji Subhash Chandra Bose and the Japanese forces

Reginald Reynolds (1905-1958) —He was a very close confidant of Mahatma Gandhi. He was an inmate of the Sevagram Ashram for some time intermittently. He was very sympathetic with the cause of the freedom of India. He was an eminent writer also. He wrote some of these books–Imperialism in India, The White Saheb in India, a Biography of Mahatma Gandhi, Cleanliness and Godliness. He championed the cause of the independence of India via several groups and associations such as- India Conciliation Group, Friends of India, the Indian Freedom Campaign. He was General Secretary of the No War Movement which was a pacifist group. He left India in 1932 and returned in 1949 i.e. after the assassination of Mahatma Gandhi. But during this absence, he was in close correspondence with the Saint and vice versa. On one ocassion, Mahatma Gandhi refused to meet other persons in the jail confinement unless Reginald was also permitted to meet him.

Iwaichi Fujiwara (March 1, 1908 – February 24, 1986)–The Japanese General Iwaichi Fujuwara was the Chief of Staff of theJapanese command namely Southern Expeditionary Army Group as Chief of Staff in 1941 during World War II. He established F. Kikan, a Japanese special operations unit, which was created by the Japanese Government with the purpose of promoting independence movements in British India, Malaya and the Netherlands East Indies. In 1943, Fujiwara and his unit were transferred to the Japanese 15th Army. Fujiwara assisted in the establishment of the Indian National Army of Netaji Subhash Bose. He had visited India in September 1941 to recruit Indian soldiers in the fight against the Allied forces during World War II.

Freda Bedi (1911-1977) —She is also known as Sister Palmo or as Galogma Karma Kechog Palmo after her conversion into Buddhism and thus she became the first Western woman to adopt Buddhism when she became Buddhist in 1972. While studying for her M. A. in Philosophy, Political Science and Economics in the St. Hughs College at the Oxford University, she came in contact with Baba Pyarelal Bedi (BPL) a Sikh coming from Lahore who had descendatory links with Guru Nanak Ji the founder of the faith. They married in a civil ceremony in June 1933 braving opposition from her family. Even the faculty took disciplinary action against her. Freda had left-weaning political thinking which developed further with her association with the Oxford Majlis where some of the nationalist minded Indian students used to meet and deliberate regularly. She also came under the influence of communist ideology which was gaining momentum at that point of time following the events in the Soviet Union. The Bedis returned to India in 1934 where she soon came under the influence of Mahatma Gandhi. She participated in the Civil Disobedience Movement and was imprisoned. She took up teaching jobs in English in Delhi. She published a quarterly magazine namely Contemporary India which expressed nationalist views. She moved on to Sri Nagar along with her husband where she developed close acquaintance with Shaikh Abdullah. She taught English in Sri Nagar also for a while. Back in Delhi, she was appointed as editor of Social Welfare magazine by the Ministry of Welfare Government of India. She also served as a member of the United Nations Social Services Planning Commission to Burma. It is during her stay here in Burma that she came under the influence of Buddhism. She learnt Vipassana system and soon became an observant Tibetan Buddhist. In 1959, following the capture of Tibet by China and in the wake of arrival of Dalai Lama and also of a large number of Tibetans in India, Freda was asked by the Prime Minister Nehru in their rehabilitation as refugees. She worked along with the Dalai Lama in the establishment of Young Lamas School in Dalhousie. She did similar work in Sikkim also. In 1972, she received full bhikshuni ordination in Hong Kong and in this manner she became the first Western woman to achieve this honor. Freda died in New Delhi on 26. 3. 1977 survived by two sons.

Some other prominent foreigners in the struggle–

A. C. C. Harvey was on the staff of the Khalsa College Amritsar during 1919-1920 and he came in contact with Mahatma Gandhi when he visited the College at that time. He was sympathetic with the Indian cause. But he did not agree with the policy of non-co-operation which he considered" not only politically wrong, but also *irreligious,* contrary to the will of God. " He suggested" the policy of co-operation, of friendly discussion, of getting together to talk over things, to explain view-points, quietly, sincerely and with desire to understand as so ably exemplified by such men as Lord Reading, Lord Irwin. " CWMG Vol. 32 page 545

Thomas Richard Duncan Greenless (1899–1966). He was born in South Africa but he was brought up and educated in England. He moved on to India and began to teach in schools in South India from 1926 onwards. He was attracted towards the Theosophical Movement of India started by Smt Annee Besant and also by the philosophy of Mahatma Gandhi. He wrote a series of 14 books on different Gospels. He wanted to do social work for the harijans and he had consulted Gandhiji in a letter as to how this could be done. Gandhi suggested that he should have to come to the Ashram to explore the possibility of" his future work for Harijans. "

Pierre Ceresole visited India in 1934 during the earth-quake in Bihar to help in the relief and rehabilitation work.

Miss Linforth worked in the Hyderabad Welfare Center which was run by an inter-communal Committee comprising Hindus, Muslims and Christians and Parsis.

Mary Ingham came to India to do village work, invited by Mary Chesley.

Some other foreigners who evinced keen interest in the aspirations of India were as follows– Florence Winterbottom, Lauri Sawyer, Dorothy Hogg, Dietrich Boenhoffer, J. Marks Williams, Nora Morell, Edmund Privat and Yvonne Privat of Switzerland, Joshua Oldfield, Mary Stopes the birth control expert, Louisette Guieyesse, Margerate Sanger, Margerate Cousins, Elanor Rathborne the British Member of Parliament, Glen E. Snyder, Leonard Elmhirst, Beverly Nichols, H. N. Brailsford, Fredrich and Francisca Standarnath, Emily Kinnaird, Nila Graham Cook, W. W. Pearson, Dr Erika Rosanthal a German lady, Gladys Owen, Donald Miller and Manay McCarthy

Chapter Fifteen
Some of the Freedom Fighters from the North Eastern States

Tirot Singh- (1802-1835) He was a chieftain of the Khasi Hills in Shillong plateau of Meghalaya State who fought the British forces with swords, bows and arrows during the Anglo-Khasi wars.

Some of the freedom fighters from Meghalaya–

Maniram Deav

Kiang Nangbah was publicly hanged on 30. 12. 1962.

Teji Maideren fought the British forces, but was captured in December 1917 and later hanged in Tezpur.

Kushal Kunwar khuagchera-He took part in the Quit India Movement of 1942. He was implicated in a train derailment case, caught and then sentenced to death.

Shoorvir Pasaltha was the first Mizo freedom fighter who sacrificed his life while resisting the British expansion in that part of the country. The British had annexed the Lushai Hills in the later part of the nineteenth century and this is how Mizoram was annexed into the British Empire but not so long as Shoorvir was alive.

Bhogeswari Phuagani took part in the Quit India Movement of 1942 and she was shot dead while taking part in a protest march.

Matmour Jamoh was a revolutionary leader from Arunachal Pradesh who was sentenced to life imprisonment by the British.

Chengiapao Kuki Doungal was a soldier in the Indian National Army of Netaji. He belonged to the Kuki tribe of Mizoram..

Ram Singh Kuka 1816-1872

Shanti Bhushan was one of the associates of Surya Sen in the Chittagong Armory. He spent ten years in the British jails. His brother Phani Bhushan was also a revolutionary.

Umesh Lal Singh was involved in the Chittagong armory case and jailed. His brother Sachindra Lal Singh was the first Chief Minister of Tripura. Umesh was elected as an MLA in 1967.

Khadendra Bhadra took part in the 1930 Civil Disobedience Movement when hardly 15 years of age.

Paona Brajabashi–Major Paona Brajabashi was one of the heroes of the Anglo-Manipur war of 1891. In the battle of 23. 4. 1891, he was killed.

Haipou Jadonang–He was a spiritual leader of the Nagas. He collectedan army and fought the British

Moje Riba-He hailed from the West Siang district of Arunachal Pradesh. He joined the Indian National Congress and soon became the president of the Arunachal Pradesh Congress Committee. He actively participated in almost all the freedom movements.

U. Kiang Nangbah–He hailed from Meghalaya and fought the British in the mid 1860s. He fought against the British interference against the tribal customs and against their evangelical activities. He resorted to the guerilla warfare system against the British forces. But then finally he was captured and hanged.

Pa Togan Sangma-He hauled from the Garo Hills of Meghalaya who was killed while fighting the British forces on 12/12/1872.

Bir Tikendrajit Singh. Born on 26. 12. 1856. He was one of the heroes of the Anglo-Manipur War of 1891 and he was called the Lion of Manipur. Manipur forces fought valiantly until they were defeated and Bir lost his life in the resistance.

Maniram Dewan– He had large tea estates in Assam. The British did not like his business empire to grow further. So they placed several restrictions upon his workings. Maniram, therefore, decided to remove the foreigners from his state of Assam. The British, however, got the ascent of his plans. He was caught and after a shame and summary trial, he was hanged on 26. 2. 1856 along with his associate Peoli Barua.

Shambhu Dan Ponglo–He belonged to the Dimasa tribe of Assam. They took part in the freedom movements.

Tyagbir Hem Baruah–25. 4. 1893-11. 8. 1945-He hailed from Sonitpur Assam. He took part in several freedom movements such as the 1921 movement when he was jailed for 6 months, movements of 1930 and 1933 when again he was jailed. A college has been instituted in Sonitpur namely Tyagbir Hem Barua College, Sonitpur.

Chapter Sixteen

Patriotic and Nationalist Inmates of the Cellular Jail

In the late eighteenth century, the British constructed a series of jails in different parts of their empire to confine their convicted persons. With the rise of nationalism and resurgent activities for their emancipation from the colonial rules and consequent deterioration in the law and order situations therein, the Empire decided to consign political prisoners also in the far off jails so that their confinement may act as a deterrent to other prospective patriots. Prisoners all over the world were treated most inhumanly. Prisons were dungeons from where no-body could come back to join their dear and near ones. Then several reformers began their crusades for jail reforms, such as Jeremy Bentham in England. The civilization of that point of time subscribed to the retributive philosophy of conviction and sentencing of the offenders. In the early stages, death sentence was the normal conviction for an offence of murder and the life imprisonment was to be awarded only in exceptional cases. Now it is just the otherwise. Today life imprisonment is the ususal conviction and sentence for a person accused for murder and death sentence has to be awarded only in ' the rarest of rare cases'. Political prisoners were considered to be in a class by and of their own. They had to be provided with no sympathetic treatment because they were supposed to be trying to strike at the very base of the authoritarian regimes. It is unbelievable today how the convicts were transported from one place to another. Not only were they handcuffed, but in many cases they were put in leg-bars of iron. Handcuffs continue even today, but leg-bars are not used very commonly. Late Justice Shri V. R. Krishna Iyer has written in a 1979 Supreme Court judgment that the undertrials should not even be hand-cuffed. World history records that political prisoners all over the world have been treated with exceptional severity. Netaji Subhash Chandra Bose has compared the Port Blair prisons with the dreaded Bastiles of France.

The British began to use the Cellular Jail extensively to deport and confine prisoners of all hues from 1857 onwards. The deportation started on 10. 3. 1858 with the arrival of the first batch of 200 political offenders or dissenters into Chatham Island within Port Blair harbor in South Andaman. The second batch of 216 prisoners arrived from Punjab. By 16 June 1858, the jail had received a total of 773 prisoners of whom 64 had died, 140 had made good their escape, 1 had committed suicide, 87 were hanged after their capture. This figure rose upto about 1, 330 prisoners by 1858. In less than two years between 1858 and 1860, about 2, 000-4, 000 freedom fighters had been confined to these jails. Sadly, many of them perished under the most agonizing living and working conditions. Although it is today possible to estimate approximately those of the political prisoners and patriots who were tortured in the Cellular Jails, there can be no correct number of those of them who have indeed suffered for their home land. So a monument has been erected there for those of the unknown inmates who perished here.

Prior to the construction of the Cellular Jail in 1896, it is said that between 1857 to 1896 i.e. during these nearly 40 years, about fifty thousand prisoners had been sent to the Cellular Jails and further that between 1896 to 1921 when the

British stopped the practice of sending prisoners to the Cellular Jail only to re-start again subsequently, yet another about forty thousands of prisoners were consigned to the Islands. It is possible that many of those thousands might not have been political prisoners and that many of them were simple convicts under the various and regular sections of the Indian Penal Code. But it is certain that it is not possible to calculate the exact number of the political prisoners from amongst them and many of them suffered incarceration here for their political views and actions. There are about 1000 of such prisoners who were kept there between 1857 to 1858.

Between 1906 to 1921, about 150 such prisoners were kept in the Cellular Jails. Between 1922 to 1931, Moppilah Prisoners 30 in number were kept in these jails. Between the period 1932 to 1938 the political prisoners 386 in number were kept in these jails. Soldiers of the Indian National Army were kept here. About 63 prisoners were shot dead here over the different periods. In this manner, the Cellular Jails have a historic record with regard to the freedom movement of India.

With the ascendancy of the freedom movement since about 1904 onwards, the British Raj deported 80 revolutionaries from Poona, in 1889 about 132 were deported, between 1909 to 1921 about 379 and many more between 1932 to 1938. There was an increase in revolutionary activities and several conspiracy cases were launched against them. The convicts from them were sent to the Cellular Jails to name a few of them- the Alipore Conspiracy Case, Nasik Conspiracy Case, the Dacca Conspiracy Case, the Banaras Conspiracy Case, the Gaya Conspiracy Case and other political cases involving the fighters.

Needless to say, the treatment of the inmates was far from human. As a result, several of them started hunger strikes for better treatment. In some cases, the inmates even committed suicides. Many attempted escapes. For example, in 1868 alone about 240 of the inmates tried to escape. 87 of them were caught and hanged summarily. In mainland India, there were protests and constant demands for better treatment to the inmates. The appeals bore some fruit. As a result, some of the inmates were transferred to other prisons in the main-land. Some of the well known inmates of the Cellular Jail are- the Savarkar brothers Vinayak and Damodar, Bhai Parmanad, Ladha Ram, Indu Bhushan Roy, Prithi Singh Azad, Pulin Das, Gurumukh Singh, Sohan Singh, Subodh Roy, Trailokyanath Chakravarty, Mahavir Singh a close friend of Sardar Bhagat Singh, Mohit Moitra, Mohan Kishor Namdev, Batukeshwar Datt and others.

Babu Ram Hari from Qadian Gurdaspur Punjab, editor of Swaraj was given life imprisonment for the offence of writing three articles which were treated by the Raj to be seditious. He spent 21 years of his life in the Cellular Jail.

Sometimes in 1937-38, many of the Indian leaders appealed to the British Government to demand more humane treatment of the Cellular inmates. Mahatma Gandhi and poet Rabindra Nath Tagore was amongst them. The appeal worked. That was the time when the Japanese threat was at its peak. The British Government repatriated the inmates. The Island was run over by the Japanese forces and in this manner, it became the first part of India to be liberated from the British rule in 1945 during the World War II. The national flag was hoisted by Netaji Subhash Chandra Bose in the Island. But the joy was short lived since the

Japanese surrendered in the War paving the way for the British to regain its control.

The Cellular Jail is now a national monument which has been dedicated to the nation by the Prime Minister Morarji Bhai Desai on 11. 2. 1979 to honor such martyrs who cannot be traced and who cannot be thus remembered.

After independence, the Andman and Nicobar Islands and the Cellular Jail premises became a tourist attraction. The Government of India has opened many facilities there. But the legacy and history of the Cellular Jail will always remain one of the most remembered and recalled folk-lore in the annals of the freedom struggle of India.

The Rangoon and Mandalay connect with the nationalist aspirations of India

The Last Mughal Bahadur Shah Zafar was exiled to Rangoon now Yangonin 1862 following his trial, conviction for life imprisonment in place of death sentence as a result of a reprieve, transported there along with his wife Zinat Mahal and two sons, probably confined in a make-shift house there where he died almost unnoticed on 7. 11. 1862 aged 87 years completely broken, ill of many ailments with such conciliatory words as that he had no place in the land of his friends. He was buried in a place behind the main gate of his place of internment. Two years later, Zinat followed him to death and finally his son Mirza Jawan Bakht from Zinat also followed them a few months thereafter. Zinat and Jawan were also buried nearby. A glorious chapter in the Mughal history of Hindustan was also being consigned to eternal peace in a far off place where hardly any-one could go to pay their tributes to them. Almost as if insult had to be added to injury, there is no certainty as to the exact place of the burial of the last Emperor of Hindustan. So Rangoon or Yangon stake a claim to be counted in the same breath as the Mandalay and Cellular Jail in Port Blair.

The trial of the Lokmanya–In the first trial of 1897, the facts are that the Collector of Poona now Pune Rand and one young military officer Lt. Ayerst were shot dead by two young men. Earlier, the Lokmanya had published an article in the paper Kesari dated 15. 06. 1897 wherein he had justified the killing of Afzal Khan by Chhatrapati Shivaji on the ground that one has to do one's duty in accordance with the teachings of Shrimad Bhagwat Gita. He also made a few such speeches in Poona. On 22. o6. 1897, Collector of Poona now Pune Rand and a young military officer LtAyerst were killed by some young men. The prosecution believed that the murders were the direct result of the incitement created by these speeches and by this article. So Tilak was accordingly tried for the offences of sedition. Justice Strachey in a trial conducted before a special jury, found him guilty of these charges, convicted and sentenced him for a term of eighteen months rigorous imprisonment. The sentence was later reduced to one year as a result of appeals from scholars and statesmen from so many places.

Not much is reported of the third trial of 1916. But enough is known of the trial of 1906. In this case, the facts are that Lokmanya had published two articles in Kesari wherein he had defended the revolutionaries Prafulla Chaki and Khudiram Bose who had attempted to kill the Chief Presidency Magistrates of Muzaffarpur Douglas Kingsford. But the attempt had resulted instead in the death of two innocent daughters of barrister Kennedy. Prafulla Chaki committed suicide. But Khudiram Bose was sentenced to death and hanged. He was 18 years of age at that time. Tilak was found guilty by the jury and the judge sentenced him to 6 years in a jail outside India. Therefore, he was incarcerated in the Mandalay Jail in Burma for six years. He spent these six years between 1908 to1914. He was released on 16. 06. 1914. His wife died during his confinement. It is during these six years that Tilak wrote his classic **Gita Rahasya** which is supposed to be the most authentic treatise on Shrimad Bhagwat Gita. It is to be noted that the British Government offered to release Lokmanya before the expiry of his regular term provided he agreed never to write such articles. He refused the offer stating that he would rather be remembered as a patriot by his people. Barrister Mohammad Ali Jinnah defended Lokmanya Tilak in his sedition case.

Netaji Subhash Chandra Bose also served a term in the infamous Mandalay Jail between 1925-1927. He was apprehended by the British Government in 1925 and sent to this jail which had the reputation of notoriety next only to the Cellular Jail.

Chapter Seventeen
Jail Literature Created by Freedom Fighters

Here are some of the jail literature created by freedom fighters while they were in imprisonments–

The story of My Deportation (1908) written in the Cellular Jail by Lala Lajpat Rai who was deported to Mandalay, Burma now Myanmar for taking part in an agrarian agitation in the Punjab. He was in exile from 9th May 1907 to the 18th November 1907. However, he was allowed to return when the Viceroy, Lord Minto, decided that there was insufficient evidence to hold him for subversion. This is an account of his jail experiences.

Tales of Prison Life (1910) is an account of his experiences in the Alipore Jail Kolkata by Sri Aurobindo (1872-1950) while facing the conspiracy of the same name.

Through Solitude and Sorrows (1910) by Shyam Sunder Chakravarty (1869-1932) is a revolutionary's prison account. He was a member of the revolutionary group Vande Mataram and some other members were Krishna Kant Mitra, Subodh Chandra Mallik, Ashwini Kumar Dutta and Manoranjan Guha Thakurta.

The Tale of My Exile 1922 has been written by Barindra Kumar Ghosh (1880-1959). He was brother of Sri Aurobindo

Twelve years of Prison Life (1924) has been written by Ullaskar Dutt. He was a convict in the Alipore Bomb Case. He was tortured in jail. As a result, he became almost insane.

Jail Life(1924) was written by Subramaniya Siva (1884-1925). He describes his jail experience. Subramanya Siva was a well known revolutionary from Tamil Nadu and hewas closely associated with V. O. Chidambaram Pillai and Subramanya Bharthi. He was arrested many times between 1908 and 1922. Later he was shifted to the Salem Jail because he had contracted leprosy.

The Indian Struggle (1920-34) In this memoir, Netaji Subhash Chandra Bose narrates his experiences of his detention in the Mandalay Jail Burma after 1925 when he was captured by the British. This is an autobiographical account of the founder of the Indian National Army Subhash Chandra Bose (1897-1945) in the Burmese Prisons contains between 1920 and 1941 for different prison terms.

Autobiography–Ram Prasad Bismil

My Experiments With Truth: An Autobiography and **Songs From Prison** are some of the works of Mahatma Gandhi while in prison. The auto-bio-graphy was written between 1927 to 1929.

Key to Health–Mahatma Gandhi started writing this book while in the Aga on 27. 8. 1942 and it was finished on 18. 12. 1942.

Mangal Prabhat –A collection of Mahatmas articles written during his days in the Yerwada Jail, Pune.

Songs from Prison is a translation of some of the great Indian saint in Jail in 1934. During his prison term in 1930, Gandhiji translated into English a number of Indian devotional poems into several languages such as Hindi, Gujarati and Marathi. He used to spend his free time in prison reading and writing. He had collected a large number of books in jails and he used to translate which ever part he felt needed translation in other books for the benefit of readers. He was incarcerated nine times in South Africa and ten times in India. He took to prison life in a very constructive manner. He used to write letters to the inmates of the Sevagram Ashram very regularly which contained necessary instructions to the inmates as to how to conduct the Ashram in a proper manner. He used to solve the personal problems of the correspondents also from the jail internments. These letters running into thousands are compiled by the Publications Division of India in hundred volumes entitled The Collected Works of Mahatma Gandhi.

The Jail Note Book has been penned by Sardar Bhagat Singh which has been published posthumously in 1994. While in jail after his conviction and pending his martyrdom, Sardar Bhagat Singh performed the amazing feat of writing his memoirs at the young age of 21 years. He left them behind after his martyrdom. They were published later on in 1994. The Note Book ran into more than three hundred pages. He had left behind the manuscript of The Jail Note Book running into more than three hundred pages which he wrote during his internment in the Central Jail Lahore.

The Spirit's Pilgrimage is an autobiographical account written by Madeleine Slade or Mirabehn 1891-1981. She was jailed several times for her part in the freedom movements. She has written their account in these memoirs.

Tarjuman al-Quran 1931 is anUrdu translation and commentary and **Ghubar-e-Khatir i.e. Sallies of Mind)** isa collection of letters written by Maulana Abul Kalam Azad.

Glimpses of World History (1934), Autobiography (1936), The Discovery of India and **A Bunch of Old Letter**s are the writings of Jawaharlal Nehru mostly while in jail. The auto-bio-graphy has been written entirely while in jail. **The Discovery of India 1944** was written in Ahmednagar fort prison between April to September 1944. It was his ninth term of imprisonment. **A Bunch of Old Letters 1958** is a collection of letters which covers a period of about three decades from 1917 upto August 1947 i.e. the achievement of Independence. It was first published in November 1958.

My Days in Prison 1934 has been written by Urmila Shastri about her jail experiences. She took active part in the movement of 1930 and was jailed for this purpose.

Fragments of a Prisoner's Diary: Letters from Jail (1940) by M. N. Roy is an account of the jail experiences of one of the founders of the Communist movement in India.

Economy of Permanence (1948) written by J. C. Kumarappa 1892-1952 to narrate his jail experiences in Nasik prison. He was made the editor of Young India by Gandhiji in 1932. He was jailed in consequence of his writings for a period of two and a half years in Nasik Prison in 1934. He wrote two books during his imprisonment, **Economy of Permanence'** and **Practice and Precepts of Jesus.**

The Story of My Lifewas written by Bhai Paramanand while in Cellular Jail in Andaman in 1920. He was arrested in connection with the Lahore Conspiracy Case and sentenced to death. The capital punishment was commuted to life imprisonment

Gita Rahasya The classic treatise on Shrimad Bhagwat Gita has been written by Lokmanya Bal Gangadhar Tilak during the internment of six years in the Mandalay Jail Burma now Mayamar. He also wrote **Letters and Other Writings** while in jail.

Memoirs of a Revolutionary -Andaman: The Indian Bastille (1939) has been written by B. K. Sinha while in the Cellular Jail Port Blair Andaman.

A Jail Diary 1944 has been written by Chakravarti Rajagopalachari Rajaji while he was in the Vellore Central Jail for a period of nearly four months from 21 - 12-1921 to 20-03-1922.

My Trip to Pakistan 1944 has been written by Yusuf Meherally (1903- 1950) who was first arrested in 1930 and sentenced to four months' imprisonment. He was again arrested in 1932 for the charges of conspiracy and sentenced to two years imprisonment. He was again arrested in connection with the Individual Satyagraha in 1940. He was arrested yet again on a charge of having defied a prohibitory order in Punjab. These are his jail experiences.

The Gandhian plan 1944 was written by the Gandhian philosopher Shriman Narayan Agarwal while in jail.

Prison Days (1946) is an autobiographical account written by Smt. ViJayalaxmi Pandit while she was in Naini Jail over a period of about ten months from August 12, 1942 to June 11, 1943.

Feathers and Stones (1946) was written by Dr. Pattabhi Sitaramayya while incarcerated for three years in the fort at

Ahmednagar, Maharashtra during the Quit India Movement in 1942. He also wroteThe History of the Congress which was published in 1935. It is considered to be an authentic account of the history of the Indian National Congress.

India Divided an Autobiography was written by Dr. Rajendra Prasad the first president of the Republic of India while he was in prison between 1942 and 1945

Thorns and Thistles: Autobiography of a Revolutionary 1948 was written by Gulab Singh who was an active member of H. S. R. A. Hindustan Socialist Republican Army HSRA, a revolutionary group, while in jail.

History of Orissa written by Dr. Harekrishna Mahtab when he was in jail along with other national leaders. He was imprisoned during the national movement for seven times i.e. for a total period of about eight years.

From Primitive Communism to Slavery has been written by S. A. Dange and published in 1949. He was one of the founders of the Communist movement in India and also one of the leading figures in the trade union movement in India. He was jailed by the British for a total period of about thirteen years.

Day to Day with Gandhi 1953 is an account of daily life in jail maintained by Mahadev Desai who was the secretary of Mahatma Gandhi for 25 years. It is a diary kept by him. **Gita According to Gandhi** was written by him when he was lodged in the Belgaum jail.

Even Behind the Bars 1961 is written by the Gandhian philosopher Kakasaheb Kalelkar. It was written by him in Gujarati and translated later in English by Sarojini Nanavati.

My Life and Struggle 1969 is an auto-bio-graphicalby account written by Khan Abdul Gaffar Khan or Badshah Khan or Frontier Gandhi while in jail.

Memoirs of an Un-repentant Communist (1975) is an account of A. S. R. Chari of his arrests and imprisonments during the freedom struggle.

A Window on the Wall Quit India Prison Diary by H. Y. Sharda who was hardly 19 years of age when he was jailed. He was jailed twice in 1942 in the Quit India Movement.

Diaries of a Freedom Fighter 2008 is written by Gudleppa Hallikeri, an Indian freedom fighter of Haveri district of Karnataka state. Hallikeri worked with Mahatma Gandhi, Mailar Mahadevappa and Sanikoppa and others.

J. C. Kumarappa-Economics of Permanence, The Practice and Precepts of Jesus and Christianity: Its Economics and Way of Life.

Jochim Alva– Men and Supermen of Hindustan

Chapter Eighteen

What Has the Government Done for the Freedom Fighters and for Their Family Members: How Are They Remembered Ceremonially

On the occasion of the celebration of the silver jubilee of the independence of the country, the Ministry of Home Affairs, the Government of India had come out with a scheme to benefit the innumerable freedom fighters and, thereafter, their eligible dependents. It is the Swatantrata Sainik Samman Pension 1980. It is supervised by the Freedom Fighters and Rehabilitation Division to the Ministry of Home Affairs. It has been re-named as the Swatantrata Sainik Samman Yojna. In addition to this scheme, there is a separate scheme for the freedom fighters who spent their times in the Cellular Jail, Andaman and Nicobar Islands during the struggle for freedom known as the Ex-Andaman Political Prisoners Pension Scheme, 1969.

The following persons are eligible for these benefis–

1. Dependents of the martyrs

2. Those who have faced imprisonments of six months or more, women and SC/ST three months

3. Those who were under-ground for a period of 6 months or were interned or externed from their districts

4. Those who suffered loss of property,

5. Those who suffered permanent incapacitations,

6. Those who suffered loss of Government jobs,

7. Those who were flogged whipped,

There is a screening committee to verify the applications for the grant of the benefits.

The beneficiaries of the scheme—The following movements and events have been recognized for the benefit of this scheme—

1. Suez Canal Army Revolt in 1943 during Quit India Movement & Ambala Cantt. Army Revolt in 1943

2. Jhansi Regiment Case in Army (1940)

3. Regiment and Azad Hind of INA.

4. Holwell Revolt Movement conducted by Netaji in 1940 at Calcutta.

5. Royal Indian Navy Mutiny, 1946.

6. Khilafat Movement.

7. Harsha China Morcha (1946-47)

8. Moplah Rebellion (1921-22)

9. Arya Samaj Movement in the erstwhile Hyderabad State (1938-39)

10. Madurai Conspiracy Case (1945-47)

11. Border Camp Cases in erstwhile Hyderabad State (1947-48)

12. The Ghadar Movement

13. The Gurdwara Reform Movement (1920-25) including:-

Taran Taran Morcha

Nankana Tragedy of Feb. 1920

The Golden Temple Ke Affairs (Morcha Chabian Saheb)

Guru Ka Bagh Morcha

Babbar Akali Movement

Jaito Morcha

Bhai Pheru Morcha; and

The Sikh Conspiracy (Golden Temple) of 1924

14. PrajaMandal Movement in the erstwhile Princely States (1939-49)

15. Kirti Kisan Movement (1927)

16. Navjavan Sabha (1926-31)

17. Quit India Movement 1942

18. INA & IIL(1942 to 1946)

19. Merger Movements in the former French and Portuguese Possessions in India.

20. Peshawar Kand in which members of the Garhwal Rifles took part

21. Read leaf Conspiracy Case (1931)

22. Chauri Chaura Kand (1922)

23. Aranya Satyagraha of Karnataka (1939-40)

24. Goa Liberation Movement

25. Kalipatnam Agitation (1941-42)

26. Kallara-Pangode Case

27. Kadakkal Riot Case

28. Chengannur Riot Case

29. Vattiyoorkavu Conference

30. Anti-Independent Travancore Movement

31. Punnapra-Vayalar Movement

32. Karivellur Movement

33. Kauvambai Movement

34. Kayyur Movement

35. Morazha Movement

37. Malabar Special Police Strike (MSP Strike)

38. Dadra Nagar Haveli Movement.

39. Goa Liberation Movement, Phase II

40. Kuka Namdhari Movement, 1871

41. Jallianwala Bagh Massacre, 1919 (Source secondary).

So far about 17200 freedom fighters of all categories have been given the benefits of pension schemes. Besides they have been given other benefits such as railway and transport facilities, telephone connections, housing facilities, medical facilities etc. It is possible that similar facilities may have been extended to several other beneficiaries since then.

Pensions for the Andaman Nicobar sufferers has been increased from Rs. 24775/ to Rs. 30000/ p. m., for outside freedom fighters it has been increased from Rs. 23085/ to Rs. 28000, p. m., for the INA warriors it has been increased from Rs. 21395, to 26000/ p. m. The pension of the freedom fighters under the general list of the Swatantrata Samman Scheme has also been increased by Rs. 5000/. p. m. Besides these pensions, the beneficiaries are also entitled to several other emoluments and facilities such as telephones, railway and transport facilities, medical assistance, residential accommodations etc. (It is possible that the pensions may have been increased since then and it is also possible that the number of these beneficiaries may be on the decline by passing of time.)

Various monuments who perpetuate the memories of the immortal heroes –

1. The Red Fort—Built during the reign of Shahjahan. It is one of the iconic buildings of national importance which carries many memories of Indian history. Bahadur Shah Zafar the Last Mughal was tried here for high treason, convicted and exiled into Mandalay, Rangoon. Three soldiers of the Indian National Army were tried here on the eve of independence.

2. The Lucknow Residency—It was built in 1800. It is one of the places from where the 1857 revolt started. It is also in the history for the Siege of Lucknow during the revolt when it was ruthlessly suppressed and thousands of the citizens and revolutionaries were killed here.

3. The MutinyMonument—It was erected by the British in 1863 in New Delhi to commemorate the English soldiers who had lost their lives in the 1857 revolt. After the independence of the country, it has been known as Ajitgarh since 1972.

4. Glorious Dead Monument Kolkata—It was built by the British Government in 1924 in the memory of the soldiers who died in the First World War.

5. The Black Hole Monument of Kolkata-It was built by the British Government to house the prisoners of war who raged war against them. Here once 123 prisoners were suffocated to death.

6. The Shaheed Minar, Kolkata—It was constructed in 1828 by the British to celebrate the victory of Sir David Ochter Lony in the Nepal War of 1814-1816. In 1969, it was named Shaheed Minar to commemorate the freedom fighters who lost their lives during the movements for independence.

7. The Aga Khan Palace—It was built by Sultan Mohammad Shah Aga Khan III in 1892 in the Yerwada locality of Poona now Pune. Aga Khan IV donated the building to the nation in 1969. Mahatma Gandhi was imprisoned here in August 1942 along with Kasturba Gandhi, Mahadev Desai and others. It contains the resting places of Mahadev Desai and Kasturba also here.

8. The Anand Bhavan of Allahabad—It was purchased by Motilal Nehru in 1930. It was the residence of the Nehru family where the meetings of the Indian National Congress were held during the movements for independence. It was dedicated to the nation by Smt. Indira Gandhi in 1970.

9. India Gate—Constructed in the early 20th century to commemorate the arrival in India of the British King Emperor George V. It commemorates those soldiers who lost their lives fighting in different arenas during the First World War and also in the Afghan Wars. There is a Tomb of the **Unknown Soldiers** inside and also **the Amar Jawan Jyoti** which was unveiled and dedicated

to the nation by Smt. Indira Gandhi on 26. 1. 1972 to commemorate those soldiers who lost their lives in the Indo-Pak war of 1971.

10. The Cellular Jail in the Port Blair Andaman Nicobar Island–This building has special importance in the annals of the freedom struggle of India. Its construction ended in1906. The British had started to use it to deport the rebels of the 1857 revolt. Thereafter, it was used to house political prisoners, revolutionaries and dissenters of the British Raj during the length and breadth of the entire struggle for freedom besides the common criminals and convicts. Netaji Subhash Chandra Bose had compared it to the Bastille of France.

11. Mani Bhavan in Mumbai—This building belonged to Ravashankar Jagjeevan Jhaveri from where Mahatma Gandhi conducted many of his several historic movements such as the Khilafat movement of 1917, the start of the Non Cooperation Movement of 1921, the Khadi movements, etc. The building was taken over by Gandhi Smarak Nidhi in 1955.

12. The Jallianwala Bagh of Amritsar—It was here that the massacre of 1919 took place. The British forces opened fire here on the command of General Dyer. 379 peaceful persons lost their lives besides many more persons suffered injuries. The meeting was being held in the wake of the draconian laws legislated by the British to suppress the aspirations for freedom.

13. The Sabarmati Ashram—Mahatma Gandhi had established this Ashram on the bank of the river of the

same name in Ahmedabad in Gujarat in 1917 on the model of his earlier ashrams in South Africa. It was earlier called the Kochrab Ashram since it was known like that earlier. The Mahatma left this ashram and moved on to Sevagram Ashram in Wardha in 1936.

14. Sevagram Ashram in Wardha–Mohandas shifted into this Ashram in 1936 perhaps for the reason that he wanted then-onwards to lead a more idyllic way of life as if far from the madding crowd. The land was contributed by Seth Jamanlal Bajaj. Since 1936 on-wards, Sevagram was nothing less than the de facto political capital of India.

15. The Birla House or now the Smriti Bhavan—This was the residence of the industrialists the Birlas. Mohandas used to reside here duringthe days of his various movements. He was assassinated here. Since then it is called the Smriti Bhavan.

16. Gowalia Tank Maidan also known as the August Kranti Maidan, Central Mumbai—It is here that Mohandas made his historic Quit India speech on 8. 8. 1942.

17. Netaji Bhawan Kolkata—It is here that the brother of Netaji Subhash Chandra Bose used to reside. Netaji made good his escape from here to escape to Japan and other places in his INA heroics.

18. Udham Singh Nagar, Rudrapur, Punjab—Revolutionary hero Sardar Udham Singh killed General Michael O'Dwyer to avenge Jallianwala Bagh. His place of residence in a district in Doaba region of Punjab has been renamed after him as Shaheed Udham Singh Nagar.

19. Sri Potti Sriramulu Nagar, Nellore in Andhra Pradesh—The place has been named after the revolutionary of the same name who was also responsible for the creation of Andhra Pradesh following his fast unto death lasting 53 days.

20. **G**andhi Nagar Ahmedabad Gujarat—It is the new capital of Gujrat named after Mahatma Gandhi.

21. Some of the Monuments for Maulana Hasrat Mohani–

    Maulana Hasrat Mohani Hostel, Aligarh,

    Maulana Hasrat Mohani Street in Thane, Maharashtra,

    Maulana Hasrat Mohani Hospital, Kanpur,

    Maulana Hasrat Mohani Girls Higher Secondary School, Calcutta now Kolkata.

22. Monuments for Lala Lajpat Rai–

    Lala Lajpat Rai College of Commerce and Economics, Mumbai,

    Lajpat Nagar Central Market, New Delhi,

    Lala Lajpat Rai Park Lajpat Nagar, New Delhi,

    Lajpat Rai Market Chandni Chowk New Delhi,

    Lala Lajpat Rai Hall IIT Kharagpur,

    Lala Lajpat Rai Hospital Hisar.

    Several roads have been named after him all over the country.

23. Commemorations for Surendra Nath Banerji

    Barrackpore Rastraguru Surendranath College

    Surendranath Mahavidyalaya

Surendranath College Calcutta now Kolkata

Surendranath Centenary School Ranchi

24. Samaldas Marg in Mumbai. Earlier it was Princess Street

25. Kranti Van–Sampatrao Pawar a sugar-cane grower from Sangli Maharashtra has built a memorial for about 700 freedom fighters and revolutionaries by this name.

26. Statue in the Krishi Bhavan, New Delhi

    Indra Nagar, Mumbai,

    Rafi Ahmed Kidwai Road, Kolkata,

27. The Sadaqat Ashram of Patna-

28. The Sodepur Ashram of Kolkata– Built by Satish Chandra Dasgupta and Hemprabha Das Gupta

Chapter Nineteen

Indian National Army or Arzi Hukumat-e-Azad Hind or the Azad Hind Fouz

Although the name of the Indian National Army or the Azad Hind Fouz is generally associated with Netaji Subhash Chandra Bose, it is also associated with the great revolutionary Ras Bihari Bose. It was formed in 1942 in South East Asia in the midst of World War II. About 75000 of the Indian forces were deployed in this region by the British Government as a part of the Allied Forces against the Axis Forces. Japan was a part of the Axis Forces. The Allied forces registered some spectacular victories in the War in the Malaysian region. But then soon the Japanese forces defeated the British Indian forces in the battle of Malay. About 40000 of the Indian troops surrendered before the Japanese commanders. Japan handed over the surrendered troops into the command of Major Mohan Singh. They formed the nucleus of the Indian National Army which was mobilized by Ras Behari Bose. But then he handed over the reins of the Army to the charismatic leader Subhash Chandra Bose. He organized the Provisional Government of Free India in 1943 and this is how he began to be called Netaji. The Indian National Army or the Azad Hind Fouz was the armed wing of the Provisional Government.

Some historians have believed that the British Government had become scarry of the desertion of the Indian troops and that they were worried about the repetition of the events of

1857. Some others have, however, suggested that the British Government had already made up their mind to quit from the Indian arena because of their exorbitant involvement in World War II. The attainment of the independence of India was a result of several contributory reasons and the glorious chapter of the Indian National Army in general and that of the Netaji in particular is definitely a hastening circumstance.

However, Japan had to suffer defeat in Burma and the untimely death of Netaji in an air-crash brought the saga of the Indian Army to a sudden close. Some of the members of the Indian National Army were later court-martialled in the historic Red Fort, convicted and sentenced for life imprisonment. But the sentences were never carried out subsequently with the attainment of the independence of India. The Indian National Congress passed a resolution to defend the officers such as Captain Lakshmi Sehgal, Prem Sehgal, Major Gurubax Singh Dhillon and Col. Shah Nawaz Khan. A team of lawyers and barristers Jawaharlal Nehru, Bhulabhai Desai, barrister Asaf Ali and Dr Kailash Nath Katju defended them.

Some of the important officers of the Indian National Army are under—Col. Prem Sehgal, Lt. Col. J. R. Bhosle, Lt. Col. M. Z. Kaiani, Major Habib-ur-Rehman, Major A. D. Jehangir, A. D. Loganathan, Abid Ali, Cyril John Slim, Malik Munawar and others.

Two of the important monuments or memorials of the Indian National Army are the I. N. A. Memorial in Moirang and the I. N. A. War Memorial in Esplanade Singapore. The clarion call of Netaji was तुम मुझे खून दो मैं तुम्हें आजादी दूंगा — you give me blood I will give you freedom.

The marching song of the Azad Hind Fouz of Netaji Subhash Chandra Bose–

क़दम क़दम बढ़ाये जा

ख़ुशी के गीत गाये जा

ये ज़िंदगी है क़ौम की

तू क़ौम पे लुटाये जा

English translation is as under-

kadam kadam badhaye ja,

Khushi ke geet gaye ja,

Yeh zindagi hai qaum ki,

Tu qaum pe lutaye ja.

That means—

go ahead each step,

Sing of happiness as you advance,

This life is meant for the motherland,

You sacrifice it for the motherland.

This is one of the favorite patriotic songs of India. Today it is the regimental marching song of the Indian Army. It was composed by Vanshidhar Shukla and set to music by Capt. Ram Singh Thakur. It was banned by the British Government in 1942.

Gurudev had written jan gan man adhinayak jay he which is today the national anthem of India. It was later translated into Hindi by Netaji himself along with some other warriors of the Fauz such as Abid Hussain. It has been composed into musical rendering by Capt. Ram Singh Thakur and sung by

Capt. Lakshmi Sehgal. This national and patriotic song is not known today. It is as under–

शुभ सुख चैन की बरसा बरसे, भारत भाग्य है जागा,

पंजाब, सिंध, गुजरात, मराठा द्रविड, उत्कल बंगा,

चंचलसागर, विंध्य हिमालय, नीला यमुना गंगा,

तेरे नित गुण गाएं तुझसे जीवन पायें,

सब जन पायें आशा I

सूरज बन कर जग पर चमके, भारत नाम सुभागा,

जय हो, जय हो, जय हो, जय जय जय जय हो I

भारत नाम सुभागा (Abridged version of the original song).

English rendering of this song is as under–

Rains of auspicious happiness fall, Bharat has awakened!

All of Punjab, Sindh, Gujarat, Maratha, Dravida, Utkala, Bengal, all the terrotories,

All the deep seas, the Vindhya, the Himalayas, the holy Yamuna and Ganges,

sing your praises, and they derive their life from you,

every one derives hope,

Just as the sun it shines over the world,

so also shines the auspicious name of India,

May you be victorious! May you be victorious! May you be victorious! May you be victorious!

(Bharat nam subhaga i.e. Name Bharat is auspicious)

All India Forward Bloc– Netaji Subhash Chandra Bose founded the All India Forward Bloc on 3. 5. 1939 following his resignation from the All India Congress Committee on 29. 4. 1939. In the Tripuri, Jabalpur annual session of the INC, Netaji defeated Pattabhi Sitaramayya who was supported by Mahatma Gandhi, Sardar Vallabh Bhai Patel, Dr. Rajendra Prasad, Acharya J. B. Kripalani and other members of the Congress Party. The Congress stalwarts wanted that there should be no casting of votes and that the President of the Party should be elected unopposed. However, Netaji wanted to inject new blood in the Party and, therefore, he wanted to be re-elected after his unanimous election in 1938. In the ensuing division of votes, Netaji defeated the Party candidate by a big margin. It is said that Mahatma Gandhi took it as a personal defeat. As a result of difference of opinion in the Party, Netaji resigned his membership and he went on to found the All India Forward Bloc. The new Party had such eminent members as S. S. Caveeshar. Lal Shankarlal, Pandit Tripathi, Khurshed Nariman and Hari Vishnu Kamat to begin with. The Party fared reasonably well in the earlier elections after independence. But now it is not much of a presence in the national politics. Its influence is mostly confined to West Bengal. However, the Forward Bloc is yet another contribution of Netaji to the country.

Ras Bihari Bose (25.5.1886-21.1.1945)--He had his early education in Suhaldaha and later in Chandranagar a French colony. It is during these formative days that he was introduced to revolutionary ideas. An attempt upon the life of Viceroy Lord Hardinge was made on 23.12.1912 which was unsuccessful. The British

Police were in his search but he escaped to Dehradun and thereafter, he escaped to Japan in 1915. He married a Japanese lady and became a Japanese citizen in the year 1923. He successfully persuaded the Japanese authorities to support the Indian cause for freedom . He founded the Indian Independence League in 1942 . British Indian soldiers were defeated by the Japanese forces in the battle grounds of Malay and Burma and they surrendered in large number of about 40 thousand . Ras Bihari galvanised them into the heralded Indian National Army or the INA on 1.9.1942 and handed over its command to Netaji Subhash Chandra Bose. Rest is a glorious part of Indian history. Ras Bihari died on 25.5.1945. The Japanese Government bestowed upon him Order of the Rising Sun. The Government of India issued a commemorative stamp in 1967 in his honor.

Chapter Twenty

Role of Men of Literature in the Freedom Movement of India

Some of the prominent men and women of literature of this era are as under–

Bankimchandra Chatterjee or Bankimchandra Chattopadhyay (27 June 1838–8 April 1894)–He was one of the harbingers of the cultural and nationalist renaissance in the nineteenth century in Bengal and from this place the fire of nationalism spreadall over the country.

Born in Kanchrapara North 24 Pargana in Bengal, Bankim had his education in Midnapore and Calcutta now Kolkata. He obtained the degree of B. A. in 1858. He was appointed as a Deputy Collector and then he was promoted as District Magistrate. He retired from Government service in 1881. During his tenure in service, he clashed with the British authorities several times. Still the British decided to honour him with a citation Companion in the Order of the Indian Empire in 1894.

Even while in Government service, Bankim Chandra wrote his novels. The first one was Durgeshnondini in 1865. He is best known for his Anandmath which came out in 1882. This is a political novel which describes a clash between the forces of the Government on the one hand and a batch of sanyasis on the other hand. The sanyasis have to suffer failure in their enterprise in the presence of the superior forces of the govt. Perhaps this is the reason why the British did not take serious notice of the novel. But then the novel contained the song **Vande Mataram.** The song was soon to achieve the status of a national song on parity with **the Jan man gan adhinayak jai hai.**

Later on, the name Vande Mataram was used by Bipin Chandra Pal and Lala Lajpat Rai for the nomenclature of their respective news-papers.

Kavi Pradeep (6 February 1915 – 11 December 1998) — The popular patriotic poet of the film industry of India namely Kavi Pradeep was born as Ramchandra Narayanji Dwivedi in Ujjain Madhya Pradesh. He had a passion for writing poems at a very young age.

In the Bomaby film industry, his first film was **Bandhan 1939**. In this film, he wrote the notable song **chal chal re naujawan** which was sung by the child-actor Suresh to the music set by Ram Chandra Pal. His next film **Kismet 1943** established him as a writer of patriotic songs which continued for the next more than sixty years until he was decorated with the prestigious Dada Saheb Phalke Award for life achievement in 1997 shortly before his death in 1998. This film had the revolutionary song— आज हिमालय की चोटी से हमने फिर पुकारा है, दूर हटो ए दुनिया वालो हिंदुस्तान हमारा है aaj Himalaya ki choti se hamne fir lalkara hai, door hato e duniya walo Hindustan hamara hai. Since this film was released under the shadow of the Quit India Movement of 1942, this song achieved special significance at that point of time. Kavi Pradeep had to go under-ground for sometime because by then he had come under the scanner of the British intelligence. In the 1941 film by name Naya Sansar, there was a patriotic song written by Kavi Pradeep एक नया संसार बसा लें Ek naya sansar basalen...which created waves all over the country. Kavi Pradeep continued with this reputation even after the attainment of independence. He composed a set of memorable patriotic songs eulogizing Mahatma Gandhi and the Indian nation-hood in the film Jagriti directed by Bimal Roy. After the Chinese aggression of September 1962, he enthralled the entire nation with his immortal rendering **ae mere vatan ke logo, jara aankhon me bhar lo paani** for which music was provided by C. Ramchandran. The song was sung by Bharat Ratna Lata Mangeshkar in the presence of Prime Minister Jawaharlal Nehru.

Sir Muhammad Iqbal (November 9, 1877 – April 21, 1938) —He is also known as Allama Iqbal. He is considered as one of the leaders of the Pakistan Movement and as one of the founders of Pakistan particularly after his famous Final Destiny of Muslims speech given by him in the annual session of the Indian Muslim League in Allahabad in 1930. He composed the Tarana-e-mili which was published in 1904 in the Urdu weekly Ittehad. This is **saare jahan se achcha Hindustan hamaara.** This patriotic song has almost the same sanctity and popularity in the nation as the other national songs. It is repeated in almost all the national functions all the times. In these nine stanzas, Allama Iqbal has eulogized his mother-land, he has described how the Indian civilization has flourished while other equally old civilisations have perished and that all the religions preach universal-brotherhood. One of its stanzas is as follows—

सारे जहाँ से अच्छा हिन्दोस्तां हमारा

हम बुलबुले हैं इसकी ये गुलिस्ताँ हमारा

The English translation is as under—

Saare jahaan se accha Hindustan hamara,

Hum bulbule hain iski, yeh gulistan hamara

Banarasidas Chaturvedi (24. 12. 1882-2. 5. 1985)–He was one of the noted poets of Hindi literature and journalist. He edited Vishal Bharat विशाल भारत. He spent many years in Fiji looking after the welfare of the indentured Indians there who were called girmitiyas. Largely because of his efforts, this system was abolished in 1920 just as it was abolished in South Africa in 1911. He was a close associate of Mahatma Gandhi. After independence, he was a Rajya Sabha member for 12 years. He was awarded the Padma Bhushan in 1973.

Ramnaresh Tripathi (4. 3. 1889–16. 1. 1962) He was one of the leading poets of that time. He propagated Hindi and attended the Hindi Sahitya Sammelan. He was a follower of Mahatma Gandhi and he went to South Africa as his emissary to look after the welfare of the British Indians there. He took part in the freedom struggle and was jailed also. He is known primarily for the following poem–

हे प्रभो ! आनंद दाता ज्ञान हमको दीजिए I

शीघ्र सारे अवगुणों से दूर हमें कीजिए I

लीजिए हमको शरण में हम सदाचारी बनें I

English translation of this poem is as under–

Hey prabhu anand-data, gyan humko deejiye,

Sheeghra sare durgunon ko dur humse kijiye.

Leejiye hamko sharan meni, ham sadachari banen.

(This is only an abridged part of the entire poem.)

He was a Gandhian philosopher and a patriotic poet. Some of his such poems are as under–

चल पड़े जिधर दो डगमग में,

चल पड़े कोटी पग उसी ओर,

पड़ गई जिधर भी एक दृष्टि,

गड गए कोटि द्रग उसी ओर... i.e. in English

Chal pade di dah mag men,

Chal pade koti pag usi or, .

Pad gai jidhar bhi ek drashti,

Gad gaye koti trag usi or...

This poem was written in praise of Mahatma Gandhi.

Viyogi Hari (1895—1988) He was a close associate of Mahatma Gandhi. He was an eminent Hindi poet and writer who wrote about 40 books. Along with Maharshi Purushottam Das Tandon, he founded the Hindi Vidyapeeth in Prayag in 1925. He worked along with the Mahatma in the fields of drive against untouchability. He edited the Harijan Sevak Hindi edition and he was a member of the Harijan Sevak Sangh. After independence, he was closely associated with Sant Acharya Vinoba Bhave in his Bhoodan Andolan. He was also associated with the Gandhi Smarak Nidhi.

Shyamlal Gupta Parshad (1896-1977). He was born in Kanpur district to Visheshwar Prasad and Kaushalya Devi. He did not join the family business and instead chose to be a teacher. He was devoted towards patriotism from very early in his life. He joined the Indian National Congress early and he rose to be the district President of the Party in 1923 which post he held for a period of 21 years. The great patriot of Kanpur

Ganesh Shankar Vidyarthi encouraged him to write a patriotic song. Accordingly he produced this immortal piece as under–

विजयी विश्व तिरंगा प्यारा, झण्डा ऊँचा रहे हमारा।

सदा शक्ति बरसाने वाला, प्रेम सुधा बरसाने वाला।

वीरों को हर्षाने वाला, मातृ भूमि का तन मन सारा।।

झण्डा ऊँचा रहे हमारा...

The English translation is as under–

Jhanda uncha rahe hamara,

Vijayi vishwa tiranga pyara,

Sada shakti barsane wala,

Prem shdha barsane wala,

Veeron ko harshane wala,

Matru bhumi ka tan man sara,

In other words–

The conqueror of the world is our tri-colour,

Let our flag alway high and above,

It showers strength to everyone all the time,

It gives the nector of love,

It provides pride to the brave,

It is the heart and pride of our motherland,

Let our flag always fly high.

This is one of the national songs of the nation. It is sung every year on all the national celebrations and it has the same sanctity as the national anthem or the Vande Mataram or some of the earlier songs written by Kavi Pradeep and the song written by Sir Iqbal. During the days of the struggle for independence, it was one of the clarion calls of the marchers on the streets carrying the trio-color while they were beaten away by the British forces. Parshad was himself imprisoned on three occasions i.e. in 1921, 1930 and in 1944 during the Quit India Movement. Parshad composed these lines in 1924, the Khanna Press of Kanpur printed and circulated them with initial 5000 copies which were immediately sold out. The Government immediately took cognizance of the song. It was first sung in a public meeting held in Phool Bagh Kanpur on 23. 4. 1924 in the presence of several leading Congress leaders such as Pt. Jawaharlal Nehru. Next it was sung in the Haripura annual session of the Indian National Congress held in 1938 by no less than the Nightingale of India Smt. Sarojini Naidu in the presence of almost all the leading members of the Party such as Mahatma Gandhi, Pt. Motilal Nehru, Dr. Rajendra Prasad, Pt. Jawaharlal Nehru, Maharshi Purushottam Das Tandon, Pt. Govind Vallabh Pant, Seth Jamnalal Bajaj, Mahadev Desai and many others.

After independence, Parshad was invited by the Government of India to sing the song on the Independence Day 1952 from the ramparts of the Red Fort. The Government of India decorated him as Padma Shree in 1969.

Bismil Azimabadi (1901—1977)–**Sarfaroshi ki tamanna ab hamare dil me hai**…The immortal revolutionary Ram Prasad Bismil had the following verses upon his lips while he was being led to his martyrdom —

सरफ़रोशी की तमन्ना अब हमारे दिल में है देखना है ज़ोर कितना बाजु-ए-कातिल में है

English translation of this poem is as under–

sarfaroshī kī tamannā ab hamāre dil meṅ hai, dekhnā hai zor kitnā bāzū-e-qātil meṅ hai. (Abridged from the original poem)

These lines have been written by Bismil Azimabadi (1901-1977) of Patna Bihar in 1921. They are associated with the valor and sacrifice of the youth of the country.

Bal Krishna Sharma Naveen –8. 12. 1897–24. 4. 1960–He was one of the front-line writers of Hindi literature, a leading journalist and a great freedom fighter. He was a contemporary of Ganesh Shankar Vidyarthi and Pt. Makhanlal Chaturvedi. He took over the editorship of the leading daily of Kanpur Pratap in 1931 following the death of Ganesh Shankar Vidyarthi as a result of a lathi-charge at the hands of the British police. He was jailed a number of times between 1921 to 1944 for his parts in the movements for freedom. He was decorated with the Padma Bhushan award shortly before his death while he was serving as a Member of Rajya Sabha from 1957. Earlier, he was elected to the first Lok Sabha after independence. A college in Shajapur MP perpetuates his memory –Bal Krishna Sharma Naveen College, Shajapur, MP.

Pandit Makhanlal Chaturvedi (1901—1978) was one of the foremost men of literature, poet, journalists and freedom-fighters of Old CP & Berar now Madhya Pradesh. He was jailed by the British Government for his patriotic poems such as the following patriotic poem—

पुष्प की अभिलाषा

चाह नहीं मैं सुरबाला के

गहनों में गूँथा जाऊँ,

चाह नहीं, प्रेमी-माला में

बिंध प्यारी को ललचाऊँ,

चाह नहीं, सम्राटों के शव

पर हे हरि, डाला जाऊँ,

चाह नहीं, देवों के सिर पर

चढ़ूँ भाग्य पर इठ लाऊँ।

मुझे तोड़ लेना वन माली!

उस पथ पर देना तुम फेंक,

मातृ भूमि पर शीश चढ़ाने

जिस पथ जावें वीर अनेक

Its English rendering is as under–

Desire of a flower

Crave not that I should decorate the ornaments of beautiful woman,

Crave not that I should be a part of garland and attract the beloved,

Crave not that I should be placed upon the wreath of emperors,

Crave not that I should praise my fortune by adorning the gods,

Oh gardener ! pluck me and throw me on that path,

On which path the brave are going to offer their heads to the motherland…

He was an active member of the Indian National Congress under the influence of Mahatma Gandhi and he took part in almost all the movements. He suffered imprisonment in 1921-

22 from 5. 7. 1921 to 1. 3. 1922 in the Bilaspur jail along with a number of other freedom fighters for his role in the Civil Disobedience Movement. It is during this incarceration, that he wrote this poem. He started his career as a school teacher. But then he moved on to the field of journalism. He edited such eminent journals as **Prabha, Pratap and Karamveer**.

Ramvriksha Benipuri—He was a man of literature, a prominent journalist and a great freedom fighter. He started his career as a journalist by contributing in the leading journaal Pratap of Kanpur in 1916. Thereafter, he contributed to a number of dailies and news journals. His writings were resplendent with patriotic fervor. He took an active part in the freedom movement and he was imprisoned for his roles in them in the years 1930-31 and 1942. He was a pioneer of democratic socialist movements which swept the country in the early 1930s. He was one of the founders of the Bihar Sociaist Party in 1931 and then of the Socialist Party in 1934 in the national canvass in the company of such stalwarts as Dr. Ram Manohar Lohia, Ashok Mehta, Jai Prakasn Narayan and others. He is notable for his contribution to the *Yuvak* journal with his revolutionary ideas. He soon came under the surveillance of the British Government. After the attainment of independence, he was elected as an MLA in 1957.

Subhadra Kumari Chouhan wrote the following poem of patriotism. It has seven stanzas, but only two are being produced here for the sake of brevity

वीरों का कैसा हो बसंत

आ रही हिमालय से पुकार

है उदधि गरजता बार-बार

प्राची पश्चिम भू नभ अपार

सब पूछ रहें हैं दिग-दिगंत-

Its English translation is as under–

How should be the spring of the brave,

Calling is coming from the Himalayas,

Trumpet is roaring like this time and again,

East West earth and the sky unlimited,

Everyone is asking the same question…

She had also written yet another poem of patriotism eulogizing the Rani Jhansi Maharani Lakshmi Bai. It should certainly rank as the most powerful depictions of the immortal Queen of Jhansi. It is as under–

सिंहासन हिल उठे राजवंशों ने भृकुटी तानी थी

बूढ़े भारत में आई फिर से नयी जवानी थी

गुमी हुई आज़ादी की कीमत सबने पहचानी थी

दूर फिरंगी को करने की सबने मन में ठानी थी

चमक उठी सन सत्तावन में, वह तलवार पुरानी थी

बुंदेले हर बोलों के मुँह हमने सुनी कहानी थी

खूब लड़ी मर्दानी वह तो झांसी वाली रानी थी…

The English version is like this–

Thrones have felt trembled and kingdoms have raised their brows,

In the old Bharat a new wave of awakening has been realized,

Everyone has recognised the value of the lost freedom,

Everyone has determined in his heart to oust the foreigners,

Has begun to shine in 1857 the sword which was old,

We have heard the story from the mouths of the Bundele bards,

One who fought like men was the queen of Jhansi…

It is a long poem running into 36 stanzas. But for the sake of brevity, only two of them are being produced here. Subhadra Kumari Chouhan and her husband Lakshman Singh Chouhan were eminent freedom –fighters who were imprisoned by the British several times for their participation in various movements. Lakshman Singh Chouhan gave up his law practice for the sake of national duty.

Mahakavi Subramania Bharti was one of the pioneers of the renaissance of Tamil literature in the early twentieth century. His compositions are resplendent with nationalist and patriotic fervor. He was a polyglot with command over 14 languages such as Sanskrit, Tamil, Hindi, English, French and others.

Born in Ettayapuram, he had his early education in Tirunelveli and Varanasi. While in Varanasi, he was influenced by the Hindu way of life, philosophy and culture. He started his career as a journalist with the Hindu, Swadesh Mitran and India. His poems soon caught the cognizance of the British authorities. He was to be arrested in 1908, so he spent the next few years in exile in Pondicherry now Puducherry till 1918. During exile, he came in contact with Sri Aurobindo and Lala Lajpat Rai. The French Government had given him asylum and protection.

In 1905, he attended the annual Congress session held in Varanasi. Here he came in contact with Sister Nivedita,

Lokmanya Bal Gangadhar Tilak, Swami Vivekanand and others. He attended the 1907 session held in Surat where the Indian National Congress was split into the Moderates and the Extremists. Subramaiyam sided with Lokmanya Tilak who was an extremist in the Congress way of thinking.

While in exile, he produced some of his classics such as Kujil Pattu, Panchali Sapatham and Kannan Pattu. On return in 1918, he was arrested by the British authorities. But then he was released under a general amnesty of 1920. All the charges against him were with-drawn by the administration. Some of his poems are as under–

On freedom–

When will the thrust for freedom slate?

When will our love of slavery die?

When will our mothers' fetters break?

When will our tribulations cease?

On social equality–

Freedom, freedom, freedom

To the Periyars, the Tiaras, the Pulyars

Freedom to the outcastes degraded

Freedom to fishermen and nomads

And to tribes in criminal trades,

Engaged in skilful work, Harming none,

Learned and wise in our land, And shall line as one.

On patriotism–

The mighty Himalaya is ours

There is no equal anywhere on earth,

The generous Ganges is ours,

Which other river can match her grace

The sacred Upnishads are ours,

What scriptures else to name with them

The sunny golden land is ours,

She is peerless, let us praise her. — (courtesy Wikipedia)

Mulk Raj Anand—Mulk Raj Anand is one of the pioneers of English prose. After early education in Amritsar, Mulk Raj obtained a Ph. D. from Cambridge University. His novels depict the rural India and the Indian ethos as prevalent in the seven lacs of villages across the country something like **Munshi Premchan**d has done in the Hindi literature. He wrote about the caste-system, untouchability, poverty and other social evils which were prevalent in the society at that point of time. Some of his books are—the Untouchable, the Village Across the Black Waters and the Sword and the Sickle. They highlight Gandhian philosophy.

Ekla chalo re…and Amar Sonar Bangla…Poet Rabindranath Tagore is one of the most celebrated names in the fields of literature and the freedom movement of the country. Yet there are some legends about Gurudev which need to be emphasized today. He was very actively involved in the mass movement against the partition of Bengal in 1905. He composed patriotic poems in praise of the unity of Bengal. He was one of the front-leaders in the renaissance of Bengal. It is due to the efforts of patriots like him that the partition of Bengal was finally annulled in 1911. These are two of such patriotic poems which he composed during that period of time. They are very popular even today. Amar Sonar Bangla is the national anthem of Bangladesh. Another similar poem of Gurudev is Banglar Mati Banglar Jol (soil of Bangla and water of Bangla) to awaken the feeling of unity in Bengal. He worked for Hindu-Muslim unity also. He started the Rakhi Utsav at that period of time whereby the two communities used to exchange rakhi amongst them-selves.

The Poet renunciated the title of Sir and the knighthood conferred upon him by the British monarch in 1913 in recognition of his Nobel Prize winning Gitanjali following the Jallainwala Bagh massacre in 1919. He established Shantiniketan in 1901 which was more of an idyllic ashram where he experimented with the ancient gurukul method of imparting education. Almost all the leading freedom fighters of that time visited Shantiniketan. Mahatma Gandhi also visited the institution. The Poet had a definition of nationalism and patriotism which was not exclusive, but which envisaged a world-citizen and a world-community in view of the fact that the country seemed to him to be on the threshold of independence and that, thereafter, the country would be a signal to the rest of the world for their political emancipation from their colonial rules.

Even in the wake of scientific progress which was taking place all over the world, the Poet dreamt that an individual will not lose his human and rational personality and that he will still then strive to work with his reasons and emotions. These lines also worked effectively in national awakening across the country. A part of the celebrated **Gitanjali** epic is as under—

Where the mind is without fear

and the head is held high;

Where knowledge is free;

Where the world has not been

broken up into fragments by

narrow domestic walls;

Where words come out from

the depth of truth;

Where tireless striving stretches

its arms towards perfection;

Where the clear stream of reason

has not lost its way into the dreary

desert sand of dead habit;

Where the mind is lead forward by thee

into ever-widening thought and action-

Into that heaven of freedom, my Father,

let my country awake.

वतन की राह अमर वतन कि नौजवान शहीद हो... In English — (i.e. towards the road of the motherland, the youngmen should be a martyr). This is from the Bombay film of the name **Shaheed** which was released in 1948. Although it is after 1947, it must have been started somewhere in 1947. The lyrics are by Raja Mehdi Ali Khan, music has been set by music director Ghulam Hyder and the voice has been rendered by Mohammad Rafi. This is one of the popular patriotic songs of that period and it is still played today on all the national days.

सुनो सुनो ए दुनिया वालो बापू की अमर कहानी**...** In English– Suno suno e duniya valo Bapu ki amar kahani...(i.e. people of the world listen to the immortal story of Bapu). This is yet another popular patriotic song of the era and it continues to be popular today. It has been sung by Mohammad Rafi.

Raghupati Sahay Firaq Gorakhpuri (28. 8. 1896—3. 3. 1982)

He is one of the leading Urdu poets of his generation. He was well versed in English, Persian and Urdu literature. He was selected for the PCS and the ICS. But at the call of Mahatma Gandhi, he gave them up and joined him in the freedom struggle. He was jailed by the British for a period of 18 months. He was professor of English literature in Allahabad University.

He was a recipient of the Soviet Land Nehru Award in 1968, Jnanpith Award in 1969, Sahitya Akademi Award for Urdu in 1970 and Padma Bhushan in 1968.

Josh Malihabadi (1898—1982)–He launched a magazine namely Kaleem in 1926 in which he wrote in favor of the independence of India. His patriotic poem **Hussain aur Inqilab** won him the title of Sher-e-Inquilab. He took active part in various movements and he was imprisoned also. He was friendly with Pt. Jawaharlal Nehru. In 1956, he migrated to Pakistan.

Sachchidanand Hiranand Vatsyayan Agyeya (7. 3. 1911—4. 4. 1987)

Sachchidanad Hiranand Vatsyayan Agyeya is primarily known in the history of the Hindi literature and more particularly in the field of Hindi poetry as a poet who experimented with the traditional form of Hindi poetry and introduced his own style of poetry which is today called New

Poetry or नई कविता. His major works are Shekhar Ek Jivani and Trishank. He was a versatile writer in the fields of poetry, short stories, accounts of travels, criticism and translations. He was awarded the Sahitya Akademi Award in 1964, Jnanpith Award in 1978 and the inter-national Golden Wreath Award in 1983. While serving his jail term, he contributed to the treasury of jail-literature by writing several short stories which were published in the Hans magazine of Munshi Premchand. He edited several weeklies before the independence of the country and after independence, he was associated with journalism as editor of Lok Nayak Jai Prakash Narayan's Everyone's Weekly from 1973 to 1974 and he was editor-in-chief of the Hindi daily namely the Nav Bharat Times later on.

Vatsyayan was of revolutionary bent. After completing his studiesin 1929, he joined the Hindustan Socialist Republican Army HSRA which was an organization of several leading revolutionaries. He was arrested, charged with sedition for helping Sardar Bhagat Singh inan attempt to escape from prison, sentenced to four years which he served till 1934 in the Amritsar, Delhi and Amritsar jails. During the Second World War in 1939, he served the British Indian Army in Kohima. He was discharged from this duty in 1946.

Vatsayayan traveled widely. He traveled Europe extensively. He taught literature in several foreign universities such as Berkeley California and Heidelberg University in Germany. Finally, he was a faculty member in the Jodhpur University. While on a visit to Japan, he came in contact with Zen Buddhism.

Some of the leading lights of literature whose works influenced the course of the movements–

Gora 1909 by Rabindranath Tagore deals with national unity and cohesion.

Bharat Bharati by Maithilisharan Gupt– a patriotic poem. Mahatma Gandhi called him Rashtra Kavi. His well known poem is as under–

जो भरा नहीं है भावों से बहती जिसमें रसधार नहीं

वह हृदय नहीं है पत्थर है जिसमें स्वदेश का प्यार नहीं ।

Its English rendering is like this–

That heart which is not filled with emotions and which does not have spirit,

That is not a heart that is stone which does not have love for the country.

He had a correspondence with Mahatma Gandhi during the freedom struggle.

Mahadevi Verma was a contemporary of Subhadra Kumari Chouhan. She composed patriotic poems.

Poet Ramdhari Singh Dinkar was a freedom fighter. He is renowned as one of the leading poets of Hindi literature. He is also reckoned as Rashtra kavi.

Following is one stanza from one of the most popular poems of Rashtra-kavi Ramdhari Singh Diinkar–

सदियों की ठण्डी-बुझी राख सुगबुगा उठी,

मिट्टी सोने का ताज पहन इठलाती है

दो राह, समय के रथ का घर्घर-नाद सुनो,

सिंहासन खाली करो कि जनता आती है ।

Smt Sarojini Naidu was not only a great patriot but also one of the prominent poetesses who was, therefore, called the Nightingale of India.

Following is one patriotic poem of Smt Sarojini Naidu—

To India–O young– through all thy immemorial years!

Rise, Mother, rise, regenerate from thy gloom,

And, like a bride high-mated with the spheres,

Beget new glories from thine ageless womb!

The nations that in fettered darkness weep

Crave the to lead them where great mornings break....

Mother, O Mother, wherefore dost thou sleep?

Arise and answer for thy children's sake!

Thy Future calls thee with a manifold sound

To crescent honors, splendors, victories vast;

Waken, O slumbering Mother and be crowned,

Who once was empress of the sovereign Past. (Source secondary).

Chapter Twenty One

On the National Flag and Other Insignia

The National Flag of India

After the uprising of 1857 and consequent transfer of power from the East India Company directly into the hands of the Crown in London, the British Government felt the necessity of having a flag for their Brightest Jewel in the Crown of the British Monarch. So they began to design one for British India. They fell upon one design which was quite similar to the flags of other British colonies. All of them had the Union Jack in the upper part of the flag. Even otherwise, the flag of England continued to be the flag of all the colonies of England including India. In the meanwhile, with the turn of tides towards nationalism and patriotism introduced into the Indian psyche by Bankim Chandra Chattopadhyaya, Swami Vivekanand, Lokmanya Bal Gangadhar Tilak and other greats, they began to feel the necessity of having a flag suitable to the Indian genius. Lokmanya suggested a design of his discretion. After the partition of Bengal in 1905, the flag of the nationalists was called the Vande Mataram flag. It had three colors, green, saffronand yellow which stood for three main religious communities of the country. The Vande Mataram flag was adopted by the Swadeshi patriots and also by the Indian National Congress. Madam Bhikaji Cama hoisted a flag in the Second International Socialist Congress in 1907. The original flag was later brought from there in India by Indulal Yagnik and it is one of the national treasures of the country.

Search for the national flag continued. **Sister Nivedita** suggested a design of her own. Annee Besant and Bal Gangadhar Tilak suggested their respective designs. In 1916, Pingali Venkayya introduced his design which is similar to the one which is in national acceptance today. It had three colors and a charkha in the centre. The design continued till 1921 when Mahatma Gandhi suggested that the three colors of our flag should rather stand for three different priorities of the country instead of standing for religious and communal considerations. Soon charkha was replaced by the chakra or the wheel of the Asoka period in the center of the flag. The flag of Pingali Venkayya was called the swaraj flag and it was used by the volunteers of the Indian National Congress on several occasions such as in the march of 1923 in Nagpur. The Indian National Congress adopted the suggestion of the Saint that the red color in the flag signified the countless sacrifices of the millions throughout these years, white stood for the purity of the countrymen in their thoughts and deeds and the green displayed the hope of the nation to usher into a better tomorrow. Since then this is how our national flag holds good. It is also believed by some others that the national flag was designed by Suraiya Badruddin Tyebji.

The Constituent Assembly of India took up the important subject of deciding upon the national flag of the country. A Committee was instituted to go into this subject. It consisted of Dr. Rajendra Prasad, Maulana Abul Kalam Azad, K. M. Munshi, Smt. Sarojini Naidu, Dr. B. R. Ambedkar and C. Rajagopalachari. They held that the swaraj flag should continue with slight modifications. As said earlier, the charkha gave way for the chakra of the Lion Capital of Asoka. But otherwise, no further changes were inserted in the swaraj design of Pingali Venkayya. On 22. 7. 1947, the Constituent Assembly of India adopted a resolution that this should be the National Flag of the Union of India.

National Song and National Anthem of India

Vande Mataram is the National Song of India. It was originally in the Bengali language and was a part of the novel of Bankim Chandra Cahattopadhyaya by the name Anandmath of the year 1870. It was first sung in the annual session of the Indian National Congress of 1896. Jadunath Bhattacharya provided the music composition. Later Maharshi Aurobindo Ghosh translated it into English.

Jana gana mana adhinayak jay he, Bharat bhagya vidhata…Is the National Anthem of India. It is a poem which was composed by Poet Rabindranath Tagore in 1911. It was originally in the Bangla language. It was set to music by Capt. Ram Singh Thakur of the Azad Hind Fouz. It was first sung on 27. 11. 1911 in the annual session of the Indian National Congress held in Calcutta.

Who coined the term Mahatma

Mohandas Karamchand Gandhi is called by many names such as Bapu, Mahatma and Father of Nation. Pt. Jawaharlal Nehru began to address him as Bapu. But it is still not clear who started to call him as Mahatma or the Great Soul although he himself was never comfortable with this address of him. On a number of occasions, he called himself as Alpatama or a small soul. Public at large began to call him Mahatma. Mohammad Ali Jinnah refused to call him Mahatma in the annual session of Congress held in Nagpur in 1920. He was booed by the audience there. He felt isolated and he gradually drifted away from the Congress ranks and file. However, on some ocassions, thereafter, he addressed him as Mahatma, but perhaps grudgingly. On the other hand, Mahatma Gandhi always called him as Quaid-e-Azam or the leader of the people. Perhaps it is he who began to call Jinnah as Quaid and it is how he began to be called in this manner by his party the Muslim League.

A reception was held to honor Mohandas and Kasturba on their return from South Africa on 11. 1. 1915 at Ghatkopar, Bombay now Mumbai. Rao Bahadur Vissanji Khimji was the President of the meeting. It is claimed by many observers that it is here that Rao Bahadur called him Mahatma. It is believed to be the first such occasion.

Many others maintain that Poet Rabindranath Tagore started this nomenclature. It is true that the Poet used to address him in this manner. But it cannot be said for sure whether the Poet was the first person to use this address.

On 27. 2. 1915, another grand reception was held in the honor of Mohandas and Kasturba who had just then returned from South Africa. It was held by Gondal Rasala, a pharmaceutical firm of the princely state of Gondal. It is believed that the royal physician of the State Jivram Sastri called him here as Mahatma.

There is yet another line of thinking which maintains that Reverend Doke called him as Mahatma when Mohandas was hardly 39 years old. Rev. Doke was a close friend of Mohandas and he is credited undoubtedly with writing the first biography of his Indian friend namely M. K. Gandhi–An Indian Patriot in South Africa.

Who invented the name the Father of Nation

It is said that Aishwarya Parashar, a ten year old girl from Lucknow filed an application under the Right to Information Act before the Prime Minister's Office PMO i.e. the Ministry of Home Affairs asking as to who had started calling Mahatma Gandhi as the Father of Nation. Her intention was to elicit the information whether there was some official order from the Government of India to this effect. The PMO did not have any answer. So they directed her to approach the National Archives of India New Delhi where she could research through the Governmental documents to elicit her information. Perhaps Aishvarya did not get her information even before the National Archives of India because there was no official order.

However, it is generally believed that Netaji Subhash Chandra Bose for the first time called him as the Father of Nation in his Singapore Radio talk on 6. 7. 1944. Smt. Sarojini Naidu also called him as such. Since then it has become customary and traditional with the countrymen to call him as the Father of Nation.

Jai Hind

It is believed by some quarters that Abdul Hasan Sofrani who belonged to Hyderabad coined the term Jai Hind. However, it is also believed by some others that Netaji Subhash Chandra Bose coined this term. But it is certain that Jai Hind was the war-cry of the Army of Netaji.

Chapter Twenty Two

Role of Business and Industry and Businessmen in the Foundation of a Strong Indian Economy

Business and industry flourished in British India in the late nineteenth and early twentieth centuries alongside the various freedom-movements. It is remarkable that the freedom-struggle was progressively dominated by Mahatma Gandhi since after his arrival on the Indian scene in January 1915. The Mahatma had a philosophy of his own with regard to the Western education, the Western civilization, the Western industrial revolution at the same time being equally respectful of the Western and the British people. He always said that the British rule had been detrimental to the interests of his countrymen, that the British industry had destroyed the indigenous and cottage industry of India and this was the reason why he advocated ruralisation of the Indian society rather than the urbanization. For this purpose he advocated spinning, weaving, carting and other cottage industries. Strangely enough, however, he did not canvas the cause of agriculture until much later in the day although India had been an agrarian society since time-immemorial. It is even argued that he was a critic of scientific advancements. He created an economic system all his own which is popularly called as the Gandhian Economy. In this system, scientific industrialisation did not have much of a chance. There was a constant agitational atmosphere all over the country because of these movements. Business and industry on the other hand necessitate peace and tranquility and order. The pioneering businessmen and industrialists of those days were patriots first before anything else. Therefore, it is indeed remarkable that there was such an amicable and peaceful co-existence between the Mahatma and the other great leaders and the various pioneers of Indian industry. The Mahatma with his doctrines of religion, ethics, spirituality and morality completely dominated the Indian scene of that era and this is precisely the reason why the various pioneers of industry found it as their way of life to align themselves in the promotion of the cause of freedom of the nation under the leadership of the Mahatma and the Indian National Congress. They donated freely to the treasures of the vanguard of the struggle i.e. the Indian National Congress. They looked after the comforts of the Mahatma even though he reduced those requirements to the level of the minimum. The Mahatma used to call himself as the ' richest poor man in the world. ' The credit goes to the nationalistic-patriotism of the founders of the modern industrial India. The doyens of the Indian industry were of course the House of Tatas, the House of Birlas, the House of Sarabhai, various Parsi Houses, the House of Seth Jamnalal Bajaj, the House of Mody, the House of Singhania, the Kirloskars, the House of Mafatlal and others. But the entire business industry and the industrialists rose to the occasion and they contributed towards the freedom movement.

By the turn of the last century, Bombay, Calcutta and Ahmedabad were the three main centers of industrial hubs in India. Ludhiana in Punjab and Kanpur, in the United Provinces now Uttar Pradesh, Ahmedabad in Gujarat were also growing up in the industrial sector. The Parsi and the Gujarati-Marwari communities were the two principal houses who engineered the industrial revolution in India. Bombay had their Tatas and the Gujarati Muslims. The Calcutta business was dominated by early British investments such as in the sectors of tea, coal and jute. The Birlas later set up their house in Calcutta. Nalini Ranjan Sarkar was yet another pioneer in Calcutta with his Indian Institutes of Technology. The Dalmias were another force to reckon with in Calcutta.

Many of the eminent businessmen and industrialists I am enumerating below are still very respectfully remembered today and, therefore, my purpose to write about them is simply to remember many of the legends about them which in my respectful opinion are not talked of today. So herein, I am writing about the great deeds of these great industrialists with the exclusive intention of bringing those great deeds and legends to the knowledge of all of us. At the same time, I consider it my responsibility to admit some possible and inadvertent errors. My purpose to include this chapter in my book is simply to bring to our memories some of the legendary contributions of the sector of industry in the building up of an independent and modern India. These pioneers are well known even today but perhaps their great deeds require to be refreshed in our memories.

Some of the pioneer industrialists of the pertinent period and their legends are as under–

Ardeshir Godraj (1868—1936)and Pirojsha Burjorie Godrej (1882-1972)–The two brothers founded the Godrej Brothers Company which is today known as the Godrej Group of Industries. Being the elder of the two, the senior Ardeshir started first as a lawyer, but then he soon discovered that he was not meant in this profession. So he then decided to continue with the family business of real estate. Ardeshir believed that the political independence of the country could not be a reality so long as the industry and business remained in the foreign monopoly. So he made up his mind that he would set up an indigenous infra-structure of Indian business and industry. After some time, his younger brother Pirojsha also joined hands with him. They set up the Godrej Brothers Company which was later to be known as the Godrej Group of Industries. Today this is one of the leading business-conglomerates of India.

Ardeshir Godrej started the manufacture of reliable locks in 1897 namely Anchor brand, world's first vegetable oil soap in 1918, steel cup-boards in 1923, soap manufacture in 1928, Pirojsha Nagar was established in Vikhroli Maharashtra in 1943 which provided residential, medical and educational facilities to the workers of the Godrej concerns and Godrej safes in 1944. After independence, the Group continued with several new ventures. In this manner, the Godrej House is one of the business houses who has carried on the good work starting earlier than the post-independence period.

In 1909, Ardeshir had been influenced by the book **Poverty of India** which had described how the Indian economy had been harmed by the foreign exploitation. Ardeshir decided that India should soon have an industry of their own. He was an ardent nationalist with close acquaintance with national leaders like Annee Besant, Poet Rabindra Nath Tagore and Mahatma Gandhi. Like some other business pioneers of the period, Ardeshier also suggested that there should be peace and safety so that trade and commerce, business and enterprise could flourish.

Jehangir Bomanji (1879—1946)–He was the son of industrialist Bomanji Dinshaw Petit who owned the Petit Mills in Bombay. He was in close touch with Mahatma Gandhi and his passive/active resistance in South Africa. He contributed generously to the funds of the South African Congress in the movements for civil rights of the British Indians there. When Mahatma Gandhi returned to India along with Kasturba in January 1915, he was one of the first to receive them in the harbor. Thereafter, he arranged a welcome-home for the Mahatma in his residence at Mount Petit Peddar Road Bombay on 12. 1. 1915. The welcome party was largely attended by Indians and the British. M. A. Jinnah was one of them.

He continued to be closely associated with the Mahatma during the period of struggle. He continued to donate generously in the Party funds. He was a member of the Bombay Legislative Council in 1927.

In the field of social service, he established J. B. Petit High School for Girls in Bombay and Bomanji Dinshaw Petit Parsee General Hospital in Cambala Bombay in 1907. He helped Sir Pherozeshah Mehta in the founding of the news-paper Bombay Chronicle.

Sir Vithaldas Damodar Thackersey (1873-1922 —He set up the textile industry. He was a member of the Imperial Council. He donated generously towards the spread of the education of women. After his death, Lady Premlila Thackersey continued this good work. She was the first Vice Chancellor of the Smt. Nathibai Damodar Thackersey Women's University, Bombay SNDT in short. She continued to donate generously. She played her part in the freedom struggle also. Mahatma Gandhi stayed in her residence Premkuty in Poona to recover his health after his fast of 21 days.

Narottam Morarjee (1877–1929)–Narottam Morarjee was one of the pioneers of steam navigation in India. Along with other pioneers Walchand Hiranand and Kilachand Devchand, he established The Scindia Steam Navigation Company Ltd in March 1919. On 19. 4. 1919, their s. s. *LOYALTY* sailed for the United Kingdom from Bombay and in this manner, it became the first Indian navigation company to cross international waters with the Indian flag atop.

Narottam started with the family business of textiles by joining the Morarjee Goculdas Mill of Bombay and the Solapur Mill of Solapur which was owned by his father Seth Morarjee Goculdas.

Amrita Hargovind Das (29.. 2. 1889—12. 12. 1964)–He was a pioneer in textile industry in Ahmedabad. He was a pioneer in the sector of education also. He founded the Ahmedabad Education Society AES in 1936 which later founded the Gujrat University in Ahmedabad. Amritlal and his brother Seth Tribhuvandas donated generously to establish H. L. College of Commerce in Gujarat in 1936. This was the first such institution of its kind in Gujarat. They contributed generously again to establish Seth Bansilal Amritlal College of Agriculture in Anand. The Society donated generously again to build up a Medical College in Gujarat and Smt. Amritlal Hargovind Das Government Ayurvedic College in Gujarat.

Seth Govindram Seksaria ——-This is a known name in the educational sector of India. Yet some legends about him need to be reiterated. Govindram Seksaria was born in

Nawalgarh Rajasthan, he lost his parents early in his life and he cameto Bombay in 1906. The entire business enterprise was monopolized at that point of time by the British capital and enterprise. So it was a challenge for the Indian entrepreneurs to rise up to the occasion by raising Indian trade and commerce and business. Seth Govindram Seksaria was one of the few businessmen to fill up this void. He is one of the pioneers in the cottage industry. Soon he shifted into other sectors also such as vegetable oil, sugar, minerals, banking, printing and motion-pictures. He founded the Bank of Rajasthan, Bombay Talkies Studio and the Bombay Hospital. He entered into the field of educational philanthropy by establishing several schools and colleges such as the Govindram Seksaria Institute of Science and Technology, Govindram Seksaria Institute of Management and Research, Govindram Seksaria College of Commerce in Wardha in 1940. Another college of Commerce was established in Jabalpur, Madhya Pradesh. Acharya Sriman Narayan was the first Principal of the Commerce College at Wardha.

Sir Purushottamdas Thakurdas—-He was one of the cotton magnates from Gujarat and an industrialist from Bombay. He was one of the signatories to the Bombay Plan which was designed to develop the future economy of India post'1947. He had earlier established the Indian Chambers of Commerce and Industry in 1927.

The Bombay Plan of 1945

Some of the leading businessmen of Bombay assembled together to build up a future plan for the economic development of India post 1947. This is known as A Brief Memorandum Outlining a Plan of Economic Development of India. The signatories were

Jehangir Ratanji Dadabhoy Tata, Ghanshyam Das Birla, Ardeshir Dalal, Sri Ram Kasturbhai Walchand, Ardeshir Dorabshaw Shroff, Sir Purushottam Thakurdas and John Mathai. The Plan recommended that the nascent Indian economy could not have flourished without state intervention and state assistance in the face of stiff competition from the private sector. So it can be said that the future system of Five Year Plans and the concept of private sector, public sector and mixed-economy owes its origin to the contents of the Bombay Plan.

Sir Cowasjee Jehangir Readymoney (1812-1878)–He belonged to a flourishing Parsi family of Bombay associated with the banking business and money-landing. He was one of the leading philanthropists of his time. He donated 200000 pounds sterlings for the establishment of the Indian Institute in London for the charitable purposes of communities of all religions and also for various purposes in Bombay. Many of the buildings in Bombay University were constructed with the help of his charity.

Laxman Kirloskar (20. 6. 1869—26. 9. 1956)—This is yet another known name in the Indian industry. He set up the well-known Kirloskar Brothers of industry in 1888 and the place is known as the Kirloskarwadi. They are head-quartered in Pune with the nomenclature the Kirloskar Group of Industry. They are today India's largest manufacturers and exporters of pumps and valves, motors and engines. The House had earned a name as one of the philanthropists during the freedom-struggle period.

Sir Sorabji Nusserwaiya Pochkhanwala (8. 9. 1881-4. 7. 1937)–He is one of the pioneers of Indian banking. He had the high ambition of establishing an indigenous bank in the country which could be genuinely called the Bank of the

Indians, Bank for the Indians and the Bank by the Indians. He had the active help of Kalianji Vardhaman Jersey. In this manner. The Central Bank of India came into being on 11 December 1911 with an initial venture capital of Rs. 50 lakhs. Sir Pherozeshah Mehta, the prominent lawyer of Bombay was its first Chairman. Today, the Central Bank of India is one of the leading banks of the country. He was one of the signatories to the Bombay Plan of 1947.

Walchand Hirachand Doshi (23 November 1882 – 8 April 1953)–Walchand Hirachand started with his family business of banking and cotton later to diversify into several sectors such as shipping and shipyard, aero-nautics and air-crafts, building construction, sugar and confectionary and others. This is today the Walchand Group of IndustriesThe patriarch founded the following— Scindia Steam Navigation Company Limited in 1919 along with Narottam Morarji and Kilachand Devchand, Hindustan Aircraft Bangalore now Bengaluru in December 19470 along with Dharamsay Mulraj Khatau and Tulsidas Kilachand known today as Hindustan Aeronautics Ltd, the Ravalgaon Sugar Firm in 1933, the Premier Automobile Ltd. Bombay now Mumbai in 1940, the national news agency of India known as the Fress Press of India along with Smt. Annee Besant and M. R. Jayakar and the Construction Company in 1926 constructed a tunnel across the Bhor Ghats to lay the railway tracks to join the Bombay-Pune route. He founded the Scindia Shipyard Ltd in Visakhapatnam in 1940—1941. It was inaugurated by Dr. Rajendra Prasad. It was nationalized by the Government of India in 1961 and today it is known as the Hindustan Shipyard Ltd.

Walchand Hirachand was an ardent nationalist to the core. He was a follower of the principles of Mahatma Gandhi and the Indian National Congress and he donated generously to the Party funds. He was able to strike a balance between the sensibilities of the British Raj whom he did not want to antagonize and the national-struggle for freedom where his affinities lay so over-whelmingly. Many of his projects were inaugurated by well-known freedom-fighters. He wanted to protect the interests of the nascent Indian industry. He believed that industrial growth required peace and safety and this is one of the reasons why he advised Gandhiji to call off the movement of 1933. He was also a signatory to the Bombay Manifesto of 1936 which did not support the socialist doctrines of Pt. Jawaharlal Nehru.

In the field of philanthropy, Walchand Hirachand can be credited with the establishment of the following educational institutions–

1. Walchand Institute of Technology, Solapur

2. Walchand College of Engineering, Sangli

3. Walchand Dale Carnegie Finishing School, Ballandur

4. Walchand College of Arts and Science, Solapur

5. Smt. Kasturbai Walchand College, Sangli

6. Seth Hirachand Nemchand Digambar Jain Boarding, Poona now Pune and

7. Walchand Public School, Sonepat.

Lala Kamlpat Singhania (7. 11. 1984–31. 5, 1937)–Yet another well known name. Lala Kamalpat Singhania is one of the leading pioneers of Indian industry hailing from Kanpur. He is the architect of the leading industrial conglomerate namely the House of the Singhanias or the JKGroup of Industries. This gigantic journey started in 1921 with the start of an humble beginning with the start of the Juggilal Kamlapat Cotton Spinning and Weaving Mills. Kamla Ice Factory 1921, JK Oil Mills 1924, JK Hosiery Factory 1929, JK Jute Mills 1931, M. P. Sugar Mills 1932, JK and JK Iron & Cotton Manufacturers Ltd. 1933 a Ltd and JK Iron & Steel Ltd 1934 followed thereafter. Today the House has expanded its shores in many other fields also such as the Raymonds garments. Padampat Singhania, Kailashpat Singhnia and Lakshmipat Singhania are the three capable sons of the patriarch Singhania.

Mafatlal Gagalbhai—He was born in 1873 in Ahmedabad. He joined the family business of his father of textile early in his life. In 1904, he collaborated with Chandulal Mahadevia and an Englishman named Arthur Shorrock in the acquisition of a mill namely Shorrock Mill. In the coming years, he acquired more mills such as in 1912 he bought a mill in Nadiad and he named it Shorrock Mill, Jaffar Ali Mill in 1916 and he named it as New Shorrock Mill and its new name was Surat Cotton Spinning and Weaving Mills.

After independence, the Group diversified in several other sectors such as information technology, chemicals, engineering and helth-care. However, today the Group is almost identical with the Arvind Denims and the Arvind Mafatlal Group.

Nalini Ranjan Sarkar (1882-1953)–Nalini Ranjan Sarkar joined the Indian National Congress early in his life and he participated in freedom movements of Mahatma Gandhi. But then he joined the Swarajya Party of C. R. Das and Motilal Nehru. It seems only a symbolic move because those who formed the Swarajya Party were all the time with the Indian National Congress and Mahatma Gandhi. But at the same time, Nalini Ranjan has the distinction of being one of the makers of modern industrial and educational Bengal.

Nalini Ranjan rose steadily in the political ladder of Bengal. He was elected as a Member of the Legislative Assembly of Bengal from 1923 to 1930 and again from 1937 to 1946. In between them, he was Mayor of Calcutta now Kolkata in 1935. He was a minister in the A. K. Fazlul Huq state Government, Member in the Viceroy's Executive Council in 1941-42, Finance Minister West Bengal in 1948 and Chief Minister of the State for some time.

In the industrial sector, he was the President of the Indian Chambers of Commerce and Industries FICCI in 1953 and also of the Bengal National Chamber of Commerce and Industry. He was a member of several committees in Bengal also at the same time. He was associated with several educational institutions such as he was the Pro Vice-Chancellor of the Calcutta University and also of the Banaras Hindu University. He held an important assignment of being the Chairman of the All India Technical Educational Committee 1946 to 1952. In this capacity, the Nalini Ranjan Committee recommended the setting up of Indian Institutes of Technology IITs in India on the lines of the Massachusetts Institutes of Technology MIT, Boston USA. This is one of the best gifts of Nalini Ranjan Sarkar to the nation.

Gujarmal Modi (9 August 1902 – 22 January 1976)–Yet another known pioneer. He was born in the family of Multani

Mal Modi and Chandi Devi. He joined the family business of sugar. Along with his brother, Kedar Nath Modi, he established the Modi Group of Companies and Industries in 1933 in a place which is now well-known as the Modinagar. With his enterprise and business, he soon built up an empire of businesses and industries. Some of them as of before the independence are as follows—

Sugar manufacturing factory in 1933, Vanaspati manufacturing mill in 1939, washing soap factory in 1940, toilet soap factory in 1941, a tin factory in 1941, Modi food products in 1941, Modi Oil Mill in 1944, a confectionary factory in 1945, a factory for paints and varnish in 1947 and a textile factory in 1948.

After independence, the Group established a spinning mill in 1957, a flour mill in 1959, a distillary in 1959, a torch manufacturing factory in 1961, a steel mill in 1964, a thread mill in 1965 and a rubber factory in 1971. The Government of India decorated him as Padma Bhushan in 1968.

Shanti Kumar Morarji (1902—1982)–He was son of Narottam Morarji one of the leading industrialists and shipping magnates of India. After the death of his father, Shanti Kumar became the Chairman of the Scindia Steamship Company which was owned along with Walchand Hirachand and Kilachand Devchand.

Shanti Kumar came in close contact with Mahatma Gandhi. He began to put on khadi clothes. His wife Sumati followed suit. They were very close to Mahatma Gandhi. Shanti Kumar helped the Congress movement just as other leading houses of industry and business had done. Many of the leading national leaders used to stay in the hospitality of Shanti Kumar in his Juhu residence. When Kasturba passed away in the Aga Khan Palace in 1942, Sumati Morarji was with the Mahatma in his hour of grief along with some other close confidants such as Lady Premlila Thackersey, Kanu Gandhi, Kamal Narayan Bajaj, his sons minus Manilal and others.

In the after-math of the 1947 exodus to and from India and Pakistan, the ships of Shanti Kumar and Shoorji Vallabhdas brought the Indians stranded in different parts of Pakistan back to India free of charges. In this manner, Shanti Kumar Morarji contributed towards the national cause.

Some other prominent houses and industrialists are the house of Dalmia, Seth Ruia who donated large tracts of lands for the construction of the Banaras Hindu University in Banaras now Varanasi, Seth Tribhuvandas Va Jivandas, Ramanlal M. Shah, Sir Chinu Bhai Madhavdas, Sir Jeejibhoy Jamshetji, Sir Harmusji Naoroji Mody, Sir Dinshaw Manecji Petit and Jehangir Dorabshaw Shroff. The House of Tatas has a very special place in the industrial history of India. They are pioneers in so many fields and they are one of the leading philanthropists of India.

Chapter Twenty Three

Role of Press and Journalists in the Freedom Movement of India

Press and journalists played a notable role in the cause of the freedom of the country. The British Government legislated the Censor Press Act 1799, Licensing Regulations 1823, Press Act of 1825, Registration Act 1867, the Vernacular Act 1878 and the Newspapers (Incitement to Offenses) Act 1908 to curb the freedom of the Indian press. Several patriots did not take this challenge lightly. They responded by founding news-papers of their own creation. These papers educated the readers with the national and patriotic needs. Many of the stalwarts of the movements were themselves devoted journalists. They themselves founded some of the mass-circulation dailies and weeklies to ignite the fire of patriotism. Indian journalism has its recorded beginning in the late eighteenth century with and it is surprising that several Englishmen were founders in this field. Some of them are as under—

William Thomas Stead (5 July 1849 – 15 April 1912) He is considered to be the father of investigative journalism. He is also called the creator of investigative journalism. He is also known as the founder of New Journalism. He edited a number of leading newspapers in the Victorian era of England. He was in the editorial board of John Morleys Pall Mall Gazette. Later he started his own Review of Reviews which published progressive views and suggestions. He was an advocate of democratic aspirations of countries which were under imperialist control such as India. He supported Indian cause for self rule, of the Indian National Congress and was an admirer of the policies of Dada Bhai Naoroji. He died in the unfortunate Titanic disaster of 1912 while on his way to New York.

James Augustus Hickey started the first printed newspaper in India in 1780 namely Bengal Gazette HICKEY'S Bengal Gazette or the Original Calcutta General Advertiser started from 10 March 1870 from Calcutta. Hickey had come from England a few years earlier. It started as a weekly.

Sulabh Samachar was started in November 1870 from Calcutta with Umanath Gupta as its editor.

The Bengal Hurakuru and Chronicle, **an** English language newspaper was started in 1795 and it lasted up to 1866.

The Calcutta Chronicle and General Advertiser was started in 1786 from Calcutta by two Englishmen namely Daniel Stuart and Joseph Cooper following the earlier launch of Hickeys journal. It was discontinued from 1790.

James Silk Buckingham was another of the British citizens to work as a pioneer in the field of Indian journalism. He highlighted not only the policies of the Government but also some of the social problems which were faced by the Indian society at that point of time. He campaigned against the tradition of sati.

Benjamin Horniman (1873-1948)–Born in Sussex England to the parents William Horniman and Sarah Horniman, after his education, Benjamin started his career in the field of journalism with Portsmouth Evening Mail in 1894. He came to India in 1906 and joined the Statesman in Calcutta as its news-editor. In

1913, he became the editor of the Bombay Chronicle which was founded by Sir Ferozeshah Mehta. He despatched dispassionate coverage of the Jallianwala Bagh atrocities to the print-media in England such as the Daily Herald which expressed the views of the Labor Party. The British Government here in India were annoyed by the free-journalism of Norniman. The Bombay Chronicle was closed for some-time and Benjamin was deported to England. Govardhan Das one of the local correspondents of the paper was sentenced for three years for the charges of sedition. There he wrote the British Administration and the Amritsar Massacre in 1920 which again raised ripples both in England and in India. However, he returned to India soon thereafter and joined the Bombay Chronicle as its editor. In 1929, he started his own the Indian National Herald and its weekly edition. He followed it up with yet another of his private ventures as the Bombay Sentinel which ran from 1933 to 1945. In 1941, he founded the Blitz along with Russi Karanjia and Dinkar Nadkarni.

The Times of India is yet another newspaper in the English language which enjoyed a mass circulation and readership. It is today one of the leading newspapers of the country.

Benjamin Horniman was sympathetic to the Indian cause.

Some of the Indian journalists and journals of the era who paved the way for independence–

Samachar Darpan 1818It was published by the Missionaries of Serampore Bengal in 1818 largely to propagate the Christian gospel. It is said to be the first Indian newspaper of an Indian language. Although some others claim that this distinction belonged to the Bengal Gazette of the same period issued by Gaurishankar Bhattacharya.

Sambad Kaumudi was founded by Raja Ram Mohan Rai in 1828 mainly as a vehicle of social change in Bengali society. It campaigned successfully against the tradition of sati and for the rehabilitation of the widows. Governor General William Bantick outlawed sati by an act of 1829. Orthodox Hindus countered by publishing **Samachar Chandrika** to propagate traditional points of view.

The Hindoo Patriot 1853 was published from Calcutta now Kolkata by Girish Chandra Ghosh from the press of Madhusudan Roy. It was later bought by Sir Ishwar Chandra Vidyasagar. The paper had witnessed the events of the revolt of 1857. It published the events of the uprising and highlighted the valor of such martyrs as Tatya Tope, Nanaji, Mangal Pandey, Rani Laxmi Bai, Thakur Kunwar Singh and others.

Indian Field 1859. Kishori Chandra Mitra started it from Calcutta now Kolkata in 1859. It later merged with the Hindoo Patriot.

Amrit Bazar Patrika – This leading news-paper was founded by brothers Sisir Kumar Ghosh and Motilal Ghosh on 20. 2. 1868 in English and Bengali languages. Tushar Kanti Ghosh the son of Sisir Kumar Ghosh was another of the well-known editors of this famed news-paper. This journal set Indian journalism in right earnest in Bengal. It was founded in Jessore which is now in Bangladesh, but it was later shifted to Calcutta. It turned into a daily from a weekly in Bengali language. The Patrika had clashes with Lord Curzon during the partition of Bengal in 1905.

The Tribune 1881 was founded by Dayal Singh Majithia from Lahore in 1881. He is also one of the founders of the Punjab National Bank.

Voice of India 1883 was founded by the Grand Old Man of India Dada Bhai Naoroji in 1883 to ventilate the aspirations of his people. It was launched in Bombay now Mumbai. It was later incorporated in his Indian Spectator.

Some of the other newspapers and journals of the nineteenth century which supported the cause of the freedom of the country–

Mirat-ul-Akhbar a Persian paperwhich was published by Raja Ram Mohan Roy from Calcutta in 1822, Rast Gaftar in Gujarati was started by Dada Bhai Naoroji in 1854 from Bombay, Som Prakash a weekly was started by Dwarkanath Vidyabhushana in 1858, Devendra Nath Tagore started **Indian Mirror** in 1862, Sir Syed Ahmad Khan started **Tahzibul-Akhlaq** to espouse the views of his community, **Prabhudda Bharatan** English monthly was started in 1896 by P. Aiyaswami, B. R. Rajam Iyer, G. Narasimhacharya and B. V. Kameshwar on behalf of Swami Vivekanand, **National Paper** was started in 1865 by **Devendranath Tagore** from Calcutta, **Bangadarshan** was started in 1873 from Calcutta by B. C. Chatterjee.

Swadeshimitran was one of the leading newspapers to be issued from Madras now Chennai. It was the first Tamil language newspaper of that region. It is the longest serving newspaper of Tamil Nadu. It was founded by G. Subramania Iyer 1881-1882. It was earlier a weekly but it became a daily since 1889. The paper aroused nationalism in the Tamil people. It was served by several eminent editors such as poet Subramania Bharti, V. V. S. Iyer and Subramania Pillai.

S. Kasturi Ranga Iyengar (15 December 1859 – 12 December 1923)–Kasturi Ranga started his career as a lawyer in Coimbatore where he was very successful. So he decided to move to Madras with a hope to do good there also. But in the High Court stage, he was not as successful as he might have dreamt of. So he changed course by joining the staff of **the Hindu** as a legal correspondent in 1885. He had great wealth. So he purchased the ownership of the Hindu in April 1905 for a valuable consideration of Rs. 75000/. At that time, the Hindu had a reasonable amount of success and circulation. Kasturi set about setting the house in order. He solicited good advertisements for the daily. In this manner, he enhanced the revenue collection of the Hindu management. He brought fresh and readable material for his readers. **The Hindu** has not looked back since then. Today Hindu has one of the largest daily popular circulation and one of the best quantitative and qualitative readership amongst national dailies. The Hindu enjoys an enviable reputation of quality journalism. Thanks mainly to its pioneer Kasturi Ranga Iyengar.

The Hindu and Kasturi Ranga had earned a great reputation during the period of struggle for independence for fearless reporting and coverage of events such as the Jallianwala Bagh atrocities. The Hindu canvassed greater autonomy for the Indians but not complete independence. Kasturi Ranga supported the Home Rule Movement of Smt. Annee Besant. But he was opposed to her promotion of J. Krishnamurti as Maitrya Buddh.

Maratha and Kesari – Lokmanya Balgangadhar Tilak founded two popular journals Maratha in Marathi language and Kesari in English. Kesari was founded in 1881. It is no exaggeration to say that these two news-papers created national fervor after the close of the up-rising of 1857. Tilak was charged for writing seditious articles in his journal and he was sentenced for six years in the Mandalay Jail in Burma. It is in this confinement that he wrote the classic **Gita Rahasya**. It is to be remembered that Tilak was defended in one of these cases by Barrister Mohammad Ali Jinnah.

Lokmanya was assisted in his pioneer work by patriots like Vishnu Shastri Chipulkar, Gopal Ganesh Agarkar and Mahadev Ballal Namjoshi. Later there arose some differences between Tilak and Agarkar and the latter founded his own paper namely Sudharak along with Narsimha Chintaman Kelkar.

Lala Lajpat Rai—Another notable name in the early Indian press is Punjab Kesari Lala Lajpat Rai. Along with Mahatma Hansraj, he started **Punjabee** from Lahore. Lalaji founded **Vande Mataram** from Lahore. The Government stopped its publication in 1927. He started another news-paper namely **People** from Lahore which was sponsored by the Servants of People Society. Lalaji was also involved with the **Hindustan Times**. It was co-owned by him along with Pandit Madan Mohan Malviya and Raja Narendra Nath. Lalaji was associated with another news-paper by name **Young India** which was printed and circulated by the India Home League of America with the purpose of propagating the cause of the freedom of the country abroad.

Young India, Harijan, Harijan Bandhu and **Harijan Sevak**—These are the news-papers which were credited to

Mahatma Gandhi. It will be no exaggeration to say that Mahatma Gandhi pioneered truly patriotic journalism in the country which was not motivated by commercial interests. He launched the **Indian Opinion** in South Africa with the intention of ventilating the aspirations of the British Indians in their fight for their civil rights. Indian Opinion did not solicit advertisements and his second son Manilal and his wife Sushila had to run it in financial difficulties.

Young India was started in 1919 and it continued till 1931. Its main purpose was to high-light the importance of non-violence in the struggle against British rule. Harijan was another weekly which was started in English in 1933. It continued till 1948. Harijan Bandhu and Harijan Sevak were in Hindi. The Marathi edition of the Harijan was published by Wardha from 1. 3. 1942. As is apparent from their names, these papers were launched with the solitary intention of high-lighting the cause of the oppressed classes of the country.

Some other prominent newspapers of the 1905 period are as follows. Madam Bhikaji Cama founded **Bande Mataram** from Paris in 1905 to propagate nationalist views from Europe. Earlier, the British had banned the poem Vande Mataram written by Bankim Chandra in his Anandmath. This led to the founding of a number of papers by this name. Sri Aurobindo also started another paper by the name **Vande Mataram** in 1905 in English from Calcutta now Kolkata. Lala Lajpat Rai also started another paper by the same name from Lahore.

The Indian Sociologist was started by **Shyamji Krishna Verma** from London in 1905 as a monthly journal to express the aspirations of his countrymen for the knowledge of the world community. The British press there was hostile to him and also to his journal.

Yugantar Patrika 1905– It was started from Calcutta in 1905 by Barindra Kumar Ghosh, Abhinash Bhattacharya and Bhupendranath Dutta in Bengali language as a weekly. The journal advocated revolutionary tactics to overthrow British rule. This journal proved to be the mouthpiece of the revolutionaries of Bengal of that point of time. The British Government came down heavily upon the journal and the revolutionaries. Editor Bhupendranath Dutta was prosecuted for the offence of sedition, he was jailed.

The Leader was started by Mahamana Madan Mohan Malviya in 1909 and it continued upto 1967. C. Y. Chintamani was one of its prominent editors.

Sandhya was started by Bramhanandan Upadhyaya in 1910 from Calcutta.

Kudi Arasu was started in 1910 by the Tamil reformer E. V. Ramaswami Naicker Periyar from Madras along with S. S. Mirajkar and K. N. Joglekar mainly to espouse the Tamil aspirations.

Swadeshabhimani –This was one of the leading newspapers of Kerala during the freedom movements. It was owned by Abdul Khader Maulvi or Vakkom Maulvi since he lived in Vakkom and also where this paper was located before moving on to Tiruanantpuram.

K. Ramakrishna Pillai (25. 5. 1878–28. 3. 1916) edited it successfully for a number of years. He was a fearless editor, a crusader against evil social practices of his society and a critic of the wrong policies of the Diwan and ruler of the princely state of Travancore. He was arrested and exiled from the state. But he later returned to revive the paper with distinction. He was an eminent writer of Malyali literature and he wrote a number of popular books in this literature.

Some other new-spapers and journals from Kerala of this period are as under. In 1920. Muhammad Khader Rahim brought out **Al Ameen** in Malyalai language which is supposed to be one of the first in this language. He was its chief editor also. This paper supported Indian fredom aspirations. Other notable papers and journals from this region are **Rajyasamachar** started by **the Missionaries of Basel Mission in 1847** from Illikunna. Like one such paper from Calcutta from the Church. The main purpose of this paper must have been the spread of the Christian gospel. **Paschimodayam** was issued from Thalasseri in 1847. **Deepika** was started in 1877. **Malayala Manoram**a was started in 1888 and it continues to be one of the most widely circulated journals all over the world still today. **Kerala Kaumudi** was started in 1911 from **Thiruvananthapuram a**nd **Mathrubhumi** from Kozhikode in 1923. **Deshabhiman** was started in 1942.

The Hitavada—It was founded by Gopal Krishna Gokhle in 1911. It is still published today from Nagpur, Bhopal, Jabalpur and Raipur being more than 100 hundred years old. It is owned by Shri Banwarilal Purohit, former Member of Parliament.

Bombay Chronicle was started by Sir Pherozeshah Mehta **in** 1913 from Bombay along with Benjamin Horniman. Sir Mehta had tried to buy Bombay Gazette in 1911 but in vain. So he launched a journal of his own. Editor Horniman edited it from 1913 to 1919 expressing the national views

Smt. Annee Besant started **New India** in 1914.

Maulana Mohammad Ali started **Comrade** in 1911 as an English language weekly. The paper espoused both the aspirations of his community and also a national programme for independence. He also started the Urdu daily **Hamdard** in 1913.

Independent– Pandit Motilal Nehru started this paper in 1919. The British Government closed it down soon in 1921 for its contents. Motilal was assisted in this work by eminent editors such as B. G. Horniman, Syed Hussain, George Joseph, Venakatraman and Mahadev Desai. For their critical views, George Joseph and Mahadev Desai were arrested by the British Government. Later Devdas Gandhi was also one of its editors.

The Socialist–It was the first socialist paper of India which was published by S. A. Dange, one of the pillars of the socialist movement of India. It was issued from 1922 as a weekly. Dange was imprisoned by the British Government for his radical views a number of times totalling an aggregate of about 13 years in their custody. Dange was one of the 32 accused persons in the Meerut Conspiracy case, he was sentenced for a term of 12 years. But the sentence was reduced to 3 years in appeal.

Mooknayak 1920 and Bahiskrit Bharat 1927 were started by Bharat Ratna Dr. B. R. Ambedkar to ventilate the cause of the suppressed classes of India.

The ***Hindustan Times*–**This is one of the leading news-papers of India even today. It was founded in 1924 by Sunder Singh Lyalpuri who started the Akali movement and the Shiromani Akali Dal in Punjab. It was inaugurated by Mahatma Gandhi on 26. 9. 1924. Pandit Madan Mohan Malviya and Master Tara Singh were two other members of the managing committee of the Hindustan Times. Later, Devdas Gandhi was one of the editors of this news-paper. It ran into financial trouble in the late 1920s. At that point of time, it was taken over by Seth Ghanshyam Das Birla. This daily newspaper is one of the leading daily newspapers of India.

Aaj was started from Banaras. Patriot and philanthropist Shiv Prasad Gupta was associated with it.

Inquilab: was started by Abdul Hamid Ansari in 1938 from Bombay.

In 1923, Swami Shraddhanand founded **Tej** with Lal Deshbandhu Gupta as editor. They published nationalist news and views. The paper was banned and confiscated a number of times.

Free Hindustan was started by Tarak Nath Das in 1936.

Hindustan Dainik in Hindi was started by Mahamana Madan Mohan Malviya in 1936.

National Herald was started from Lucknow in 1938. It was the Associated Journals Ltd and it was owned by Young India Ltd Company of the Indian National Congress. It served as an expression of the policies of the Indian National Congress during the movement days. It was founded by Pt. JawaharLal Nehru. The British Government banned it for its views during the 1942 Quit India Movement. It was, however, re-started later in 1945. K. Ramarao was its first editor. Pt. Jawaharlal Nehru served as its international correspondent. Feroze Gandhi was one of its Managing Directors.

Pothan Joseph– He was one of the eminent editors of his time. He edited such leading news-papers as **The Voice of**

India, The Indian National Herald, The Indian Mail, The Hindustan Times, The Indian Express and the **Dawn.**

Ramnath Goenka (22. 4. 1904–5. 10. 1991)– He founded the Indian Express in 1932 and **the Indian Express Group** which published a large number of publications in various regional languages and also in English. In 1941, he was elected as the President of the National News-paper Editors Association. He was a Member of the Constituent Assembly of India. In the pre -independence days, he confronted the British Raj with his nationalist views.

The Free Press Journal– An English language daily which was founded by Swaminathan Sadanand in 1928 from Mumbai. The paper supported the cause of the freedom of India. It also supported the cause of the Jew doctors who fled from Germany in the wake of Nazi persecution to practise medicine in India.

Satish Chandra Mukherjee (1865-1948) edited Dawn and Young India. **Urdu newspapers, journals and journalists –**

The Urdu Press

In the freedom struggle of India, the Urdu press has played a very important role in the mass awakening of the people towards national aspirations. They dissaminated general information about the events of the struggle. In consequence, their editors and publishers suffered at the hands of the Government. The Urdu and the Persisn press was very active even during the troubled times of 1857.

The first Urdu paper was **Jam-e-Jahan-Nama** started by Harihar Datta in 1822. The second Urdu paper was started in 1850 by Munshi Harshukh Rai.

Maulvi Mohammad Baqr edited **Urdu Akhbar** during the 1857 period. He was killed by the British for his nationalist views. **Payam-e- Azadi** was published in 1857 both in Hindi and Urdu calling upon the Indians to fight the British occupation. The paper was confiscated by the Government. Other editors of the same period to suffer were **Jamaluddin editor** Sadiqul Akhbar who was sentenced to three years. Munir Shikohabadi, **editor of Gulshan-e-Naubahar** was sent to the Nicobar jails. First Hindi daily **Samachar Sudhavarshan** and **UrduDoorbeen** and **Persian Sultan-ul-Akbar** faced trial in 1857 for publishing news of the uprising and for publishing a farman of Bahadur Shah Zafar calling people to revolt against the British. **Shola-i-Tur,** Khair Khuwahan-i-Khulqand Akhbarul Alam published nationalist news and views. There were about 35 Urdu newspapers during the early period of the revolt of 1857. But many of them were closed down by the East India Company.

Urdu papers supported the freedom call from abroad also. Some of them are **Aina-e-Saudagiri London 1887**, Tarjuman-e-Shauq **Constintinpole** 1878, **Sultan-ul-Akhbar Turkey, Hindustan London 1884, Hurriyat Tashkent 1914, Talwar Berlin 1910, Hindustani San Francisco** 1914, **Yaad-e-Watan New York** 1923. Munshi Sajjad Hussain, editor of Awadh Punch of 1877 promoted communal harmony.

During the days of freedom movements, **editor** Abdul Qayyum Ansari **of** Bihar based Urdu paper**s Al-Islah and Urdu monthly Musawa**t opposed partition of the country. **Editor** Syed Hussain was India's voice from abroad via newspapers. Maulvi Sanaullah Khan started a nationalist Urdu newspaper **Watan** in 1902 and it continued upto 1935.

Some of the papers who supported the Pakistan movement later on. Many of them earlier stood for the independence of India–

Dawn– It was in the forefront of the Pakistan Movement. It was founded by Mohammad Ali Jinnah on 26. 10. 1941 and it started publication and circulation w. e. f. 12. 10. 1942. Jinnah had declared that the main purpose of Dawn would be to advocate the Pakistan cause amongst its readership and that it would become the mouthpiece of the Indian Muslim League. The editors truly lived upto the aspirations of their leader.

Manshoor a Urdu weekly in support of the Pakistan movement was started in 1938 by Syed Hasan Riaz in 1938 from Delhi as an organ of the Muslim League.

Morning News appeared from Calcutta in 1943 to support the Pakistan cause.

The New Times was published from Lahore to support the programme of the Muslim League.

In short, we can say that the news-papers and journals in India have played a very constructive role in the freedom movement of India.

Chapter Twenty Four
Miscellaneous Subjects

Here is a supplement of the names of some other great freedom fighters.

Some of the leading Islamic divines associated with the freedom movements of India——Maulana Khifayatullah, Maulana Ahmed Sayeed Dehlavi, Maulana Habibur Rahman Ludhianavi, Mufti Mohammad Naim Ludhianavi, Maulana Ataullah Shah Bukhari, Maulana Fakhruddun Moradabadi, Maulana Hifzur Rahman Seoharwi, Mufti Atiqur Rahman Usmani, Maulana Muhammad Shahid Fakhiri, Maulana Sayyid Muhammad Mian Deobandi, Maulana Abdul Qadir Qasuri, Maulana Muhammad Qadir Qasuri, Maulana Muhammad Sadiq Karachvi, Maulana Abdul Aziz Gujranwala and Maulana Bashi Ahmad.

Uzair Gul Peshavari- (1886-1989)– He was an eminent Islamic scholar and a freedom fighter who took part in the Silk Letter Movement.

Anupriya Barua and Sudhalata Datta organized a women's force in Assam. They were part of the Indian Red Cross and they helped the wounded freedom-fighters.

Managini Hazee 73 years old satyagrahi of Tamluk division of Midnapore was leading a procession during the 1942 Quit India Movement when she was killed in the police firing.

Manmohini Sehgal, Parvati Devi, Lakshmi Devi, Amrit Kaur and **Pushpa Gujral** are some of the other prominent women freedom-fighters of Punjab.

Anusuiya Bai Kale was yet another prominent worker from Uttar Pradesh during the 1942 Quit India Movement.

In Dharwad, Karnataka, girl student Bamakka, Hemlata and Galwadi hoisted the Congress flag in the courtroom and they appealed to the lawyers to leave their work during the Quit India Movement of 1942.

Annapurna Maharana daughter of freedom fighters Ramadevi and Gopabandhu Choudhury participated in the Quit India Movement of 1942.

Mrs. M. K. Chidambaram and Miss Saraswati were elected Chair-person and Secretary of theIndian Independence League of the Azad Hind Fauj in 1943.

Vinod Kinariwala (1924-1942) took part in the Quit India Movement of 1942. He was killed in the police firing at age 18 years.

Benoy Basu 22, and Badal Gupta 18 were killed in police firing after the killing of Col. N. S. Simpson. Parwati Giri participated in the Quit India Movement of 1942.

Some of the Gandhian supporters who took active part in the movements–

Valji Govindji Desai, Vasumati Pandit, Gangabehn Vaidya, Vanmala, Totaram Sondhiya, Balak Bisen Secretary to Mahatma Gandhi and others.

This is certainly not the exhaustive list of the forgotten freedom fighters. It is almost impossible to trace all of them. I have made a sincere effort to find out as many of them as possible. For example, in the Cellular Jail, thousands of freedom fighters were lodged who were inhumanly tortured there, many of whom could never return to the mainland, many of whom were hanged and many attempted unsuccessfully to escape. Memorials have been erected in their sacred memory. Their names are available in those lists. Similarly, a number of freedom fighters were kept in the jails in Aden and in the Mandalay Jail in Burma, now Myanmar. We pay homage to them silently. That there were such great patriots and supreme sacrificers who willingly chose to lay down their lives so that the next generation may live peacefully, that there were from amongst us such persons who could sacrifice their studies and jobs to exert pressure upon the foreign rulers to quit this country, that there were brave women who sacrificed their comforts so that their illustrious husbands could serve the patriotic interests, that there were several freedom fighters who refused to accept pensionary benefits and stately decorations saying that they had not endured their sacrifices for some remunatory returns. It is equally necessary to reiterate the patriotic services of the business community who so adroitly balanced their commercial interests with their national duties so that the movements might not suffer for lack of funds and who, therefore, succeeded in laying the foundation of a strong economy. Eminent doctors and physicians were also not to be left behind in the hour of need. Intellectuals and journalists also played their respective roles by arousing patriotic and nationalist fervor in the hearts of the millions of their countrymen and women. Not only is it necessary to recollect these forgotten names, but it is equally important to remind ourselves of several legends about the freedom fighters who are not forgotten today.

What are the contributions of these well-known patriots in the diverse fields which need to be recollected by us. This has been one of my solemn efforts in this book.

Look at the sacrifices of these valiant warriors for whom their countrymen were first before themselves. So many of them languished in the British jails for decades suffering all types of tortures. Surendra Sai spent 36 yearrs in jails of the East India Company in 1806. Rani Veli Nachiar is reported to have applied for the first time the human-bomb technique in 1780 while her valiant warrior Kuyilli doused her body with inflammables and jumped into the arsenal of the Company. It is disheartening to learn that several of our brave freedom fighter-revolutionaries had to struggle to manage even the basic necessities of daily life for themselves and for their family members. Some of them had to survive on petty jobs immediately after their releases after a decade or so of tortuous incarcerations. It has also to be brought to our fresh memory that the efforts of so many of these devoted sacrificers were foiled by some betrayors. Who knows that the revolutionaries might have succeeded at least reasonably if not fully had it not been for these acts of betrayal. In the din of the discharge of our daily assignments and onerous responsibilities both within the confines of our families and in the outside world of our societies and communities, let us still find some time out to recall these legendary deeds of our braves.

This book **Forgotten Heroes and Legends of the Freedom Movement of India** is an humble effort to pay tributes to these countless supreme sacrificers from amongst all walks of life. This book is a compilation of their names as far as it could be possible, their short biographies, their deeds and contributions without any claim for infallibility from errors, incompletions and scope for improvements. But my sincere desire is apparent. With these preliminary observations, may I place this humble effort at the hands of my esteemed readers with a fervent hope, trust and expectation that they will find some merit in my work. The nation is celebrating the 75th year of their independence. Let this book be a tribute to these patriotic sons and daughters and citizens of the motherland from all walks of life.

Other Books Written by the Author

1. Role of Lawyers, religion and history
    In the freedom movement of India
    And in the subsequent birth of Pakistan

2. Wisdom of Mahatma Gandhi,

3. Kasturba Gandhi: the Silent Sufferer,

4. हरिशंकर परसाई:चिंतन एवं लेखन,
    (Harishankar Parsai: Chintan evam Lekhan)

5. Mahatma Gandhi: the Social Reformer,

6. A Tale of Three Lawyers
    Mahatma Mohandas Karamchand Gandhi
    Quaid-e-Azam Mohammad Ali Jinnah and
    Bharat Ratna Dr. Bhimrao Ramji Ambedkar.

7. अभी हाल ही में –भाग १ (abhi haal hi mein -bhag 1)

8. अभी हाल ही में –भाग २ (abhi haal hi mein- bhag 2)

Bibliography

1. An Autobiography–Pandit Jawaharlal Nehru,

2. Collected Works of Mahatma Gandhi, Publications Division of India, New Delhi.

Footnotes

Chapter 7

    1. An Autobiography- Jawaharlal Nehru pages 105 and 106

Chapter 12

    1. An Autobiography- My Experiments With Truth, M. K. Gandhi page 167

    2. An Autobiography- My Experiments With Truth, M. K. Gandhi page 168

Chapter 13

    1. Collected Works of Mahatma Gandhi Vol. 36 page 215

Chapter 14

    1. Collected Works of Mahatma Gandhi Vol. 32 page 545

www.ingramcontent.com/pod-product-compliance
Lightning Source LLC
Chambersburg PA
CBHW070742160726

48004CB00001B/13